NORTHERN LIGHTS

NORTHERN LIGHTS

A HISTORY OF THE ARCTIC SCOTS

EDWARD J. COWAN

PEGASUS BOOKS
NEW YORK LONDON

NORTHERN LIGHTS

Pegasus Books, Ltd.
148 West 37th Street, 13th Floor
New York, NY 10018

First Pegasus Books cloth edition September 2023

ISBN: 978-1-63936-270-7

10 9 8 7 6 5 4 3 2 1

Printed in the United States of America
Distributed by Simon & Schuster
www.pegasusbooks.com

CONTENTS

PLATES

Plate section 1

PREFACE

Surprisingly, the remarkable story of the Scottish role in the discovery of the Northwest Passage, following the demise of Napoleon through to the outbreak of the Crimean War, has never been told. The first official postwar Arctic expedition by a much reduced British Navy was captained by the veteran John Ross from Stranraer, accompanied by his nephew, Midshipman James Clark Ross, who would become the most experienced arctician of his generation, discoverer of the Magnetic North Pole and, later, leader of a remarkable four-year venture to Antarctica. John Ross, a true hellraiser and extrovert, failed in his quest in 1818, consequently attracting much hostile criticism, but ten years later he and James spent fifty-four months of enforced exile in Prince Regent Inlet and the Gulf of Boothia. Since many believed the Rosses and their crew had perished, their experience somewhat foreshadowed the fate of Arctic explorer John Franklin and his expedition of 1845–9. The latter's forays overland to the 'Hyperborean Sea' were undertaken with the support of Dr John Richardson of Dumfries, a remarkable individual who demonstrated that he was possessed of the 'right stuff', an accidental cannibal and executioner of a murderer, as well as a most engaging natural historian. The fourth notable Arctic Scot was Orkney's national hero, John Rae, who discovered the first evidence of Franklin's demise. Scots whose contributions are also assessed include the temperamental Hudson's Bay Company fur trader Thomas Simpson from Dingwall, the Scotophile Joseph Bellot, the sole Frenchman on a ship full of Scots in one of the harshest places on earth, and his captain from Canada, William Kennedy, who discovered and named the Bellot Strait in the Frenchman's honour.

Scots were particularly fascinated by the Inuit, with whom they cooperated and enjoyed good relations on the whole, depending on their knowledge of the environment in many crucial cases. John Ross named a group of Greenlanders (Inughuit) 'the Arctic Highlanders', who lived in a region so far north that it had previously been believed human existence there was impossible. All Scots learned a great deal about Inughuit, Kalaallit and Inuit survival, hunting, country food, clothing, local customs and language, as well as the building of snow houses.

Scots–Irish are included, especially those with Scottish surnames, such as Leopold McClintock. The whalers also played an important part, particularly William Penny of Peterhead, who undertook the first maritime search for Franklin, and who took his wife to the north, where she became the first known European woman to over-winter on Baffin Island. Another wife who made a considerable impact was Lady Jane Franklin, who was loyal to a fault where her husband was concerned. She committed a great deal of love, energy and money to the searches for the lost Franklin expedition, becoming largely responsible for the apotheosis of her husband.

The major aim of this book is to properly return their nationality and their achievements to these Arctic Scots, who are still usually identified as English by modern writers. A theme running throughout the book is the conflict between Scottish common sense and English exceptionalism. I had the good fortune to visit many of the places mentioned in the text and I have been privileged to meet and become friends with some of the leading authorities on the Arctic.

Ted Cowan

EDITOR'S NOTE

A Personal Message

Edward 'Ted' Cowan loved the North, he loved the Arctic, but most of all he loved Scotland and dedicated a large chunk of his life to teaching and inspiring countless others to love it too. In his youth he devoured the classic texts of exploration and adventure, from Knud Rasmussen and Roald Amundsen to Fridtjof Nansen and Peter Freuchen. During his academic career – at the universities of Edinburgh, Guelph and Glasgow – Ted developed expertise in Viking and early Norse history, Icelandic Sagas and an unrivalled breadth of knowledge of Scottish history. A fortuitous invitation in 1995, to guide and lecture aboard an expedition ship around Scotland with a Canadian tour company, Adventure Canada, would later open the door to fulfil a lifetime ambition: to travel to Svalbard, Alaska, Greenland and the Canadian Arctic. With me, his wife, we were fortunate to make numerous trips around Scotland and throughout the Arctic regions together, largely thanks to our associations with this wonderful expeditionary tour company – and for that we were/are both truly grateful. To say these opportunities changed our lives may sound corny or cliched but it is heartfelt and honest. The warm welcome and hospitality given to us from people across the Inuit Nunangat is also not forgotten.

In the early hours of 2 January 2022 Ted left this world, with me by his side, and I will never recover from this loss. Before he died, he had recently completed a full draft of a book – this book – on the Scottish story of Arctic exploration in the first half of the nineteenth century. Birlinn had agreed to publish it and I am thankful to them for honouring this agreement. However, it also meant that I was now responsible for taking the manuscript through the revision and proofreading stages, a process that has been bittersweet and challenging for me beyond measure. I could hear Ted's voice in every line and, where I was required to modify, alter or add additional text I have tried to stay true to his voice. I hope he is happy with my input and adjustments. If there are any errors, I take full responsibility.

Lizanne Henderson Cowan

Ted Cowan and Mathew Nuqingaq (artist and Inuit culturalist),
guiding with Adventure Canada through the Northwest Passage, Nunavut
(Photograph by Lizanne Henderson © padeapix)

The land retains an identity of its own, still deeper and more subtle than we can know. Our obligation toward it then becomes simple: to approach with an uncalculating mind, with an attitude of regard. To try to sense the range and variety of its expression – its weather and colors and animals. To intend from the beginning to preserve some of the mystery within it as a kind of wisdom to be experienced, not questioned. And to be alert for its openings, for that moment when something sacred reveals itself within the mundane, and you know the land knows you are there.

Barry Lopez, *Arctic Dreams* (1986)

A NOTE ON TERMINOLOGY

In the age of European exploration of Greenland and the North American Arctic, from the sixteenth to the nineteenth centuries, the indigenous inhabitants were known to Europeans as Esquimaux or Eskimo. The exact origin and etymology of the term is uncertain, often assumed to derive from an Amerindian word meaning 'flesh eaters' or 'eaters of raw meat'. An alternative derivation is from an Algonquian (Montagnais) Innu-aimun word meaning 'one who laces snowshoes'. In the 1970s the Inuit Circumpolar Council (ICC) took the decision to reject the term 'Eskimo' in favour of 'Inuit' to describe the indigenous peoples living across the Inuit Nunangat and beyond, including the Inupiat, Yupik (Alaska), Inuit, Inuvialiut (Canada), Kalaallit (Greenland) and Yupik (Russia). While 'Eskimo' is still used to denote the Eskimo–Aleut language group, Inuit (plural, meaning 'the people') and Inuk (singular) is generally the preferred name.

The indigenous peoples of Kalaallit Nunaat (known also as Greenland since Norse explorer Erik the Red established a colony there in the tenth century) are Inuit but generally refer to themselves as Kalaallit (west coast), Tunumiit (east coast), and Inughuit (north), the latter formerly known as 'Polar Eskimo' or, as referred to by Sir John Ross, the 'Arctic Highlanders'.

Today, the Inuit Nunangat of Canada consist of four main regions: Inuvialiut (Northwest Territories), Nunavik (Northern Québec), Nunatsiavut (Labrador) and Nunavut (a territory since 1999). The primary language across the Canadian Arctic is Inuktitut, Inupiaq in Alaska and Kalaallisut in Greenland.

LHC

ABBREVIATIONS

DCB   *Dictionary of Canadian Biography* (online), University of Toronto/
         Université Laval: http://www.biographi.ca/en/

EIC   East India Company

HBC   Hudson's Bay Company

NSA   *The New Statistical Account of Scotland 1834–1845* (online):
         https://stataccscot.edina.ac.uk/static/statacc/dist/home

NWC   North-West Company

ODNB   *Oxford Dictionary of National Biography* (online), Oxford
         University Press: https://www.oxforddnb.com/

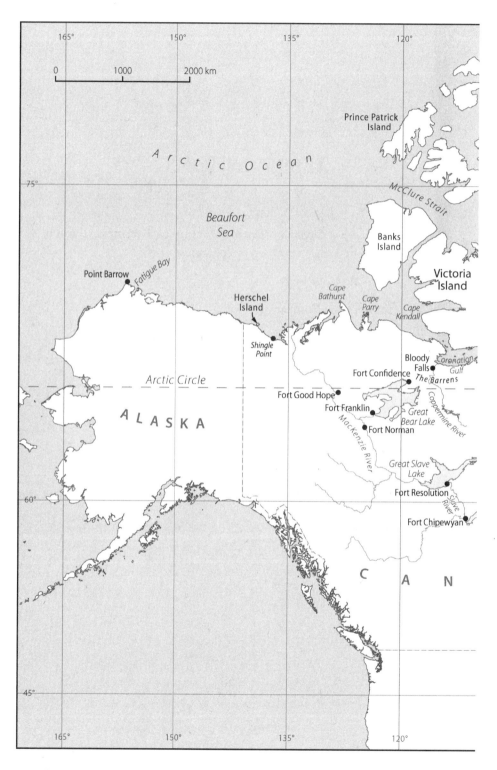

The search for the Northwest Passage: key places related to the expeditions

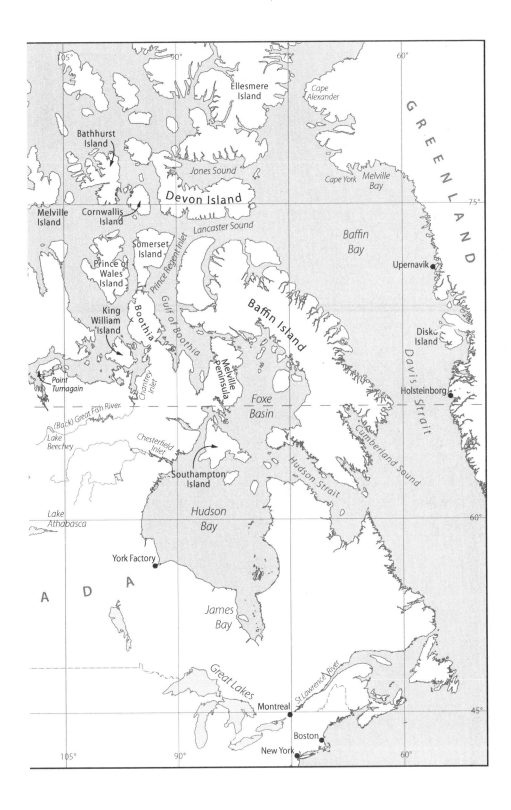

GREENLAND

Ellesmere
Island

Cape
Alexander

Bathurst
Island

Jones Sound

Cape York   Melville
Bay

Devon Island

Melville
Island

Cornwallis
Island

Lancaster Sound

Baffin
Bay

Somerset
Island

Prince of
Wales
Island

Prince Regent Inlet

Gulf of Boothia

Boothia

Baffin Island

Upernavik

King
William
Island

Melville
Peninsula

Disko
Island

Chantrey
Inlet

Point
Turnagain

(Back) Great Fish River.

Foxe
Basin

Davis Strait

Holsteinborg

Cumberland Sound

Lake
Beechey

Chesterfield
Inlet

Southampton
Island

Hudson Strait

Lake
Athabasca

Hudson
Bay

A   D   A

York Factory

James
Bay

Great Lakes

St Lawrence River

Montreal

Boston

New York

105°   90°   75°   60°

75°

60°

45°

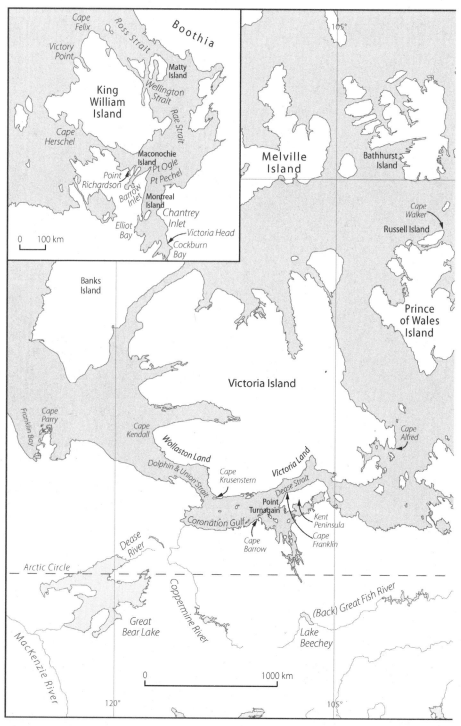

The search for the Northwest Passage and the lost Franklin expedition: more detailed map of the area around Boothia and King William Island

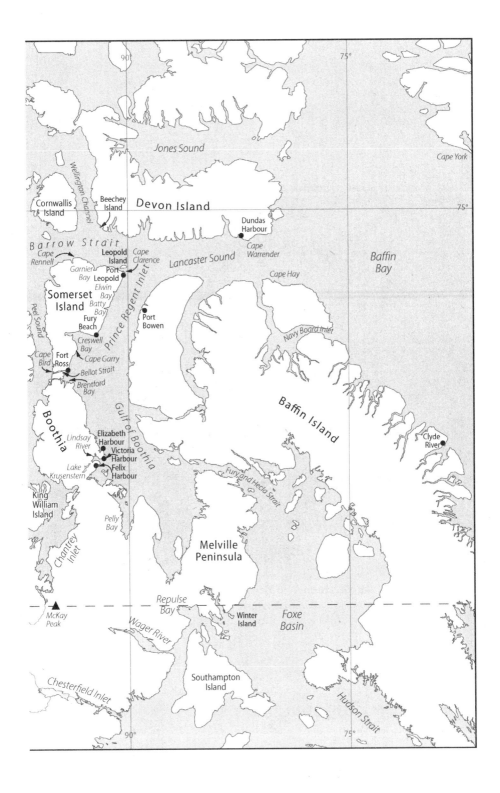

'Taking Possession', from John Ross, *Narrative of a Second Voyage in Search of the North-West Passage* (London, 1835)

1

THE ARCTIC SCOTS
Hyperborean Awakenings

Five thousand years, unvisited, unknown,
Greenland lay slumbering in the frozen zone –
While heaven's resplendent host pursued their way
To light the wolf and eagle to their prey.

James Montgomery[1]

The involvement of Scots in the Arctic is a phenomenon that has not so far received a great deal of attention, but investigation of their ideas, ambitions, achievements and collective biographies, through consideration of their communal Arctic experiences in the creation of a Scottish prosopography, may shed some light on the matter. According to the Icelandic sagas, the Scots were present when Norwegian ships were exploring the coasts of Greenland (Kalaallit Nunaat) and the North Atlantic in Viking times, when some of them encountered the Thule people (ancestors of the Inuit) for the first time, pejoratively calling them Skraelings. In the sixteenth and seventeenth centuries Scots were prominent in the Danish–Norwegian navy and army. Notably John Cunningham became the governor of north Norway, in which capacity he was responsible for 'voyages of inspection' in the western and northern seas, which gave him some control over fishing and whaling.[2] Scots retained their interest in the riches of the ocean in the eighteenth century: in search of trade routes to the Pacific, explorer Alexander Mackenzie reached for the (mythical) Hyperborean Sea, named by the ancient Greeks for giants who lived beyond the North Wind.

Few Scots were involved in the first scientific naval expedition in search of the North Pole in 1773, a venture inspired by reports to the Royal Society in London that the Dutch had sailed within one degree of the target, an untruth which served to galvanise the society into action. The king entrusted two bomb-ships to Constantine J. Phipps, seconded by the splendidly named Skeffington Lutwidge. The expedition was not remarkable, though two noteworthy expeditionaries were aboard. Olaudah Equiano, the famous African who wrote one of the first published autobiographies by a slave,[3] was a close associate of Dr Charles Irving, born at Holywood, Dumfriesshire. The latter was the naval surgeon aboard *Racehorse* and inventor of a 'marine chair' intended to compensate for the vessel's motion when calculating celestial measurements. The two first met when Equiano worked as a hairdresser in London, and Equiano joined Irving on *Racehorse*. He was Irving's assistant when the doctor perfected his method of transforming seawater into fresh water, an achievement rewarded by parliament with a grant of £5,000. Irving was anti-slavery and after the voyage he again employed Equiano, presumably for his knowledge of the area and language, when he attempted to establish a sugar plantation on the Mosquito Shore, which was to be organised on 'humane lines', generating 'amelioration of servitude'.[4]

Scots remained involved in Arctic exploration during its 'most classical period', from the time of Captain James Cook to the mysterious disappearance of the Franklin expedition of 1845, eventually part-resolved in the late 1850s. Three out of four of the greatest British Arctic explorers of the nineteenth century came from Dumfries and Galloway in the south-west of Scotland: the incomparable, pugnacious and talented John Ross, an outspoken extrovert from Stranraer (see Chapter 2); his nephew James Clark Ross (JCR), one of the most experienced Arctic and Antarctic explorers of his generation, much more reserved than his uncle, with wide scientific interests and a deep consuming passion for the culture of the Inuit (see Chapter 3); and Dr John Richardson, a brave explorer, natural historian and doctor, as well as a controversial figure (see Chapters 4 and 5). The fourth was from the other end of the country: John Rae, also a doctor, Orkney's national hero, admired as an unrivalled, non-indigenous expert on snow-shoes and a consummate arctician (see Chapter 9).[5]

Another notable Arctic Scot of this era was Captain David Buchan, of unknown birthplace, who, with Englishman John Franklin, failed when tasked with reaching the North Pole by way of Spitsbergen in 1818 (see Chapter 2).[6] Sadly conflicted, though not devoid of acuity, was Thomas Simpson from Dingwall, cousin of Governor George Simpson of the Hudson's Bay Company (HBC), who was arguably the most powerful Scot in the world at the time, effectively viceroy of most of British North America. Thomas's hatred of the Métis, mixed race people, led to his death in 1840 after the HBC expedition of 1836–9 (see Chapter 8).

Many Scots, Orcadians and Shetlanders served in the Navy, while they also heavily, and famously, populated the fur trade, notably HBC.[7] Largely unsung in journals of exploration were significant numbers of impressive individuals from the ranks of the whaling industry. Although the Navy tended to look down upon them, whalers were often employed as first and second mates, or sailing-masters, since they had acquired hard-earned experience of the northern seas. Scottish whalers were based at Leith, Dundee, Aberdeen and Peterhead; important English centres were London, Hull and Grimsby. The Gray family of Peterhead had the longest-known association in Britain with whaling. David Gray commanded his first ship in 1811; Alexander, David's second grandson, captained his last whaler in 1890, going on to command *Discovery* and *Pelican* on the Great Lakes in the employ of the HBC.[8] Scots had little experience of the Arctic but they displayed a huge appetite to learn, achieving, with whaler support, less regimentation and more creativity than the more rigidly controlled officers and men of the British Navy. They gained further advantage through cooperation with the HBC, which, alongside the whalers, brought them into much closer contact with the First Nations and Inuit. The first known European woman to over-winter on Baffin Island was Margaret Penny, wife of the distinguished Scottish whaler William Penny, 'a forthright Scottish Man of the People';[9] she kept the ship's journal and was left in charge while Penny was off scoping possible whaling grounds. He was contracted by Lady Franklin in the search for her missing husband and his men, as was William Kennedy, the son of an Orcadian Chief Factor and a Cree mother. He controversially insisted upon appointing Lieutenant Joseph René Bellot of the French Navy as his second-in-command (see Chapter 11).

Medical doctors were also to the fore on whaleships: some were penurious students, while others were fully fledged physicians often as, or more, interested in natural history and the sciences than they were in medicine per se. A late example was Edinburgh-born and educated Arthur Conan Doyle, creator of Sherlock Holmes. He volunteered for service on a whaling ship in 1880, and later reported 'I came of age at 80 degrees north latitude'.[10] A number of ships' doctors mentioned in this book studied at Scotland's other well-regarded universities under professors who attracted students from all over the world.

Several explorers wrote books about their Arctic experiences. Some of these (including John Franklin) can be accused of Eurocentric snobbery, understanding little of the ways of the indigenous population. The latter accusation has become increasingly common among American and Canadian commentators in recent years. It is depressing to read the sort of hogwash of which an American academic was capable as recently as 2017. With reference to British Arctic expeditions, post 1815, David Welky writes:

> Their rigid military mind-sets . . . discouraged them from adopting native methods of survival, negating any positive impact from their innovations in equipment. In a ludicrous display of stubbornness, officials wore Royal Navy uniforms instead of furs, ate tinned food instead of fresh meat, slept in tents instead of snow houses, and pulled sledges by hand instead of using dog teams. Such obstinacy resulted in a string of futile expeditions and over 100 deaths during the mid-nineteenth century.[11]

While there is undoubtedly a sliver of truth in some of these tired clichés regarding the Navy, the actions and attitudes of most Scottish voyagers challenged these assumptions. The deaths mentioned in the quotation refer to the 129 comprising Franklin's final expedition. Although his ships *Erebus* and *Terror* have recently been recovered with great fanfare by the Canadians, the demise of Franklin, undoubtedly a sadly prejudiced individual, is still not well understood. The Navy's main problems arose from the ignorance shown by a top-heavy, wilful and insensitive administration whose benighted members believed they could conquer the Arctic as effortlessly as they supposedly ruled the waves but few, if any, British expeditions could match the utterly pointless disasters in the later futile American search for Croker Land. It is ludicrous that modern writers should still be trying to depict heroic, patriotic Americans attempting to tame the Arctic, while in reality their supposed 'rugged explorers', Peary and Cook, both appear to have faked their accounts of having separately conquered the North Pole.

While John Franklin's preference was to operate as an imperialist with (like Robert E. Peary) a disdain for indigenous peoples, most Scots understood their essential dependence upon the Inuit, the Greenlanders (Inughuit and Kalaallit) and the First Nations (see Chapter 7). They had a strong track-record in this respect: Canadian historians Sylvia Van Kirk and the late Professor Gillies Ross have argued that 'the Scots in particular showed a special aptitude for getting along with native people'.[12] Among the Arctic whalers, 'William Penny stood out for his ability to recognize valuable traits and capabilities in the Inuit population and for his eagerness to learn from their knowledge.'[13] From early days, Scots displayed a remarkable ethnological interest in indigenous peoples that they never really lost. This is not to deny that Scots occasionally committed appalling atrocities, as other participants did, but on the whole the British imperial experiment in the Arctic was virtually bloodless. It should also not be forgotten that there was an element of mutual exploitation involved in the relationships. Scots may have assumed that they were the superiors, calling the shots, but the Inuit and the First Nations harboured similar reciprocal assumptions about their own role.

*

Luminaries with visions for what is now Western Canada included such individuals as Captain James Cook, Alexander Mackenzie from the island of Lewis, Captain George Vancouver and geographer Alexander Dalrymple. Mackenzie was the 'true (white) father' of New Caledonia west of the Rockies, even if he did not name it as such. In 1774, he emigrated to Canada, later joining the North-West Company (NWC). When he moved out west, he was determined to find a route across the Rockies to the Pacific. The potential value of such a discovery was obvious, extending as it did 'the boundaries of geographic science', adding 'new countries to the realms of British commerce'. His personal quest was initiated by 'commercial views', but he also possessed 'an inquisitive mind and enterprising spirit', a strong physical constitution and a supreme confidence in his own abilities. Plans were underway by 1788, at which date, following 'the custom of the country', Mackenzie had married Catt, or Kitty, a woman of the First Nations. His instructions from NWC were to travel 'in a bark canoe in search of a Passage by Water through the N.W. Continent of America from Athabasca to the Pacific Ocean in Summer 1789'.[14]

Mackenzie's first expedition took him down the river that now bears his name, to the Beaufort Sea, whence he briefly considered venturing westwards to the Pacific, his intended target. In the Slavey language the Mackenzie is *Deh-cho*, big river, appropriately, since it is the longest river in Canada and is second only to the Mississippi in the size of its drainage basin. His journal contains much of interest about his relations with the First Nations, but his reportage is often rather vague and even difficult to follow. He confessed, 'I am much at a loss here how to act, being certain that my going further in this Direction will not answer the Purpose of which the Voyage was intended, as it is evident these Waters must empty themselves into the Northern Ocean', but he decided to continue, to 'satisfy peoples Curiosity tho [sic] not their Intentions'. Consequently, he spent four nights on Whale Island before returning to the mainland. He complained that his expedition was hardly mentioned and there is a tradition that he named the Mackenzie 'River of Disappointment', though that claim has been challenged. To his credit, Mackenzie does seem to have been conscious of gaps in his own competence, convincing him of the need to visit London in order to hone essential skills in surveying, navigation, magnetism and mensuration, which all later explorers were required to master. Hundreds, if not thousands, of Scots would follow him into the west and north to the wilderness named, for a time, New Caledonia.

The British interest in the Pacific shore can be traced to Francis Drake's naming an indeterminate portion of California as New Albion in 1579. Two hundred years later Captain James Cook, whose father was a Scottish farm-servant from Ednam in the Scottish Borders, a detail that most of his biographers ignore, sailed to Oregon in 1776, having been commissioned to find the Northwest Passage from the Pacific. He made his way along the coast of what is now British Columbia, exploring Nootka Inlet on the west side of Vancouver Island, thence along the coast of the Alaskan littoral and through the Bering Sea to Icy Cape, beyond which he was defeated by a wall of ice some ten to twelve feet high. His instructions had allowed him to over-winter in some suitable location before moving on to Kamchatka the following year. In preparation for a winter berth he read the translation by a Scottish doctor, James Grieve, of Stepan Krasheninnikov's *History of Kamtschatka*, which described such an unalluring place that Cook fatefully decided in favour of Hawai'i, where he was killed in February 1779.[15]

George Vancouver was in turn charged – among other matters on his epic voyage of 1791–5 – with finding likely settlement sites on the north-west coast. He was cruising the Inside Passage at the same time as Mackenzie was pursuing his second quest. Scots who sailed with Vancouver included two of his shipmasters, William Broughton and James Johnstone, who, following the American Robert Gray's discovery of the Columbia River, crossed the river's treacherous bar, to sail 100 miles inland. Gray had named the mighty river rather feebly after his ship, *Columbia Rediviva*. When Alexander Cranstoun, Vancouver's surgeon, fell sick, his duties were transferred to Archibald Menzies, the expedition's botanist, after whom the Douglas Fir, *Pseudotsuga menziesii*, is named;[16] both of these men were Scottish. Midshipmen included Charles Stuart, son of the Earl of Bute, and

John Stewart, a nephew of Admiral Elphinstone. Young Bute was completely incensed by Vancouver's flogging of a fellow midshipman, protesting that if he ever suffered the same ignominy, he would cut his own throat rather than live with the disgrace; his presence, however, doubtless inspired the naming of Bute Inlet and Arran rapids.[17] Naval Scots were not numerous; rather it was Yankees who were to become 'Lords of the Pacific',[18] but a continent was revealed by a handful of ships navigating the vastness of the Pacific. On this occasion, since there was no rendezvous between voyagers and voyageurs, there was to be no celebratory ceilidh on the *Columbia*, no jamboree on the Georgia Strait. Nonetheless it is worth stressing that the approach to the Arctic was overland, via fur trade routes, as well as by sea.

Alexander Mackenzie realised he had little hope of success without local input. One of the impressions to be gained from his journal is that he and his party were passed on from one group of First Nations to another as if they were commodities themselves, like pieces of trade silver or lumps of iron, which some found appealing and others did not. In a much-quoted passage discussing his second expedition, Mackenzie relates how he was asked, 'What can be the reason that you are so particular and anxious in your inquiries of us respecting a knowledge of this country: Do not you white men know everything in the world?' Initially taken aback, he replied that he and his companions 'certainly were acquainted with the principal circumstances of every part of the world'; they knew the position of the sea and their own location but they did not understand the obstacles which were so well known to locals. 'Thus I fortunately preserved the impression in their minds, of the superiority of white people over themselves.'[19] Whether he convinced his questioners is a moot point since they would have presumably considered that, given Mackenzie's predicament, knowledge of a locality was more pertinent than that of all the world.

Despite Mackenzie's arrogant assumptions it was, of course, the superior local knowledge of the residents that guided the Norwesters about where to diverge overland from the river, along trails which would bring them out to the ocean at Bella Coola. A brief foray into the tidal sounds allowed the explorer to inscribe a rock with the proud boast 'Alexander Mackenzie, from Canada, by land, 22 July 1793'.[20] There on the Pacific edge, Mackenzie realised his true dream. Had he been there some fifty days earlier he might have confronted none other than George Vancouver, who, according to local information, had fired upon the inhabitants. Thus Mackenzie would have met Macubah, as the First Nations called Vancouver, supposing this identification to be correct;[21] instead he was forced to beat a hasty retreat from the unwelcome attentions of hostiles.

Everywhere Scots went, they networked with the existing inhabitants. Mackenzie's published works reveal his compelling interest in customs, culture, artefacts and language. In time, however, he would lament that the ancient way of life was under serious attack, rather like that of his own heritage in Gaelic-speaking Lewis, he may have thought. Much of the land west of the Great Lakes was in a state of degradation. Smallpox – spread by the whites – was taking a severe toll. He believed that missionaries had done untold harm, while the loutish and criminal behaviour of the fur traders had poisoned relations with the native population. Worst of all, many of the *indigines* had a great fondness for alcohol, which the traders, including himself on occasion, were only too pleased to indulge. Traders were scarcely less savage than the supposedly worst of the First Nations.[22] In addition many bands had become hopelessly dependent upon hand-outs from the fur companies. Furthermore, many First Nations' sacred customs had become contaminated: pipe-smoking, for example, had a ritual and religious significance, while whites treated it as a purely recreational activity.[23]

Mackenzie did his best to persuade the British authorities to act expeditiously in protecting their interests on the Pacific rim. The discovery of a sea passage from the Atlantic to the Pacific had long excited the interest of governments and individual enterprise, but he considered that his own efforts proved 'the non-existence of a practicable passage by sea, and the existence of one through the continent'. Since the trade was much too vast to be handled by individuals, he recommended an association between NWC and HBC, a new enterprise based on the Columbia River to exploit the rich harvest of the Pacific slope. Thus Britain would obtain control of the entire fur trade along the 49th parallel, to which could be added:

> the fishing in both seas, and the markets in the four quarters of the globe. Such would be the field for commercial enterprise, and incalculable would be the produce of it, when supported by the credit and capital which Great Britain so pre-eminently possesses.[24]

Mackenzie's views were positively influenced by those of Alexander Dalrymple, hydrographer, geographer and indefatigable advocate of numerous commercial and imperial schemes, the younger brother of the Scottish historian Lord Hailes.[25] Dalrymple, in a pamphlet on the subject, wrote that by the eighteenth century the quest was for a route *through* America. There was not much activity after the founding of HBC in 1670 until parliament offered a reward of £10,000 for the discovery of the Northwest Passage, but HBC employees were 'very averse' to northern expeditions due to the difficulty, 'almost amounting to an impossibility', of constraining men at a distance to execute anything contrary to their inclination'. Mackenzie's intention was to persuade the HBC and East India Company (EIC) that they could work together in the exploitation of sea-otter skins, which were in great demand in China, as were furs of all kinds, but the British Government was to remain disgracefully uninterested in its Pacific frontier.

The conclusion of the Napoleonic War in 1815 introduced an era of paradoxes and economic recession. The British Government no longer had any need for the number of men in the services. In 1798 there had been 120,000 men in the British Navy at an annual cost of £13,644,000.[26] Largely due to Sir John Barrow, Second Secretary to the Admiralty, the search for the Northwest Passage became more frenzied after 1815, allegedly as a way to train men for naval deployment.

Polar recruits should be 'of a cheerful disposition, free from disease', 'without blemish and without spot' and 'inured to the life of a sailor'. Ideally, they should be aged between 20 and 32, of middle stature with well-proportioned bodies, 'strong and active, with a well-developed, capacious chest, sound heart and lungs', organs which even in normal conditions are the most severely taxed. They required 'stout muscular limbs, with a light active gait' and they should not harbour any constitutional or hereditary disease.[27] For some these were tall orders. They also had to be free, but the press-gangs were still feared, and Irishmen especially were viewed as potentially troublesome. The Spithead and Nore mutinies in the Royal Navy at the end of the eighteenth century preserved a nervous memory, rendering impressment legal until 1835; indeed, according to some authorities it was never formally abolished.

*

The period from 1815 to c.1860 was obviously one of profound transition when attitudes to politics, monarchy and authority underwent great changes. Technology was revolutionised and an eccentric naval captain by the name of John Ross from Stranraer in south-west Scotland was one of the first to advocate the Navy's adoption of steamships.[28] It was also a period when a British obsession became an international one and dead heroes were elevated far above survivors. The craze for ice was part of the fantasy but there was interest also in its practical applications, for example food preservation through refrigeration. The greater public became fascinated by Arctic poems and tales, from *The Ancient Mariner* to *Frankenstein*. The search for the Magnetic North Pole became a quest for a grail of a kind, while the understanding of electromagnetism intrigued many, as it eluded more.

William Scoresby, born 1789, was the son of a Grimsby whaler of the same name who at one point founded the 'Greenock Whale and Fishing Company' with three businessmen from that Clyde port. Scoresby junior was one of the most remarkable men of his generation, studying natural history and chemistry at Edinburgh University with Professor Robert Jameson, to whom he dedicated his classic two-volume *Account of the Arctic Regions with a History and Description of the Northern Whale-Fishery* (1820), which has been lauded as 'the foundation stone of Arctic science'. He combined book learning with his practical experience of the whaling industry inherited from his father. His books remain essential reading for anyone truly interested in the Arctic, which he first visited when he was eleven years old in 1790, going on to command at least fifteen voyages. Two years in the Navy convinced him to thereafter avoid the Senior Service. In 1817 he reported information, originating from whalers, about unprecedented amounts of clear, ice-free water in Baffin Bay and hence an opportunity to seek the Northwest Passage, even though by then all knew it offered virtually no real commercial prospects. Scoresby had experienced the volatility of the Arctic weather and oceanography at first hand and so was not making any suggestions about climate warming as such. Any hopes of improved conditions were swiftly shattered. Scoresby would have been delighted to captain a naval exploratory vessel and was well qualified for the task, but he fell foul of John Barrow, who excluded him from the Admiralty's renewed Arctic searches for a passage in 1818 and 1819.[29] Despite the lack of support from Barrow, Scoresby completed his survey of Greenland's shoreline in 1822 and published his *Journal of a Voyage to the Northern Whale Fishery* (1823). However, in 1823, he made his last Arctic voyage following the death of his first wife and the combined economic impact of declining numbers of whales in Greenland waters. Shunned by the Navy's Arctic explorations, Scoresby turned to a new vocation studying theology at Cambridge. His biographers[30] wittily referred to the great minds that influenced him at Edinburgh as 'The Northern Lights', namely the group that included, among others, geologist James Hutton, scientist Joseph Black, natural historians Robert Jameson and John Richardson, natural philosopher John Playfair and mathematician and theologian John Leslie from Fife, who in 1810 was the first to demonstrate the artificial creation of ice.[31] To these, Joseph Banks and many others were added.

Scoresby's early studies of snow led him to discover that no two crystals were exactly identical. He begins his *Account of the Arctic Regions* with a discussion of a possible sea communication between the Atlantic and the Pacific, quoting the maxim 'What we wish to be true, we readily believe', reviewing expeditions from earliest times to those of Buchan and Franklin in 1818. He reports his own research and experience in Svalbard, Jan Mayen Island and other islands to provide a hydrographical survey of the Greenland Sea on such aspects as water colour, transparency, specific gravity and salt content, together with temperature, depth and pressure, as well as currents and waves. He writes at length about ice, atmospherology and natural history, backing up all of his assertions with tables, measurements and observations. He describes the devastating effects of cold on the human body. His second book is given over entirely to the whaling industry. No such comprehensive surveys as those had ever before appeared.

Another subject that exercised Scoresby became known as the Magnetic Crusade, rather a grandiose title but an appropriate one, as the subject of the Earth's magnetism gripped the scientific world in the eighteenth and nineteenth centuries. Andrew Lambert has argued, with pardonable exaggeration, that the Arctic expeditions were 'a global attempt to measure, catalogue and control the natural world that it might be reduced to order, placed under the British flag and exploited for commercial gain'.[32] Scoresby asserted that greater understanding of the magnetism phenomenon would be of crucial benefit to navigators and chart-makers: hourly observations should be made of the fluctuations of magnetic variation, dip and intensity. On agreed days all European observatories should observe during twenty-four successive hours, simultaneously, and at intervals of not more than five minutes. It was recommended that this should be done six times a year, later reduced to four. Further research was needed worldwide on land and at sea. Since there was very little information about these matters in the southern hemisphere an expedition was urgently required. Special measuring implements were acquired, refined or invented for the tasks ahead. Many thought that terrestrial magnetism was a phantom. Others such as John Ross never actually quite understood it; in 1818 his ignorance greatly embarrassed his nephew.[33]

Everything was orchestrated through the various learned societies in London: the Royal Society, the Geological Society, the Geographical Society and the British Association for the Advancement of Science. At the heart of all of these endeavours was Sir Roderick Murchison, born at Muir of Ord, Ross-shire, sometime soldier, who was rescued from a frivolous life of hunting and shooting by Sir Humphry Davy. Davy converted him to geology, a study at which he excelled, leading to specialisation in coal and an influential book entitled *The Silurian System*. Murchison collaborated with John Barrow and, with the support of magneteer Edward Sabine and naval hydrographer Francis Beaufort, he organised Arctic expeditions that were largely concerned with terrestrial magnetism. It had long been noted that the compass, invented by the Chinese in the first century AD, was affected by the magnetic field of the Earth, which varied in different places, depending upon activity in the Earth's core. Disruption can be caused by sun-flares or electromagnetic storms. Solar influence is also manifested in the 'Aurora', the Aurora Borealis or 'Northern Lights'. These matters were of crucial interest to mariners as a possible means of predicting magnetic variation through understanding of the dip, defined as 'the angle which the direction of the magnetic needle at any place makes with the horizon'. The dipping-needle was 'mounted so as to be capable of moving in a vertical plane about its centre of gravity, and thus indicating by its dip the direction of the earth's magnetism'.[34] The process could be interrupted by the iron in the ship's reinforced head or bow, or indeed anything else metallic on board. The father of British geomagnetism was William Gilbert from Essex, who in 1600 published his *De Magnete* (full English title, *On the Magnet, Magnetic Bodies and the Great Magnet of the Earth*). His researches revealed that the Earth, which itself acts as a giant magnet, has two magnetic poles. Many prominent scientists, including Baron von Humbolt, joined the magnet men. J.F.W. Herschel on behalf of the British Association for the Advancement of Science urged that the three elements,

> the horizontal direction, the dip, and the intensity (recently realised) require to be precisely ascertained before the magnetic state of any given situation on the globe can be said to be fully determined. Nor can either of them, theoretically speaking, be said to be more important than the others, though the direction, on account of its immediate use to navigators, has hitherto had the greatest stress laid upon it, and has been reduced into elaborate charts.[35]

*

During the period characterised as the Enlightenment, the hunt for knowledge of all kinds was insatiable, though until recently Canadian historical research appeared to lag some distance behind the US in that regard, a situation that is now receiving some academic attention. As Canadian confidence grew, so too did research into science, technology and natural history.[36]

This was an era when the poet Allan Cunningham, for one, celebrated the freedom of sail and sea, of life on the ocean wave, though his sea-going experience was limited to trips between his native Dumfriesshire and London. His family resided at Sandhead on the opposite bank of the River Nith to Ellisland, whose sometime tenant was Robert Burns. Their landlord was Patrick Miller of Dalswinton who, with William Symington, an engineer from Leadhills, famously trialled the first demonstration of the potential of steamships, on tiny Dalswinton Loch in 1788. Witnesses confirmed that the event attracted a large crowd of locals, who turned it into something of a festive occasion, but unfortunately for those who assume that Burns must have been there, he almost certainly was not. Cunningham favoured wind over steam:

> A wet sheet and a flowing sea,
> A wind that follows fast,
> And fills the white and rustling sail,
> And bends the gallant mast;
> And bends the gallant mast, my boys,
> While, like the eagle free,
> Away the good ship flies and leaves
> Old England on the lee.[37]

None other than Sir Walter Scott believed this was 'among the best songs going' and many agreed. However, in the Arctic, the image of the free-flying eagle would dramatically freeze when ships were stationary for eleven months of the year, ice-bound and only to be moved, if at all, by human muscle and sweat. To get anywhere they had to be manhandled by warping, towing or tacking. Warping involved attaching a hawser to the ice ahead of the ship and hauling it by use of the capstan. Towing was done by the ship's boats, as rowers hauled the ship behind them. A combination of the two was known as kedging. During the 1812 War, the American ship *Constitution*, which appeared to be trapped in Annapolis harbour, outwitted a British squadron by kedging for three days in flat water, en route to Boston.[38] Tracking required the ship's company to pull the ship on ropes. Sawing through the ice was the most effective, if exhausting, way to free an ice-bound ship, or to create a dock that might hold two ships abreast, or even to create a canal through which the ship could be manipulated.

A further quixotic aspect of the age was that Vice-Admiral Nelson was hero-worshipped for disobeying orders, while the unfortunate Admiral John Byng was executed in 1757 for his best efforts, despite inadequate resources. Equally striking is the memorialisation of all the Dundas and Melville names that appear on maps of the Canadian Arctic. Henry Dundas, Viscount Melville, and his son, Robert Dundas, were both, in succession, First Lords of the Admiralty. Both also controlled the Scottish political machine and hence also a great deal of patronage that, rightly or wrongly, included the appointment of fellow Scots to naval office. Naval officers such as John Ross could do well out of the spoils of war, only to be faced with austerity when hostilities ended. Although in 1818 the Arctic appeared to offer little in the way of riches, it was nonetheless considered important to 'Take Possession', resulting in the vast northern territories claimed by the British and later handed on to Canada. The process involved a short ceremony in which the captain or his delegated officers 'took possession of the country', claimed in the name of the monarch. A flagstaff was normally erected and often a toast was shared by those present. The 'flagstaff' was occasionally fashioned out of rocks to form a pillar but in the harsh conditions of the Arctic such constructions were often short-lived. At times the possession process was conducted as a celebration involving a number of men, at others a rushed job so that those involved could take shelter from the elements as quickly as possible. The badly flawed credo of *Terra Nullius* (nobody's land or empty land) was assumed, as in the Antipodes, and, of course, the rights of the Inuit were not considered.

The aforementioned John Barrow, born in Ulverston, Lancashire, the son of a tanner, became known as Britain's original and most accomplished civil servant, later knighted for his services. Like many of his professional ilk he was expert at flattering his superiors and bullying his underlings. He was to play an important part in the life of John Ross and other explorers. He was offered the position of Second Secretary to the Admiralty by Lord Melville, a post that he retained until 1845. He has been described as a bureaucrat *par excellence*, but an ambitious one who detected great advantage for his country in exploration. He wrote several books and a lifetime achievement of 195 articles for the *Quarterly Review*, founded in Edinburgh by John Murray to challenge the phenomenal popularity of the Whig *Edinburgh*

Review. When elected to the Royal Society he became acquainted with Sir Joseph Banks, veteran of Cook's circumnavigation of the world, whom he assisted to become 'the father of global exploration'.[39] However, Barrow was literally a closet explorer who had very little personal experience of the Arctic and other exotic places to which he sent favoured representatives. He was also a single-minded autocrat with a waspish tongue, a vicious pen, a great conceit of himself and an unattractive tendency to blame others for his own failings.

John Wilson Croker (1780–1857), Irishman and an arch Tory, was appointed First Secretary to the Admiralty in 1809, a post he retained until 1830. He had an unenviable reputation for self-aggrandisement and the manufacture of enemies, as a staunch reactionary in defence of conservatism. His adopted daughter, Nony, married John Barrow's son, George. Notoriously John Ross was to give Croker's name to a non-existent range of mountains that he incorrectly identified in Lancaster Sound, off Baffin Bay. Croker also enjoyed a career as a writer though he was not enthusiastic about fiction, reputedly preferring 'an ounce of fact to a ton of imagination'.

It is something of an irony that a famous literary monster and the most professional British Arctic expedition hitherto conceived should be launched in the same year. John Croker reviewed a publication of 1818 in the *Quarterly* which introduced one Victor Frankenstein to the world. The author was the eighteen-year-old Mary Shelley, who with her lover Percy, the well-known Romantic poet, and their son, had holidayed on the shores of Lake Geneva with her half-sister Claire Clairmont and Dr John Polidori, personal physician to an outrageous individual who in literary and visceral terms might be regarded as the foster-father of Frankenstein, namely George Gordon, Lord Byron. It was probably Byron who suggested that the group amuse themselves by holding a story-writing competition about ghosts. Mary's monster and his maker were the result. However, her name did not appear as author until 1823, the earliest reviewers assuming (inevitably) that the author was a man, an imaginative writer, with a poor grasp of plot and construction. The pages of the novella are damp with endless deaths and tears. There is too much of the 'the man of feeling' for modern tastes. The science is bogus but, to the uninitiated, believable. As a specimen of literature, *Frankenstein* may be one of the most over-hyped productions ever to appear on undergraduate reading lists because it seems to invoke so many contemporary metaphors, despite its brevity, while remaining relevant and accessible through so many botched cinematic versions of an already unstable text.

The story begins, ends and is told by whaleship Captain Robert Walton who, somewhere in the far north, takes on board a man in a bad way who proceeds to relate his experiences. He is Frankenstein himself, who has learned to kill in order to generate life, and who is, of course, the creator of the nameless monster. As Croker indicates, the education of the monster is just plain daft. He listens outside a cottage window to the learning expounded within, acquiring a complete education worthy of a Scottish Enlightenment *philosophe*: 'He learns to think, to talk, to read prose and verse; he becomes acquainted with geography, history, natural philosophy' and the French language. He soon reads Plutarch, Milton and Goethe's *The Sorrows of Werter*. He is intent upon having revenge on Frankenstein for creating him in the first place, by murdering the latter's brother, bride and best friend as well as contriving the deaths of innocent nursery maids, but the desire for vengeance explodes when the 'scientist' refuses to create a mate for him.

Clearly the dangerously deranged monster must die and a chase begins as the creature is pursued by his maker to the Arctic. Croker wittily observes that 'as our *Review* [i.e. the *Quarterly*] has not yet enlightened mankind upon the real state of the North Pole, he directs his course thither as a sure place of solitude and security; but Frankenstein who probably had read Mr Daines Barrington and Colonel Beaufoy on the subject' follows him, 'the monster flying on a sledge drawn by dogs according to the Colonel's proposition'.[40] Frankenstein is rescued by Walton, as described in Letter Four of the text, but dies soon after he has narrated his astonishing tale. The monster turns up as funerary rites are proclaimed, to announce that he will incinerate himself on a funeral pyre, though where he will find enough wood is not discussed; hopefully there was a driftwood bay handy. Thus, according to Croker the reader is left at the end of the tale, wearied 'after a struggle between laughter and loathing, in doubt whether the head or the heart of the author be the most diseased'.[41]

Just as interesting are the opposed views of Mary Shelley and mariners on the nature of the Arctic. Mary, who had never been there, regarded it as a place of everlasting light, while Captain John Ross dreaded its recurring darkness.

*

This book does not intend to suggest that the Scots were superior to others in the annals of Arctic exploration but it does promote the view that they played a major role in the Franklin era. Multiculturalism is the future and while it is essential to preserve and share heritage and history it is pointless to privilege some cultures over others. For some two hundred years it has been common for writers specialising in the Arctic or Antarctic, whether in Canada, the USA, England or elsewhere, to render Scots invisible by representing them as English. I propose that we restore national identities to all of those whose true origins have been obscured. Irish, often with Scottish surnames, were also involved, for example Francis Leopold McClintock, who eventually found extensive, if incomplete, evidence of the fate of the Franklin expedition.

In what follows, the awakening of the Scots to the magnificence and dread of the hyperborean regions – as places of discovery, of inspiration and, regrettably, of exploitation – will be traced, with particular emphasis on the first half of the nineteenth century until the desperate, and at times frenzied, search for the beleaguered Franklin and his crew. On witnessing the Northern Lights during his second expedition to the Arctic, James Clark Ross was inspired to compose a poem in 1820, expressing his awe of this spectacle, which might serve well to encapsulate the fascination the Scottish explorers discussed in this book held for the far north:

> High quiv'ring in the air, as shadows fly,
> The Northern Lights adorn the azure sky . . .
> The blaze of grandeur fired my youthful blood,
> Deep in th'o'erwhelming maze of Nature's laws,
> Midst her mysterious gloom I sought the cause.
> But vain the search! inscrutable to man
> Thy works have been, O God! since time began,
> And still shall be – Then let the thought expire
> As late the splendour of Aurora's fire
> To dark Oblivion sank, in wasting flame,
> Like the dim shadows of departed fame!

John Ross Capt. R.N.

This Portrait is presented Gratis to the Purchasers of Nº 1 of Bell's Weekly Magazine.

Admiral Sir John Ross, by Day and Haghe, no date
(National Galleries of Scotland. Given by Sir Hew Hamilton Dalrymple 1940 /
Purchased 1884 / Presented by Dr J.H. Tallent 1947)

2

JOHN ROSS'S EXPEDITION OF 1818

Thy way is in the sea, and thy path in the great waters; and
thy footsteps are not known.

Psalms 77:19

John Ross asserted that few voyages of discovery had excited more general
interest at their outset than that of 1818. He cautioned that his nautical
education had taught him to act and not to question; 'to obey orders as
far as possible, not to discuss probabilities, or examine philosophical or
unphilosophical speculations'. He claimed that his chronicle of the 1818
enterprise was intended as little more than the journal of a seaman, lacking
in elegance of composition, narratorial entertainment or memorable adventure. Modesty did not become Ross any more than controversy avoided him.
His book *A Voyage of Discovery* (1819) was condemned in a vicious review by
John Barrow two months before it was published, part of a storm of literary
onslaught and professional jealousy as tempestuous as the worst meteorological disturbances encountered in the Arctic today.

Ross was born on 24 June 1777 at Soulseat, Wigtownshire, the manse of
his father, who was minister of the parish of Inch, neighbouring Stranraer.[1]
He was the youngest of four brothers.[2] The future explorer left his *Memoirs*
(1838) to posterity; this book contained a frequently confused and confusing
account of his career, but was clearly designed to show that he had 'the right
stuff'. Whether it represents fiction or fact, it conveys some idea of Ross's
personality and the view he had of himself. His parents had just returned
from a visit to the Isle of Man when he was born, a fanciful prognosis that
he was 'destined for a sailor', as well as displaying a disposition for mischief
and the water. At the age of six he was fighting older and bigger boys, earning
thrashings from his father.

He attributed his ability to withstand cold in later life to running about
barefoot as a child, a claim that could have been made by most Scottish

children at that time. At age nine he joined the Royal Navy and was assigned to HMS *Pearl* but did not go to sea.[3] Instead his first action involved a smuggler in Luce Bay, a confrontation in which he suffered a leg wound from a pistol. He spent a year at Ayr Academy; 'at the time the boys mutinied and kept the masters out by blocking up the school with snowballs', an incident typical of his mischievious practices. He boasted of having organised a raid on his Latin master's fruit trees. The unfortunate teacher on another occasion was bound hand and foot by the pupils until he promised that he would no longer beat them. The dominie gave up on Ross as 'uncontrollable . . . the head of all mischief'. John also posed as a prostitute in order to foil an unpopular local shopkeeper. It was definitely time that he returned to his ship. Thus Ross, having demonstrated that he could climb to the masthead and sail a boat, properly went to sea in 1790, having been demoted, much to his chagrin, from midshipman to cabin boy, apprentice to a merchant ship out of Greenock bound for Jamaica.

There were seven passengers, two women, four gentlemen and a farmer's son from Inch who was escaping ill use from his stepmother; he sold his father's horse to pay for his passage. The captain died of yellow fever in Jamaica. Other sufferers among the crew asked Ross to write letters for them to their sweethearts. Archibald McFadzean from Campbelltown died after signing his letter, but before it was sealed. Ross provided a postscript: 'I was taken ill of the fever this morning. I died at 12 o'clock and was buried at 6 this evening'! On returning to Scotland he enjoyed sexual adventures in Islay but what stands out in his account is the matter-of-fact way in which he describes violence at the hands of teachers and naval personnel. A Miss Kepping, with whom he formed some kind of attachment, was punished by a teacher for refusing to identify the perpetrators of a prank. She suffered twelve slaps on her hand, resulting in blistering. In return Ross organised a gang of boys and two sailors who trashed the teacher's study and destroyed his valuable scientific instruments. Ross took part in three voyages to the West Indies and three to the Baltic, 'all of us gentlemen's sons, sent to sea under the mistaken idea of preparing us for the Navy or India service'. They were expected to find their sea legs on merchant ships but their privileged backgrounds seem to have rendered them disrespectful of authority. Ross escaped a flogging for near-mutiny through a chance meeting with a lieutenant who knew his father; he made his peace with an alcoholic captain whom he saved from drowning.[4]

Gaps in his memoir severely limit its usefulness. He claimed to have no interest in the Navy during peace-time since the prospects for both promotion and prize money were remote. Family influence assisted in his appointment to the East India Company ship *Queen* in 1794. He was involved in the suppression of at least two more mutinies, and went through the traditional 'crossing the line' ceremony at the Equator with Mr and Mrs Neptune, as he sailed to India, surviving a ferocious storm in the Bay of Bengal. He thrashed two sailors who challenged him to a fist fight. Sailing homewards from Madras the boatswain announced, 'We have a new face on the mainyard!' A sailor had forgotten his trousers before climbing aloft thus exhibiting his 'bare stern'. A scandalised lady passenger fled to her cabin. Less amusing were outbreaks of scurvy which spread throughout the ship. Two hyenas died when they escaped their cages. Shortly afterwards an elephant that was also part of the cargo died, probably not of natural causes but because the crew bitterly resented the amount of fresh water the beast consumed. Back on land, Ross won a duel, rather a fashionable activity at the time. He was preparing to flee to France when he learned the supposed victim had survived.

On the outbreak of the Napoleonic wars in 1803 he sailed on HMS *Grampus* under the flag of Rear Admiral Sir James Saumarez, who that year received the Order of the Bath, the Freedom of the City of London and a parliamentary annuity of £1,200 a year for his naval services. Ross remained with him until he was promoted to commander in 1812. He was attached to the Swedish Navy for a time, becoming a knight of the Swedish Order of the Sword and learning the language, serving in the North Sea, the White Sea and Scottish waters. Having personally suffered (or claimed) a total of thirteen wounds, including two broken legs, a bayonet through his body and five sabre cuts to his head, he was imprisoned by the French. He married Christian Adair in 1816, using significant rewards of prize money to build their home at Northwest Castle, Stranraer. If he could have afforded the luxury, Ross might have settled in to genteel retirement now that the Napoleonic wars were over, but he was hopeless in matters financial and his restless spirit remained hyperactive. Much to his delight, he was about to embark on a second career as an Arctic explorer.

On 16 December 1817 Ross was ordered by a fellow Scot, Sir George Hope, a Lord of Admiralty, to London. Two weeks later, four ships were commissioned for two separate expeditions with the aim of searching for a Northwest Passage. Ross was given command of *Isabella*, 'the most proper ship for the senior officer', while *Alexander* would be commanded by Lieutenant William Edward Parry, soon to make a great name for himself in Arctic annals. The other two ships were *Dorothea*, captained by David Buchan, and *Trent*, commanded by Lieutenant John Franklin. They were to be sent via Spitsbergen to discover the North Pole and, if successful, according to their instructions – as breezy as they were bold – they were to proceed to the Bering Strait. The Buchan expedition was a fiasco (see pages 52–8).

Isabella's officers included Scots William Robertson, William Thom (the purser), A.M. Skene (admiralty midshipman), and Ross's nephew, seventeen-year-old midshipman James Clark Ross, son of George Ross. There were no confirmed Scots on *Alexander*, though John Allison, master and Greenland pilot, may have been one. Members of the crew such as carpenter, sailmaker, cook and able seamen as well as marines were infrequently named.

During the following month, elaborate reinforcement of the vessels was undertaken to strengthen them against the ice. Equipment and spares were carefully stowed. Beds were constructed in such a way that they could be used to assemble a dwelling in the event of shipwreck. Particular attention was paid to ventilation. There was a cloth roof to be used for over-wintering. There were five whale boats, an ice boat, ice anchors, ice saws, ice axes, ice spurs, ice poles and pole hooks, whale lances, harpoons, knives, rifles, seven-barrelled guns, carronades and enough powder and shot for three years. Presents for local inhabitants encountered in Greenland and Canada included brass kettles, cutlery, axes, knives, lengths of flannel, mirrors, needles, vermillion, cutlasses, scarlet-milled caps, swords, red thread, scissors, razors, pistols, rifles, snuff, soap, pikes, iron hoops, beads, cowrie shells and umbrellas. Inevitably the cargo included 129 gallons each of gin and brandy though there is no evidence that Ross ever inflicted either of these upon the indigenous peoples. He considered himself a pragmatic supporter of temperance in the Navy, on which he later published a pamphlet, but he was not a teetotaller, simply believing that water was more refreshing than grog for men who were habitually expending large amounts of energy.[5]

Isabella was provided with a well-stocked library containing mainly items about previous Arctic expeditions. Literacy was an important feature of nineteenth-century voyages; close attention was paid to previous accounts, while journals and narratives were compiled with future explorers very much in mind. One of Franklin's editors in a stimulating discussion examines the uses that publications such as those of Ross, Franklin and others were intended to serve.[6] They were 'public' accounts of expeditions designed to satisfy a public thirst for travelogues and exotica while serving to promote the authors in the eyes of their superiors. Hopefully they would also generate quite satisfactory revenues from book sales. There were, in addition, journals that were internal to the Navy and not for public consumption. Ross pored over available material concerning William Baffin's voyages and he carefully studied Crantz's *History of Greenland*, as well as such classics as Hearne's and Mackenzie's overland travels to the Polar Sea and the voyages of Cook and Vancouver. Works on Iceland and Patagonia, as well as books on geology and mineralogy, were also devoured.

Isabella boasted the latest in sophisticated measuring equipment, since mensuration was a naval obsession just as magnetism would shortly become a national, and international, fixation – seven chronometers for calculating latitude, at least twelve compasses as well as several dipping needles, thermometers, barometers, a hygrometer, a hydrometer, a micrometer and a sympiesometer, which was a type of barometer invented by Adie of Edinburgh. Also included was 'Electrical Apparatus invented by Sir H. Davy' and a gadget for retrieving sea-water from depths greater than eight fathoms, not forgetting 'Trengrouse's apparatus for saving lives'. Each man was provided with special warm clothing including a flushing jacket made from a type of wool first developed at the Dutch port of Flushing, a monkey jacket (or sailor jacket), red shirts, a pair of flushing trousers, swan-skin (i.e. flannel) drawers, coarse woollen stockings, sea boots, scarlet and fawn caps, mitts, fur caps, 'comfortables' or scarfs, and ankle shoes.

Ross was deeply concerned throughout his career that his men should enjoy an adequate diet. For a total of fifty men over a possible period of twenty-six lunar months *Isabella* was supplied with 18,200 pounds each of bread and of flour, 1,300 pieces of beef each weighing eight pounds, 2,600 six-pound pieces of pork, 1,000 pounds of suet, 600 of raisins, 1,950 of cocoa, 3,900 of sugar, 162 bushels of peas and 30 of oatmeal. 700 gallons of wine, 1,925 of spirits, 325 of vinegar together with 2,275 pounds of lemon juice and equivalent poundage of sugar to make it palatable, as well as 1,329 pounds of molasses, were also put aboard. In addition the ship carried comparatively modest amounts of herbs and vegetables which were dwarfed by 3,200 pounds of preserved meats and 1,300 quarts of vegetable soup and the same amount of concentrated soup. Pickled walnuts and cabbage made for some variety; 69 iron tanks for the storage of provisions were distributed between the four vessels.[7]

Clearly 'nothing was neglected which could be conducive to the health and comfort of those who volunteered to serve on this enterprise'. Payment ranged from £46 per month for the captain to £3 for an able seaman. A surgeon earned just over £39 per month, a midshipman over £6, a carpenter £6 and a cook £4. There were fifty-seven persons in total aboard *Isabella* and forty-one on *Alexander*. One 'Eskimaux' was paid £3. This was the colourful Inuk John Sacheuse (or Sackhouse, sometimes known as Zakaeus), born in south-east Greenland, who, having been converted to Christianity, stowed away on a whaler bound for Leith where his kayaking displays became popular. In Edinburgh he studied painting with the liberal-minded portrait and landscape artist Alexander Nasmyth, who had been a friend of Robert Burns and steam-promotor Patrick Miller of Dalswinton, both deceased by that time. Ross hired Sacheuse as interpreter, praising his 'meritorious conduct' and fulsomely lauding his linguistic skills. Ross's onboard 'man of science' was Captain Edward Sabine of the Royal Artillery, 'a gentleman well-skilled in astronomy, natural history and various branches of knowledge, to assist you in making such observations as may tend to the improvement of geography and navigation and the advancement of science in general'.[8] If Sacheuse acted effectively as the expedition's pacifier, Sabine, who later became a major leader of the terrestrial magnetism movement, notably contributed to Ross's personal maelstrom. Ross's nephew, James, would also incur avuncular wrath when he became enmeshed, as did Sabine, in machinations orchestrated by John Barrow.

The 'Official Instructions' given to Ross stated that 'an attempt should be made to discover a Northern Passage, by sea, from the Atlantic to the Pacific Ocean' but he had a personal interest in ascertaining the extent of the great bay named for William Baffin who discovered it in 1616, one of the great luminaries of Arctic exploration, the first Englishman to record longitude. Baffin made several voyages to the ice in Canada, Greenland and Spitsbergen. He experimented with the compass, charted Baffin Bay and almost discovered Lancaster Sound. Narratives of some of his ventures have survived but by 1818 many of his achievements had been queried probably due to a naval sense of superiority as the service professionalised. Ross felt considerable empathy for him, although there was no mention of Baffin in his 'Instructions'. He was ordered to pass through the Davis Strait in search of a current flowing from the north or north-west, which, if in existence, he should then follow to the north before heading west round the north-east corner of the American continent. Alexander Fisher, assistant surgeon on *Alexander*, was convinced that a passage existed, based on the experiences of Hearne and Mackenzie.[9]

It was assumed that Ross would proceed directly to the Pacific via the Bering Strait. If no westward passage was found he was to sail north to ascertain whether Greenland was an island or part of America. He was specifically forbidden to over-winter, quitting the Davis Strait by 1 October. It was hoped that he would improve knowledge of the geography and hydrology of the Arctic regions, 'of which so little is hitherto known, and contribute to the advancement of science and natural knowledge'. Although commercial and colonial opportunism had often been a major motivation for the voyages of discovery, the acquisition of scientific knowledge had also always been an important factor. There was much to learn for it is evident that no-one suspected the vexed existence of the numerous Arctic islands, the second largest archipelago in the world, which would prove, during the next half century or so, the cruellest of nature's mazes, a frozen labyrinth of incomparable complexity compounded by seemingly endless day or perpetual night.

A master and mate 'of whale-fishing vessels, well experienced in those seas' were to be appointed to each of the expedition ships. Some advice was given about what little was known concerning ice conditions and currents, the potential dangers of which were not minimised. If they found clear water they were to pass through it to the Pacific and thence to Kamchatka whence they were to send their charts and other documents to London via St Petersburg. Crews were then to rest in Hawai'i or New Albion (California), before returning east through the passage. If that was not possible they were to return via Cape Horn. Before leaving Shetland, on their way north from London, Ross was to make arrangements with Buchan concerning a rendezvous in the Pacific. Their confidence and ambition were breathtaking. Instructions were issued about taking over any damaged expedition ships and any of their crews that had become disabled. If they failed to approach the passage because of ice-block, they were to sail as far up the coast of West Greenland as they could, looking for indications of a way through to the north. Otherwise they were to explore the east coast of America and any intermediate islands, making drawings and surveys of the geography, and taking numerous readings, measurements and scientific observations. As well as such obvious subjects as the weather and all aspects of the sea, they were to study magnetism and the influence of magnetic force, atmospheric electricity and the Aurora Borealis upon the needle. They were also to investigate refraction, the dip of the horizon and the contents of the sea-bed, the last using a new instrument designed for the purpose. One further possibility was the need to over-winter in the Davis Strait, in which event they were to cultivate friendships with 'either Eskimaux or Indians' living locally, while looking out for signs of hostility.[10]

In early April 1818 the ships were inspected by the Duke of Clarence, the future William IV, known as 'the sailor king'. Ross does not mention the accidental drowning of the superintendent of Sheerness Harbour on 19 April,[11] perhaps because it was regarded as an ill omen at the start of the voyage. By 25 April, after some delays, the ships had exited the Thames, and the maritime pilot (who helped them manoeuvre out of the harbour) disembarked at Cromer. The next day was Sunday and the occasion, as was the case throughout Ross's expeditionary career, for divine service.

They arrived in Lerwick, Shetland four days later, where they recruited a volunteer from an excise cruiser, as well as a cook and a fiddler. They were also hospitably entertained by William Mouat of Gardie House on the island of Bressay, who offered facilities to erect a portable observatory and thus an opportunity to test their instruments and take measurements. Bad weather detained them longer than they wished, though they enjoyed visits from local worthies. A valuable acquisition was a bullock presented by Mouat, taken aboard ship and consumed a couple of days later. Fisher, assistant surgeon on *Alexander*, amused himself by writing a brief ethnography of Shetland and its inhabitants. According to him the women were excellent knitters but in the countryside many were little better than beasts of burden while, among the men, anyone who could pull an oar signed up for the Greenland fishery. *Dorothea* and *Trent*, bound for Spitsbergen (Svalbard), 'the latter in a leaky state', arrived just before the other two ships left. So *Isabella* and *Alexander* on 3 May bade farewell 'to the last vestige of our native land, with a voyage of uncertain length before us; and it was not with hearts unmoved that we left these shores', sailing past Whalsay and through Yell Sound. The rhetoric indicates that the myth-maker was already at work.

As the ships headed west-north-west the crew took soundings and tested equipment. *Isabella's* carpenter was busily constructing 'what the sailors call a crow's-nest, a kind of hurricane-house, fixed at the mast-head, to screen the look-out men from the weather; its form is cylindrical'.[12] On the Sabbath the men were given religious tracts to read. Inability to take soundings in deep water disproved the existence of Baffin's sunken land of Buss (marked on many charts since Martin Frobisher's explorations in the sixteenth century), thus confirming the doubts of the whalers. Others had questioned the existence of Buss; Ross was the first to offer conclusive proof that their scepticism was valid. On 26 May the expeditionaries, 100 miles west of Greenland, observed their first iceberg, considered a symbol of good luck since it appeared to resemble the lion and unicorn of the royal arms. Fisher recorded the 'magnificent spectacle appearing like an immense rock of white marble rising out of the sea'. Like most folk who have visited the Arctic, words failed him on encountering his first bergs.

Ross thought nothing could exceed the beauty of 'calm and delightfully serene' long-light nights in the Arctic, 'presenting the appearance of summer with the reality of winter'. He reported that, night and day, icebergs glittered 'with a vividness of colour beyond the power of art to represent'. Copper capsules containing messages and accurate positions, in several languages, were thrown overboard at regular intervals – highly unreliable 'Ocean Mail' as few were ever recovered. Equipment and scientific instruments were tested. A 'mud-machine' took samples as the crews adjusted to snowfalls, endless light and drift ice. On tying up on a grounded iceberg the crews encountered their first Greenlander, who told them the berg was left over from the previous year. A seal was shot, weighing 850 pounds and yielding 30 gallons of oil. All the while, measurements were laboriously and scrupulously carried out, to the point of utter tedium. The ships were primarily survey vessels laying down charts of the greatest possible accuracy for future voyagers. In this respect there is a huge difference between the actions of Ross's contingent and those of later controversial explorers such as Robert E. Peary and James Cook, whose readings were seriously challenged, dismissed by some as invention.

On 11 June they fell in with some whalers, one from Dundee, the rest from Hull, all of whom had been ice-bound for two weeks, but who reported open sea west of Disko. Both naval ships were tacked, warped and towed through the pack ice in company with several other whalers. At Whale, or Kronprins, Island, they met the Danish governor, Inspector Flushe, his wife, six other Danes and a hundred 'Eskimaux' employed in seal and whale hunting. Flushe reported that the previous winter had been severe; many harbours that should have been open remained frozen, and the way to the north was blocked. The populace had been reduced to eating their dogs. Such accounts confounded the previous year's optimistic reports of clear water, the authors of which appeared to have been 'guided rather by their imaginations' than any real knowledge of local conditions. Ross jocularly and ironically recalled reading articles before sailing, predicting that the English climate would come to rival that of Italy and 'every peasant would make his wine, where he now with difficulty reared his apple trees'.[13] Such Hesperidean fantasies are today part of serious global warming.

Around Hare Island, Ross viewed some forty-five whalers trapped in the ice. The portable observatory was erected on land to determine latitude at

70°26'17' N. Seven hundred icebergs were in sight, all cradled in a semi-circle of islands connected to a wall of ice. Ross's powers of seamanship were tested when the iceberg to which they had anchored was suddenly driven westward, but later *Isabella* was at the mercy of the tide for hours, slowly warping her way through the ice. From Four Point Island her crew beheld vast amounts of ice, as well as a deserted Danish whaling station and a whaleship's surgeon collecting human skulls. Finding clear water, *Isabella* was towed for a time, only to be trapped in shallow water, while *Alexander* grounded, both being rescued by whalemen laboriously manipulating hawsers. Worsening conditions did not permit the crew to recover from the exertions of several days, essentially manhandling their vessels in desperate conditions. Muscles were stretched once more as the ships were warped into a breeze. The whalers were confident that easterly winds would enable them to sail north, Mr Lawson of *Majestic* advising that they keep between the ice and Greenland.

Weather conditions improved once the ships left the district of Avanersuaq (Northwest Greenland). A shore party, which included James Ross, went in search of habitations, tidal observations and natural history specimens. John Ross named Cape York in honour of the royal duke's birthday. Next day he discovered mysterious crimson cliffs, on which the snow was stained red, a phenomenon which generated much controversy and ridicule when the ships returned home, though later validated by several independent observers. James Ross and surgeon Beverley were in a party sent to secure samples of the red snow which they speculated was caused by vegetable matter. They were correct. Peary called it a 'red banner of the Arctic',[14] the colour deriving from an alga, *Protococcus nivalis*, but it provided another excuse to lampoon Ross. Soon they passed Cape Dudley Digges, named by Baffin, where they noted a considerable swell and water clear of ice north-westwards. Six miles to the north a large glacier was seen as they approached Wolstenholme Island where Ross had been falsely led to believe he would find the 'King of the Inuit', a pleasure he was forced to forgo because of the lateness of the season and the anticipation that he was on the verge of solving the issue of the Northwest Passage. The most impressive part of the voyage so far had been the encounter with the Inughuit, named by Ross 'the Arctic Highlanders', an enlightening exercise in relativism (see Chapter 7). He named Dalrymple Rock for the Earl of Stair, while a southerly cape honoured the Duke of Atholl.

Improving weather opened a channel in the ice through which the naval ships threaded, accompanied by a number of whalers, to be confronted by a veritable forest of huge icebergs concealing false passages and inlets which necessitated back-tracking and endless patience. The whole of July was taken up with this relentlessly tedious activity as wood and ice were engaged in a daily battle for survival. Ross used part of the time to design a new deep-sea clamm, as he named it, to secure sea-bed samples, jettisoning the other model. The first whale was spotted as the first whaleship was crushed in the ice. Ross barely noticed the event but Fisher was much more forthcoming. Forty whalers began the killing. The whaleship *Three Brothers* of Hull was trapped between two ice floes 'which closed on her with such violence that she was cut right in two' though fortunately no lives were lost since the crew escaped onto the ice.

> Let any one consider the violence of the shock which must ensue from the meeting of two floes, each perhaps several miles in circumference, and three feet thick, and these moving in in contrary directions, at the rate of a mile, or a mile and a half, an hour, and he will readily conceive the little chance a ship would have of withstanding the enormous pressure which would be upon her, were she to be caught in such a situation.[15]

Isabella was almost crushed in a narrow channel but fortunately rose above the ice, to be hauled into clear water, while *Alexander* followed, having been similarly extricated. Both literally inched northwards as crews sawed through ice flows and then warped the ships through the channels. On 17 July, through fog and frustration they eventually reached a conspicuous sea-mark, the Devil's Thumb, a distinctive pinnacle 1,791 feet high in northwest Greenland, at latitude 74°30' N. but it was barely visible because of the weather. And so they continued as muscle, sinew and ingenuity strove to overcome the forces of nature. A fruitless polar bear hunt involving the assistant surgeon Beverley, accompanied by midshipmen Skene and James Ross, offered some diversion. A little later, surgical assistance was provided for the whaling master of *Everthorpe*, who had been severely lacerated by a bear.

At last the ships met open water and were able to raise the sails. They were now, allegedly, as far north as any whalers had been known to venture, but calm weather demanded 'towing, sweeping and warping the ships along'. Towing involved just that. The entire crew was placed on the ice, pulling a rope attached to the fore-mast; care had to be taken that the rope was not severed by sharp ice. To relieve the monumental boredom of the task the fiddler led the procession, generating much mirth and wit as he occasionally fell through holes in the ice, as did the odd crewman. So this fleet of the frozen wastes, *Isabella*, *Alexander* and some thirty whalers, painfully advanced, to win clear water. Between latitudes 75° and 76° Ross named Melville's Monument 'from gratitude to the late lamented Viscount (Sir George Hope) from whom I received my first commission in His Majesty's Navy', and Melville's Bay, 'from respect to the present First Lord of the Admiralty', Robert Dundas, 2nd Viscount Melville. Sychophancy could prove a useful, if tedious, tool! Thus two of Scotland's supreme political managers were commemorated in the far north of Baffin Bay.

More importantly, in the new and unexploited killing waters, Ross was able to report the presence of numerous whales that had never been hunted, though he was almost certainly mistaken in making that claim because whalers had undoubtedly tested the waters long before. An island was named for Mr Thom, purser of *Isabella*. James Ross took part in a whale hunt though his uncle seemed unexpectedly affected by the creature's appalling death, 'rolling and writhing in dreadful agony, lashing the sea from side to side with tail and fins, till he expired'. The blubber was saved for purposes of light and fuel should the ships become trapped for the winter. Fisher devoted several pages to a close description of the dead whale. The whaleship *Bon Accord* of Aberdeen then went into the same pool and killed five whales. Letters were sent with the whaler as it prepared to return south, 'parting with three cheers'.[16]

Ross is silent on the matter of exchanging personnel with the whalers, for one reason or another, as mentioned by Fisher. A seaman suffering from mental derangement, epilepsy and suicidal tendencies was swapped for one, John Gordon, aboard *Equestris* of Hull. There were other exchanges with *Royal George*, *Everthorpe* and *Dexterity*. These men, either ill or unsuitable for service, were replaced by volunteers from the whaleships.[17]

The ships continued to push northwards, noting auks, whales and narwhal. Each ship was tracked part way, but it was necessary to suspend a boat from the jib-boom, which was rolled by two seamen raising a wave ahead to break the ice. A freshening breeze in clear water permitted the luxury of travel at five or six miles per hour, 'a velocity we had not experienced for several months'.

Isabella became trapped between a rapidly passing berg and a fixed flow, subject to swirling pressure which bent her beams and threatened to crush her. Suddenly the hull rose several feet, but the ice, 6 feet thick, broke, placing extreme pressure on the bow and driving her towards *Alexander*. All attempts to avoid fouling one another were futile; 'the ice-anchors and cables broke one after another, and the sterns of the two ships came so violently into contact, as to crush to pieces a boat that could not be removed in time'. The collision was so violent that Ross feared for the masts, but when the ice fortuitously receded the two vessels passed one another. In a last parting drama the bower anchors of both ships became entangled so that, ripped from their respective bows, their lines linked both until *Alexander*'s broke.[18] Heavy snow, a fierce gale and rapidly moving ice added to their woes. As a large ice field was bearing down on the ships, all hands were immediately ordered to saw docks for shelter, but the ice was too thick. Fisher is presumably referring to the same confusing situation in his description of the tangling of the ships. While they were attempting to warp between icebergs and the icefield, the two crashed together forcing the latter fifty feet up the side of the former, 'where it suddenly broke, the elevated part falling back on the rest with a terrible crash, and overwhelming with its ruins the very spot we had previously chosen for our safety'. Secure once more, the exhausted men were given extra rations and grog, before starting to repair the damage. Whaling veterans opined that a whaleship in such a situation would have been crushed to atoms; earlier measures to reinforce the two ships had proved themselves. Four officers investigated Bushnan Island, where they found Inuit graves and a small piece of heath-bush burned at one end, identified by Sacheuse as a lamp-trimmer.

Ross was now forced to make passage for the north-west due to the situation of the ice but on 9 August the expeditionaries were introduced to one of the highlights of the entire voyage when, to their amazement, they detected men on the ice. It was thought impossible that humans could live at such a latitude. The encounter was sensational, and Ross, perhaps surprisingly given what we know of his character and attitudes, was enchanted by the people he dubbed the 'Arctic Highlanders', who became known to the world as the Etah Inughuit. They have also been named the Greenlandic Inuit, the Smith Sound Inuit and 'Polar Eskimos'. This is a fraught subject for an outsider as is so much of Inuit and Kalaallit culture, language and belief. The approach taken here is to view the Greenlanders and the Inuit through the eyes of Ross and his successors as they perceived the peoples of the Arctic. Those of us who have no wish to pretend knowledge that we do not have must await much needed studies written by the remarkable Inuit themselves rather than by interlopers who have traditionally far too often regarded them as exotic objects of research. (On the Inuit see Chapter 7.)[19]

*

It was 18 August 1818. During the next week or so *Isabella's* captain appeared to spend much of his time confirming Baffin's discoveries at the top of the vast bay named for him.

The ships continued northwards, as promising winds were confounded by dense fog. At all times compass readings and sea-bed soundings were taken. All were agreed, however, after several officers had been engaged on scanning the horizon from the masthead, that there was no passage through to the north, that, beyond the ice, the land was continuous. According to Ross:

> The ardour existing at home for the discovery of a north-west passage, and the confidence with which the supposed situation of such an opening has been transferred to one spot as fast as it was found not to exist in another, render it necessary to recapitulate the circumstances which disprove its existence in this place, which forms the northernmost extremity of Baffin's Bay . . . Even if it be imagined that some narrow Strait may exist through these mountains, it is evident, that it must for ever be unnavigable, and that there is not even a chance of ascertaining its existence, since all approach to the bottoms of these bays is prevented by the ice which fills them to so great a depth, and appears never to have moved from its station.[20]

Why John Ross should have been so dogmatic about such matters is puzzling. As his biographer ruefully remarks, he 'had an unfortunate knack of stating his opinion in uncompromising terms on matters which he was later proved to be wrong'.[21] He was, however, about to make the most unfortunate and famous misjudgement of his career.

The party was now on the west side of Baffin Bay, where Ross named Cape Clarence for yet another royal. Ice and fog made the going exceedingly difficult as they painfully moved southwards. Approaching Jones Sound they picked up a piece of driftwood with nails in it. Seals were numerous and they found the prints of a very large polar bear. The night of 24 August was the first to display a sunset since 7 June, 'thus terminating a day, which consisted of 1,872 hours, and giving us warning of the approach of a long and dreary winter'.[22]

Cobourg Bay was completely occupied by a glacier dropping from a mountain chain; its capes were named for Captain James Horsburg, a Scottish hydrographer from Fife, and the distinguished naval officer Sir George Cockburn (1772–1853), Admiral of the Fleet, veteran of the French wars and mastermind of the burning of the White House during the 1812 War. Further south, Banks Bay honoured the president of the Royal Society. The ships made 36 miles in 24 hours despite difficult ice conditions, *Isabella* at times forcing a passage for the subsequent *Alexander*. Ice and water-depth had to be watched at all times, the ships tacking between bergs and following channels that presented themselves, often requiring warping. Since *Alexander* was much the slower vessel, observations were often made and readings taken while she caught up. Presently they found themselves experiencing a considerable swell in the open sea, but the shore was still packed with ice and the season was drawing on. Soon they found themselves in the mouth of a channel, judged to be 45 miles wide, with mountains to the north and south. In the space between west and south-west there was open water, ice-free save for a few bergs, and out of sight of land; as we now know, they had arrived at Lancaster Sound.

As they beat to the westward carrying all sail, 'the wind died away, the weather became mild and warm, the water much smoother, and the atmosphere clear and serene'. The mountains on each side of the Strait, being clear of clouds, displayed various beautiful tints. Their situation occasioned much speculation but 'the general opinion was that it was only an inlet'. Captain Sabine, armed with Baffin's account, opined that they were in Lancaster Sound, but that there was no hope of a passage until they sailed further south to Cumberland Sound. To use his words there was 'no indication of a passage', 'no appearance of a current', 'no driftwood' and 'no swell from the northwest'. Or so Ross alleged in the first edition of his book *A Voyage of Discovery*, though these lines were suppressed in the second. Others, crowding the masthead and the crow's nest, were more hopeful, but the matter was still unresolved at sunset. At 4am the officers of the watch spotted land across the inlet, but before Ross could view the scene, fog obscured it. Thereafter he saw

a high ridge of mountains, extending across the bottom of the inlet. This chain appeared extremely high in the centre, and those towards the north had, at times, the appearance of islands, being insulated by the fog at their bases. Although a passage seemed hopeless, I was determined to explore it completely, as the wind was favourable and therefore continued all sail.[23]

Mr Beverley, assistant surgeon – described as the most 'sanguine', hopeful or confident of them all – also viewed land across the bay from the crow's nest, but Ross was still intent on exploring further, handicapped though he was by the absence of *Alexander* trailing far behind. A footnote in the second edition, absent from the first, states that Midshipman John Bushnan distinctly saw ice extending a distance of 35 miles from the island to the land. That a man of Ross's seniority should have invoked a midshipman's testimony is as incredible as it is out of character. At 3pm on 31 August some clearing was reported at the bottom of the bay. What followed is best reported in Ross's own words:

I immediately went on deck and soon after it completely cleared for about ten minutes, when I distinctly saw the land round the bottom of the bay, forming a chain of mountains connected with those which extended along the north and south sides. This land appeared to be at the distance of eight leagues; and Mr Lewis the Master, and James Haig, leading seaman, being sent for, they took its bearings, which were inserted in the log . . . At this moment I saw a continuity of ice, at the distance of seven miles, extending from one side of the bay to the other, between the nearest cape to the north, which I named after Sir George Warrender, and that to the south, which was named after Viscount Castlereagh. The mountains, which occupied the centre, in a north and south direction, were named Croker's Mountains after the Secretary to the Admiralty. The south-west corner, which formed a spacious bay, completely occupied by ice, was named Barrow's Bay; it is bounded on the south by Cape Rosamond, which is a head-land, that projects eastward from the high land in the centre. The north corner, which was the last I had made out, was a deep inlet; and as it answered exactly to the latitude given by Baffin of Lancaster Sound, I have no doubt that it was the same, and consider it a most remarkable instance of the accuracy of that able navigator.[24]

The weather having worsened, Ross tacked to join *Alexander* 8 miles behind, and the two ships stood to the south-east. Prudence dictated further withdrawal. At Cape Byam, Martin, James Ross and Skene (both midshipmen) were despatched 'to take possession of the country'. There was surely something strange about this, since normally it was a function that should have been entrusted to a more senior officer. John Ross made a point of explaining that he was employed on board, 'in sounding and in trying the temperature of the water', which he described – almost defensively we may think – as 'important objects', although such activities had taken place almost daily since departing Shetland. He did take soundings at 1,000 fathoms, recovering soft mud and worms with the clamm, and a starfish entangled in the sounding line. And he did order Lieutenant Parry to follow on as commander of the shore party, but why was Parry not given the task in the first place? They went through the usual ceremony, making the claim in the name of the king, and erecting a flagstaff. Several hours were spent collecting natural history specimens. The scenery, for a change, was of some interest: rivers, valleys, grass and wild flowers, deer, fox, ermine and hares.

This section of Ross's account smacks of special pleading. He referred to his official instructions, which had ordered him to pay particular attention to the currents, and to look for the north-east point of America 'or, in other words, the north-west passage, about the seventy-second degree of latitude'. Since he had found no current in the recent inlet, or anywhere to the north of it, he naturally assumed that it would exist to the south. He had fully obeyed his orders 'to stand well to the north'. He was also instructed to quit the ice on 1 October at the latest.

> I had only one month left for my operations in which month the nights are long and according to a fair calculation not more than two days clear weather out of seven could be expected. It may therefore with propriety be stated that I had only eight days remaining to explore the remainder of Baffin's Bay, a distance of above 400 miles. Of this space nearly 200 miles had never been examined, a range, including the supposed place of discontinuity of the continent, being that to which my attention had been particularly called, and where the imaginary current, which was to be my guide, was to be expected.

He was anxious to continue with the exploration of the coast even after any hopes of finding the passage were surrendered. In his view he had persevered in the search despite the absence of current, driftwood or any other indication of the north-west route, 'until I actually saw the barrier of high mountains, and the continuity of ice, which put the question at rest'. This he considered fortunate, since it enabled him to explore the east side of Baffin Island. Because *Alexander* was so far behind, it was not thought necessary to check for corroborative sightings, but one of her officers of the watch claimed to have actually seen land at the bottom of the bay. There is a surrealist element to Ross's account because, by the time it appeared, he had already been accused of incompetence, and there had been a bitter row between participants in the voyage, as well as sedentary critics who never had seen, and never would see, the Arctic. Fierce controversy also emerged about who, and who did not, agree with his assessment of the 'inlet'. There would be a parliamentary enquiry on the matter, as well as several publications. To some he was the man who found the Northwest Passage and came home. In his own defence, the second 1819 edition of John Ross's *Voyage of Discovery* was an attempt to have the last word. By the time he wrote it, Parry had already set out on another expedition of which Ross honestly and uncompromisingly wrote:

> Should it prove that a passage exists where I have supposed the land to be continuous, I shall unite with others at rejoicing at this extension of our geographical knowledge, without feeling any disappointment that there has been reserved for others that success which no one can command, but for which our best exertions were made.[25]

These words are in the second edition of Ross's *Voyage of Discovery*, but are completely absent in the first. Nonetheless there is a nobility about that statement which does John Ross great credit. A proud man who yet knew, at least once, when to bow his head.

Ross and his men followed 'numbers of birds of the guillemot kind', flying south and thither, avoiding treacherous tongues of ice that extended, underwater, out to sea. The voyage was not yet over but it is sometimes possible to detect the author's enthusiasm flagging a little. For example, 2 September: 'nothing of consequence happened during these 24 hours, nor was any observation made worthy of remark'.[26] Progressing southwards he named Pond's Bay (now Pond Inlet) for the Astronomer Royal, as well as capes Bowen and McCulloch, the latter for the geologist at home who would repay Ross by dismissing his geological samples as disappointing because they were carelessly collected. He remained convinced that there could be no passage between latitudes 73°33' and 72°. He was able to test his deep-sea clamm in 1,050 fathoms of calm waters, which meant the line was 'perfectly perpendicular'. It took 27 minutes to descend and an hour to pull it back up.

He gave the name North Galloway to land believed hitherto unseen by any earlier navigators. Doubtless moved by a sense of nostalgia for his own locale he also named Cargenholm, Hamilton's Bay and Cape Eglinton, and Scott's Bay for the novelist. Part of the coast was dubbed New Ayr, in which was situated Ardrossan Bay with nearby a Horse Island, reminiscent of that back home. Inuit remains, a dwelling and part of a skull were found on Agnes Island, which was claimed for the crown. He named Clyde River, Haig's Island, Bute Island and Cape Broughton. Of other features and places similarly esteemed, Adair (Cape) is a Galloway name, as is Agnew (Cape) of the Lochnaw family, while Borthwick may be named for the naval captain from Locharwoods, Dumfries. Loch Ryan is obvious and the McDoualls (Cape) are another ancient Galloway clan. Cape Murdoch may be named for a Murdoch of Portpatrick. Ross indulged in the geographical 'Scotching of the Arctic' with an enthusiasm that was highly likely to upset his superiors because he was honouring men – worse, Scotsmen – often considered non-entities of whom they had never heard, thus disrespecting the great and the good similarly honoured.[27]

Parry, Ross and Bushnan measured a large iceberg which was 4,169 yards long, 3,869 broad and 51 feet high grounded in 61 fathoms. They passed another large berg,

> on which there was a large bird of the falcon kind and a bear; the former immediately flew away, but the latter, after looking at us for some time, climbed to the top, apparently with the intention of jumping into the sea from it, but, on finding it was too high, he descended, and when at a short distance from the lower edge, he plunged into the sea; several shots were fired at him, but the distance was too great for the balls to take effect and he escaped.[28]

Winter was now truly upon them as observations on wind and weather intensified while they bore southwards. Returning to London via Shetland, on reaching Leith, Ross reported with justifiable pride:

> Not an instance of punishment has taken place in this ship, nor has there been an officer, or man, on the sick list; and it is with a feeling

not to be expressed that I have to conclude this letter, by reporting that the service has been performed, and the expedition, I had the honour to command, has returned, without the loss of a man.[29]

John Ross had proved genuinely solicitous of the wellbeing of his men. After the *Isabella* and *Alexander* entangling episode, he reported that throughout the day every single officer and man was employed, noting that 'their zeal and activity under the severest fatigues could only be equalled by their patience and fortitude', fully justifying his expectations of them in the hour of danger.[30] Discipline was essential to the health of his men. Sometimes the 'tedious and often laborious progress through the ice' kept the crew occupied for several days and nights without rest. On such occasions an extra meal of preserved meat served at midnight seemed to keep them going, aided by the light nights. He thought that such measures also prevented against scurvy, as did a diet of vegetables, replaced with lemon juice when they were used up. Ross was also aware of the virtues of variety and fresh food. Little auks, or dovekies, were shot as often as possible for the pot. On one occasion 1,500 were taken to be preserved in ice; some were made into a broth which tasted like hare soup. This food too would defend against scurvy. When the men were soaked, they were made to change into dry clothes, since it was believed that there was some connection between dampness and scurvy. Special caps were issued, lined with flannel and proofed, and long enough to protect the neck and shoulders. Through such measures, according to their captain, 'no crews were ever in higher health or spirits'.

Ross claimed and believed that his expedition had been a great success. He had extended geographical horizons. The existence of a huge bay from Disko to Cumberland Sound had been proved but the claim that he had 'set at rest for ever the question of a north-west passage in this direction' was, of course, hopelessly wrong. The re-discovery of Baffin Bay had exonerated the reputation of a worthy explorer, whose achievements had been expunged from geographical records and his bay treated as 'a phantom of the imagination'. Ross would soon regard Baffin himself as something of a kindred spirit. In addition, he had demonstrated the potential for whaling to the north of Baffin Bay, the whales being large, numerous and tame, since they had never been much disturbed, and thus easier to catch, all of which information the whalers would already have possessed. He believed that if the whaling ships were better supplied they could stay on the grounds for an additional two weeks and thus prolong the hunting season to the benefit of all involved. He also advocated establishing a fur trade, since foxes seemed to abound and, in his view (possibly erroneous), there was little evidence that the Inuit used the fur themselves, although they were quite expert at trapping the animals.[31] There were other trading possibilities since there would be secure markets for narwhal ivory and the teeth of bears and walrus, which could be exchanged for knives, nails, harpoon heads and various cheap and useful tools and utensils, 'both to the great benefit of the merchant, and to that of this secluded race of people'.[32] Modern sensitivities may be offended by all of these suggestions but as a man of his time this disciple of Adam Smith believed that trade was the foundation of civilisation.

*

John Ross arrived back in London on 16 November 1818. A week later he dined with Lord Melville in the company of John Barrow, Second Secretary to the Admiralty, who recounted a familiar reminiscence about having been, as a boy, to Greenland on a whaleship. When Ross shook his head, Lady Melville asked Barrow the name of his ship, but he could not recall it, nor that of its captain. He did remember that it sailed out of Whitehaven, a port on the English side of the Solway, famous for having been attacked by John Paul Jones from Galloway, who fought on the American side during the Revolution. 'Whitehaven is a small dry harbour', interjected Ross; 'no whaler ever sailed out of that'. According to Ross's recollection, Barrow, having been caught in a boastful lie, 'coloured up to the eyes, while the whole company burst out in laughter but from that moment Barrow was my bitter enemy'. In fact, some whalers did sail from Whitehaven, and Barrow did visit Greenland, but the post-prandial anecdote rings true and seems characteristic of both men. Ross had another tale about Barrow stomping out of the office of the publisher John Murray, after Ross had criticised his grammar, saying he would have nothing more to do with him. If true, this was tactless on Ross's part because Barrow had arranged for Murray to publish the account of his recent voyage. Whatever the source of their mutual dislike, 'my friend Mr Barrow', as introduced by Ross, was friend no more.

In fairness, Ross's memory, when convenient, was not always the best. He claimed that he declined the command of a second expedition because of his wife's delicate condition; their only child died on the same day Ross returned to London. Elsewhere he blamed his eyesight for his refusal; however, it seems unlikely he was ever offered the post in view of his emphatic denial of the existence of the Northwest Passage. Ross could massage the truth as well as anyone. One of the issues on which Barrow criticised Ross was that the latter referred to himself throughout his account as 'captain' although in reality he was a commander. He was promoted to captain on 7 December not, as has often been assumed, for his Arctic activities but, as M.J. Ross points out, for his general service record. Conventionally Ross's promotion would have been planned months before this; his name would not have been added to the list at short notice.

While in Shetland, before he returned to London after the 1818 expedition, Lieutenant Parry, who was to be rewarded with the command of the 1819 expedition, wrote to his parents that it was obvious they had not sailed through the Northwest Passage since they had been away so briefly, 'but', he added, 'I know it is in existence, and not very hard to find. This opinion of mine, which is not lightly formed, must on no account be uttered out of our family; and I am sure it will not when I assure you every future prospect of mine depends upon its being kept secret.'[33] The Times had reported as early as 13 November 'the final close of attempts to discover the North Pole', gleefully reporting that there was no Northwest Passage. An anonymous letter written by an officer of Alexander and published in Blackwood's Edinburgh Magazine argued that no member of the expedition would hazard such an assertion due to lack of proper competence in the matter, though he opined that the west side of Baffin Bay comprised 'a great cluster or archipelago of islands. Beyond which is the polar sea; but whether all, or any, of these straits are, or are not, navigable, is a question that yet remains to be decided.'[34] Sabine thought it unlikely that the public would be satisfied in the matter, 'I do not see this thing passing over without a very complete inquiry and certain dissatisfaction', though he thought he could avoid involvement if he held his tongue.[35] Evidently he did not, for in mid December Ross asked some of his officers to recollect Captain Sabine's statements concerning Lancaster Sound. William Robertson, one of the officers, had frequently heard Sabine say that there was no passage in Lancaster or in any other sound in Baffin's Bay, urging that the expedition should focus upon Cumberland Sound. William Thom, the purser, went further, asserting that it was a notorious fact that the officers had completely given up all idea of a passage at that point and consequently all interest therein had 'entirely subsided'. The officer of the watch on Alexander, Midshipman Bisson, wrote a letter in support at Ross's request, a truly astonishing development for a man of Ross's pride, self-esteem and consciousness of rank, for whom a midshipman was virtually beneath contempt.

Assistant surgeon Alexander Fisher explained that, since *Alexander* was three or four miles behind *Isabella*, 'we could not see anything like land at the bottom of the inlet, nor was the weather well calculated at the time for seeing any object at a great distance . . . Ocular demonstration would certainly have been very satisfactory to us, on a point in which we were so much interested; but we must be content that all in Isabella were fully convinced of the continuity of land at the bottom of this inlet.' To back up his recollections he supplied a copy of *Alexander*'s log for 31 August in an appendix to his *Journal of a Voyage*.[36]

The most devastating attack of all came in an unattributed, but authorially obvious, review by Barrow, in the *Quarterly Review*. The piece shows Barrow at his disgraceful worst, as an arrogant, carnaptious, sarcastic and petulant spoiler who did not hesitate to attempt the destruction of another in support of his own often ill-informed ideas. Whereas he passed off David Buchan's lack of success in his part of the 1818 expedition as accidental, he asserted that, 'of the other we hardly know in what terms to speak', scornfully dismissing virtually all that Ross had written: Ross's descriptions of icebergs were wrong, his sketches laughable, the designation 'Arctic Highlanders' ludicrous and red snow a phantom. Barrow could not understand why a Navy man (a captain no less, though nonesuch at the time) should pay so much attention to the views of an artillery captain, namely Sabine. Ross's published view of the bay and chart of the land in Lancaster Sound did not agree with his text and in any case could not have been properly executed in a turn-around of ten minutes without reference to the views of his officers. Barrow rejected Ross's arguments about the currents mentioned in his instructions as the reason for quitting Lancaster Sound so soon. 'A strange infatuation seems to have taken possession of his mind', he wrote, 'impenetrably dull or intentionally perverse must anyone be who could mistake the meaning of this part of them'. The instructions, he asserted, were completely misunderstood by Ross, who was not directed to leave the water by 31 August or the ice by 1 October. The Scot was compared unfavourably and unfairly with earlier explorers such as Columbus, Cook and Vancouver, although this inadvertently put him in the gallery with some of the greatest explorers. 'A voyage of discovery implies danger; but a mere voyage like his round the shore of Baffin's Bay, in the three summer months, may be considered a voyage of pleasure.' If the latter assertion was unforgivable, there was room for disagreement about the instructions. Other points can be dismissed as the speculations of a querulous malcontent, yet the mystery of why Ross departed 'the Gateway to the Passage' in such haste has never been explained. He was, after all, 'an excellent and accomplished navigator, a man of considerable intellectual power, a Scotchman, and not one to accept his facts on the endorsement of his imagination'.[37] He also genuinely did want to discover the Northwest Passage, though he may have been convinced that if it was discovered it would remain useless as a trade route.

There is considerable mention of currents in the 'Instructions' but they are not as clear as Barrow pretended. The document states that, because of uncertain knowledge about the ice and sea of Davis Strait, no specific information existed for Ross's guidance. Hence 'the time and manner of proceeding to fufil the ulterior object of your destination, in places where impediments may occur, must be left entirely to your discretion'. Ross's zeal and skill were fully acknowledged but, despite Barrow's denial, he was told to leave the ice by 1 October at the latest.

*

George Cruikshank, a Londoner very proud to be a Scot, and a talented caricaturist, influenced by pantomime and witty venom, celebrated Ross's return with an engraving entitled *Landing the Treasures, or Results of the Polar Expedition!!!* (1819), a truly fascinating lampoon (see Plate 5). A corpulent gent on the extreme left is probably John Barrow, who snidely remarks 'I think as how we have Bears, Gulls, Savages, Chump Wood [fake wood], Stones and Puppies enough without going to the North Pole for them.' To his right a black fiddler with a wooden leg sings 'O Captain he is come to town, doodle doodle dandy / How you do Sir: hope see you well Sir?!!' Next in the line of figures is John Ross himself with a false nose, followed by similarly noseless sailors carrying a dead polar bear covered in yellow stars – an astronomical reference to the Great Bear, *Ursa Major* – that might also allude to wounds, since, notoriously, the killing of that magnificent creature required multiple shots. The individual situated at the bear's rear mutters 'Tis a good thing I've lost my nose.' He is not alone. It was a trope of Arctic travel that noses froze first. All the Arctic veterans featured in the print have lost their proboscises but this may also be an allusion to the Inuit custom of nose-pulling as a greeting. Both Ross and the wee man behind him (possibly James Clark Ross, a midshipman at this point) wear ruffled shirts.

In the background of the image is the British Museum, founded in 1753 and soon to undergo substantial expansion. Three small excited figures dance on the museum roof. Left to right the first says 'Huzza! They have got *Ursa Major* as I live Huzza! Huzza!' The next cries 'I see! I see it! by Jupiter!! I'll cling to it like a leech. Huzza! huzza!! Huzza'. The third shouts 'I see Jack Frost! I see Jack Frost!! Huzza! with the N. Pole in his hand Huzza', which might possibly refer to the Inuk man at the end of the line holding a narwhal tusk, who is probably John Sacheuse.

A wraith-like soldier halfway along the line seems to be sticking his bayonet into the backside of a gull, labelled 'Sabini' (Sabine's Gull), a reference which obviously points to Captain Edward Sabine of the Royal Artillery. A man with a cocked hat is possibly William Parry. To the right of a barrel, labelled 'Red Snow' and marked B.M., the wag helping to support a chunk of 'Esquimaux Wood for BM' says to the black man behind him 'I say Snowball, mind you don't tread on my heels' to receive the reply 'No, No, Massa Billy and mind you no tread on my toes' (note – he does not have toes, or feet, but possibly has two wooden legs). The black man carries on his head a can with the label 'worms found in the intestines of a seal by a volunteer'. Behind him is a white man also carrying a large box on his head inscribed 'Moluscoe for the British Museum' as he asks 'Who the hell's to carry the big stone?' A package onshore is labelled 'Granite', doubtless representing Ross's report of a 'very large piece of granite' floating on a piece of ice, which sank when he tried to capture it.[38] The joke here is the supposedly ludicrous claim that such a huge chunk of granite would float at all.

The 'savage' bringing up the rear, Cruickshank's cartoon of an Inuk, carries a lance 'made from the horn of a unicorn used as a walking stick' (i.e. a narwhal tusk). He sports crazy hair and a tutu possibly made from polar bear fur. Under his arm, the Inuk carries a portfolio of drawings by John Sacheuse, which supports the idea that the Inuk and the Inuit interpreter are one and the same. In 1818/19 most folk would have no idea of what an Inuk looked like and the racism was inevitable. At the far right, three men in a jolly boat are discussing sled-dogs, which they appear to be unloading. One asks, 'If they kill the dogs & stuff'em! What will they do with Jack Frost?' to which his mate replies 'Cut his throat & stuff him also I supposes'. A possible reading of this is that the Inuk is symbolically referred to as 'Jack Frost' – identified by the spectator on the museum roof as the man with the North Pole (narwhal tusk) – whose fate, like the live dogs destined for the taxidermist, is being jokingly regarded as just another 'specimen' for the Arctic collection. It is as difficult to capture the significance of the various references as it is to discover the extent of the print's circulation. Copies were sold as single sheets or in pamphlets, and also appeared in newsprints. Would it be going too far to suggest that Ross had a hand in creating the piece since most of the items supposedly ridiculed were actually genuine, making Barrow the butt of the satire?[39]

Ross was also greeted on his return by satirisation in a publication early in 1819 entitled *Munchausen at the Pole; or The Surprising and Wonderful Adventures of a Voyage of Discovery* (a reference to writer Rudolf Erich Raspe's *Baron Munchausen* stories first published in English in 1785). It featured a ship stranded three miles into an iceberg, red snow, the Lost Tribes of Israel and the legendary eleventh-century Irish king Brian Boru, as well as such treasures for display in London as 'an amphibious Esquimaux' and a cable made from a Greenlander's beard.[40] A French professor, Frédéric Regard, refers to Ross as 'the Scottish Punchinello' in homage to Punch of *commedia dell'arte* fame, on no particular basis.[41]

The *Edinburgh Review* was among those in support of Ross who, it claimed, had performed his duty 'with great diligence, courage and ability'; it told his story clearly and honestly, adding, with some feeling, 'it is not for us to reconcile the doubts of those who disbelieve, with the testimony of those who have seen'. The reviewer thought the directions concerning currents to have been wrong in the first place, satisfied that Ross had disproved the existence of the Northwest Passage, claiming that its champions had persecuted him in a disgraceful manner: 'we leave it to those who have so acted, to determine, and show by their conduct, whether the unwillingness to abandon their hypothesis, has not been a stronger motive for this pertinacity than the advancement of science'.[42]

There was further unseemly squabbling about who wrote or said what and when. Sabine offered to complete his papers and return them to Ross for publication in his book but when *Voyage of Discovery* appeared the soldier complained that the tables of magnetic measurement were described as 'furnished by Mr James Ross', who later signed a statement acknowledging that they had been copied from papers supplied by Sabine. The latter objected that the tables were, in fact, incomplete and inaccurate, as were Ross's remarks on the Inuit language, which were also copied from a paper by Sabine, printed correctly in the *Quarterly Journal of Science and Arts*. Sabine was sure that Ross had said more than once that he alone had seen the land and that he had never mentioned the barrier of ice until his book was published. In any case, 'land seen for a short time by a single individual, at a very considerable distance, on a very unfavourable day . . . would not be considered as decisive evidence on our return', a view with which it is difficult to disagree. Parry, in letters to his parents, betrayed his personal deviousness in slyly undermining 'the blundering Ross', confiding that Barrow believed there was enough evidence in Sabine's treatise to justify the court-martialling of Ross – a completely unfounded accusation – and that a forthcoming pamphlet by Ross would include extracts from a letter that Sabine wrote to his sister, 'which Ross looked over on board the *Isabella*, while lying on the table and which called him a stupid fellow! How *low* must such a man be fallen'! This was nothing more than malicious gossip which proved that Parry truly was 'Barrow's Boy', seeking and obtaining the secretary's favour in the hope of future preferment, which duly paid off when he was given command of the 1819 expedition.

The saddest aspect of the whole unsavoury business was the rift that temporarily emerged between John Ross and his nephew who, he wrote, 'had sided with the Barrow party against me, and but for the entreaties of Mrs Ross I would have turned him out of the service for having been the author of a malicious and false report. He [James], however, made it out that he had been taken in by Sabine and made an affidavit to that effect.' Young James was in a rather difficult position since he had served with his uncle on all his ships, but particularly *Isabella*, enjoying a somewhat privileged situation as midshipman. At the same time he was shrewd enough to realise that future advancement might be adversely affected through the same relationship, should his reputation somehow be tarnished through association with his uncle. It is also possible that at sea he tried to somewhat distance himself on occasion from John in the banter of comradeship with his shipmates. When Sabine published his pamphlet both Rosses were called to a naval hearing. James, who appeared first, reported to his uncle:

> I came to town the first opportunity with the intention of acquainting you with any part of yesterday's examination that you might desire, and more particularly with one part which as you would not see me today I think it is right I should send you by letter, that you may be aware of what has passed on the only point on which any *stress* was made at the end of the examination.

He was questioned about who was present when magnetic observations took place. He responded that he had assisted both Sabine and Ross at different times, but, noting that Ross was non-interferingly present several times when Sabine acted, he could only recall one occasion on which his uncle took the readings.

> Mr Croker, after all was over, said to me alone – now Mr Ross it turns all upon this – whether you say it was Captain Sabine assisted by you who took these observations . . . for Captain Ross has differed from you on this point . . . I hope that, when the Admiralty see clearly that you took one set and Captain Sabine the others, that all differences will be settled. I have again thought over all I said to the Admiralty and have still reason to be satisfied that I have asserted nothing contrary to the affidavit I took . . . and am not conscious of a single point in which I have said anything to your prejudice.

When John, who had either not seen or chosen to ignore James's letter, appeared the next day, he was apoplectic, rushing in with a statement, although advised that he might first wish to hear the evidence already given. He claimed James Ross was his 'greatest enemy ever since he knew Captain Sabine'. A most serious conspiracy existed during the voyage and still existed against himself. He alleged that when James had hesitated to make the affidavit though 'there was nothing in it but what he could and ought to swear', he offered to let James take the affidavit away and alter it in any way he pleased but if he refused, he would take him before a magistrate. He believed that before he appeared at the enquiry James had met with Parry. John added that he mentioned this 'to show that Mr James Ross, tho' his nephew, is not his friend'. Next day John intimated that he wished to withdraw the accusations made against James. His nephew's brother had assured him that there was no conspiracy between James, Parry and Sabine. He also retracted the charge, 'relative to the combination [hostile association]' during the voyage, which was 'probably nothing more than the difference which arose from a Land Officer being embarked with the Sea Officers and produced no injury to the service'. The affidavit so often mentioned was never produced, John asserting that it remained in James's possession.[43]

Many have been puzzled by Ross's retreat from Lancaster Sound, which was his decision and his responsibility alone. As he told Sabine in a letter, a ship's commander neither requires nor asks for advice. To do so, he thought, would encourage subversion of discipline and even the possibility of mutiny: 'one alone should rule'. No further explanation was necessary. In *Barrow's*

Boys Fleming suggests that the weather played a part: freezing fog turned everything white and sculpted non-existent images, including mountain ranges. He is correct; in such conditions it is possible to conjure shapes and objects that cannot possibly be where they are supposedly seen, but, as he argues, a naval professional such as Ross, with experience of fog, should have been aware of these phenomena. Another of Fleming's suggestions is that Ross did not understand the full effects of refraction, a slightly more convincing idea. He also believes that Ross was the sort of captain who could not abide contradiction from his subordinates and so resented any hint that he should proceed further.[44] This makes sense from what we know of Ross's character: thrawn, invincible and certain of his own judgement. He retained these characteristics throughout the painful intrigues and disappointments of his return but there were to be indications in the future that he modified his behaviour somewhat. It is noteworthy that this episode did no damage whatsoever to James Ross. In fact it benefited him because it showed that he could be his own man though torn over the issue of loyalty to his uncle, who was also, be it remembered, his commanding officer. James's Arctic career was well and truly launched when he was appointed to Parry's expedition the following year. John Ross, though he had to eat humble pie, even in the introduction to the second edition of his book, must have thought he was surrounded by some of the most lamentable ingrates in creation.[45]

Ross has not been allowed to rest. Professor Frédéric Regard has come riding into the literature to tell us that Ross's career was a tragi-comedy, the understanding of which he seeks to illuminate utilising a crucial weapon, namely rhetoric, through the application of which 'the literary critic's inquiry becomes necessary to the historian's'.[46] The professor neatly incorporates 'the icy fields of credibility' in the title of his article but this, in a Scottish context, is hardly news. In Scotland, literature and history, in the language of the Scots, emerged at the same moment in John Barbour's celebrated fourteenth-century poem *Brus*, which rehearsed the saga of Scottish independence, feeding history into oral sources such as ballad, song, early printings and chapbooks. Medieval Lowland Scots often referred to their language as 'Inglis' but they certainly did not thereby identify themselves as English. Barbour, like Ross, though five centuries earlier, knew a good deal about rhetoric, as did most literate Scots, women and men.[47] The first Regius Chair of Rhetoric and Belles Lettres, and hence of English Literature, was founded at Edinburgh University in 1762. The country as a whole produced a wide range of writers, poets – even literate historians – in the flow of the centuries from Gavin Douglas, William Dunbar and Robert Henryson through to Allan Ramsay, James Thomson, James 'Ossian' Macpherson, Robert Burns and Walter Scott. The generation to which the Scottish explorers belonged was that of the Enlightenment, which hosted the richest output of publication in all fields ever achieved until that point in British history.

Professor Regard asserts that 'on the recommendation of his friend Sir George Hope, who was of Scottish descent, the Scotsman Ross was appointed to the *Isabell*. Already the critic is clumsily taking sides; can we imagine that nationality would have been mentioned at all if the subject was English? Furthermore, Hope was not just 'of Scottish descent'; he was unquestionably Scottish, the grandson of a peer. His parents were married in Linlithgow and his own son tried unsuccessfully to establish a special uniform for Scots in the Navy. Any word relating to 'Scot' has apparently become *un mot péjoratif,* according to Regard, who asserts that Ross became 'the inevitable emissary victim, the scapegoat to be sacrificed on the altar of national pride'. Might this be a wee bit rhetorical? Which nation and whose pride?

Of course books were the way to advertise achievements but it surely cannot be denied that of the expeditionary books published in the 1820s Ross's stood out because it contained anguish, heart, heroism and the discovery of a lost culture. Barrow – sensitive to nation and pride – disagreed. According to Barrow's scathing account of Ross's 1818 expedition, Lord Hope's *protégé* was not fit for his task; to ram home the idea of Scottish collusion, Hope is mentioned repeatedly. Barrow then struck with his *pièce de résistance*. While he was away, Ross had been promoted captain for past services but Barrow claimed it was a reward for 'a few months voyage of pleasure round the shores of Davis Strait and Baffin's Bay . . . a voyage which any two of the Yacht Club would easily accomplish in five months'. His remarks were disgraceful. Barrow, after all, had commissioned Ross as expedition captain, yet he acted as if the Scot was guilty of sabotage; he would have known perfectly well that he was twisting fact to Ross's disadvantage. The 'British sublime masculinity'[48] (an excellent term) which he was so keen to promote was not a quality he personally possessed.

Regard recounts Ross's many successes during the voyage but he tends to move back and forth between 1818 and his four-year residence in Prince Regent Inlet (see Chapter 6). As a literal-minded historian I prefer to observe the limits of chronology; the Ross of 1829 was different in many respects from the captain of 1818. Ross was a talented writer and I tend to disagree with those who see his 'journal of a seaman' as disingenuously naïve;

it is also perfectly possible to view his remarks on Lord Hope, who signed Ross's orders on his deathbed, as sincere: both can be seen as pertinent to the personality of a civilised Scottish gentleman. Much that Regard considers contrived in Ross's writing, actions and opinions seems to me to represent no more than a Scot, admittedly somewhat eccentric, devoted to the acquisition of 'useful knowledge', genuinely fascinated by contact with another culture and willing to shed his pretensions and conceits in the interests of friendship and understanding. Regard states that the scene of 'Greenlandic Mulattoes [Ouch!] dancing Scotch reels on the deck of a British ship – a perfect symbol of the porosity and potential hybridization of low, popular cultures . . . seems to be given such an unexpected importance in Ross's narrative that one may well suspect that it probably enabled the author, a Scottish officer of low extraction to stage . . . a sort of paroxysm of cultural, racial and social confusion'. 'Low extraction' was not a term a Scot would use; Ross was the son of a minister, one of the most highly regarded professions in Scotland. On Navy ships, dance was a common and popular recreation. Why on earth would a man wish to 'enable a paroxysm of confusion' unless he was a deluded American president or a clueless academic?

Regard's reading of the Inuk Sacheuse seems to me to be as awry as his assessment of Ross. He detects significance in Ross calling Sacheuse 'Jack' instead of 'John', which seems misleading (though 'Jock' would have been more appropriate!). The use of familiar names and the suppression of inhibition are two indications that a ceilidh, in Scotland or an Inuit village, is going really well. In some of his remarks Regard displays the gaze of an Englishman, in this case the seriously prejudiced John Barrow, who wilfully demotes the Scot. In the process, Regard contrives the negation of his own thesis. History is not about taking sides; it is about assessing evidence and reaching conclusions, preferably without the potentially misleading intrusions, and hence fictions, of literary criticism. He ends on 'taking possession', apparently affirming Barrow's dismissal of the ceremony as 'silly' the more so when the object is 'worthless . . . a barren, uninhabited country covered with ice and snow. The coast becomes peopled with unprolific names chiefly from Scotland; and among the rest the territory is divided into a couple of Scotch counties.' However, he notes that Barrow applauded the British (or should that be English?) acquisition of domains or lands in other parts of the world, and later Brits and Canadians would be grateful for Ross's energetic activities.

Both Barrow and Regard differentiate between history-making British officers and backward-looking peoples, the Greenlanders and the Scottish

Highlanders combining to form the Arctic Highlanders, the formula for an indistinct mass of 'otherized aliens'. Regard closes his article with the unexpected revelation that a man from Stranraer, such as Ross, would have denied his nationality! The professor is seriously mistaken in asserting 'it should be remembered . . . that in the early nineteenth century a Lowlander like Ross – he was from Stranraer, situated in the extreme southwestern portion of Scotland – would not have described himself as Scot but as English'. *Mon Dieu!* How Ross must have wished to claim respectability like Barrow, the son of a tanner from Ulverston in the southern Lake District. In Scotland the rise from humble origins to distinguished positions was greatly admired and not uncommon. Our professor is not only wrong, but careless, drawing upon another academic, Robert Young, who is also inattentive to his sources. The latter, discussing the phenomenon of Saxonism, reports that '*many* [my italics] Lowlanders do not describe themselves as Scots', but as English, citing a sentence from Thomas Carlyle which included the words 'us poor English'. There is nothing surprising about a Scottish author (Carlyle) living in London, writing in English for an English-speaking audience at home and abroad, temporarily invoking Englishness, especially one who regarded his youthful Scotch background 'as merely an effete and outdated northern variant of Englishness', but his reverence for Teutonism did not turn him into a German. What was important, as Robert Louis Stevenson stressed, was the 'strong Scots accent of the mind'. Both professors are guilty of making elementary mistakes that would be unworthy of undergraduates and which inevitably raise questions about the validity of some of their other claims. In time Carlyle would become one of the best-known Scots in the world, who was, loathe him or love him, an extremely gifted writer and thinker who far too often displayed a Scottish-inspired cantankerousness, but in 1818 his first book was twenty years away.[49]

Ross had an exemplary war record. He was chosen for the voyage because he stood out in a legion of worthy candidates who had honed their skills in conflict. At every turn Ross displays the stamp of his indelible Scottishness. It must be understood that throughout his life he enjoyed being outrageous, a unique character whose actions may not have always been admirable but were generally memorable. He was a sailor that other seamen were keen to meet and even cherish. To others the fact that he was a pain in the neck did not negate his achievements. He had a highly developed sense of humour. Barrow, like many men in high places, had absolutely none and little awareness of irony. Their feud would fuel their respective fires for the rest of their lives. The secretary levelled many other criticisms at Ross including a base insinuation imputing personal cowardice, a treacherous intention to thwart the wishes of Government and violation of the sacred duties he owed his king. Reasonably enough, Ross refused to answer such slanders: 'I am not reduced to so low an estimate of myself as to think it necessary to vindicate my character from such contemptible aspersions. I have served my country *faithfully*, I trust, however imperfectly, and she will not require from me the humiliation of *proving* that I have done so.'[50]

The future Lady Franklin first met John Ross in early 1819. She reported 'He is short, stout, sailor-looking & not very gentlemanly in his person, but his manners & his language are perfectly so; his features are coarse & thick, his eyes grey, his complexion ruddy & his hair of a reddish sandy hue. Yet nothwithstanding his lack of beauty, he has a great deal of intelligence, benevolence & good humour in his countenance'. She thought he was about fifty (actually forty-two) with a much younger wife, Christy Adair, small, slender and rather pretty. The Adairs were an old Galloway family. Christy's eyes, wild and staring, gave her the look of 'Affright personified'.[51] Whether her husband was responsible for her condition is not recorded, but she had wed a man who was to become known as the most reviled, most eccentric and most famous of the Arctic explorers of his era.

*

Captain David Buchan (1780–1838) represented the other wing of the 1818 expedition but neglected to supply any account of his North Pole venture, and none appeared until 1843 when Frederick W. Beechey published his narrative, anxious that 'this voyage, which was conducted with great zeal and perseverance, and attended with a result, if not successful, at least honourable to the nation, should be handed down to posterity'. Beechey, a veteran of earlier Arctic expeditions and sometime explorer of the north coast of Africa, had enjoyed ample opportunity to reflect on the affair and he could not resist including some remarks on other post-1818 ventures. He had supplied words and pictures for the panorama of Buchan's attempt, exhibited in the 'large rotunda of Henry Aston Barker', Leicester Square.[52] Such panoramas were very popular with the British public. They displayed large paintings of Arctic scenes as well as artefacts brought back by individuals from expeditions. These were arranged as a sequence showing topography and seascapes or events of particular interest and the panoramas often proved very profitable.[53] However, by 1843 the reading public had much greater expectations of exploration literature than it had done fifteen years earlier.

It is not known where in Scotland David Buchan was born. By 1806 he was a lieutenant in the Royal Navy and throughout his career he was closely associated with Newfoundland, where he was charged with two expeditions to contact the remnants of the Beothuk nation. Though sympathetic to their plight, he was forced on both occasions to withdraw fearing possible hostile exchanges would jeopardise future relations. After his polar adventure he returned to Newfoundland (sometimes referred to as 'the Rock'), where he continued to be concerned about the Beothuk, becoming sheriff in 1825. He probably died at sea in an East India Company ship sailing from Calcutta in 1838. Buchan gave his approval to Beechey's book project. His only regret in failing to publish himself was 'the privation of making the public acquainted with my entire approbation of the conduct of the officers and seamen I had the honour to command', according to a letter he wrote in 1834. Why Beechey delayed publication until 1843 is not known.

In this half of the 1818 expedition, Buchan was commander of *Dorothea*, 370 tons, while John Franklin was in charge of the 250-ton *Trent*. Their orders were to proceed to the Spitsbergen seas, passing northwards between Greenland and the archipelago. 'As navigation among ice may be considered as an art to be acquired only by practice, we have directed that there be appointed to each of the ships . . . a master and a mate of whaling vessels, well experienced in those seas, from whose knowledge and skill you may derive considerable assistance.'[54] Because of imperfect knowledge, no specific instructions could be given about the sea beyond Spitsbergen; the captains were to rely upon their own discretion. The admiralty commissioners, relying on reports from whalers that the sea should be free of ice north of latitude 83°5' N or 84°00' N, were intent that the best endeavours should be exercised to reach the North Pole. If such proved possible they were to remain in the vicinity for a few days, making observations, especially concerning magnetic variation, atmospherical electricity, currents and ocean depths. On quitting the Pole they should head directly for Bering Strait but, if it was blocked, then they should head south-west between Greenland and the east coast of America into Baffin Bay. If the Pole should prove completely unattainable they were to make directly for Bering Strait, 'recollecting that, although it is highly desirable, with a view to the interests of science, and the extension of natural knowledge that you should reach the Pole, yet the passage between the Atlantic and Pacific is the main object of your mission'.

If the sea to the west of Spitsbergen was impassable they were to attempt a route south and west, in search of a passage between the oceans, seeking, if possible, to pass over, or near, the Pole. Over-wintering was to be avoided, particularly in the seas north of Spitsbergen, 'concerning which we are in a state of entire ignorance'. Having arrived at the Bering Strait they were to pass to the Pacific and make their way to Kamchatka; the remainder of their orders were identical to those issued to John Ross about delivering documents to the Russian Governor in St Petersburg for forwarding to London. They too should proceed to Hawai'i or California for some rest. A possible rendezvous in the Pacific was to be arranged with Captain Ross.

Spitsbergen (now Svalbard) is an archipelago where adjectives soon become redundant when visitors are consumed by the magic of the place, but it never fulfilled its promise so far as the search for the Northwest Passage was concerned. This was the first official expedition since the scientific naval expedition in search of the North Pole in 1773. The 'spirit of discovery only slumbered while wars were won', pursued with 'an ardour worthy of a great maritime nation'.[55] No Arctic land had so far been discovered between the Russian archipelago Nova Zembla (Novaya Zemlya) and Spitsbergen, nor between the latter and Greenland. Many believed, indeed strenuously argued, that by breaking through a belt of ice, an open sea around the North Pole and new routes would be discovered. On *Dorothea*, William G. Borland (assistant surgeon), Peter Bruce (Greenland master) and George Crawford (mate) were probably Scots. The *Trent* complement included Andrew Reid (mate), Alexander Gilfillan (assistant surgeon), George Fyfe (Greenland master) and James Bowden (carpenter). There were forty-three seamen and marines on *Dorothea*, supported by twenty-eight on *Trent*.

The ships set sail from London on 21 April 1818, arriving in Shetland on 1 May when a leak on *Trent* had to be investigated. Its source could not be determined but the continuous effort involved in manning the pump unnerved the crew, while local Shetlanders who might have been expected to sign on as part of the crew, regarded the problem as unpropitious. The Arctic Circle was crossed on 14 May when constant daylight was first experienced, initially energising, but also irksome if sleeping arrangements were not managed carefully. Soon after their first snowfall the ships passed Bear Island with its evocatively named Mount Misery. The first ice, combined with a low sun and refraction, created illusory formations which fascinated the crews as they identified a grotto, a cavern, a church and more familiar structures, which, however beautiful they appeared, soon threatened the ships. Clearing the first ice they were met by south Spitsbergen and a violent gale. Ice, which accumulated on planks, ropes and bowsprits, had to be hacked off with axes. Some were in favour of attacking the ice immediately in search of a passage but Buchan, 'who had some experience in this matter, very wisely abstained from so rash an enterprise, and reserved his vessel for a more promising occasion'; he decided to linger for a few days in Magdalena Fjord. Off Rotge Hill, named for little auks, they marvelled at the numbers of birds – it was calculated that four million of them were on the wing at one time,[56] prompting comparisons with Audubon's billion-plus passenger pigeons in Ohio, the last of which died in 1914. It was possible to kill 30 auks with one shot. Other sights have inspired visitors ever since – the glaciers, the 'Hanging Iceberg' and the 'Waggon-Way', named for the moraines on the glacier which resemble a paved road when viewed from afar.[57]

Once anchored, boats were sent off to different parts of the bay for survey work. For the first time it was possible to take stock of the Arctic land-scape. 'We were particularly struck with the brilliancy of the atmosphere, the peaceful novelty of the scene, and the grandeur of the various objects with which Nature has stored these unfrequented regions.' They were also greatly awed by the fearful fragility of the stupendous glaciers. The sound of a single gunshot would invariably send massive chunks of ice crashing into the sea. In poor weather there was nothing 'more dreary than the appearance of the shores of Spitzbergen' but, when fine, 'all nature seems to acknowledge the glorious sunshine, and the animated part of creation to set no bounds to its delight'.[58] Modern visitors would agree. The welcome noise of birds and mammals by day contrasted with the stunning silence of the bright polar night. Here one realised that man was the intruder, in territory seldom visited by humans. Walruses crowded the boats that hunted them, trans-forming the human predators into potential prey. The sea-horses, however, were almost always the losers, with kills of a thousand in seven hours being reported by earlier expeditionaries.

Red-stained snow was seen but was not thought to resemble that noted by John Ross.[59] Buchan welcomed some Russian hunters who arrived by boat, exchanging gifts. An officer of *Dorothea* accompanied them back to their wooden hut, where 'in this retired spot, probably the most northern and most desolate habitation of our globe', he observed 'a spirit of devotion rarely exercised in civilized countries'. Before entering their hut the hunters kneeled at the threshold to pray, 'an instance of the beneficial effect which seclusion from the busy world, and a contemplation of the works of Nature, almost invariably produce upon the hearts of even the most uneducated part of mankind'. These men, the Pomors (Sea People) from the White Sea region, were almost the last of their kind, quitting Spitsbergen in the 1820s. Hardy souls, since the sixteenth century they had visited throughout the winter, some remaining permanently, to hunt furs – peltry – and 'morses teeth', the ivory tusks of walrus, uplifted annually by merchants from Archangel. Winters can of course be bitter but to this day settlers in Svalbard point out that it is much easier to travel around in winter than it is in summer whether by ski, dog-sled or skidoo.

On quitting Magdalena Fjord, the expedition found the northern ice in a somewhat less solid condition than that described by Phipps and still highly challenging. Rising gales twice drove them into the ice pack. Searching for a way through, the ships were towed by the boats to avoid being driven onto the ice by the heavy swell. *Trent* broke loose but suffered no damage, though both vessels, despite the crews' best efforts, were eventually forced into the ice. They now experienced the effect of the swell on floes, crushed into brash ice, as a strange see-saw motion impacted on the ships, caught 'amidst this giddy element', bowsprits pointed at the larger floes to avoid broadside collision. The men passed an uneasy night, those on *Trent* diverted by manning the pump. They fell in with some whalers who informed Buchan of compacted ice to the west in which fifteen Greenlanders were beset. The captain, deciding that his best course was to sail as close to the land as possible, made for Prince Charles Foreland (Prins Karls Forlandet) where 'the Three Crowns' were sighted, most conveniently viewed today from the scientific research village of Ny-Ålesund in Kongsfjorden. Beechey was mystified by the name, as many folk still are, since there are five peaks not three, while the mountains bear no resemblance whatsoever to crowns. The modern explanation is that the Tre Kroner are named for the three Scandinavian countries, Dana, Nora and Svea.[60] The voyagers retreated to Cloven Cliff, Klovningen – as its name suggests, an island with a cleft in the middle of it – on the north-west corner of Spitsbergen, passing eastwards to Red Bay. It was noted that they were now at a point where most previous expeditions had been halted and where they were themselves beset, attached to floes, for thirteen days. As some compensation, the persistent leak on *Trent* was discovered and promptly fixed.

An off-ship excursion party met acute difficulties when they became lost, enveloped as they were in thick fog; some fell through the ice while others drifted helplessly on floes. They fired shots to attract attention but were so cold, wet and depressed that they prepared for the worst. After 18 hours, rescue arrived in the shape of George Fyfe and George Kirby, master and mate of *Trent*, respectively. Further diversion was provided when a polar bear, wounded by three shots, seized one of his tormentors by his thigh.[61] Another bear suffered a wound to *his* leg, which, to the wonder of observers, he rubbed in the snow to staunch the flow of blood. Yet another was seen to mimic the movements of a walrus as he unsuccessfully attempted a kill. There were further trials on the ice and further animal hunts, while observations of the behaviour of bears, walruses, seals, whales and narwhals afforded some interest. Again they managed to clear the ice, making for Fair Haven. At Vogel Sang (Fuglesangen, an island north of Spitsbergen) they killed forty reindeer; some were shot but others were driven into the sea to be hunted from boats. They captured four alive but they had to be put down when they injured themselves by thrashing round on deck. Eider ducks made easy prey, defending their nests until dispatched with sticks.

On 6 July the ships reached latitude 80°19' N but were again repulsed by the ice. Overnight it unexpectedly slackened as channels opened in favourable directions. 'Captain Buchan, whose patience had been severely tried, and whose perseverance through the most disheartening circumstances had never once relaxed, but, on the contrary, had been such as to inspire the fullest confidence in the minds of every person under his command, lost not a moment in directing his vessel towards one of those channels in the most determined manner', spreading as much of canvas as the mast would bear. The ships made good progress as men were posted along the side of the canals to give assistance at awkward bends or turnings. Beechey thought that a talented artist might do justice to the heartening scene, which he declined to spoil by attempting to describe it. But yet again there was rapid change as the ice began to close once more. Buchan attempted to progress by the weary and soul-destroying ploy of tracking and warping.[62] They reached their most northerly point at 80°34' N. During the next two days they realised that, despite their energetic efforts, the current was driving them southwards. As they laboriously advanced (as they thought) to the north, they were actually carried further south. Renewed fierce pressure from the ice seriously damaged both vessels. The crews realised that the Pole was once again unattainable. For nine days of painful and excruciating boredom they exerted every sinew to free their ships. When open water was eventually attained, Buchan steered eastwards. After the frustration of the ice the ships appeared to bound through the water 'and every passing wave brought with it a peculiar gratification'. However, well aware that east had always proved the futile direction of impassable ice, he then decided to set west for Greenland – and an almighty storm.

Trapped between a furious sea and the ice edge, the ships competed with huge chunks of ice and bergs, which resulted in 'many very heavy concussions'.[63] *Dorothea* took refuge inside the ice, 'a practice resorted to by whalers in extreme cases, as their only chance of escaping destruction'. *Trent* was eventually forced to follow suit but, fearing that she was less robust than her sister, the crew first hung a kind of shield of metal plates and walrus skins suspended around the ship's sides, and at the bow, with the aim of giving it some protection in the event of a broadside collision with the ice.

Throughout, the crews displayed calmness, resolution and fortitude, as the ships were tossed from one chunk of ice to another. Against the odds, when imminent destruction had seemed inevitable, both ships survived, though so badly battered as to be rendered useless. They limped into Fair Haven; when approaching, *Trent* struck a sunken rock so hard that, but for their recent contest with the elements, it would have caused great alarm, 'but it now passed off without much attention'.[64]

The storm damage essentially killed off the expedition. *Dorothea* was much more badly damaged than *Trent*. Buchan considered whether he should follow his orders and abandon his ship while taking command of *Trent*. Franklin, for his part, requested permission to continue with the quest for the Pole. Either of these options would have entailed *Dorothea* returning home unaccompanied, possibly endangering the lives of the men. Furthermore, if he had taken over *Trent*, Buchan worried that he would have been seen as trying to avoid dangers to which he was abandoning his crew. In the event Buchan decided to remain with his ship, which would limp home with her sister. He thus took the noble option.

The ships were anchored in the lee of Danskøya (Dane's Island). In the few remaining days Fisher conducted various experiments and observations on the island. Franklin and Beechey drew up a plan of the port and the adjacent islands. The opportunity was taken to explore the surrounding area by sea, collecting information on the geography, topography and glaciology of Spitsbergen. They marvelled at the sight of icebergs calving, describing the loud cracking sound, which heralded the shearing off from the main glacier and the frenetic turbulence of the water. Four miles away Buchan was supervising the careening of *Dorothea* when the shock of the after-wave struck, necessitating the rapid release of the tackles holding down the upturned ship to avert total destruction.[65] There is much padding in the last two chapters of Beechey's account. He relates that when the ships left Spitsbergen on 30 August they were originally headed north, since Buchan was minded to sail for a glimpse of Greenland, but fog and ice, as well as *Dorothea's* condition, dictated retreat. They arrived in England on 22 October.

It is unfortunate that in this narrative the commander's voice is hardly detectable. Buchan refrained from publishing his own journal, considering that it contained insufficient material of interest to the general reader. Beechey was intent upon 'scrupulously preserving [Buchan's] opinions upon every point of difficulty which occurred, and by giving his sentiments on every important event'. His text was submitted to the captain, who found it in 'perfect accordance' with his views. The voyagers had demonstrated once more the existence of a great ice barrier extending from Nova Zembla to Greenland. 'There is no advantage at all adequate to the labour, to be gained by the wearisome operation of endeavouring to force a passage through the ice in the manner attempted by Captain Buchan.' Some earlier explorers in much smaller ships had enjoyed greater fortune. Indeed Beechey pointed out that chance played a great part in success or failure in the Arctic, a question of the right place at the right time in the right conditions. Buchan's attempt had coincided with a most unfavourable season. Sailing ships were not well suited to the ice. Nonetheless Beechey did not consider the quest to be 'entirely hopeless'. Well-intentioned though he was about portraying Buchan in the best possible light, he was far too reliant upon hindsight and contemporary debates to achieve that end. He favoured another attempt because Buchan had only shown that success was not practicable in the year he was commissioned. Furthermore, his ships were cruelly damaged just at the seasonal point when the seas were becoming most open. Also, Beechey was optimistic about the potential of steam, in 1843 if not in 1818; steam would set ships free, or so, at least, he hoped.[66]

David Buchan's achievement should not be minimised. He had shown himself a determined leader who demonstrated outstanding seamanship in desperate conditions. Bolstered by his Newfoundland experience he also took a bold approach to the ice. Apart from the whalers under his command, none of his crew had ever been to the Arctic and few of them could have had any idea of the appalling conditions created by sea and ice. Most importantly of all, he had shown that it was possible to survive such elemental experience. Had he written his own account he might have been able to communicate the novelty, wonder and strangeness of it all rather in the manner of John

Ross. It was not Beechey's fault that he felt compelled to make reference to later voyages because by 1843 he had to meet the expectations of the reading public whose acquaintance with the Arctic had been steadily growing while becoming ever more demanding of thrills, adventure and above all success. David Buchan is well deserving of the recognition that has long eluded him.

Portrait of Commander James Clark Ross, by John R. Wildman, 1834
(National Maritime Museum, public domain, via Wikimedia Commons)

3

THE ARCTIC APPRENTICESHIP
OF JAMES CLARK ROSS

The William Parry Expeditions of the 1820s

How much have I then to be thankful for as regards my
worldly happiness – my advancement in the profession which
I love has been most rapid, and less than 16 years after leaving
school I find myself a Commander in the Navy.[1]

It is somewhat difficult to see James Clark Ross as his own man, overshadowed as he always appears to be by his more colourful uncle, yet he was arguably the greatest polar explorer of the nineteenth century or any other. The attempt will here be made to isolate JCR, the individual, in part, by consulting reports mentioning his activities on the Parry voyages of the 1820s. James was born in 1800, the third son of George Ross, elder brother of John. George, who had studied the merchant trade in the Netherlands, moved to London shortly after the death of his father, the Rev. Andrew, in 1787. He married Christian Clark, daughter of Dr James Clark of Kirkcudbright in 1796. His maternal grandmother, Mrs Corsane, wrote to 26-year-old George congratulating him on taking parental charge of his brothers and setting them up on career paths, as well as having himself commenced a successful business in trade, while retaining the parental lands and buying more. Such promise, however, was not realised. Throughout his life George was to experience severe financial difficulties. He traded in London as a wine and spirit merchant and it was probably there that James was born. He also had property interests in the West Indies, where he spent much of his time, but he was declared bankrupt in 1801 and again in 1810. Ever seeking the perfect business opportunity, he was to pursue a number of scams and phantom schemes. As late as 1848, when charged with insolvency and fraud, he produced letters received in 1800, testifying to his part in suppressing a London grain riot.[2] In Stranraer he would have been known as a chancer.

James was sent to Chislehurst Academy, London. At age twelve he became a first-class volunteer on *Briseis*, of which his uncle John was commander, and with whom he continued to serve until the expedition of 1818 and later. When William Edward Parry undertook his triumphant Arctic expedition of 1819–20, James sailed as midshipman. Uncle John wrote to James just before he set off: 'I may with truth assure you that my affection is no less than that of parent to you', despite the recent falling out which may have made James feel quite relieved to escape Uncle John's clutches.[3]

Parry was given command of two ships for the 1819 expedition: *Hecla*, a bomb (i.e. a vessel strongly reinforced with additional timbers), which he regarded as 'perfection'; and *Griper*, a gun brig of 180 tons sailed by a subordinate, Lieutenant Matthew Liddon. They sailed on 11 May, charged with discovering a Northwest Passage through the Arctic Ocean from the Atlantic to the Pacific. Edward Sabine accompanied Parry, as did a Greenland master, a Greenland mate and several other officers, including Lieutenant Frederick W. Beechey (1796–1856), who had been Franklin's second-in-command on *Trent* in 1818 and who would belatedly write a favourable account of Captain David Buchan's performance on that same voyage. When they reached the American coast they were to erect a flagpole attached to a bottle message giving some account of their progress and future intentions for the attention of Lieutenant Franklin, who was leading an overland expedition at the same time (see Chapter 4). If they reached the Bering Strait they were to proceed to Kamchatka, from where they were to forward copies of their journals to St Petersburg for onward transmission to London. They were then to head for Hawai'i or Canton to refit before striking for home.

Scots on Parry's *Hecla* included Lieutenant Andrew Reid; James Skeoch, assistant surgeon; midshipmen James Clark Ross and John Henderson. Other members of the crew included Greenland Master John Allison and Greenland Mate George Crawford; the ship total was sixty. On *Griper* were Allan McLaren, assistant surgeon, Greenland Master George Fife and Greenland Mate Alexander Elder. The ship total was fifty-eight. There were seven marines, including a sergeant and a corporal on each ship. The ships sailed via Orkney encountering their first ice off Cape Farewell. They spotted their first whale, which, due to the configuration of the ice, was forced to descend tail-foremost; at one point eighty-two whales were observed in a single day. Scots had been whaling since the Bronze Age, the industry approaching commercialisation in the mid seventeenth century. The *Griper* crew killed a polar bear, which sank in the sea. Knowing of the bear's phenomenal sense of smell, mariners often attracted them with fried herring.

Parry crashed through the imaginary Croker Mountains, metaphorically wiping them off the charts, while naming, penetrating and briefly exploring Prince Regent Inlet, which, he opined, might one day be found to offer a communication between Repulse Bay and Hudson Bay. They would return to the Inlet before long, and James Ross would come to know it very well. The ships ploughed the Polar Sea, discovering the southern coasts of Cornwallis Island and Bathurst Island en route to Melville Island and Winter Harbour, where they spent almost a year. Luck and skill had bought them the key to the Pacific. Parry attributed their good fortune to God and to having pitched upon Lancaster Sound, 'where one outlet to the Polar Sea exists'. Future expeditions would have to investigate lower latitudes.[4]

When, earlier, Sabine and the two doctors landed on Byam Martin Island (which neighboured Melville) to inspect the flora and fauna, the skeletons of large mammals and ruined dwellings of the Inuit, James Ross accompanied them, something of a favour we may think and probably indicative of his existing interest in natural history.[5]

Parry's team were to learn quickly about the realities and discomforts of Arctic travel as the ships became the first known British naval vessels to over-winter in the nineteenth-century Arctic. Consequently there was much to report whether memorable, novel, curious, mundane or unexpected. Parry noted that on 26 October there was enough sunlight to permit reading and writing in his cabin between 9.30am and 2.30am; 'that cheering orb of this great world, both eye and soul' was seen above the horizon for the last time on 4 November and did not re-appear until 8 February, though JCR reported seeing it from the mast-head at noon on 11 November. As daylight withdrew, the wolves advanced 'howling most piteously' but offering relief from the sound of silence, a sound 'far different from that peaceable composure which characterizes the landscape of a cultivated country; it was the death-like stillness of the most dreary desolation, and the total absence of animated existence'. However, it was noted that sound travelled over long distances in the Arctic. The men soon learned the danger of exposing human skin to metallic touch; instruments quickly iced up while human bodies adjusted surprisingly swiftly to changes in temperature.

Parry had novel ideas about heating, cleanliness, health, exercise and 'good order', as well as an abiding interest in magnetism, natural history, topography, geology and geography. He grew mustard and cress in his cabin to provide a modicum of an anti-scorbutic to ease the first signs of scurvy contracted by the gunner of *Hecla*. The *North Georgia Gazette and Winter Chronicle*, edited weekly by Sabine, provided welcome distraction. Plays and skits were performed fortnightly, James Ross taking occasional female roles featuring such characters as Miss Grantham and Corinna, as well as Mrs Bruin in *The Mayor of Garratt*, and Poll in *The North-West Passage or the Voyage Finished*, eventually graduating to a male role as Colonel Tivy in *Bon Ton*, but posing as Ann Lovely in *A Bold Stroke for a Wife*. Some of these were rerun.[6] Young James thus showed himself to be a rather fun-loving, even extrovert, individual unlike the rather dour character he later became.

James had been entrusted by Parry with scoping possible ship-berthing sites for the winter; during the weary ten months at Winter Harbour he was heavily involved with others in recording 6,862 lunar observations, finessing the measurement of longitude, working with Parry, Sabine, the first lieutenant and the purser W.H. Hooper. This was invaluable experience for one in his position and a chance to build on the skills to which he had been introduced, mainly by Sabine, during the 1818 expedition. He also continued with his natural history interests. A plant, *Geum rossii*, was named for him. He was likewise honoured by the naming of Ross's gull, a small dove-like bird which he discovered. He collected other avian specimens and small mammals for taxidermy. Parry named Point Ross in his honour. On his return to Britain, James was made a fellow of the Linnean Society and was promoted to lieutenant.

The greatest enemy to be overcome during the long winter, next to cold, was ennui. When weather allowed, the men were encouraged to exercise or to perform tasks around the ships. Punishments were rarely mentioned since most captains wished to stress the contentedness and communitarianism of their men, but two marines guilty of drunkeness were each given thirty-six lashes. Snow-blindness was countered by gauze inserted in spectacle frames or attached to headgear. A few more sailors suffered from scurvy but overall it was successfully treated. It was believed that the disease was caused by 'slush', the skimmings or grease from the water in which salt beef was boiled, a perk traditionally given to the cook.[7] When that individual on *Hecla* was caught supplying the stuff to crew members he was exposed and disgraced before the whole ship's company and forced to wear a badge on his back ridiculing him for his misdemeanour, a form of shaming. Scurvy remained a problem throughout the expedition and beyond the period discussed in this book, though it was well understood that it could be kept at bay by the supply of fresh food, such as the ptarmigan that re-appeared at the end of winter, doubly hailed as a sign of spring and as relief for patients. So efficacous was the meat that Parry ordered every bird killed to be treated as public property issued to officers and ships' companies alike without distinction, a practice that became known on shipboard as 'game laws', an ironic term since these laws in Britain were all about privilege, social rank and exclusivity.[8] When the winter finally ended and the ice broke up, Parry tried to explore west-wards towards Banks Island but progress was hindered by ice, and they were unable to leave the harbour until August. To avoid risking another winter in the Arctic, the expedition returned to England in October 1820.

Parry's achievements on this expedition were undoubtedly memorable, not least for having crossed the 110° W meridian, which qualified him for a government bounty of £5,000, one fifth of which was due to the captain. However, the *Edinburgh Review* remained loyal to John Ross, who had ventured into Baffin Bay, proving some of the claims of William Baffin two hundred years earlier. He had conquered the Davis Strait without any recent predecessor to aid him, following a track which in 1820 saw the wreck of fourteen Greenland whalers, as well as indicating places where a passage was impossible, from all of which Parry benefited. The Arctic archipelago was the perfect place to point out that no man is an island. We all depend on those who went before, just as those who come after rely on present achievements, which they in turn will develop. Parry's unpleasant side was revealed when John Ross sent him a letter of congratulation on his success. The conqueror of the Croker Mountains told his parents that, among many such letters, Ross's was 'the most ardent and I doubt not, the most sincere . . . I propose to have it framed and glazed and then put it into the British Museum . . . I will answer him at my leisure – quite civilly, but so as to prevent the possibility of his bringing on a correspondence which is the game he now wants to play'. In fact, Ross seems to have been quite sincere, thanking Parry for the helpful assistance he had extended to James.[9] There was no need for such a model Christian as Parry to behave so uncharitably.

*

James was signed up for Parry's next expedition of 1821 to 1823, which charged the commander with two ships: *Hecla* from the previous voyage, to be captained by George Francis Lyon, and *Fury*, a ship of exactly the same size, entrusted to Parry as expedition leader. There were sixty men on *Fury*,

65

including twenty able seamen. Scots were James Skeoch, assistant surgeon; John Henderson, midshipman; George Fiddis, carpenter; John Allison, Greenland master; and George Crawford, 'worthy old Greenland mate', with forty-three 'inferior officers and men'. Midshipman Francis Crozier, an Irishman who, following Franklin's death, became leader of his doomed expedition, was also aboard. George Francis Lyon, an Englishman, enjoyed the unusual distinction of having been sent by John Barrow in search of the Niger River, spending two years in North Africa and the Sudan. Among the fifty-eight men on *Hecla*, Scots included Allan McLaren, assistant surgeon; George Fyfe, greatly valued Greenland master who died on the eve of return; and Alexander Elder, Greenland mate who sailed with Ross in 1818 and also died on the eve of return.

Lyon was appointed as a naturalist and artist but Parry specifically commended young Ross who, 'from the commencement of the voyage, undertook in addition to his other duties, to superintend the preservation of stuffed specimens of birds and other animals: a task requiring a degree of taste as well as of skill and attention, which perhaps persons accustomed to these matters can alone duly appreciate', a remarkably fulsome assessment of JCR's talents. Ross was also given some responsibility for the Abstract of the Meteorological Register. Lyon does not mention him in his journal, although Ross features quite prominently in Parry's *Journal*. Lyon was an interesting character and a popular figure as well as an entertaining writer with a passion for discovering and recording the life and culture of the Inuit. He believed with Baffin that 'God, which is greater than either ice or tide, always delivered us'.[10]

Parry's instructions were to lead *Fury* and *Hecla* in searching for a passage from the Atlantic to the Pacific as in his previous commission, with the addition of the *Nautilis* transport that was to convey supplies to the Davis Strait and return. The Rev. George Fisher replaced Sabine as scientist. According to James Ross, Sabine was universally detested for his quarrels with the officers 'and will yet prove most likely be hauled over the coals if he does not mind his p's and q's'. John Bushnan was along as assistant surveyor and artist, 'on Fury only'. An improved heating system was devised for the ships, and a new contrivance that melted snow for consumption, together with enhanced food storage and better anti-scorbutics.

The expedition set off on 8 May 1821, reaching Orkney a month later. On 1 July *Nautilis* returned home from the Davis Strait, the bergs multiplied, the glorious sea birds flew and the Brits contemplated a fog-bound scene, 'indescribably dreary and disageeable . . . utter barrenness and desolation'.[11] In Hudson Strait they encountered two HBC ships beset in the ice. Next day another ship appeared, *Lord Wellington*, carrying 160 settlers for the Earl of Selkirk's Red River colony. Moving west, the explorers passed the Saddleback Mountain, shortly thereafter meeting Inuit who wanted to trade but, as usual on such occasions, the presumptious Europeans considered the local inhabitants to be a bunch of thieves whose persons were as filthy as the nauseous food they consumed. One feature on an island reminded Parry of 'the Mormond Hills over Buchan Ness', Aberdeenshire. He and Ross took a gig to sound the channel off Southampton Island. The surviving Inuit archaeology of Repulse Bay was most impressive. When Parry was indisposed, James stood in for him. Otherwise he was frequently chosen for short explorations, often accompanying the captain. He was rewarded when Parry named Ross Bay 'in compliment to the gentleman who had accompanied me during during the whole of this examination'. Throughout their journey they found piles of stones at Inuit sites and some stones that appeared to be built into cairns, giving them the look of men in the distance. But the words 'inuksuk' or *inuksuit* (the Inuktitut term for a constructed stone landmark or cairn conveying various meanings to travellers) do not appear in their records. Another group of Inuit, more amenable and less rambunctious than those they had met earlier, were also interested in trading.

The expeditionaries settled in a bay of Winter Island. Plays were revived and some entertainment was provided by a phantasmagoria. Schools were run on both ships nightly. Parry and Fisher set up a portable observatory. Only one man was sick, John Reid, carpenter's mate. Walking was encouraged when weather allowed and finger-posts were erected near the bay to guide folk who were lost or overtaken by the elements. It was discovered that a type of shrimp would completely devour meats until only a clean skeleton was left, thus neatly providing anatomical specimens of various creatures. All the men were supplied with snow-boots made with cloth and cork, which unlike leather footwear allowed the free circulation of blood. The Auroras were spectacular, while Sirius, the Dog Star, exhibited the most beautiful violet and blue suffusions. They had never seen anything so brilliant, 'the play of prismatic colours in a cut diamond' inspiring Parry to compose an eloquent celebration of the event. The company organised soirées reminding the men of home. Sometimes a fiddler played for dancing, which was not unusual, since at this period, even in Britain, probably more men danced publicly than women. For example, dancing for prizes at Highland Games in the nineteenth century was by men; females did not take over until the next century. The Inuit from a nearby village often joined in with their own songs, reciprocated by the sailors on violin, flute and voice. In addition, musical parties were held in the cabins of Parry or Lyon. The captain asserted that nobody was bored. There can be no doubt that the presence of the extremely friendly Inuit greatly shortened the winter.

The Inuit women were fascinated by Lyon's evocative portraits of them and their men; some of them sang for him. A talented woman named Iligliuk drew detailed maps for the kabloonas (foreigners), indicating a possible route westwards beyond the Melville Peninsula to a land named Akkoolee, inhabited by many Inuit on the shores of a vast ocean. The artistic abilities of an Inuk named Toolooak reminded Parry of the talents of 'John Sackhouse'. Indeed, both races showed great respect to each other, the best evidence for which survives in Lyon's excellent drawings of the polar people. He depicts both women and men most sympathetically. The women are beautiful, the men handsome, and all are confident as they go about their tasks or pose for his pencil. Lyon attempted a brief recce across the Melville Peninsula but his party was promptly defeated by ferocious weather and frostbite. He sledged with huskies, making 'the first long journey performed by a naval officer with dog-drawn sledges', thus disproving the oft-repeated accusation that the Navy dismissed canine traction in favour of human draught.[12] JCR also tried his hand at sledging. He must have been fascinated by the prolonged exposure to the Inuit because he clearly developed a deep interest in their culture and ethnology. Parry and Lyon both produced modest ethnologies of the Inuit and the Inuktitut language, in which JCR became fluent.

The first death occured in mid May when James Pringle, a seaman on *Hecla*, fell from the mizzen top-mast. William Souter, quartermaster on *Fury*, sent to sick bay by Ross, soon also died, as did John Reid, carpenter's mate. All three bore Scottish names. The soul-destroying pain of cutting out – physically separating the ships from the ice – began in June. 'Nothing could exceed the alacrity with which this laborious work was undertaken, and continued daily from six in the morning till eight at night, with the intermission only of meal-times'. The crew's voices could be heard 'mingling with the cheerful though fantastic songs with which the Greenland sailors are accustomed at once to beguile their labour, and to keep the necessary time in the action of sawing the ice. The whole prospect, together with the hopes and associations excited by it, was to persons cooped up as we had been, exhilarating almost beyond conception'[13] or so, at least, thought Parry, who no doubt shared the exhilaration of release but who probably had never attempted to saw ice in his life.

Lyon made a short trip of four days to acquire fish from a new band of Inuit and in particular the 'remarkably intelligent and energetic man named Toolemak'. Parry had tried kayaking; Lyon attempted dog-sledging. He also shared his food with his Inuit hosts and tried a small sample of the contents of caribou stomachs, *nerooka*, 'on the principle that no man who wishes to conciliate or inquire into the manners of savages should refuse to fare as they do'. The sailors had eleven dogs pulling their sledge. The lead-dog responded instantly to the commands of the driver, who did not beat it but repeatedly talked to it and called it by name. 'It was beautiful to observe the sledges racing to the same object, the dogs and men in full cry, and the vehicles splashing through the water with the velocity of rival stage-coaches.' He then visited a village where their wet clothes were taken from them to be dried. His hosts' endless questions kept him awake but he eventually fell asleep, awakening in great warmth to find himself covered by a large deerskin under which lay his host, 'his two wives and their favourite puppy, all fast asleep and stark naked'. He was treated to a nose-rubbing, *koonik*, ceremony and then distributed sewing needles to all the females present, 'having extracted kooniks from all the prettiest in return'. He taught the Inuit leap-frog; 'even women with children at their backs would not be outdone by the men'. Before he left, he was given two tattoos, one from his host's oldest wife and one from his youngest, an unusual compliment. Lyon had proved himself a perfect and thoroughly appreciative guest.

Parry was anxious to discover the accuracy of Iligliuk's maps once the ships were eventually free of the ice, following the coast of the Melville Peninsula up towards Igloolik. The narrow strait named Fury and Hecla was still blocked, as it had been earlier. Midshipman Crozier was sent in a small boat with two marines to establish whether there was a permanent current in the strait. After three days, Ross was sent after him with fresh supplies and instructions to find out if the north shore of the strait was insular. Other probes proved equally unhelpful. In September Ross was again sent with two assistants to measure tides and currents. Parry probably had John Ross's disgrace in mind, worried that he too might be blamed for polar phantoms. En route to Igloolik, *Fury* was beset by heavy ice but *Hecla* was spared. Meanwhile Lyon, ever the romantic, discovered 'a fairy-like grotto', an object of little interest to his practical colleagues, we may think. At Igloolik they once again encountered the Inuit, who were delighted that Parry planned to over-winter there.

As usual, the winter produced little of import save that JCR and Parry often studied the heavens together. It was noted that the Inuit hunted walrus, and the efficiency of their fox traps was admired. The explorers shared their medicinal knowledge with Inuit who were sick, inevitably moving on to discuss burial practices and death customs. Parry, unusually, had an Inuk lashed for theft. Close attention was paid to the crew's diet. In April, plans were made for their eventual departure. There was also time for a rather odd experiment which concluded that nine dogs belonging to Lyon dragged 1,611 pounds a distance of 1,750 yards in nine minutes!

It was becoming clear that the voyage was effectively over due to hostile weather, the persistent presence of ice in the vicinity of the Melville Peninsula, the absence of abundant game and the increasing cases of scurvy. Alexander Elder, Greenland mate of *Hecla*, died of a pulmonary disease while George Fife, master of the same ship, was killed by scurvy; both were Scots. Parry consulted the doctors and Lyon about whether another year in the north should be contemplated but all agreed, in written statements, that they should make for home. Moving south they were still encountering ice problems but they received a great welcome in Shetland, Parry and Fisher moving on to the Admiralty, London, on 18 October 1823.

*

At the end of June 1824 James Ross was second lieutenant on *Fury* for the third voyage to the Arctic in search of the Northwest Passage, entering Lancaster Sound and travelling south to explore the coastline. At the same time Franklin and John Richardson were completing their surveys of the American coast (see Chapter 4). Franklin was expected to travel eastwards on *Hecla* from the Coppermine River to Icy Cape where he would rendezvous with Frederick Beechey, who was to sail in *Blossom* all the way through the South Atlantic, round Cape Horn to the Pacific and north to Bering Strait and Russian America. The ambition of the planners in London, led by Barrow, was, once again, almost beyond belief. At Disko, James Ross met and instantly became friends with Lieutenant Holboll of the Danish Navy who, for two years, had been carrying out scientific research for his government.

Lyon was charged with the unenviable task of sailing to Repulse Bay in *Griper*, described as 'a vessel of such lubberly, shameful construction as to baffle the ingenuity of the most ingenious seaman in England to do anything with her'. He was something of a cultural tourist, visiting the 'Druidical remains' – the Standing Stones at Stenness – from where he enjoyed a view of the Ring of Brodgar, surely one of the first of the Arctic travellers to remark in print on the brilliant archaeology of Orkney. He also purchased two ponies, presumably with some intention of seeing how they tolerated the ship conditions and also those of the Arctic. They became very popular with the crew, who were devastated that they had to be killed due to food-stuff shortage.[14]

The first indications that the expedition was to encounter numerous problems were when it took the Baffin contingent eight weeks to reach Lancaster Sound in desperate ice and fog conditions. The icebergs were between 100 and 200 feet high. The ships advanced only 70 miles in a month, 'heaving, warping or sawing' their way through the ice. 'Sallying', using boats to break the ice ahead of the ships, was also used. A new capstan performed well but snapping hawsers injured some of the men. All contests with the ice were very hard on the crew. So bad was the situation that Parry thought of turning back to England. Having just entered Prince Regent Inlet, they were swept out again by wind and ice but managed to re-establish sufficient control to berth at Port Bowen on the east shore of the inlet, where they remained for the winter.

Parry pointed out that the success of exploration often depended on the 'little things'. In this regard, adequate and proper clothing was crucial. For example, for the prevention of lumbago to which seamen were particularly liable 'from their well-known habit of leaving their loins imperfectly clothed', he recommended that all men wore under their clothes 'a canvas belt a foot broad, lined with flannel and having straps that go over the shoulder'. Many whalers used these but some prejudiced officers and men scoffed at 'wearing stays'. It was believed that damp bedclothes encouraged scurvy, so warmth, dryness and air circulation were important. Once again a school was organised teaching reading, writing and religion but there was no longer enthusiasm for plays. Instead masques proved popular in which participants dressed up, acting as different characters from history or literature, Parry celebrating 'masquerades without licentiousness – carnivals without excess'. Like many pious individuals, his tolerance for fun or gaiety was severely limited.

JCR became involved in a small village of huts and little houses created for scientific experiments. Again he and Parry spent a good deal of time contemplating the heavens. Virtually all visitors to the Arctic look forward to the performances of the Aurora Borealis and the 'merry dancers' ('heavenly dancers' in the song 'The Northern Lights of Old Aberdeen', which was first published in 1952 having been written by an English couple who had never been to Aberdeen). On one occasion Ross was lucky enough to observe five meteors or falling stars in the space of fifteen minutes. His description of the event was published by Parry. Since so few of Ross's words have survived it seems appropriate to quote him here.

> The two first fell in quick succesion, probably not more than two minutes apart. The third appeared about eight minutes after these, and exceeded in brilliancy any of the surrounding stars. It took a direction from near B Tauri (the Bull), and passing slowly towards the Pleiades, left behind it sparks like the tail of a rocket, these being visible for a few seconds after the meteor appeared to break, which it did close to the Pleiades . . . it passed to the eastward, and disappeared half way between B Tauri and Gemini . . . The fifth of these meteors . . . was more dim than the rest, and of a red colour like Aldebaran. There was a faint appearance of the Aurora to the westward near the horizon.[15]

When Parry's rheumatism recurred, Ross substituted for him on magnetic readings, known as the 'needles'. There were diversions. One man fleeing from a bear fell over a vertical cliff and was lucky to survive. The time of year when the men became most impatient was in March as the light was returning but the snow still stubbornly fell. A whale-hunt was organised to obtain the mammals' oil; Ross was credited with killing a small one. However, he must have been a happy man when his superior sent him with four men to explore northwards along the shore of Prince Regent's Inlet in order to make an accurate survey and to check the sites visited in 1819, noting any variation in the measurement of latitude and longitude since that date. He reported the welcome news that the sea was clear 22 miles north of Port Bowen. From the Cape York hills there was no indication of ice at all. He spotted innumerable ducks, dovekies, loons, kittiwakes and ivory gulls.[16] He and his men also found traces of Inuit occupation. This was important because the locals always understood the best places for shelter and habitation sites far better than British naval officers. What had once been occupied in the past might be so again in the future, a principle understood worldwide by many conquerors and, unfortunately, most attentive would-be colonists.

On Parry's order, the company crossed to the west side of Prince Regent's Inlet hoping for some surveying opportunities and appropriate means of egress. This proved another trial due to the strength of the ice. For a time both ships appeared vulnerable but ultimately it was *Fury* that succumbed, badly damaged and trapped in ice. There was much frenetic activity as her cargo was taken off and stored on shore. Since the idea was to lighten her in order to carry out repairs, *Fury*'s spars, sails, boats and other equipment were also taken off. Some of the men were totally exhausted to the point that they could no longer comprehend orders. *Fury* was 'hove down' – turned on her side to investigate the damage below her waterline. Repairs seemed impossible and in any case ice and wind once again refused to co-operate. To make a long story short – and Parry *did* make a long story out of the episode – the danger to *Hecla* and the crippled state of her sister-ship inevitably led to *Fury*'s abandonment at Fury Point, creating a remarkable 'free emporium' of usable stores for future expeditions.

Parry took great care to consult his officers, including James Ross, whenever he had to make a decision. He also discussed several other factors of less import but still relevant to the outcome. In these respects he was quite unlike the single-minded, defiant JCR and it is tempting to suspect that it was the treatment John Ross received that rendered Parry quite so timid; he who had once been so critical of the Scot could now perhaps empathise with him. Barrow, as usual, was full of opinion based on unfathomable ignorance. For example, he was certain that the open sea was preferable to hugging the coast, pronouncing that 'we speak from some little experience' in asserting that the danger of becoming immobilised was 'very trifling indeed'. Parry was indignant that the Admiralty was attempting 'to let the blame for failure lie on any shoulders but their own'. It was also to blame for Lyon's problems with *Griper*, responsible as it was for 'the principal, original and most glaring faults'.[17] Throughout his career, Barrow's achievements were many but his credibility was rendered suspect when his schemes and demands were not realised. He needed successes just as much as, if not more than, ambitious naval officers. One way to advance his polar politics was to review, ahead of publication, printed Arctic journals that he had personally edited, a ploy of which John Ross's book fell foul.

The Naval Secretary foresaw that soon the geography of America's Arctic coast would be fully discovered and adventurous Englishmen would reach for 'the very northern extremity of the earth's axis' by way of Spitsbergen, which was not exactly a new idea, but a very attractive one because for long the 'European Arctic' had attracted voyagers from different parts of the continent.

*

After his 1824–5 expedition, William Edward Parry informed Robert Dundas, 2nd Viscount Melville, First Lord of the Admiralty, that the North Pole might be conquered by using sledge-boats which could cross ice and water. Several authorities, including Scoresby and other whalers had suggested that to the north of Seven Islands the ice was 'flat and unbroken'. According to Parry, the idea of the boats had originated with Franklin, doubtless due to his experience in Spitsbergen and Canada, though Scoresby had suggested that sledges, drawn by dogs or reindeer, could be adapted as boats, and even fitted with sails which might double as tents.[18] For his 1827 North Polar expedition Parry was given command of *Hecla*. The boats were duly commissioned, 'having great flatness of floor, with the extreme breadth carried well forward and aft, and possessing the utmost buoyancy, as well as capacity for storage'.[19] They were 20 feet long with a maximum width of 7 feet. Charles Macintosh's recently invented (1823) waterproof canvas was attached to a frame of ash and hickory, which was then covered in fir planking three quarters of an inch thick, in turn felted with oak cladding of similar thickness. Steel sledge-runners were fixed to each side of the shallow keel. In addition two wheels, 5 feet in diameter, with a small steering wheel aft, 'like a bath chair', were added to each boat, though they later proved useless. A hide rope was attached to both runners, and to it two horse-hair ropes were tied, for hauling. Broad leather shoulder belts were provided for each member of the crew: ten seamen and two marines, commanded by two officers. Each boat had a bamboo mast 19 feet long, a tanned duck sail which doubled as an awning, with fourteen paddles and a steering oar. The plan was to leave north Spitsbergen at the beginning of June, travelling to the Pole, and returning within ninety days. With equipment and supplies the weight worked out at 268 pounds per man, excluding four 26-pound sledges.

It is not difficult to imagine that the usual official Admiralty instructions were based on a draft provided by Parry himself. One officer, Lieutenant Foster, was to survey the northern and eastern coasts of Spitsbergen, taking the customary measurements and estimating the potential for whaling before the Pole seekers set out. JCR was once again present.

Hecla was towed down the Thames on 25 March 1827. Viscount Melville boarded briefly to wish everyone well. Excellent weather conditions enabled the ship to reach Hammerfest by 17 April. Another planned innovation was to use reindeer to pull the boats over the ice, an idea first mooted by Colonel Mark Beaufoy, who sent questionnaires to Russia,[20] but the animals had not yet been delivered to the community, giving the seamen the opportunity to practise on their newly purchased snow-shoes. On 23 April the king's birthday was celebrated and a couple of days were spent training eight reindeer when they eventually appeared. Each required four pounds of moss per day – somewhat bulky fuel – but Parry, who was much taken with the animals of whom he had the highest expectations, reported that they could survive for six days without food, that they consumed snow and bedded down happily on ice. He confessed that, the more attached he became to them, 'the more painful became the idea of the necessity . . . of ultimately having recourse to them as provision for ourselves'.[21]

On 2 May they met their first ice. Four days later at latitude 77° N they greeted two whalers from Peterhead and later one from Hull, all of whom reported that ice conditions seemed heavier than usual. In company with some twelve Greenlanders they 'bored' through the ice to sight Spitsbergen at Prince Charles Foreland. By 14 May they passed Magdalene Bay, arriving off Haluytodden which they rounded, seeking anchorage in Smeerenburg Harbour, filled with one unbroken floe of ice to which they made fast. They sought refuge from fierce gales by driving *Hecla* into the pack ice at about the same place where they reckoned *Dorothea* had been so damaged in 1818. Thus sheltered they drifted to Cloven Cliff and along the north coast to Red Beach. JCR was sent out to investigate the cause of the 'redness' but could not land. Excellent fresh water was available in ice hummocks but ice pressure was less benign. When Ross was able to reach the shore he found it to be composed of brownish red-tinged clay-slate. He also discovered two graves dated 1741 and 1762.

An attempt to launch the boats proved futile. Ross went off to explore the ice some five miles from the ship but reported unfavourably. Worried that time was passing, Parry briefly considered using only one boat for the Pole attempt, with a double crew, an idea later abandoned. Much labour was involved in depositing food caches on Red Beach and at other places for the return journey.

Departure was again delayed because of ice conditions that endangered *Hecla*, tied to a floe and helplessly having to go wherever the ice took her, potentially and most worryingly, dragging her into the shallows. The ice teased them by opening up and then closing again, the men straining to warp the ship around its berg in order to avoid possibly fatal accumulations. *Hecla* was effectively beset for twenty-four days but still she could not find a secure berth as the conditions refused to co-operate. Parry consumed many journal pages describing his hapless ship at the mercy of the to-ing and fro-ing of the ice; little wonder that he began 'to entertain the most serious apprehensions as related to the accomplishment of our principal object'.[22] At last on 19 June they found a berth in Treurenberg Bay at a spot they unsurprisingly named Hecla Cove, sawing open a canal.

They were now ready to depart. Parry and surgeon Charles James Beverley (from Fort Augustus) were in one boat, *Enterprise*, Ross and midshipman Edward Bird in the other, *Endeavour*. Food dumps were placed on Walden Island and Low Island for the return. Having already been tortured by ice conditions they decided to dispense with reindeer, sledge-wheels and snow-shoes, although the snow-shoes furnished material for four supply-sledges.[23] To the cheers of shipmates, the boats departed on 22 June. In recounting the journey, Parry remarked wherever possible on features of interest – topography, ice conditions, driftwood, natural history and anything else that took his fancy. He sensibly opined, for example, that walruses were never the first to make an attack.

They initially made encouraging progress, travelling by night to avoid the glare of the midday sun and thus snow-blindness. There was also a better chance of using the warmth of restful 'day-time' to dry clothes, while there was less melt water around at night. However, the men found twenty-four hours of sunlight disorienting, as indeed it is. Some complained that they never knew night from day during the whole excursion.

After sleep, the 'day' began with prayers and a discarding of 'sleeping dresses' in favour of travelling clothes, dry or wet; clothes usually became wet within fifteen minutes in any case. Breakfast consisted of cocoa and biscuit followed by about five and a half hours of travel, a one-hour break, up to six more hours on the move, dinner and post-prandial conversation, storytelling and smoking before turning in for seven hours' sleep. The daily allowance was 10 ounces of biscuit, 9 oz of pemmican, 1 oz of cocoa which made a pint, and 1 gill of rum. Each man was given 3 oz of tobacco per week. There was much rain and much fog. Ice fragments, dubbed 'penknives', cut boots and feet.[24] Hummocks rendered the handling and manoeuvring of the boats very difficult and tiresome. Laborious portages involved several trips back and forth to bring forward supplies, and often ice hazards and obstacles necessitated roundabout routes. Six hours of severe toil might accomplish an advance of one and a quarter miles. Better weather brought little relief as the ice was frequently uncrossable. When landing on a floe, Ross and Parry would generally go ahead, together or separately, to scout a route. Then the portaging would re-commence; 'thus we proceeded for nine miles out of every ten'. Parry became very critical of reports such as that of Ludwidge about 'one continuous plain of smooth, unbroken ice, bounded only by the horizon'! The sledge-runners often sank in deep snow or water, or became jammed. Once it took two hours to cover 100 yards. One bonus was slight diet enhancement as birds were shot quite regularly but birds became rarer the further north they advanced.

Since the Royal Society of Edinburgh had nominated 17 July as one of the days for simultaneous weather observations the party obliged with 'an hourly register of every phenomenon which came under our notice'.[25] That day, eleven hours of effort accomplished barely four miles. The exhausted men were somewhat refreshed by dining off a small seal. Next day several men suffered eye problems, donning shades against incipient snow-blindness. Twelve hours gained them just three miles. The following day they travelled more than ten miles to find themselves less than five miles north of where they had been three days earlier. To make matters worse, the ice collapsed and several men fell through it. No-one was killed and no supplies were lost but the episode engendered further gloom. Parry's eyes were so badly affected that Ross took over as sole pioneer or scout. He was injured dragging the boat when he was trapped between the gunwhale and an ice hummock, suffering numbness and sickness but he soon recovered.

Parry and Ross, like Buchan, now had to recognise the inevitable, namely that the struggle against the current was futile. They could make no headway against a southerly drift of four miles per day. Their furthest north was calculated at latitude 82°45' N, an achievement 'considerably beyond that mentioned in any other well-authenticated record'.[26] They were permitted a day of rest before turning south. Progress remained laborious but confident. By 5 August they observed what the whalers called the 'tree-ing' of the ice, when refraction creates the illusion that ice has been raised in a sheer wall above the horizon, a condition often believed to indicate clear water, though not in this case.

James Ross shot a bear, which was immediately cooked, many of the crew gratefully gorging on the meat. Weather and ice conditions remained deplorably difficult but when more open water was ultimately reached they resorted to riding on a floe to avoid loose ice. Another bear was killed but this time the quantities consumed were strictly controlled. Parry archly wrote that they had to move to another part of the floe 'for the sake of cleanliness and comfort' since the portion they occupied had become 'so like an Eskimaux establishment'. Following a last meal at the edge they finally quit the ice on 11 August after an abode of forty-eight days, to paddle 50 miles towards Table Island, again in adverse and uncomfortable, even painful, conditions. On reaching the rock to the north of Table Island, where supplies had been left, it was discovered that the bears had eaten 100 pounds of bread. The men, replete with bear meat, joked that 'Bruin was only square with us'. However, they did find such luxuries as sugar and lemon-juice, which were immediately dispensed to a few crew members who were showing signs of scurvy, with pleasing results. There were also messages informing them that *Hecla* had been grounded in the ice break-up, though successfully hauled off and repaired by attentive officers and crew. Unable to land on Table Island, they struck for Walden in a snowstorm, making landfall after fifty-six hours on the go, forty-eight of them in the boats. The men bore 'that wildness in their looks which usually accompanies excessive fatigue', seemingly unable to comprehend orders. After rest, Ross was sent to the north-east of the island to recover a boat left there for their return. In recognition of Ross's talents and his role in the expedition, Parry announced that he had named 'the islet which lies off Little Table Island, and which is interesting as being the northernmost land upon the globe', after the lieutenant, 'for I believe no individual can have exerted himself more strenuously to rob it of this distinction'.[27]

The final mention of Ross on the 1827 expedition concerns his long walk on Low Island in the company of Mr Beverley but no details are forthcoming. Parry's boats were prevented for several days, by wind and sea, from re-joining *Hecla*; the reunion transpired on 21 August to a 'warm and cordial welcome, which can alone be felt, and not described'. The captain claimed to have covered a total of 1,127 miles, almost the same distance from Spitsbergen to the Pole and back. The boats had performed admirably in the most severe conditions, suffering no damage whatsoever. The sole casualty was the whaling master, Crawford, who suffered from dropsy and died on the return voyage. Parry praised the 'cheerful alacrity and unwearied zeal' of both officers and men but lamented that twenty times as much rain fell that summer as in any other he had spent in the polar regions.

Further observations and surveys were made in Treurenberg Bay, notably of the graves at Eolusneset. All were impressed by the good weather in the bay compared to that which they had recently experienced to the north, and by the strikingly different weather conditions to be experienced on land and sea. Their ship left its name on Heclahuken. On 30 August they sailed around Hakluyt's Headland to the open sea, receiving favourable winds to clear Spitsbergen, but were thereafter detained by southerlies and south-westerlies that kept them from Shetland for two weeks. Bad weather also hit them in Fair Isle and Orkney where Parry left *Hecla* to join a Revenue cutter *Chichester*, bound for Inverness. From there he went on to London, arriving 29 September, with *Hecla* following on 6 October.

Parry concluded, unsurprisingly, that the objective of the enterprise remained 'of still more difficult attainment than was before supposed'. The plan had been reasonable enough but it was ruined by ice conditions. A boat of sufficient size to combat water and ice would have to be too large to be powered by dogs or reindeer. The incessant launching and hauling up of the boats, eight or ten times daily – and on one occasion seventeen times – could only be accomplished by humans. The management of animals would take too much time, while their food supplies would take up too much space. The possibility of setting out earlier was negated by the consequent need to over-winter on the north coast of Spitsbergen, a solution which would weaken the men and render the acquisition of moss for the deer impossible. Another problem was that provisions were insufficient 'to support the strength of men living constantly in the open air, exposed to wet and cold for at least twelve hours a day, seldom enjoying the luxury of a warm meal, and having to perform the kind of labour' to which they were subject. Rations would have to be increased by at least one third, adding to transportation difficulties. Another difficulty was that earlier accounts of the state of the ice were completely misleading, probably due to reporters viewing the ice from afar, or above, from the crow's nest or high up on mountains. Rain compounded the problem. All noted clear water in August that would have made possible, it was believed, the attainment of latitude 83° N by the end of the month. Whether a safe return might have been possible was not mentioned. One rather surprising and regrettable omission in Parry's account is the absence of a name-list of *Hecla*'s crew, perhaps reflecting a sense of his own superiority.

It is seldom possible to recover information about the inner life of James Ross. Mostly we have to rely on unsatisfactory scraps about him as reflected in the thoughts and actions of others, but M.J. Ross supplies a couple of valuable exceptions that shed some light on James the man. His father and uncle did not approve of the individual who wished to marry his sister Isabella, whereas James knew her suitor, a solicitor William Spence, with whom she was much in love. He admitted that Spence was not 'one of the brightest characters in the world, but rather the contrary'. However, he was a quiet, good-hearted, domesticated sort of man capable of bringing Isabella happiness. Importantly he also had an income of £400 to £500 per annum. James sent a letter to his father George in July 1824 from the Whalefish Islands announcing the couple were to be wed in August and looked forward to a happy marriage, which apparently it was. Having rather taken charge of affairs in the absence of his unreliable father in the Caribbean, James had sorted out an important family matter. On the same day James also wrote to John Ross about the marriage, adding that on this day twelve years ago 'I first embarked under your care and this awakens the most gratifying recollection of the many advantages I have derived from your paternal protection'. On 1 January 1828 James confided to his diary that the previous year had 'opened upon me in doubt, anxiety and hope'. The summer following was a time of fatigue, hardship and privation and the Autumn was a mixture of hope and fear, the close bringing 'promotion, happiness and peace'.

But has my advancement in Religion been equal to [that in the Navy] or in any way been such as to express my gratitude for worldly advantages which I have received? Alas, I feel I have much to answer for which has yet to be expressed, for as the blessings of earthly goods increase, so does my advancement & achievement seem to be too retrograde.

The good things and the enjoyment of this world engage too much of my time and leave me hardly enough to reflect on the folly and madness of thus pursuing the pleasures of this world which is today, and tomorrow may be no more, and of neglecting those things which belong to my eternal peace. O God, I beseech Thee to grant me the assistance of thy Holy Spirit to amend my life and to [give?] myself entirely to Thee, my Creator. Pardon and end my first sins and failures for the sake of thy Blessed son Jesus Christ our Lord and enable me to lead a new life. Strengthen, O God, my faith in thy mercy through Christ, deeply impress me with a grateful remembrance of his death and finally in Death assure me of thy mercy and of a glorious resurrection into the mansions of eternal peace for Christ's sake. Amen.[28]

Almost all of the explorers discussed in this book believed that God travelled to the Arctic with them, keeping them safe, secure and superior.

Portrait of Sir John Richardson, painted by Thomas Phillips,
engraved by Edward Finden, 1828
(Public domain, via Wikipedia Commons)

4

THE TRIALS AND TRIBULATIONS OF DR JOHN RICHARDSON

The Coppermine Expedition of 1819–1822

Over the cloud-bridge of illusion lies the path of human
progress.

Fridtjof Nansen

It was Saturday 29 September 1821. A party of exhausted, frozen explorers
had reached a point on the Coppermine River in northern Canada that they
named Obstruction Rapid because it was blocking their way; it was impera-
tive that they crossed it as they made for their base. They were starving,
having subsisted on putrid venison, deer bones, antlers and a lichen known
as *tripe-de-roche* (rock tripe) scraped off rocks, as well as a few blueberries and
cranberries that appeared in patches of snow. They were introduced to *Arbutus
uva ursi* (variously known as wortleberry, foxberry and checkerberry), a plant
with the alarming property of turning urine black. Despondency had rendered the men surly and disobedient, eliciting unflattering remarks from the
officers about the treachery of the voyageurs (canoe transportation workers
in the fur trade) who were guilty only of questioning the competence of the
naval officers, responsible as they undoubtedly were for the dangerous plight
in which they found themselves. The men constructed a raft of willows.
When that failed, the group's doctor and scientist stepped forward.

> I proposed to swim across with a line and to haul the raft over
> . . . I had advanced but a little distance from the bank with a line
> around my middle when I lost the power of moving my arms
> through the cold. I was then obliged to turn upon my back and had
> nearly reached the opposite shore in that position, when my legs
> also became powerless and I sank to the bottom. The men hauling

upon the line however, I immediately came to the surface again and regaining my recollection, was enabled by keeping in my breath as much as possible, to remain above water until I was drawn ashore. Being then rolled up in a blanket and placed before a good fire of willows I recovered tolerably in the course of the evening . . .[1]

To add to his woes, a knife lying on the riverbank cut his foot to the bone, laming him for some time thereafter though he neglected to mention the injury in his journal. He claimed that in normal circumstances he would not have hesitated to plunge into water at below 38 °F, but he was so skinny (to the Canadians *maigre*) that he had little resistance to cold. To wade into an Arctic river at the best of times feels like leg amputation. Total immersion does not actually feel as cold but drains energy alarmingly. The swimmer later wrote that what he assumed would be his last thoughts were of his wife, Mary Stiven of Leith, and his mother.

The man concerned, John Richardson of Dumfries (1787–1865), was lucky to survive. He is one of the Scottish explorers slowly gaining some recognition, in Canada, if not in Scotland. His hometown, metropolitan centre of south-west Scotland, was a prosperous little burgh on the Nith estuary, which meets the sea in the Solway Firth, Dumfries's gateway to north-west England and the world, including the American colonies, from which the port one year imported more tobacco than Glasgow. Robert Burns described the place as 'Maggie on the Banks o Nith, a place wi pride eneuch'. John's father, Gabriel, a wealthy brewer and sometime provost, was a neighbour of the bard in Nith Place. As an exciseman, Burns successfully petitioned the Dumfries magistrates to lower the local tax on Richardson's beer. Burns encouraged young Richardson to memorise the Paraphrases, doubtless reinforcing the profound faith in God which would sustain him throughout life. Young John and Burns's eldest son, Robert, enrolled at Dumfries Grammar School on the same day, prompting the bard, who was always rather preoccupied with posthumous fame, to wonder which of the boys would prove the greater man. Robert, who showed a talent for classics and mathematics, eventually gained a post in the London Stamp Office. John became an accomplished medical doctor, naval officer, explorer, naturalist, chief physician to Haslar Naval Hospital, the largest brick-built hospital in the world at the time, hospital inspector, health care reformer and author of the remarkable *Fauna Boreali-Americana* series, the first major empirical study of North American polar and sub-polar natural history. His friends and associates included Charles Darwin, T.H. Huxley, the botanist William Jackson Hooker, and just about everyone among his contemporaries who was interested in biology and the natural world. He retained a lifelong devotion to the Scottish ballads, medieval Scottish verse and Burns's poetry. When he retired he spent a considerable amount of time extracting such material for what became the *Oxford English Dictionary*.

Richardson's childhood was spent in a kind of laboratory that prepared him for life. The River Nith was only a few yards from the family home; a little further placed him in the countryside. Nature then, as now, provided the major diversion for rural children. The hills, woods and meadows around Dumfries were complemented by visits to relatives at Kirkhouse of Kirkbean on the Solway coast. There young Richardson would have heard about the activities of John Paul Jones, who attacked his homeland on behalf of the Americans during their Revolution; Richardson was perhaps as fascinated by Jones's adventurous exploits as he was repelled by his traitorous escapades. Jones grew up on the estate of William Craik of Arbigland, noted agricultural improver, linguist and man of enlightenment. William's son James became the personal physician and confidant of George Washington. He came from the same parish as the naval scientist and investigator of latitude Admiral John Campbell. Richard Oswald, a notorious participant in the nefarious slave trade of the British empire, owned the local estate of Cavens; as principal British negotiator he helped deliver the Treaty of Paris of 1783 which ended the American war.

In 1800 Richardson was apprenticed to his maternal uncle, James Mundell, a prominent Dumfries surgeon. On Mundell's death he joined the practice of Samuel Shortridge, who arranged for him to attend classes at Edinburgh University. After two years he became house surgeon at Dumfries Infirmary, returning to the university to take a fifteen-minute examination as surgeon. He had already advised his mother that the Navy was looking for assistant surgeons and he was soon London-bound where he met up with several 'Doonhamers' (Dumfriesians) including Robert Burns Jr. He passed his exams with the Royal College of Surgeons (London) and with the Transport Board at the Admiralty. Through the intervention, or better the patronage, of a Lord of Admiralty, Sir William Johnston Hope of the Annandale family, he was appointed to the frigate *Nymphe* and embarked on what would prove to be a glittering naval career. His subsequent twelve years at sea are not part of his Arctic story but perhaps a few aspects which influenced his later experience may be indicated.

His various assignments over the next six years took him to Denmark, Portugal, Spain, the African coast, Bermuda, Nova Scotia, Quebec, Sicily, Algiers, Sweden, Orkney and America. Mostly he was fortunate to secure happy ships but one exception was *Blossom*, a small ship which he joined in 1808. The purser poisoned the mind of a suspicious captain concerning the loyalty of his officers, whom he suspected of plotting against him while, in reality, according to Richardson, they 'were amusing themselves writing sonnets'. The nervous commander arrested the first and second lieutenants penning them up in the little ship, imagining that all on board were 'mutinous and enemies'; both officers had to be hospitalised on reaching home port. They were court-martialled, as was Richardson, who told his father: 'never were charges so groundless brought before a court, and it was the evident opinion of every member and witness of the trial that the unfortunate commander was not in his right mind'. He was angered that the guilty captain was merely dismissed from the ship, noting there was a great difference between the trials of lieutenants and captains because the court trying the latter comprised officers who had 'a fellow feeling for each other'. On another occasion he experienced a ship on which the leader and his subordinates were at loggerheads, a situation breeding general uneasiness.[2] Such accounts are interesting in view of the general stress of shipboard existence which is often suppressed in the voyaging literature. The next sailing on *Blossom* was a great contrast because the captain was Francis Beaufort, inventor of the Beaufort scale (wind force scale), who was to become a lifelong friend of Richardson.

In letters home, the doctor communicated graphic descriptions of life on board ship. On shore leave, he cultivated the patronage of the Earl of Galloway. At Mahon, Minorca, he was delighted when he met an old schoolfriend named McGhie, 'the most intimate of my acquaintances in Dumfries'. 1812 found him in Sweden and then, in *Cruiser*, he was chasing privateers in Orkney during the 1812 war with America. However, he confessed that he was losing his taste for the sea and considered taking over Shortridge's practice in Dumfries, before concluding that he could not afford to give up his naval pay. After his time on *Cruiser* he studied in London before visiting Dumfries over the winter of 1813–14, finding time to call on his brother Peter at Disdow in Galloway. Lochenbreck, one of his favourite fishing lochs, was nearby which, like the Nith, inspired his interest in ichthyology. He temporarily parted company with the Navy when he was appointed surgeon to the first battalion of Royal Marines then serving in America.

His first experience of land warfare did not impress him. He deplored the 'predatory system of warfare which serves to degrade the British character without materially injuring the enemy'. In Georgia he was again critical of the way British troops mercilessly looted and destroyed enemy property. With the American war well over and Waterloo won, Richardson, like so many of his naval colleagues, went on to half pay, enabling him to fulfil his long-held ambition to complete his medical studies, during 1815–17, through intensive lectures and the completion of a thesis on yellow fever. For a time, he practised at 36 Constitution Street, Leith; his disappointment with this was partly sweetened by marrying Mary Stiven, a local girl.

They had been wed for just short of a year when John Barrow, responding to Richardson's application to join a planned expedition to northern America, contacted him. He was invited to 'undertake to collect and preserve specimens of minerals, plants and animals', potentially a rich harvest since the country had never been visited by a naturalist. To Richardson's delight, Barrow had consulted MacVey Napier, editor of the *Encyclopaedia Britannica* and the *Edinburgh Review*, as to his suitability for the post. He was invited to meet Sir Joseph Banks, who introduced him to J.E. Gray of the British Museum. The doctor accepted the post with alacrity, swiftly arranging to renew his acquaintance with Professor Robert Jameson at Edinburgh University, who allowed him to attend his lectures for free. He saw the opportunity for advancement and for becoming acquainted with 'many scientific men and those at the head of naval affairs'. His prescience was immaculate.[3]

*

The Coppermine expedition of 1819 to 1822, which on arrival in North America would involve overland travel to Great Slave Lake followed by travel along the Coppermine River, was a peculiar episode in the annals of polar exploration. Thanks to John Barrow's wrong-headed planning, four Navy personnel and their captain John Franklin were to be placed as passengers on a Hudson's Bay Company ship which was engaged on the regular spring voyage to transport HBC hopefuls, colonists and supplies to York Factory, a port on the south-west coast of Hudson Bay. Franklin had enjoyed the good fortune to be briefed and advised by Sir Alexander Mackenzie (just in time, for he died in 1820). Dr John Richardson was appointed as surgeon and naturalist. I make no apology for foregrounding Richardson in this investigation because he appears a much more useful team participant than his dismal leader, Franklin, without whom the enterprise would have proved much less of a hazard and incomparably more successful.

John Franklin enjoyed a varied and interesting career after he joined the Navy at the age of fourteen in 1800, almost immediately pitched into the Battle of Copenhagen, with Horatio Nelson second-in-command, thereafter joining Matthew Flinders' *Investigator* as a midshipman bound for Australia. On returning he was assigned to *Bellerophon* and was one of only seven survivors when forty died in 'the slaughter pen' of the quarterdeck during the Battle of Trafalgar. He was involved in the war of 1812. Throughout this period he studied magnetism.[4] By the time he led the Coppermine expedition in 1819–22 he had a very respectable curriculum vitae, a growing reputation and the first brush with his nemesis. However, it is impossible to agree with Andrew Lambert that Franklin 'demonstrated a rare talent for leadership'.[5] He displayed all of the characteristics that should have ensured his Arctic career ended at the same time as his second expedition; his first was to Spitsbergen in 1818 (see Chapter 3).

This contingent of the 1819 expedition was to explore the northern coast of America from the mouth of the Coppermine River to the east, mapping latitudes and longitudes and the trending of the coast to the eastern extremity of the continent, as well as providing detailed geographical information that might be of value to Captain Parry who, unknown to the overlanders, was at that time deep into the western Arctic. All of the usual daily measurements of air, water, winds and weather were to be noted, together with observing 'the dip and variation of the magnetic needle and the intensity of magnetic force in particular in association with the Aurora Borealis'. Franklin was also to investigate the regional source of copper, which was of potential commercial and scientific interest.[6] Once in the north, the party of newcomers was to be greatly enlarged, courtesy of HBC.

The HBC ship *Prince of Wales*, supported by two consorts, *Eddystone* and *Wear*, sailed from Gravesend on 23 May 1819. After delays in sailing, the ship eventually reached Orkney in early June 1819. There they were supposed to recruit additional men but succeeded in attracting only four, an estimated 1,200 having been enticed to man 300 ships exploiting the *muc* (expanded shoals of herring). According to an unimpressed Franklin, other potential Orkney employees were worried about the Arctic dangers, the pay and the chances of a safe return. They clearly did not share his confidence of success, prompting him to tactlessly and misleadingly compare their attitudes to those of fearless English seamen, who allegedly entered upon any enterprise however hazardous.

Franklin and Richardson's professional colleagues included George Back (1796–1878), born in Cheshire, who had fought in Spain, was captured by the French and on release served on the North American station. Back had volunteered on the Spitsbergen expedition of David Buchan and John Franklin. He was delighted to join Franklin once again on his journey to the Polar Sea but he literally missed the boat at Yarmouth, necessitating a lengthy journey by the Northern Mail coach to Edinburgh and a gig to Thurso on the Pentland Firth. En route he encountered two 'bibulous Scots' at Bonar Bridge, one of whom provided hospitality. As Back wrote, 'I have a vivid recollection of the plentiful Highland breakfast enjoyed in his company and that of his very pretty daughter, whose regular and intelligent features haunted me for many a long month afterwards in the cheerless forests of America.' Since the Stromness ferry was cancelled due to bad weather he chartered Old Andrew, a well-known smuggler, to make the crossing, sent off by an admiring crowd and the skirl of bagpipes. Two girls who accompanied him on the rough sea were very sick, clinging to Back, 'in their agony, with a tenacity quite irresistible'.[7] That night he joined *Prince of Wales* and his fellow officers, who were enjoying a ball aboard ship, ignoring Franklin's advice that he should rest after his exhausting journey of nine nights, thus displaying the stamina and energy for which he became famous. He was to prove himself a crucial resourceful expeditionary adjunct, as well as a talented artist.

Another companion was Midshipman Robert Hood, born in Portarlington, Ireland, who had served in the Baltic, the Mediterranean, the English Channel, Algiers and the Cape of Good Hope. He was appointed to Franklin's adventure in order to make drawings and paintings of the landscape, natives and examples of natural history as directed by Richardson. Completing the British contingent was John Hepburn, born at Whitekirk, East Lothian, a cowherd before he became a seaman sailing between Newcastle and London; having become involved in the transatlantic trade he was captured by an American privateer. He served on Franklin's *Trent* in 1819 and was to prove then, as on future voyages, a highly dependable and able asset. In Canada, Willard Ferdinand Wentzel, a trader, was appointed by the HBC to assist the group; he would accompany them to the Coppermine River. Richardson told his wife that Franklin was 'a steady, religious, and cheerful man and altogether an honour to his profession'. Franklin later praised Richardson to whom was due the 'exclusive merit of collections and observations in the department of Natural History'. The two were to become lifelong friends but, though unstated by the loyal doctor, Franklin must have at times severely tried his patience.

When the *Prince of Wales* reached the Pentland Firth and Stromness on 3 June, Richardson and Franklin visited a ship belonging to the Moravian Missionary Society, bound for Labrador. They picked up a few words of German and Inuktitut, Franklin gratefully receiving a copy of St John's Gospel in the latter language. Two weeks later they again set sail. Collisions with icebergs and a confrontation with an enormous cliff, as well as a heavy swell, dismayed everyone on board. The ship's pumps could not cope with the invasive sea, a situation worsened by heavy gales that split the sails. As they neared land, the Inuit came out to barter, in kayaks and umiaks (open skin-boats). They offered oil, walrus-teeth, whalebone, clothes made of seal-skin and models of animals and kayaks. Richardson and Franklin seized an opportunity, when taking fresh water on board, to briefly visit the Labrador shore. The harbour at York Flats was reached on 30 August, seven miles from York Factory.

As already noted, the HBC was stacked with Scots and Orcadians, but the explorers had arrived in the midst of a civil war between rival Scottish bands, those in HBC and their rivals in North West Company (NWC). Both fur-trading companies were concerned that the arrival of numerous colonists, such as Gaelic-speaking Highlanders sponsored by the Earl of Selkirk, an ambitious coloniser from Kirkcudbright, seemed to herald the beginning of the end for the trade. NWC was on the point of disappearing. Since some of its luminaries were prisoners at York Factory when the visitors arrived, Franklin ordered his men to refrain from becoming involved in any way. The governor at York Factory was very helpful, securing a boat for the newcomers though there was not sufficient room for all of their supplies, some of which they had to leave behind, with a promise that they would be sent on in due course. Guns, cheers and the good wishes of all, accompanied their departure as they began their journey 'into the interior of America'. Almost immediately they confronted the tiresome reality of river travel as the crew 'had to commence tracking, or dragging the boat by a line to which they were harnessed'. The high banks were slippery underfoot due to the rains and fallen trees impeding their progress, hardly the conditions that sailors would have expected. The rivers along which they travelled were sur-veyed, mapped and sketched by Back and Hood. Wrapped in buffalo robes, they slept well that first night.

Next day, though the scenery was impressive, 'it appeared desolate from the want of human species. The stillness was so great that even the twittering of the *whiskey-johneesh*, or cinereous (ash-grey) crow, caused us to start'.

They were joined by three other HBC boats, all sharing the misery of river travel due to low water and rapids, since the boats had to be lifted over boulders and brash ice, which involved the men jumping into the shallow water. Their heavy boat fell behind, the others refusing to take some of their cargo, while the guides frequently followed the wrong channels. Portaging was an unpleasant necessary evil, the loads often too ambitious. The men were permanently soaked in freezing water as they almost became at one with the detritus of the river. However, they were reinvigorated when they reached the Dramstone marking the end of the dreary ascent of the Hill (Hayes) River: 'we complied with the custom from whence it derives its name'. Franklin, who knew nothing about the environment, blamed the First Nations and the voyageurs for forest fires, not realising, as the residents probably did, that conflagration was part of Nature's renewal plan.[8]

Franklin's *Narrative of a Journey* may be a somewhat pedantic and even tedious publication, not to mention lengthy, since it runs to 768 pages, but it is an invaluable account, much of which has had to be reluctantly jettisoned here, since the present discussion focuses on Richardson, who contributed to, and enhanced, the work. Both he and Franklin were the inheritors of Enlightenment ideas and were keen to impart and communicate useful knowledge of all kinds. Like them, Hood noted that the First Nations were possessed of great curiosity, which might easily be directed to the attainment of such knowledge, though he sadly devalued his assessment by havering on about their ideas concerning matters of personal hygiene.[9]

Their route took them to Norway House and along the north coast of Lake Winnipeg to the mouth of the Saskatchewan, which they followed as far as Little River, leading them to Pine Island Lake and so to Cumberland House, their arrival coinciding with the onset of winter. Franklin could not resist recounting stories of cannibalism among the natives, of men and women reduced to feeding upon the bodies of their own family.[10]

All along the trail they had encountered First Nations folk who were ill and suffering. Franklin regretted that the Europeans had not taught them the perniciousness 'of the grief that produces total inactivity', nor had they been furnished with any of the consolations 'which the Christian religion never fails to afford'. However, he thought that such expectations were misplaced in 'persons who have permitted their own off-spring, the half-casts, to remain in lamentable ignorance on a subject of such vital importance'. The assumed superiority of European beliefs was doubtless in evidence at the boozy celebrations on Christmas Day and at New Year loyally observed in the fur trade. In a New Year letter to his father Richardson reported that everything had gone remarkably smoothly: 'I am afraid that we shall not meet with any difficulties sufficient to ornament a narrative.'[11] How wrong he was!

Franklin decided to proceed to Athabasca, accompanied by Back and Hepburn, to make further preparations concerning the expedition, while Richardson and Hood remained at Cumberland House until spring, when they would convey supplies in two canoes to Fort Chipewyan. Richardson provided an overview of the Cree people, many of whom fatally suffered from European diseases such as whooping-cough and measles. Others were so weakened that they could neither hunt nor fish. One warrior who lost his son was so distraught that he refused to eat, eliciting Richardson's observation that 'misery may harden a disposition naturally bad, but it never fails to soften the heart of a good man'.[12] Another problem was alcoholism. While inevitably criticising some aspects of Cree society, Richardson is in the main interested in their culture and sympathetic to their problems, often caused by the invasive 'whites'. He discusses the Métis, or Bois-Brûlés (the mixed bloods), and he is particularly interested in the role and treatment of women, as well as different tribes among the First Nations.[13] He also discusses the disorder of goitre (enlarged thyroid gland frequently associated with iodine deficiency) that he attributes to drinking river-water. He writes to his wife in March 1820, reflecting that the snowdrops and crocuses would now be decorating the 'good old town' of Edinburgh. By way of contrast, there is a sameness about the landscape at Cumberland House. Log houses can barely be distinguished from fallen trees. 'Where there is no art, Nature loses half her charms.' He continues:

> The screams of a famished raven, or the crash of a lofty pine, rending through the intenseness of the frost, are the only sounds that invade the solemn silence. When in my walks I have accidentally met one of my companions in this dreary solitude, his figure, emerging from the shade, has conveyed, with irresistible force, to my mind, the idea of rising from the grave. I have often admired the pictures our great poets have drawn of absolute solitude, but never felt their full force till now. What must be the situation of a human being, 'alone on the wide wide sea!' How dreadful if without faith in God! An atheist could not dwell alone in the forests of America.[14]

Richardson and Hood met up with their fellows at Fort Chipewyan on 13 July. Franklin was relieved and delighted that they brought some men from Cumberland. He paid off and sent home the recruits he had picked up in Orkney. The final contingent comprised sixteen Canadians–voyageurs, 'our worthy and only *English* attendant John Hepburn' (he was, of course, Scottish), one Chipewyan woman and two Inuit interpreters who were to join at Great Slave Lake.[15] All were plagued by mosquitoes to such an extent as to make even the reader itch.[16]

On departing Fort Chipewyan the voyageurs received their 'customary dram'. All seemed cheerful despite a serious shortfall in supplies due to mix-ups originating in the fur trade fallout, as well as a cruel accident when the foreman of a canoe was lost at Otter Portage.[17] They paddled to the Slave River, passing many rapids, to arrive at Old Fort Providence on Great Slave Lake. There, with great ceremony, they met the distinguished chief of the Copper Indians, Akaicho (Akaitcho) or Big Foot, who welcomed them with a smoke, a glass and a speech, expressing his love for the visitors, but also his disappointment that a 'great medicine chief' who reportedly could restore the dead to life (presumably Richardson) did not in fact possess these powers. Franklin then indicated that the greatest chief in the world and sovereign of trading companies, the friend of peace and every nation, had sent him and his companions to trade with his 'children in the north'. He was charged with finding a passage by sea that would enable big ships to transport great quantities of goods. He was also interested in the produce and people of the north and asked for the help of the natives in providing food. He insisted that hostilities between First Nations and Inuit must cease. In return, Akaicho would be rewarded with clothing, ammunition, tobacco and other goods. This was a welcome suggestion, but Akaicho warned that the Inuit were very treacherous. His elder brother Cascathry, who claimed to have accompanied Samuel Hearne (1745–1792) to the Polar Sea in 1771, obligingly drew a map of the Coppermine River. While natives and new-comers were enjoying a dance, the tent shared by Franklin and Richardson caught fire. Hepburn, who was resting inside, threw some gunpowder clear of the flame and rescued some of the baggage. They tried to conceal the accident from 'the fickle minds of the Indians' without success, Akaicho insisting that any other misfortunes should be communicated. The dance continued on the advice of Wentzel (the trader appointed by HBC to accompany the group) lest the fire was construed as a bad omen.[18]

On 3 August 1820 the expedition set out for the north, 'through a line of country not previously visited by any European',[19] paddling and portaging up the Yellowknife, known to the locals as the River of the Toothless Fish, before crossing Lake Prosperous, which was part of the river that became more engorged with rapids the further they progressed, convincing Franklin that it would never make a canoe route. Richardson treated a sick native boy. The lack of food caused some considerable discontent among the voyageurs, leading Franklin to stress the danger of insubordination, threatening heavy punishment on any who refused to go on. He had some sympathy for the conditions they had to tolerate but was apprehensive that the Canadians would try to take advantage of him if they could. Deer meat and fish quenched further dissidence as the men set about the building of Fort Enterprise on Winter Lake. The original plan had been to continue to the Coppermine River and thence to the sea if passable but Franklin was talked out of that idea by Akaicho, Cascathry and the voyageurs. Instead, Back and Hood were sent off to explore the approaches to the river. Back then returned to Providence in search of supplies that were supposed to have been forwarded to Enterprise. Scarcity of sustenance was to plague all of Franklin's party and was to kill too many of them. When the Brits proposed to cut down a pine tree that was particularly valued by the First Nations, they desisted, an episode that suggests Franklin was not a totally unreasonable man if sensibly advised.

What survives of Richardson's journal begins on 21 August 1820; it is somewhat reminiscent of a natural history tour as he describes scenery, shrubs, plants, fish, reindeer and birds. By 1 October he has achieved a list of forty-two different lichen. A snowstorm prevents observation of a solar eclipse. He and Franklin, with Cascathry, commence a 'pedestrian excursion' to the Coppermine. They sleep, each under a single blanket, beside a fire in the open air. Cascathry strips to the skin, toasts himself at the fire, and instantly succumbs to repose, under a deerskin. Their progress is slowed when Franklin rekindles an old painful wound in his ankle, and they return to Fort Enterprise after only six days on the trail. There the doctor learns of the not unexpected death of his father, 'a tender parent and indulgent friend'. He died before receiving John's last letter in which he explained that he had agreed to participate in the expedition because it held out the prospect 'of rendering me ultimately more able to be of use to those whose absence I so much regret, and whose advantage I value far beyond my own comfort'. In another letter he attempted to comfort his mother who also mourned her youngest son's death in Jamaica, 'a land where the traffic in their fellow-creatures has debased the nature of its inhabitants, and where the lust of sordid gain snapped asunder the holy bonds of religion'.

To his brother Peter at Disdow he humorously described the journey from Fort Enterprise to Point Lake in a suitably 'hamely' style. There were twenty-three folk in the motley crew, recalling Chaucer's Pilgrims. His description would certainly be dismissed as sexist and racist at the present time, but Richardson, by the standards of his own day, was less infected by both these prejudices than many of his contemporaries. The letter affords a rare chance to see an example of his humour. He describes the party marching in single file – Belanger *le gros* exulting in his strength; Belanger *le rouge*; little Perrault; Jean Baptiste Adam, the interpreter, with an overloaded sledge and a second sledge, crammed with plunder, for his beloved wife Angelique. Richardson was particularly impressed by Angelique, carrying a big stick and wearing red stockings, whom he compared to the goddess Hecate and Scott's Meg Merrilies, or indeed to the most fantastic of Shakespeare's weird sisters. In his imagination Scotland was not far away.[20]

Adriana Craciun makes much of this passage in Richardson's letter, especially of the lines, quoted below in my italics, which are excised in McIllraith's biography of Richardson:

> The most prominent figure . . . of the whole, because the most unearthly, was mother Adam. She came striding along supported by a stick which towered over the heads of all others; a pair of red stockings and various other items of her garb heightened the peculiarities of her figure; and as to her gait, it was similar to nothing I had ever before seen. Sometimes I was tempted to compare her to Hecate, sometimes to Meg Merrilies. Not that she had mind enough to be a powerful sorceress, or majesty sufficient for a commanding presence, but because she appeared to be rather a creature of the imagination than a reality – *I think however that she might have been more aptly considered a fit companion for Frankenstein's [monster] chef d'oeuvre, as she had this in common with that vision of Byshe Shelly, that* every member of body seemed to have belonged to *fifteen* different individuals and *so* to have been formed by a random association into a sort of semblance of the human form; but from want of proper animation the extremities never acted in concert, and the distorted spine which composed the centre, now bent to this side now to that, according as the leg which described

the greater or the smaller circle was in motion, while the arms played up and down to preserve something like equilibrium, but with the involuntary and convulsive motions of the most fantastic of Shakespeare's weird sisters in the height of her frenzy.[21]

Professor Craciun is to be congratulated on picking up on the pious minister McIllraith's omissions but both writers make the point that mother Adam, wife of the interpreter, was 'rather a creature of the imagination than a reality'. The passage does not show that Richardson had actually read the Shelley novelette – he most likely perused Croker's review (see Chapter 1) – but he is the only explorer known to have mentioned *Frankenstein*, which, of course, was partly set in the Arctic. He was also greatly indebted to Scott's *Guy Mannering*, published in 1815, which he obviously *had* read. Early in the novel Mannering encounters the magnificent Meg Merrilies, 'Full six feet high' dressed in a man's greatcoat and carrying a sloe-thorn cudgel. At other times she wore a large piece of red cotton wrapped around her head like a turban. Characterised as 'harlot, thief, witch and gipsy' she also appeared with a long red cloak and a staff in her hand, headed with a spear-point.[22] Whenever she appears she illuminates a rather dull novel.

One story Richardson did not tell was of the rivalry between Back and Hood over Cascathry's daughter, Greenstockings, so-called because of the colour of her clothing. She was recognised by all as a great beauty who at the age of fifteen had already been married twice. Both Back and Hood fell for her, the latter becoming the father of her child. Competition between the two had become so fierce that they were preparing to fight a duel. Hepburn claimed that when he learned about it he withdrew the charges from their pistols at night, and Franklin sent Back out of harm's way, to seek supplies at Fort Chipewyan. It was probably to this affair that Franklin referred when he wrote to Back in November 1820:

We get on very well *en famille*, not a single dispute or unpleasant word. You will hear of the change that has taken place in family affairs. Perhaps you were prepared to expect the pleasure of having a female companion in your room. Hood says he will inform you of the circumstance, I need not therefore enlarge upon the subject.[23]

The younger Back comes across as something of a Lothario. It can be assumed that as a narcissist and adventurer he would not have been ecstatic about the development of events. 'Loser' was not in his vocabulary. Fourteen years later, Back met 'my old acquaintance and Indian belle . . . Greenstockings'. When he called to her she laughed and said she was an old woman now, but to him she was still the beauty of her tribe. It is quite touching that these two individuals could still meet up with such pleasure after so many years. In 1823 a census recorded the orphaned daughter of Lieutenant Hood. It is also delightful to learn that Robert Hood who, because of his unfortunate ailments, often appears as a rather sad colourless person in the journals, was actually a determined character who could outmatch his rival.[24] It should be added that neither officer offended the cultural mores of the Copper people.

Richardson wrote a substantial description of reindeer (caribou), simply called deer by Brits, which would later be recycled in *Fauna Boreali-Americana*. He worked on similar accounts of ptarmigan, loon, the hawk-owl and the hare. He studied igloo construction, providing a plan of same. A journal entry for 8 May, 'a fly seen', heralded the advent of better weather. Richardson had plenty of time for some doctoring – for example of Cascathry's wife. There was apparently not much worth reporting in his journal, save disagreements with Akaicho, who tried to gain some leverage by refusing to lead the explorers to the sea, but all was well as they set off for the Coppermine on 4 June. Akaicho followed ten days later.

The doctor and a First Nations 'conjuror' both treated an old Indian suffering from kidney stone, each using his own techniques. Another elderly ethnic, known as the 'Hermaphrodite', was hired by Akaicho as a guide. The men were expected to transport 180 pounds weight each; several suffered from serious irritation, hardness and swelling of the thighs, causing lameness, so the loads had to be reduced. Back thought a hill named Rock-nest bore an exact resemblance to Salisbury Crags, Edinburgh.[25] They had now reached the Coppermine and the stunning scenery on its banks, quickly plunging their canoes into rapids some two miles long. Much more rough water was encountered before they reached the sea, involving exhausting portages along the banks. Canoeing Canadian waters is undoubtedly one of the most exhilarating and rewarding of activities but the price is the stress and strain of portage, even today when the loads are nothing compared with those experienced in 1821. It took just two days short of two weeks to reach the head of Bloody Falls, named by Samuel Hearne, who claimed to have witnessed the massacre there of local Inuit by the Chipewyan. Those in the Franklin party seem to have been rather unnerved by the place. Richardson alleged that 'the ground is still strewed with human skulls and as it is over-grown with rank grass, appears to be avoided as a place of encampment'.[26] Certainly Akaicho was highly suspicious, as were his kindred, of the Inuit, whose leader was Terregannoeuck, 'White Fox'. The latter's folk fished at the Falls every year in July. 'None of this tribe had ever seen white people before, but they had heard of them.'[27] Today there is nothing sinister about the place. If anything, it is energising, as fast-flowing water usually is; some fifteen kilometres to the north-east the river abandons the American continent as it enters the Hyperborean Sea, close to the Richardson River and Richardson Bay. It is now believed that Hearne was not actually at Bloody Falls, that he knew the story but was at another site.

This first-known cruise by Europeans along part of the northern coast of North America was rather a dismal affair. In his journal Richardson seems to strain to report items of interest and much of the space is taken up with natural history and measurements of one kind or another, both essential. He wrote as a naturalist but he was also attempting to give future explorers some idea of fresh food supplies available in the shape of reindeer and fish such as salmon, trout, Pacific herrings and Arctic flounders. John Ross was by no means alone in commending the virtues of country food in maintaining health (see Chapter 2). The voyageurs refused to consume a bear, alleging that it suffered some kind of illness, though in fact they had an aversion to the meat, but the Brits found its paws excellent eating. All tucked into two other ursine banquets but in general food supplies were low and the pemmican was found to be mouldy. There were plenty of signs of Inuit activity but no Inuit were to be seen.

The Barrens, whether on sea or land, was a dangerously depressing place. The men became openly critical of the officers. Weather, cold, the pitiless coast and shattered canoes, together with scarcity of food, conspired to convince them that to attempt further travel was 'little short of madness'. Indeed, the voyageurs had 'assumed the privilege of thinking for their commanding officer', hoping to persuade him of their cause by ceasing to hunt altogether. Franklin reluctantly conceded but he, Back and Richardson went 10 miles further to reach Point Turnagain.

Franklin had intended to go back to the mouth of the Coppermine but, all things considered, he thought that everyone would have a better chance of success if they made for the Hood River, following it inland and crossing overland to the Coppermine, a very bad decision. They remained on a raging sea, running before a strong wind, for 25 miles. 'The privation of food under which our voyageurs were at present labouring, absorbed every other terror, otherwise the most eloquence would not have induced them to attempt such a powerful traverse'.[28] They landed on an open beach with such force that the head of one of the canoes was split, but all the men were safe. Next day they crossed Bathurst Inlet to Barry's Isles where they found deer and relief from their hunger. A further paddle took them to the Hood estuary and a strenuous portage up the river. 'Our Canadians may be said to have in general shewed considerable courage in bearing the dangers of the sea, magnified to them by their novelty, but they could not restrain their expressions of joy on quitting it'. The sea was as alien to the voyageurs as pedestrianism was to sailors. The dual predicament was neatly expressed in the ballad 'I once Loved a Lass':

> The men of the forest, they askit of me
> How many strawberries grow in the salt sea?
> I askit them back with a tear in my e'e
> How many ships sail through the forest?

Those who suffered most on this bungled expedition and who are too often still overlooked, especially by commentators engaged in micro-studies of Franklin, were the voyageurs:

Joseph Peltier	Michel Teroahauté (Iroquois)
Gabriel Beauparlant	Mathew Pelonquin (Credit)
Francais Samandre	Solomon Belanger (*le gros*)
Vincenza Fontano	Joseph Bennoit
Registe Vaillant	Joseph Gagné
Jean Baptiste Parent	Pierre Dumas
Jean Baptiste Belanger (*le rouge*)	Joseph Forcier
Jean Baptiste Belleau	Ignace Perrault
Emanuel Cournoyée	

The interpreters were Pierre St Germain ('Pierez'), Jean Baptiste Adam and Chipewyan Bois-Brûlés (unnamed).

The elements did not spare them. 'Weather extremely cold . . . ground a foot deep with snow . . . our garments stiffened by the frost . . . tents a very insufficient shelter from the rain . . . no means of making a fire . . . the wind blowing so keen that no one could keep his hands long out of his mittens . . .

99

Franklin from exhaustion and sudden exposure to the cold wind was seized with a fainting fit'.[29] All joyous thoughts were outlawed. They had to cross the Burnside River one at a time in the sole remaining canoe.[30] They found some food in hares, partridges and a slab of ox meat rescued from a pack of wolves; later they killed a musk-ox.

Walking became much more difficult and treacherous as the snow deepened, and downright dangerous on sloping surfaces covered with large 'angular' stones. The hunters managed to kill another musk-ox, which gave them a decent meal, but next day they were back to the *tripe-de-roche*. When trying to cross the Burnside River the canoe conveying Franklin, Pierez and Belanger was upset in the rapid, in which they stood with water up to their waists. Pierez emptied the water out of the canoe, replacing it with Franklin's personage and then joining him, only to be returned to the water when the canoe sank. Belanger was left standing on a rock but eventually managed to grab a rope attached to a canoe which dragged him 'perfectly senseless through the rapid'. He was stripped and rolled up in a blanket with two mates until he recovered after some hours. In the accident Franklin's journal was lost, along with some of his scientific observations; in addition, they were now canoe-less. In the aptly named Barrens, they were forced to devour deer bones and skin. 'They also ate several of their old shoes' giving Franklin the near laudatory name he would receive on returning home – 'the man who ate his boots': actually moccasins that, as Houston points out, did have a nutritive value. Franklin mentions the consumption of 'roasted leather', while Richardson wrote that once boiled it was 'greedily devoured'. In time of famine the First Nations were known to eat their moccasins and robes, which preserved modest food value because the leather was 'untreated and untanned'.[31]

The hunters were once again severely critical of their superiors. A raft was made out of willows bound in faggots but Solomon Belanger failed to make the crossing. Richardson, as described at the start of the chapter, also made the attempt but had to admit defeat. Franklin was gone for three hours, trying to walk half a mile to visit Pierez before the deep snow completely sapped his strength. At last, Pierez St Germain fashioned a canoe, described as a cockleshell by Houston, from the painted canvas in which they wrapped their bedding, thus enabling a wet crossing for all, one by one, and further discomfort for there was insufficient wood to dry clothing and blankets. Back, Pierez, Beauparlant and Belanger *le gros* (Solomon Belanger) decided to move ahead in search of Akaicho and his followers, who they hoped could supply life-saving food supplies. Next day all were fatigued, stumbling around almost in slow motion. Credit (Mathew Pelonquin), who had to carry the officers' tent, was incapable of standing by the time they reached their encampment. He suffered an adverse reaction to *tripe-de-roche*, as did Vaillant and Hood. Departing at nine next morning they encountered a strong piercing gale, snow and drifts. By noon, Credit and Vaillant were so shattered they could barely move. Others were too weak to render assistance. The men urged Franklin to allow them to abandon their loads and make for Fort Enterprise where they intended to winter. Richardson volunteered to remain with John Hepburn to look after Hood, who could barely walk. Franklin initially rejected his suggestion, though he had little choice but to agree. The weather closed in after Franklin and his supporters departed, forcing Richardson, Hood and Hepburn to remain at rest, reading portions of religious works to one another, notably *Bickersteth's Scripture Helps*. They were inspired with 'a strong sense of the omnipresence of a beneficent God', reflecting on their past lives and hope for the future.[32]

Next day the still weak Hood remained in bed while Hepburn cut willows for the fire and Richardson in vain sought supplies of *tripe-de-roche*. On his return to the campsite, Richardson was greeted by the Iroquois, Michel Teroahauté, delivering a note from Franklin. It indicated that the captain was sending Jean Baptiste Belanger and Teroahauté back to join the doctor, recommending a clump of pine trees only a mile away as an alternative campsite. Both naval officers familiarly addressed and referred to Teroahauté as Michel, presumably in place of his more confusing (to English speakers) French surname. Here, in nomenclature, I follow their example. Michel claimed to have lost his way, spending the night in the snow, but he now offered to share a hare and a partridge, for which the recipients praised the Lord, Hood offering a share of his buffalo robe and Richardson a shirt to their benefactor. Hepburn exclaimed that he would love this man if he did not 'tell lies like the others'. Meanwhile Belanger had 'gone astray', a claim which Richardson soon had some reason to doubt.

Next day, Richardson, Hepburn and Michel moved some of the heavier items to the pines, subsequently returning to the tent, though Michel decided to stay where he was, having been loaned a hatchet. He did not appear next morning and when the three arrived at the pines, he was not there either. Hepburn went back for the tent, his return coinciding with the advent of Michel, explaining that he had been hunting deer and had found the remains of a wolf killed by an antler (possible but unlikely), a portion of which he donated to the group. According to Richardson 'we implicitly believed this story then, but afterwards became convinced from circumstances, the detail of which may be spared, that it must have been a portion of the body of Belanger or Perrault'. On the question that possible murder was involved or whether the bodies were found in the snow, Franklin later opined that both had been 'sacrificed', hence the need for the hatchet, which is not a weapon associated with the butchering of caribou, but is useful for breaking down frozen meat, or so they later reasoned. Michel then disappeared for another couple of days, proving evasive when questioned on his return, though he did indicate he was considering making directly for Fort Enterprise. Again, he spent the day supposedly hunting. And so, the bluff and counter-bluff continued. Hood's health further deteriorated, exacerbated by starvation and cold winds. The three expeditionaries tried to keep up their spirits but, 'with the decay of our strength, our minds decayed, we were no longer able to bear the contemplation of the horrors that surrounded us. Each of us . . . excused himself from so doing by a desire of not shocking the feelings of others, for we were sensible of one another's weakness of intellect though blind to our own'.[33] They were notably religious, praying each morning and night to the Supreme Being.

Michel refused to co-operate, threatening to leave them. When Hood attempted to remind him of his obligations he vented his anger in a crazed reply: 'It is no use hunting, there are no animals, you had better kill and eat me'. Richardson preserved the unusual detail that Michel had spotted three caribou but could not follow them 'from having wet his foot in a small stream of water thinly covered with ice, and being consequently obliged to come to the fire'. However, that night he slept in the tent, possibly to avoid the dreaded fate that he himself had predicted.

The following morning, Sunday 20 October, Michel, obviously still apprehensive, refused to go hunting, lingering at the fire, 'under the pretence of cleaning his gun'. Richardson went off to gather some *tripe-de-roche*. Hood and Michel were arguing, while Hepburn was cutting down a tree. Soon after, the doctor heard a shot, followed a short time later by Hepburn calling him in great alarm; he had found a lifeless Hood with a ball in his forehead. Richardson at first suspected suicide but on later inspection discovered that the victim had been shot in the back of the head, the muzzle of the gun having set fire to Hood's night-cap. The gun clearly could not have inflicted such a wound unless fired by another person. Michel claimed he did not witness the killing. Hepburn assumed it was discharged during cleaning but reported that Hood and Michel argued fiercely before the shot was fired.

By the time Michel called him, about ten minutes had passed. The body was placed in a clump of willows and Richardson conducted a funeral service at evening prayers; he was impressed that the victim had been reading *Scripture Helps* at the very moment of his death, a detail which does not sit very well with the report of the loud quarrel between the hunter and the midshipman. Though Richardson, despite his suspicions, did not openly accuse Michel, the latter 'repeatedly protested he was incapable of committing such an act'. Despite his poor understanding of English, the hunter tried to prevent conversation between Richardson and Hepburn.

Michel bedded down in the tent that night but unsurprisingly none of the three could sleep. Next day they shared a kill of partridges supplied by Michel. As they planned to follow Franklin they were alarmed by Michel's gestures and conduct, muttering his distaste for going to Fort Enterprise and threatening Hepburn, whom he accused of telling stories against him. He also directed his wrath towards Richardson, who he claimed was completely in his power. Richardson reported that 'He gave vent to several expressions of hatred towards the white people, or as he termed us in the idiom of the voyagers, the French, some of whom, he said, had killed and eaten his uncle and two of his relations'. When Michel paused to gather some *tripe-de-roche* the other two were enabled to talk to one another for the first time without interference. Their decision was almost inevitable. In their weakened state they were no match for the hunter, Richardson reckoning that he was armed with a gun, two pistols, an Indian bayonet and a knife. Hepburn had taken the precaution of loading a pistol for Richardson that morning. They believed that Michel had not moved against them because he did not know the way to Fort Enterprise, so consequently they urged him to follow Franklin's trail, to no avail. Hepburn offered to act as executioner but the senior officer present insisted the role was his.

> I determined, as I was thoroughly convinced of the necessity of such a dreadful act, to take the whole responsibility upon myself; and immediately upon Michel's coming up, I put an end to his life by shooting him through the head with a pistol. Had my own life alone been threatened, I would not have purchased it by such a measure; but I considered myself as intrusted also with the protection of Hepburn's, a man who, by his humane attention and devotedness, had so endeared himself to me, that I felt more anxiety for his safety than for my own.[34]

Richardson described the incident in detail in order that his readers might understand why he felt compelled to deprive 'a fellow-creature of life'. He wrote of the dead man's previous excellent conduct and respect for the officers. Indeed, they had discussed rewarding him for his good service when they reached Fort Enterprise. However, he believed that because he did not enjoy the divine truths of Christianity, he was unable to 'withstand the pressure of severe distress', to Richardson a powerful explanation, if somewhat less so to posterity, though it is of considerable interest that the doctor acknowledged his victim's mental dislocation. Much later he stated that over half the party perished including Hood, 'under most distressing circumstances which are related at length in Sir John Franklin's narrative of the journey'.[35] A week later, after a nightmarish hike involving deep snow, extreme cold and an exhausting haul through large stones over which Richardson fell more than twenty times until he was unable to stand, the two men, thanks to John Hepburn's amazing reserves of strength, staggered into Fort Enterprise. There can be little doubt that John, as he now called him, saved Richardson's life, though Hepburn later told Joseph Bellot that both he and Richardson suffered irreparable injury to their constitutions. Hepburn 'had a sort of dropsy . . . he was all bloated, his hair perished, his nails broke etc'. They were incapable of speech, 'inarticulate sounds, issuing from the nose like grunts'.[36]

The killing of Michel was the most notorious episode in Richardson's career. He wrote a separate report on the event which was sent back to London; it was later published in Franklin's *Narrative*.[37] It undoubtedly shows signs of being doctored by both Richardson and Franklin. While the long trek from York Factory to the Arctic Sea inspired much to admire in individual effort, accomplishment and even heroism, the establishment back in England understood very little about the conditions in the far north; the entire expedition could be summed up in the Scots word *boorach*, meaning a shambles. The Navy had no understanding of how the HBC was run, no consideration of the company's relationship with the First Nations and the voyageurs. Men trained for the sea should never have been expected to tackle the sheer vastness of Canada north of the Great Lakes. The Navy men were possessed of disparaging assessments of Orkneymen and Canadians alike, who were just as ignorant of the expectations of the Royal Navy as the Navy was of them. The voyageurs, for example, were happy to work for Navy payments but they had no time for, or understanding of, naval discipline.

Richardson's biographer, Robert E. Johnson, agreed with his hero that all went reasonably well until the early appearance of winter at the beginning of September 1821, but like others he deplored the cost in human life. Of the twenty men who participated in the expedition, eleven died, an unforgivable number of casualties. George Simpson, imported from Scotland to Canada to rebuild the fortunes of the HBC, learned from Back that the objectives of the expedition were unlikely to be realised 'from a want of unanimity among themselves'. Simpson considered that the project had been undertaken without mature consideration or proper arrangements, famously criticising Franklin's 'lack of physical powers for the labour of moderate voyaging in this country'. It was not his fault that he did not look like an explorer, being very stout and only 5 foot 6 inches tall. He allegedly demanded food and tea three times a day. Furthermore 'with the utmost exertion he cannot walk above eight miles in one day'. It turned out that Franklin's health was not up to the rigours encountered.[38] Indeed, following the dismal experiences and incompetence of the first overland expedition, Franklin should never have been allowed to command again.

Willard-Ferdinand Wentzel of the HBC nursed a dislike of the British explorers: 'They acted on some occasions imprudently, injudiciously and showed in one particular case an unpardonable want of conduct'.[39] Whether this last comment referred to the Teroahauté tragedy is not known but Wentzel reported Back's view that events had taken place which 'must remain unknowable'. He was also of the opinion that it was unlikely that an 'authentic account' of their activities would ever emerge in England. He accused Richardson in particular of 'unpardonable want of conduct', and he seems to have believed that the murder of Michel richly merited that Richardson be punished.[40] As his editor has sensibly indicated, Franklin's ethnocentrism was a further barrier to mutual understanding. The other officers were not as single-minded as Franklin in the matter of naval culture. Richardson's mask dropped from time to time since almost all educated persons in Georgian Britain held racist views. For example, he apparently shared Franklin's opinions on the supposed treachery of subordinates.

The people, however, through despondency, had become careless and disobedient, they had ceased to dread punishment or hope for reward and it is a melancholy truth that gratitude for past favours or a sense of duty seldom influence the conduct of a Canadian voyager. Although they beheld their officers suffering even in a greater degree than themselves, yet they considered the want of food as dissolving all ties between us, and they had not scrupled to steal from us [the officers] part of the meat which had been allotted to us with impartiality. In consequence of this total want of discipline, much time was lost in halting and firing guns to call in stragglers.[41]

He also asserted that many shots were fired at partridges with few results; an alternative explanation was that the hunters chose not to add their kill to the common stock. It is disappointing that Richardson wrote these words and we may assume that weakness caused by hunger briefly overshadowed his innate sense of decency. The voyageurs' contracts stipulated that sufficient quantities of food were to be supplied by Franklin as part of their payment. Richardson had no right to assert that the voyageurs were thieving or ungrateful, and his claim that the officers suffered more than the 'watermen' was patent nonsense. Possibly, in all of this, he temporarily deferred too much to Franklin. It is perhaps surprising that none of the officers felt seriously threatened by the protesters who, well-armed as they were, could easily have outnumbered them, with fatal consequences.

In general Richardson adopted a common-sense approach, enhanced by a genuine interest in the ethnology of the folk he encountered, a quality shared by many Scots of his generation, who acquired some idea of a Scottish democratic quotient, inherited from the Kirk, Scottish history and Scottish literature. This is not to argue Scottish exceptionalism, for undoubtedly there were Scottish deviants in the ranks of HBC, to look no further; in any case most Scots are happy to admit that, as the saying goes, 'there are bad folk in every clan'.

Richardson was the son of the Provost of Dumfries, a wealthy brewer, but he was also a member of a generation of achievers. He chose medicine as his career but there was an over-production of doctors in Scotland due to the excellence of the country's universities, and in any case most folk could not afford the consultation charges.[42] Richardson, like many of his professional colleagues, looked to military service as an alternative to domestic medical practice. Both career paths served to elevate his social status but, while he was ambitious, he never seems to have deliberately sought fame. He regarded nature as a manifestation of the glory of God, which extended to a sincere interest in his fellow human beings, and thus in general he kept his feet firmly planted on the ground. He was a lifelong devotee of Robert Burns but he demonstrated a desire and ability to move with the times.

Franklin, however, was a true English imperialist who believed the 'jolly tars' to be superior to any similar force on the planet. The Navy demanded obedience but the voyageurs were jealous of their traditional dues and did not hesitate to openly criticise their leaders. Many disputes concerned the lack of food, 'the Canadians never exercising reflection unless they are hungry'. When they refused to work, Franklin threatened them with the heaviest punishment; according to Midshipman Back, he vowed to 'blow their brains out'.[43] There was an ongoing war of a kind between Brits and Canadians over sustenance. Some of the voyageurs, or perhaps all of them, had secondary occupations as hunters; from the end of August 1821 their activities appeared chaotic. The men were so heavily loaded that they had no spare capacity for carrying chunks of buffalo meat. Men who expected eight pounds of meat daily were given half a partridge each for breakfast. Hunters went off unsupervised and disappeared for a time, not always to great effect; the scanty supply of animal food affected everyone. Pierre St Germain presented each of the officers with a small piece of meat from his own allowance. 'It was received with great thankfulness and such an act of self denial and kindness, being totally unexpected in a Canadian, filled our eyes with tears'.[44] This was pure Henry Mackenzie, the famed Scottish 'Man of Feeling'. On this occasion Richardson presumably shared in the emotion but his attitude and that of his associates was racist; privileged officers should not have been tearfully taking food out of the mouths of starving voyageurs.

Credit (Pelonquin) kept going off on his own, reappearing when he felt like it. The party attempted to subsist on singed deerskin. The situation deteriorated when it was discovered that a misreading had taken them off course and there was still nothing to eat. 'A gloom spread over every countenance'; the men were desperate and 'perfectly regardless of the commands of their officers'. By 25 September it was their eleventh day without meat. Having killed five small deer, the men petitioned for, and were granted, a day's rest but they should not have had to take the initiative; the officers ought to have read the signs and responded appropriately. And so the misery persisted. Credit brought in the antlers and backbone of a deer killed in the summer. They divided up the putrid spinal marrow, 'so acrid as to excoriate the lips' and they also devoured the bones rendered friable in the fire, a ghastly, tragic, mocking 'Barrens Supper'!

Was Richardson's action with regard to Michel Teroahauté justified? The doctor was a devout Christian, an Evangelical, who on many occasions displayed sympathy for his companions whether British, First Nations, Métis or Inuit. He communicated daily with God, who would have certainly been consulted about the action deemed necessary regarding Teroahauté. Indeed, he sought counsel with the Almighty in every difficulty, who in return 'permitted his heart to be touched with a sense of my duty', stating in a later letter that 'in our strength we can do nothing, and it is only by His permission that we succeed in any attempt that we make'.[45] Hood would probably have agreed. He told his father in another missive that Richardson was 'a very acute and good man' but despite the latter's cryptic account, suspecting the source of the supposed chunk of wolf that Teroahauté recovered, Richardson and his companions were clearly guilty of unwitting cannibalism. Richardson claimed that if he had been alone he might have acted differently, presumably avoiding the execution, but it is difficult to suggest what option he had. He was doubtless as exhausted and temporarily unhinged to some degree by the conditions of weather and starvation, as all of the others. The exception was Hepburn, who was shortly to demonstrate that he still possessed reserves which saved Richardson's life. The Navy was on Richardson's side since its regulations called for death as the punishment for many crimes far short of murder, but Teroahauté was not a naval employee. Richardson's God would presumably have supported his action, which, although Mosaic law was redundant, was intended to preserve two lives through the destruction of one. We have to wonder if there was something in the doctor's instrument-case, or medical cabinet, which could have been used to disable or incapacitate the victim, allowing the fitter Hepburn to drag him to Fort Enterprise where he might have been handed over to HBC, possibly to meet the same fate. The doctor's account was fully supported by Franklin for many of whose deficiencies he more than adequately compensated.

Adriana Craciun cleverly challenges the assumptions and cultural values of Richardson's world and our own when she describes the doctor as 'a killer and probably a cannibal'.[46] Most of us who aspire to some kind of re-creation of the past attempt shorthand characterisations of persons and historical eras and thus are just as guilty of gross (if not always as revealing) distortion as Craciun. Richardson was neither a willing murderer nor a habitual cannibal. A true test would be to ask what he would have done if the roles of Hood and Teroahauté were reversed, but surely he would have 'acted differently'. The Iroquois and the voyageurs were regarded as expendable in a way that the Brits were not, and generations of readers have undoubtedly nodded when encountering the passage in question. In any case death held no terrors for the devout. Hood expected to die. According to Richardson, 'the calmness with which he contemplated the probable termination of a life of uncommon promise, and the patience and fortitude with which he sustained unparalleled bodily sufferings can only be known to the companions of his distresses'. What is truly remarkable is that the authorities and the critics did not make nearly the same fuss about the issue of cannibalism as was later directed at John Rae for suggesting that the practice played a part in the Franklin disaster. Robert Johnson in his biography preserves the anecdote that when Richardson visited Glasgow in 1828 the eleven-year-old J.D. Hooker followed him around, fascinated by a person who seemed more than human, longing to ask him about Teroahauté's death but strictly forbidden to do so by his parents.

Franklin told Richardson in August 1823 that Barrow had heard from 'three quarters' that some persons considered that 'you have not made it sufficiently clear that Michel actually murdered poor Hood', nor had he explained 'the dreadful necessity to which you were reduced by taking away the life of Michel'. Although Barrow considered that he had stated the case positively, he asked Franklin to advise Richardson of the propriety of reconsidering that part of his *Narrative*, adding 'if you can', some additional points that would satisfy the objectors. He thought this would best be done 'by dwelling a little more on the steps you took'. The critics had to be few because Franklin had never heard any of these rumours; indeed, most people believed the doctor had acted in a proper and necessitous manner. Barrow recommended that any additions should be short for the forthcoming reprint. He had fully argued against the doubters but he feared 'if these men are evil disposed they may chatter on these points with others who will receive it on their authority without even reading the account in the *Narrative*, much more give themselves time to reason on the grounds offered in justification of the fact'. Naval officialdom was doing its utmost to defend its servant. A generation later, attitudes were rather different as John Rae discovered to his cost.

*

Fort Enterprise was 'an abode of misery' in a ruinous condition. Franklin was dangerously weak as were the remaining voyageurs, the others having departed in search of Akaicho and his promised food reserves. The hollow and sepulchral sound of the voices of those who remained 'produced nearly as great horror to us as our emaciated appearance did on them', prompting

Richardson to urge that they adopt a more cheerful tone. They subsisted (barely) on deer skins and the larvae of warble flies. The voyageurs Peltier and Samandre were very weak, unable to cut firewood; two days later they were dead. Adam the interpreter suffered painfully from oedema, which Richardson treated. Both Hepburn and Richardson felt themselves to be failing. Hepburn's legs swelled alarmingly; in 1851 he told Joseph Bellot that he thought both men suffered permanent damage: 'He was all bloated, his hair perished, his nails broke etc. Inarticulate sounds, issuing from the nose like grunts, were the only means of conversation.'[47]

First Nations arrived on 7 November with supplies of dried meat and fat, also providing fires and general assistance, which greatly impressed Richardson. But the rescued suffered from distention of the stomach due to the sudden consumption of meat. Adam made great progress in recovery while for Franklin and Richardson progress was much slower. They became suspicious when their benefactors suddenly departed, fearing abandonment, but it turned out that they went off to attempt speedier delivery of further supplies. On 16 November the group abandoned Fort Enterprise, their deliverers providing every imaginable assistance: from lending their own snow-shoes to cooking and supporting their weakened charges against falling, 'evincing a degree of humanity that would have done honour to the most civilized nation'. Next day they took the greatest care to massage the parts of Franklin's face affected by frostbite. But the Brits were less impressed by the actions of the Fop, a colourful, if brutal, Red Knife, who regularly beat up his young wife. They felt that he received deserved injury when his gun burst, wounding his wrist. As they moved south they encountered many herds of caribou. They soon reached a First Nations village whose inhabitants catered for their every need. Such care continued when they were welcomed by Akaicho, whose rewards or payments for food supplies negotiated with Franklin were delayed by NWC. At Fort Providence Franklin assured the chief that the dues or debts would be paid by the autumn. The delay did not greatly perturb Akaicho, who noted 'the world goes badly, all are poor. You are poor, the traders appear to be poor, I and my party are poor likewise . . . I do not regret having supplied you with provisions, for a Red Knife can never permit a White man to suffer from want on his lands, without flying to his aid'. He added, humorously, that this was the first time 'the White people have been indebted to the Red Knife Indians!'. On 19 December the explorers reached Fort Resolution to be greeted by chief trader Robert McVicar, whose hospitality they enjoyed for the next five months.

A canoe bearing the payments and supplies that Franklin owed Akaicho arrived just as the naval party was preparing to leave. The captain was pleased to add rifles and ammunition to the awards. He and his men then advanced to Fort Chipewyan where they met Wenzel. From Norway House they sent the voyageurs down to Montreal while the naval contingent went on to York Factory. 'Thus terminated our long, fatiguing, and disastrous travels in North America, having journeyed by water and by land including our navigation of the Polar Sea, 5,550 miles'.[48]

John Richardson supplied several sections to Franklin's *Narrative* as well as 'Geognostical Observations', 'Remarks on the Aurora Borealis', 'Notice of the Fishes' and 'Botanical Appendix'. He was given a great deal of responsibility considering this was his first Arctic outing and he can take the credit for ensuring that the expedition did not turn out any more disastrous than it actually was. When required he provided excellent medical care, outstanding surveying skills, a steady aim, sympathy for the native peoples and a remarkable grasp of natural history – mammals, insects, fish, birds and plants – perhaps his greatest achievement, since, as Stuart Houston has demonstrated, many of his specimens had never been previously recorded. He encountered medical conditions that were new to him. He learned much about food and diet, matters of crucial concern to all Arctic explorers. With his naval colleagues he greatly expanded knowledge of Arctic geography and he was a fine map-maker. Climatology was another of his interests, a subject in its infancy at the time. Above all he had an open-minded appetite for experiences of all kinds that life might throw at him. These unfortunately included cannibalism and the execution of a murderous psychotic, as well as close contact with the dead and the dying in the graveyard that was the Barrens, though it is difficult to assess the impact these horrendous occurrences had upon him. His Arctic career will be further explored later in this book. He deserves to be much better known in Scotland; there is presently a remarkable and lamentable ignorance about his achievements, even in his own home town of Dumfries, though he has recently been memorialised in a street name and, in 2019, I had the pleasure of unveiling a small plaque at Dumfries Academy, formerly the Grammar School, which he and Robert Burns junior attended.

Lestris Richardsonii, from John Richardson, *Fauna Boreali-Americana*
(London, 1829)

Corvina Richardsonii, from John Richardson, *Fauna Boreali-Americana*
(London, 1829)

5

BOREAL NATURALIST

John Richardson's Role in the Franklin Expedition of 1825–1827

My duty will be to collect minerals, plants and animals. The country has never been visited by a naturalist, and presents a rich harvest.

John Richardson

After the initial disasters over which Franklin presided during the 1819–22 Coppermine expedition, he should have been banned from further ventures, but having, for some unfathomable reason, been given another chance, he was determined to make a success of his second expedition to the shores of Arctic America in 1825, taking care to personally supervise the arrangements. Essential supplies such as pemmican were shipped from England to New York where their onward transmission was organised by chief trader Robert McVicar of HBC. Eighteen voyageurs manned three small 'north canoes', received at Lake Athabasca by Peter Dease, who was charged with assembling supplies of fish, while providing buildings for the expeditionaries at Great Bear Lake. Franklin also arranged for two large canoes to be readied at Penetanguishene, the Navy's base on Lake Huron, thus gaining ten days on the usual route from Montreal and the addition of thirty-three voyageurs. William McGillivray of HBC provided much practical advice from afar. A range of scientific instruments was also put together – electrometers, hygrometers, thermometers and a photometer, as well as sextants, artificial horizons, altitude instruments, compasses and a dipping-needle.

Two waterproof 'dresses' for each man were manufactured by Macintosh of Glasgow. Gun-locks were tempered to withstand cold temperatures, supported by broad Indian daggers which could be used as bayonets; ample ammunition was supplied. Food supplies were carefully wrapped in three layers of waterproof canvas. The usual paraphernalia were also readied:

cartridge-paper for plant specimens, fishing tackle and a range of goods for trading with the residents, as well as tools such as saws, ice-chisels and 'trenching irons to break open the beaver lodges'.

Many purchasers of Franklin's *Narrative of a Second Expedition* must have been rather dissatisfied because it is rather thin on genuine Arctic material and somewhat brief compared to others. Franklin experienced most of the action in encountering hostile Inuit, probably due to his assumptions and prejudices, while Richardson appears to have met with few real difficulties in his part of the expedition. There are fairly obvious signs of padding, and the descriptions of New York, city and state, contain material that could have been dropped; even though it is not without interest, much of it would have been familiar to devourers of travel literature by 1825.

On 12 February 1825, John Franklin, John Richardson, George Back, naturalist Thomas Drummond, cartographer and naval officer Edward Kendall and four marines sailed from Liverpool for New York on the packet-ship *Columbia*, arriving twenty-seven days later. After a week of hospitality from the city's finest, they moved on. Richardson was amused that distinction of rank 'seemed to be preserved more tenaciously in the republican United States than in monarchical Britain'. A steamboat conveyed them up the Hudson, stopping off en route at West Point. At Albany they met General De Witt Clinton, Governor of New York State, regarded by Richardson as 'a polished gentleman of great scientific attainments'. They heard a sermon from a Dr Christie, who prayed for their success in the north. They then boarded three coaches bound for Lewiston, accompanied by the British Consul to New York, James Buchanan, who was Scotch-Irish. He re-arranged his schedule so that he could accompany the visitors to Canada. Another new acquaintance was Cadwallader David Colden, a member of the New York Senate, whose much more famous grandfather and namesake was the son of the minister of Duns, Berwickshire, student of medicine at Edinburgh University, scientist and philosopher, deservedly regarded as being at the forefront of the American Enlightenment.[1]

Crossing the Niagara they reached Queenstown and from there the Falls that Oscar Wilde would later famously define as 'every American Bride's second greatest disappointment'! Richardson was kinder, more dignified and more awe-struck: 'It is a stupendous monument of the power of the Creator of the universe, who wields at will an element that mocks the strength of man'.[2]

Canada, it seems, did not impress him, offering miserable roads and thinly settled country, as they proceeded by way of Lake Simcoe and the

Natawasaga River to Lake Huron and Penetanguishene, which they left on 23 April, arriving at Fort William on 10 May, where they swapped their big boats for four river boats. This fort on Lake Superior was named for the Scot William McGillivray of NWC. Washington Irving, whose father hailed from Shapinsay, Orkney, gained fame and international recognition as one of America's early novelists. He was proud of his Scottish heritage, memorably describing the annual councils at Fort William as 'transplanted clan gatherings' attended by the chief traders of the fur companies, Scottish 'hyperborean nabobs' dressed in all their traditional finery.[3]

Franklin and Richardson pushed ahead, leaving the others to follow them to Cumberland House (the HBC's first inland fur-trading post situated on the Saskatchewan River). Dry weather had resulted in poor water flows, which created severe difficulties in negotiating the Methy Portage (an old fur trader route) because of the amount of cargo the men had to carry over the 12 miles and more, tortured by mosquitoes. When they reached Fort Chipewyan on Lake of the Hills (Lake Athabasca), their thoughts turned to Alexander Mackenzie, the first Euro-Canadian to cross Canada from sea to shining sea. From there they went on to Great Slave Lake and the hospitality (again) of Robert McVicar, from Islay, a Chief Trader of HBC, who had made such a favourable impression on Richardson on the first expedition. Two days later the doctor was off down the Mackenzie River, through Fort Simpson, Fort Norman and up the Bear Lake River to Fort Franklin, in process of being built on the western shore of Great Bear Lake, where his early arrival surprised Chief Trader Dease. When Franklin followed, he continued down the Mackenzie to Garry's Island, 30 miles beyond Whale Island, the furthest point reached by Mackenzie. There Franklin unfurled a flag made by his late wife, whose not unexpected death he had learned of in April. He joined Richardson at Fort Franklin on 6 September; since leaving New York on 26 March they had travelled 5,160 miles.

The doctor seemed quite gratified that 'the greater part of our men, amounting in all to twenty-five, are Scotchmen, and very well behaved'. The music of the bagpipes doubtless soothed their potentially savage souls. When the staff at an American inn were reluctant to quit their warm beds in order to make a late supper, James Buchanan sent in Wilson the piper, marching through the building playing the 'Gathering of the Clans', 'before the landlord, his wife, and five or six female attendants, hurried forth'.[4] Many Americans who had blamed the greed of Scottish Tobacco Lords for the Revolution, were now positively influenced by aspects of Scottish history, culture and literature. John Quincy Adams, elected in 1825 just as the Franklin party arrived in New York, was the first President to be associated with the song 'Hail to the Chief', based on lines from Sir Walter Scott's poem 'The Lady of the Lake'. Come the spring, after over-wintering at Fort Franklin, the group would eventually divide into two expeditions: Franklin leading a party westwards towards the Bering Strait and Richardson leading another eastwards along the Mackenzie and Coppermine rivers. Scots assigned to Franklin's boat *Lion* included William Duncan (cockswain), George Wilson (marine and piper), Archibald Stewart (soldier), Neil MacDonald (voyageur) and Gustavus Aird (bowman), while George Back in *Reliance* had only three Scots – Charles Mackenzie (bowman) and two middlemen, Alexander Currie and Robert Spence. In Richardson's party, Richardson in *Dolphin* had only one fellow-countryman, John McLellan (bowman), while Kendall in *Union* hosted four or five – John McLeay (coxswain), George Munroe (bowman), John McDuffey and George Harkness – the origins of William Money (marine) are uncertain. Another Scot, naturalist Thomas Drummond, born at Inverarity, Forfarshire (now Angus), would not join either expedition as he was left at Cumberland House to botanise along the Saskatchewan River and into the Rockies. Drummond had studied at Glasgow University with William Jackson Hooker, Professor of Botany, who recommended him to Franklin as a suitable assistant for Richardson. In a letter written while at Fort William, Richardson described Drummond as 'the most indefatigable collector of specimens of natural history I have ever seen'. In the same letter he noted that Edward Kendall 'is an exact picture of Captain Franklin, in size, face and temper'.[5]

There was an altercation when the Scottish Highlanders in the party objected to their description as *Montagnards*, or 'natives of the mountainous lands', coincidently the same designation the voyageurs used for the Dogribs, a branch of the Chipewyan. Racism raised its ugly head as the Gaels responded by attacking the voyageurs; the Dogribs became involved and instantly rumours spread like wildfire among the First Nations alleging the whites planned to destroy them, but soon tempers cooled as quickly as they had risen.[6] The ethnic diversity at Fort Franklin was noteworthy. In addition to the Europeans and the First Nations, there were Inuit, two of whom, interpreters Tattannoeuck, known as Augustus, and Ooligbuck, were to play invaluable roles in this second expedition to the northern Canadian coast.[7]

As soon as he arrived at Bear Lake, Richardson was off to explore some two hundred miles of its shoreline. He wrote to his mother emphasising how well things were going and explaining that his sister Margaret's gift of a bottle of pickles, and another containing cayenne pepper, had survived the long journey. He asked after Margaret, teasingly requesting that she communicate 'all the gossip of Mouswald', the tiny village where she lived, just outside Dumfries. He wrote again to tell her that portraits of Franklin and him had been painted before they departed. England seemed to be in the throes of an industrial and technological craze which would extend to Scotland if only the country had enough money 'to play the fool with'. One such craze, photography, was in its infancy; by the 1840s Franklin and several of his officers had been immortalised by the daguerreotype, which sometimes produced an almost ghost-like and portentous image. Soon Scots such as David Brewster and Robert Adamson were at the forefront of experimentation with cameras.[8]

In a letter to his sister, Richardson said he could not find a word to express 'the romantic attachment which a Scotchman, in his wanderings, feels towards the land of his birth, conjoined with the canny wisdom which prevents her, Scotia, from following the vagaries of her flaunting sister of the south', nor did he approve of Englishmen who were impudent enough to describe the land of the mountain and the flood as a 'beggarlie country'. His own news noted that the Dogribs were off to new hunting grounds. Their chief's wife had delivered her own son that morning and was back at her usual tasks an hour or two later. Meanwhile Peter Dease's wife had given birth to a daughter. They were to celebrate Christmas and New Year, when voyageur wives and First Nations ladies dressed in all their finery. The males were from all over Scotland and England as well as France and Canada. Some Inuit also appeared. Richardson begged his mother for gossipy letters from Annandale which brought to remembrance 'so many persons and things of bygone times'.[9]

The month of May arrived with a sense of occasion. Richardson and Kendall returned from another survey of Bear Lake and the height of the land. The former's report was included in Franklin's *Narrative of a Second Expedition*. On 6 May swans were seen and on successive days there appeared a goose, two ducks and some gulls. According to Franklin, the geese were of the kind 'to our shame denominated Bastards by the Voyageurs' (known as bustards to the rest of us); they were followed by snow geese and greater-white fronted geese, as well as smaller waterbirds. The first mosquitoes were much less welcome. By month's end, sweet coltsfoot and white anemones were plentiful.

Preparations were made in June concerning the two expeditions east and west, reminding everyone that either or both might meet up with British ships already in the Arctic. Franklin assigned fourteen men to his two west-bound boats, *Lion* and *Reliance*, and ten to Richardson's eastbound *Dolphin* and *Union*.[10] The earlier problems with canoes were not to be repeated. Franklin was proud of having designed three boats based on the model of the Northwest canoe (which he thoughtlessly described as the North American canoe), built from timbers of mahogany and ash. The largest was 26 feet long and 5 feet wide, the others 2 feet shorter and 2 inches less in width. Construction in England was supervised by Captain David Buchan, late of *Dorothea* and the abortive polar expedition. Another Scot, of the distinguished Eskdale family, near Langholm, Lieutenant Colonel Pasley, designed a light vessel, 9 feet long, 4 feet 4 inches wide, made from ash and Macintosh's waterproof canvas. It could be stored in three parcels and assembled in only twenty minutes, resembling half a 'walnutshell', the name by which it came to be known.[11] 'Several ladies who had honoured the trial of the boats with their presence fearlessly embarked in it, and were paddled across the Thames in a fresh breeze.'[12] This ancestor of modern inflatable zodiacs was designed to avoid incidents like Richardson's experience on the Coppermine River in 1821.

*

There is no doubt that the explorations of 1825–7 were very much more efficiently organised than the earlier effort. HBC had absorbed NWC by 1821 and its executives were much more willing and able than they had been before to lend assistance. In the event, these voyages appear somewhat tame after the agonies suffered in 1821, though Franklin reported a catalogue of danger and discomfort. The initiative for the follow-up expedition was Franklin's, who advocated the completion of the survey covering the coast from Alaska in the west to Point Turnagain in the east. He must have been shrewdly aware that his ideas mirrored Barrow's. His 'official instructions' reflected his suggestions that his own expedition should explore the northern coast of America from the mouth of the Mackenzie River to the Bering Strait, having established a base at Great Bear Lake from where he was to develop friendly relations with the local Inuit.[13] He was then to follow the coast westwards to Icy Cape where he could expect to rendezvous with Captain Beechey, in *Blossom*, thus possibly returning home via the Pacific. Richardson was to head eastwards to the Coppermine but if supplies were short he was to investigate the Rocky Mountains, the Copper Mountains and the shores of Great Bear Lake, researching plants and minerals, with a view to completing knowledge of the natural history of North America. Richardson's escape route, if required, would involve Captain Parry's ships *Fury* and *Hecla*, though he could not know that both ships, in 1825, were ice-locked in Prince Regent Inlet, where *Fury* was abandoned, while *Hecla* was soon bound for home. Franklin also ordered François Beaulieu, Yellowknife chief and interpreter, to meet the Richardson party at Dease River on the north-east of Great Bear Lake in the autumn on his way back from the Coppermine. Beaulieu had accompanied Alexander Mackenzie on his overland trek to the Pacific in 1793 and had persuaded Franklin to over-winter at Great Bear Lake on the earlier expedition. He was quite a character, who became a Christian and monogamous for the first time at the age of 79. He died aged 100 in 1872.[14]

Both parties spent the last night together at the appropriately named Point Separation in the Mackenzie estuary. On 4 July each party went its own way. Franklin's contingent, in *Lion* and *Reliance*, discovered a large encampment of Inuit on one island in the estuary. As the Inuit set out to meet them, Franklin prepared presents and possible trade goods, while cannily telling his crew to check their weapons. Almost immediately his boats grounded in the mud of the Mackenzie, a situation of which the Inuit, with an estimated 250 men, took advantage. Under Franklin's command were eight Scots: Duncan, Aird, Wilson, Stewart, McDonald, Mackenzie, Currie and Spence. Franklin, with interpreter Augustus, planned to visit the Inuit ahead of his men, but the Inuit soon began to attack. Augustus courageously faced down forty armed men with a mixture of cajolery and threat, warning them of scuppering opportunities for trade and also of the power of gunfire. The Inuit threatened with knives, allegedly intending to murder all in Franklin's party as they advanced. Ropes and rigging on the boats were cut. Augustus and Duncan were sent to examine the state of the ice to the west. Each side remained wary of the other. When ashore the Brits were plagued by mosquitoes and swampy ground; fog and rain were abundant. Augustus took a shivering fit when he plunged into cold water in pursuit of a deer. Piper Wilson saved the day by giving him some of his own clothes.

Travelling west along the coast, on 31 July they reached Point Demarcation, 'the boundary between the British and Russian dominions on the northern coast of America', and a place much frequented by the Inuit. Despite its potentially romantic name, the scenery, as on much of the western coast, was dismal, worsened by persistent bad weather. Franklin, later discovering that Beechey and his ship *Blossom* were 160 miles further west, claimed that no 'difficulties, dangers, or discouraging circumstances would have lessened his determination to advance' but he should have been grateful for his ignorance since Beechey later reported that the natives were as hostile as the weather.[15] In 374 miles of the coast Franklin had not found one viable harbour. On the return journey they were attacked by the First Nations. When Franklin's party returned to the Mackenzie estuary, great alarm was caused by reports communicated by Barbue, chief of the Loucheux, that Franklin and Richardson had been killed. The story seems to have originated in the violent death of another chief somewhere on the coast. The rumour probably did not reach Richardson, but Franklin, fearing the worst, namely that the Loucheux and the Inuit were allying against him, sent men east to investigate.[16] Franklin was highly critical of the HBC agent Dease, of whom he observed 'the making of difficulties seems to be a component of (his) condition', which reportedly included having failed to collect firewood for the winter; consequently everyone experienced 'a voyage of unceasing anxiety'.[17]

*

Richardson's party sent off the 'westerners' with three hearty huzzas before embarking themselves in *Dolphin* and *Union* to travel eastwards. The Scots were Richardson himself, McLellan, McLeay, Munroe, McDuffey and Harkness. They traversed uninteresting flats enlivened by the welcome sound and actions of sand martins, the deadly enemies of mosquitoes. Along the coast were many signs of abandoned Inuit camps. The cartographer Kendall prepared a message in hieroglyphics designed to indicate friendship by depicting gift-giving to the Inuit. Richardson named an insular gravesite Sacred Island. Approaching Richards Island they noted tents and skin canoes. The doctor had previously agreed with the Inuk guide Ooligbuck that the two of them should approach alone, all guns having been hidden but handy for use if required. Two women saw them as they went ashore, sounding the alarm to their people, who debouched from their tents semi-naked. Once they realised that the Navy wished to trade, the Inuit seemed to understand, but they became more aggressive as they saw what was on offer. Ooligbuck, realising they were 'very bad people', hoisted Richardson on his back and into the boat. The entire population appeared to follow them in their kayaks and umiaks. Some gradually resumed trading, 'showing much tact in their commerce with us', wrote Richardson, 'circumstances which have been held by an eminent historian [William Robertson, principal of Edinburgh

University] to be evidences of a considerable progress towards civilization'. Robertson shared Adam Smith's view that trade had a crucial impact in bringing civilisations, nations and peoples together. The Inuit offered only one article at a time, exchanged names with the visitors, admired the wooden canoes and their rudders and named Richardson's telescope 'far eyes', which was also their designation for their own snow-shades. The doctor and some of his crew reciprocated the interest, enjoying 'the glances that could scarcely be misconstrued' of some of the women and noting their clothing and hair styles. Richardson suggested that they chose to live in villages because they needed the numbers of men required to hunt whales. He compared the Inuit use of the fist to the *waddie* of New South Wales; in one-to-one fights both cultures exchanged blows, in turn, until one fell down. Both also used throwing sticks for 'discharging their spears'. He derived this information from Peter Cunningham's 'entertaining work' *Two Years in New South Wales*.[18]

The Inuit delighted in demonstrating the swiftness and versatility of their kayaks. They placed their paddles to form a kind of bridge/springboard that enabled them to leap from kayak to wooden boat. They grabbed and rocked the boats, threatening to tip out the occupants. Eventually, as the Inuit became more boisterous, the Brits armed themselves in preparation for the worst, but their attackers backed off, while remaining very interested in plunder. There were many Inuit campsites as the party advanced eastwards. Richardson was minded to tolerate their mischievous activities by trying to gain their trust, particularly because the weather conditions were such that he thought his men might need to encamp, conceivably requiring their assistance. For their part the Inuit thought the naval boats resembled umiaks, almost exclusively managed by women in Inuit culture, asking Ooligbuck if all the white women had beards! The interpreter's contribution was limited because he did not speak English but he did convince the Inuit that the visitors were of a friendly disposition. Rain, changeable winds, *Union* breaking her moorings, and concerns about a possible Inuit attack, all made sleep impossible.

Various objects placed in bundles and suspended on poles outside Inuit houses included 'spear-heads and ice chisels made from the tooth of the narwhal and spoons of musk-ox horn'. The Inuit hunted the white whale (beluga), narwhal and black whale (northern right whale) as well as seals. Capelin were plentiful and simple to catch. On 10 July the party had now reached the true mouth of the Mackenzie, noticing two or three Inuit who appeared to be shadowing them. Strong winds over the next couple of days forced them to remain at their mooring place, their boredom slightly alleviated by observing the antics of two black foxes. Two elderly Inuit visited, seeking friendship and trade, admitting it was they who had been observing them. By 13 July moderate winds allowed the party to continue their course. On Atkinson Island, named by Kendall, they found seventeen houses and one large building, 27-foot square, with the skulls of twenty-one whales placed around the base. They had little idea of its purpose but suggestions were an assembly hall and an eating room. Kendall illustrated the site, and Richardson wrote that 'the general attention to comfort in the construction of the village, and the erection of a building of such magnitude, are evidences of no small progress towards civilization'.[19]

Moving on, they heard the sound of breakers confirming they were now at sea but they were now hampered by fog and rain. At Browell Cove Richardson found thrift and several other plants familiar from Scottish hills. At a place they named Harrowby Bay some Inuit looked to be intent upon attack until they were persuaded that the intruders wished to barter. As they set sail again, Kendall designed a kind of barricade on the boats to prevent stealing while aiding defence, but they were somewhat dumbfounded when three umiaks, each rowed by two women with a third steering, proved they could outrun the naval vessels. The women danced 'in their slender boats' so energetically as to prompt fears of capsizing; their entreaties to stay over were for a time successful, according to Richardson. Ooligbuck demonstrated the use of the gun to which the Inuit gave the same name as to their whale-harpoons (not divulged).

By 18 July they had reached Cape Bathurst, named for an English peer. The record of bestowing the names of British nonentities on often obscure Arctic sites ultimately becomes extremely tedious because the individuals so honoured are often deservedly long forgotten, while some of the place-named sites are difficult to distinguish. The modern Inuit initiative in reclaiming names from, and for, their own culture is therefore to be sincerely welcomed. We may name the Mackenzie River with a certain amount of pride in an individual who worked hard at reaching the Arctic Ocean and then the Pacific but we must acknowledge, as he did himself, that he could not have succeeded without the aid of the First Nations and hence the native name is to be preferred. In the Slavey language the Mackenzie is De-Cho, big river, which is apt because it is the longest in Canada. It is not helpful or interesting to be told that 'in the forenoon we passed the mouths of two small rivers which were designated after Sir Henry Jardine, Bart., King's

Remembrancer in the Court of Exchequer for Scotland; and Dr Burnett Commissioner of the Victualling Board'.[20] It was Kendall's responsibility to make sense of it all by mapping their journey, and hence the features of land and sea, for posterity.[21]

Richardson reckoned on 21 July that they were halfway between Point Separation and the Coppermine River. Further east he named the great bay after Franklin. Soon they detected the northern extremity of the promontory that was named Cape Parry, leaving a letter under a cairn there for Parry, should he be passing. Emerging from yet more fog, Richardson named an island honouring Hugh Clapperton 'the undaunted explorer of central Africa'. Clapperton, born in Annan, Dumfriesshire, became a lieutenant in the Royal Navy before embarking on his African adventures 1822–5. Fourteen miles from Clapperton Island, Richardson named a cape after Captain G.F. Lyon, who had earlier attempted to travel, like Clapperton, to Bornu and the River Niger.

Coxswain McLeay killed a deer shortly after they quit Cape Lyon. This man was something of a hunter for this was not his only kill, venison being most welcome to his associates. A hill in the Melville Range honoured Professor William Jackson Hooker. They were now encountering significant amounts of ice such as to make the sails redundant, necessitating the use of oars and poles. Also, the tides rose much higher than they had to the west. *Union* was almost crushed between two large ice floes, *Dolphin* having sailed through only two minutes earlier; her turn came a little later when she escaped with only a few cracked planks. The ice remained a worry until Kendall reported that the main shore was inclining to the south-east, which indicated that the Coppermine could not be far away. Richardson named what he thought was a large island for William Hyde Wollaston, the scientist who discovered palladium and rhodium. Previously Wollaston Land, it is now known as the Wollaston Peninsula on the south-west of Victoria Island. Richardson also named the open water to the south, leading to Coronation Gulf, after his two boats, the Dolphin and Union Strait, now often regarded as marking the western termination of the Northwest Passage.

The crew were buoyed by the 'favourable trending of the coast', but *Dolphin* was once again damaged by ice which broke a timber and some planks, forcing them ashore for repairs. Back at sea, the fierce eddies and large masses of ice drove them back to the land with thoughts of Scylla and Charybdis, the fierce sea monsters of Homer's *Odyssey*, perhaps something of an exaggeration but every respectable account of an Arctic voyage requires a ferocious storm! Richardson and Kendall took a walk, gratified that there would now be plenty of time to reach Great Bear Lake before the bad weather arrived. They considered that Dolphin and Union Strait would be dangerous to shipping because of hidden rocks. 'Walnut' Pasley was rewarded with a bay named for him, and a cape was named for the Russian explorer and world circumnavigator Adam Johann von Krusenstern.

While out walking, Richardson noted that the Inuit marked prominent sites 'by erecting piles of stones similar to the cairns built for landmarks by the shepherds of Scotland'. One of the doctor's final commemorations was for Kendall, with another named for Captain Back. Since Richardson River, named by Franklin, had proved to be a dry ravine, Franklin transferred the name to a bay at the mouth of the Coppermine. Richardson was able to pleasantly surprise his men by telling them that a 'short traverse would bring them to the river'. Throughout the voyage, as might have been expected, the doctor noted all kinds of information about plants, animals and birds.

On 9 August the party entered the boats for the 11-mile journey in extremely low water levels to Bloody Falls, where they abandoned Dolphin and Union and any other surplus gear, but retained the Pasley boat. The tents were pitched and articles that would prove valuable to the Inuit were placed within. Shortly thereafter the 'Walnut' was also abandoned. Three days later 'Whisky John' (or 'whisky jack', a Canadian jay) was seen for the first time since the Mackenzie: 'The country was, in general, naked'. Sand-flies were irritating, partridges so tame they could be killed with stones. McLeay's game store performed well, regularly stocked up as it was by fresh kills of venison. On 15 August the party reached Dease River, where they met up with three Hare Indians known to Richardson from the previous autumn; they had been hunting in the area hoping to run across the expeditionaries, for whom they had brought food supplies. But there was no sign of Yellowknife chief and interpreter François Beaulieu, who had been told by Franklin to set out on 6 August remaining at Dease River on the Great Bear Lake until 20 September. HBC Highlanders were impressed by Kendall and Richardson's accuracy of navigation across the Barrens, ensuring that there was not a single mile of 'unnecessary walking',[22] unlike in 1821, they might have added.

There was a convention of setting trees on fire to send messages, signifying the presence of explorers to the First Nations and vice-versa. One fire spread to the Navy campsite, causing some excitement. There was good fishing on the lake while the Indians brought in supplies of fresh meat such as deer and musk-ox. Richardson was becoming impatient because if Beaulieu did not arrive with boats they would have a 300-mile hike around the lake to reach Fort Franklin. He sent half his party, including McLeay, McDuffie, McLellan, Gillet the coxswain and Ooligbuck 'on a distant hunting excursion' to Limestone Point some distance west of Dease River. When Beaulieu duly arrived on 24 August, having been delayed by bad weather, he was accompanied by four voyageurs, four Chipewyan hunters and ten Dogribs with wives and children, amounting to some thirty people. Since there was no sign of the five already sent, Kendall and Richardson went in search of them and they were eventually found at Haldane River. The party once again reunited, Richardson exchanged canoes with Beaulieu and set off again, arriving back at Fort Franklin on 1 September 1826 after an absence of seventy-one days and having traversed a distance of 1,980 miles. He was pleased by the performance of his crew, especially Ooligbuck, 'our good-natured and faithful Esquimaux friend' whose 'attachment to us was never doubtful'. He was also very impressed by the qualities of Lieutenant Ned Kendall.

*

The major concerns throughout the exploration of the coast, shared by both Franklin and Richardson, were distrust of the Inuit and the fear of possible violence, but though the Inuit purloined the odd item, they never came to blows or caused bloodshed. The Inuit idea seems to have been to scare their enemies into submission. It was commendable of both the expedition leaders to attempt contact, backed up solely by their respective Inuit interpreters, but the true violence appears to have been latent in the naval officers, despite the fact that they were the intruders or invaders.

Franklin's racism came to the fore once more on discovering that the Dogribs had failed to provide sufficient food supplies due to the 'indolence and apathy which mark the character of this tribe'. He sent five men to remedy the deficit by fishing. Beaulieu also returned with welcome dried meat but he was keen to leave the expedition, departing with seventeen followers. Kendall collected stores, clothing and mail from Fort Norman. Winter set in, the last ducks departing in mid October. Franklin began to plan his own departure. He was delighted that the local residents were beginning to build houses on the model of those at Fort Franklin.

A Dogrib murdered his wife's lover, bringing the number of homicides around Great Bear Lake to roughly thirty since the trading post was established there in 1799, a depressing indication of kabloona influence upon the local population, but a circumstance to which the invaders were blind.

Franklin collected some traditional tales while Dease investigated First Nations beliefs in a Great Spirit 'who created everything, both us and the world for our use'. They thought the Spirit lived among the white men, to whom he was kind, so that some people there never died and warm winds always blew from the south. Some confided that they considered their medicine men did a poor job in not consulting 'the master of life', who would give them better lives and banish death, but 'He does not inhabit our lands'. Christmas and New Year were celebrated in style. The two Hare Indians who had earlier relieved Richardson at Great Bear Lake were rewarded with medals. In January a temperature of 58 degrees below zero was recorded, the lowest they had ever experienced.

Franklin left the fort on 20 February 1827. The desertion of the First Nations in his party reinforced his prejudices. He found shelter and sustenance at Fort Simpson, where he arranged for HBC to take some of his spare stores at valuation. In March he pressed on in his 'cariole', a small one-man carriage-like sledge pulled by dogs. He took with him goat and lynx skins and those of smaller birds and animals for the natural history collection. At Fort Resolution he stopped to greet Robert McVicar again. Three months earlier, in December 1826, Richardson had left the fort to join Thomas Drummond on the Saskatchewan River. Franklin noted in passing that the Chipewyans and Copper Indians were using dogs, rather than their wives, as the mode of traction for their sledges. Also, they no longer beat their spouses as cruelly as in the past: 'in the comparative tenderness with which they now treat the sex, they have made the first and greatest step to all moral and general improvement', a development he attributed to the presence of HBC, an explanation not entirely convincing. At Fort Chipewyan he noted further improvements since HBC had stopped importing spirits into the district. The hunters were paid partially in clothing. The Sabbath was 'ordered to be properly observed' and vegetables were now cultivated. The self-congratulatory tone may have been premature. A few years earlier the attempt to impose alien values on the population may have been responsible for the phenomenon of the 'Manlike Woman', a Chipewyan transgender prophet, who predicted a kind of First Nations' apocalypse, a case that clearly fascinated Franklin.[23]

On 18 June 1827, having reached Cumberland House, Franklin met with Richardson, whom he had not seen for eleven months. He also encountered the indefatigable Thomas Drummond, who impressed him so much that Franklin was moved to include Drummond's report in his *Narrative of a Second Expedition*. Six weeks after Drummond arrived at Cumberland

House, in June 1825, he had joined the brigade of traders for the Columbia, arriving from York Factory, accompanying them for 260 miles to Carlton House. The unsettled state of the First Nations convinced him to remain with the brigade until it reached the Rockies. The swampy, wooded country on the route to Fort Assiniboine necessitated the abandonment of some luggage, leaving him with paper for drying plants, a few shirts and a blanket. He spent the winter with almost nothing to do, living in a hut made from the branches of trees since he did not have a tent, while depending on a hunter who brought him scant supplies at irregular intervals. As the weather improved, he made for the Columbia Road Portage where he was abandoned by the hunter and thus forced to botanise locally. Finding another hunter/ guide to lead him to Smoking River, he again almost starved, noting that the hunter's wife, 'a young half-breed woman, bore the abstinence with indifference, although she had two infant sons at the breast'. He was able to make a quick trip across the mountains to examine the vegetation and enjoy the superior climate. In the spring he received a message from Richardson inviting him to meet at Carlton House. Again, he suffered from hunger and snow-blindness, soon cured when he met the doctor. In all, Drummond reckoned he had collected 1,500 species of plants, 150 birds, 50 quadrupeds and 'a considerable number of insects'. In 1824–5 he published an exsiccate (dried samples) of mosses, *Musci scotici*, in two volumes.

Franklin, followed a couple of days later by Richardson, left Cumberland House for Norway House, arriving on 24 June 1827. Here, Franklin remarks, almost as if it was an expected daily occurrence, they met Mr Douglas,

> who had been sent to the Columbia River by the Horticultural Society, as a Collector of Natural History, and who had recently crossed the Rocky Mountains, for purpose of proceeding to England from Hudson's Bay. This gentleman being desirous of occupying himself previous to the arrival of the ship, in making an addition to his collection from the neighbourhood of the Red River Colony, I felt happy in being able to give him a conveyance, in the canoe with Dr Richardson and myself, through Lake Winnipeg, to Fort Alexander, where he met another canoe that was going to the colony.[24]

This was David Douglas, a botanist and naturalist from Perthshire. He had arrived at the mouth of the Columbia in 1825, accompanied by John Scoular,

a Glasgow surgeon. All the way to York factory Douglas was tripping over
fellow-countrymen in one of the greatest wildernesses in the world; as I have
suggested elsewhere, the Scots haunted their own metaphor.[25] One of his
encounters involved the famous buffalo wrestler Finan Macdonald, captain
of the militia in Glengarry County, Ontario, and a Canadian MP. Charged
by a buffalo, Douglas was believed to be dead but as he later explained he
survived by holding on to the beast's 'wig'! Franklin helped him to Norway
House, where he was treated by Richardson.[26]

They said goodbye to Augustus at Norway House. Franklin thought the
interpreter's tears showed the strength of his feelings, and the affection was
mutual. Ooligbuck also communicated through Augustus that he would
quit his family and country at any time for another expedition. In much
more time than it takes to tell, the explorers reached Montreal, New York
and finally Liverpool on 26 September 1827. They had been gone for two
years, seven and a half months. Back, Kendall and Drummond followed
a full month later, bringing tragic news of the death of Archibald Stewart
from consumption and of Gustavus Aird from drowning on the Slave River.
Franklin had desperately hoped to be able to report that on this expedition
nobody died, but that was not to be.

*

Richardson returned to full-time doctoring. He was appointed Chief
Medical Officer of the new Melville Naval Hospital at Chatham, a position
in which he was recognised as a particularly hard worker, setting standards
which he expected his subordinates to replicate. He continued to think
about exploration: 'I have practically shown that ten men are sufficient to
navigate two boats along an equal extent of Arctic coast.' An earlier commanding officer of the hospital had been James Lind from Edinburgh,
who researched scurvy and fevers, the latter partly inspiring the subject of
Richardson's own doctoral thesis on yellow fever; scurvy was a concern of all
naval captains of the eighteenth and nineteenth centuries, as it had been for
a millennium. In 1753 Lind published his research in *A Treatise of Scurvy*,
which showed the efficacy of citrus fruits in overcoming the disease. This too
was known, but Lind's work was based on empirical evidence enabling his
biographer to state that 'he set other researchers on the path to a practical
cure for scurvy'.[27] Richardson introduced the practice of having all patients
visited by a surgeon daily before breakfast. Dr Joseph Dalton Hooker, who
worked under him, admired his bedside manner: 'His words of accost [on

first approach], whether of recognition, sympathy or congratulation, were wonderfully few and pithy, and he had a clever way of questioning, that drew from the patient much more information than he apparently sought', about his staff as well as the sick.[28] A possible suggested link with his home town was Crichton Royal Hospital, Dumfries, opened in 1839 by Elizabeth Crichton as 'a lunatic asylum', since Richardson initiated the treatment of mentally disturbed sailors when he was promoted to Physician of the Fleets at the Royal Naval Hospital Haslar at Gosport. He was an early user of ether anaesthesia, the first public demonstration of which took place in Boston on 16 October 1846, where it was witnessed by, among others, ship's surgeon Dr William Fraser of Dumfries, who arrived back home on 16 December, heading straight for Dumfries Royal Infirmary. There within two days it was used by a surgeon named William Scott to amputate a leg, the first such operation in the UK or Europe.[29] Since Richardson adopted ether early, the link with Dumfries is intriguing. He set up research centres at Chatham and Haslar for the investigation of all aspects of natural history, a subject that would prove to be his magnificent lasting memorial.

The first volume of his *Fauna Boreali-Americana* was published in 1829, the last in 1837, four splendid books, the first on quadrupeds, the second on birds (a collaboration with William Swainson), the third on ichthyology, which Richardson wrote alone – he was probably the world's greatest authority on fish in his day – and lastly insects, *Entomologia Boreali Americana*, a subject of considerable complexity, which he wrote in collaboration with the Rev. William Kirby. All were published 'Under The Authority Of The Right Honourable The Secretary Of State For Colonial Affairs'. He described the first volume as a 'sketch' because his exploration duties did not provide very much time for the serious study of natural history. His technique in compiling his Northern Zoology is to describe the creature's size, shape, colouring, teeth and peculiarities. 'I am at a loss to imagine how [the American marsh-shrew] procures a subsistence during the six months of the year in which the countries it inhabits are covered with snow.'

In a lengthy section on bears he provides fascinating information on First Nation beliefs concerning the killing and consumption of the animals, drawing also on evidence from Russia and Lapland about ceremonial custom and folklore. He points out that some tribes refuse to consume bear meat; HBC collects around a thousand bear pelts per annum but the demand is declining since muffs are no longer fashionable in Europe; skins that fetched between twenty and forty guineas now sell for less than forty shillings. Richardson heard a story from Cascathry on the first expedition of how the old warrior saw a large bear on the other side of a stream studying him. His only defence was to address him. 'Oh Bear! I never did you any harm; I have always had the highest respect for you and your relations, and never killed any of them except through necessity. Go away Bear, and let me alone, and I promise not to molest you'. The bear walked off. He was a grizzly, a designation which Richardson did not favour, preferring 'Barren-ground bear'. Richardson introduces *Ursus maritimus*, the polar or sea bear, by recounting the vicious attack by one of the crew of Barentz's ship in 1594. No pacificatory language is mentioned on this occasion. Two men were mangled to death, before the bear, still relishing his prey, was shot in the eye. A Scot in the party finished him off with his sabre. Today the sight of polar bears roaming along the shore, or a mother swimming with her cubs in search of food, is becoming rarer each year. Although they continue to provide utterly iconic encounters with the Arctic, tragically, in all probability, not for much longer.

Other points of information mentioned by Richardson in volume 1 of his *Fauna Boreali-Americana* include that 100,000 skins of martins are taken annually in the fur countries. The First Nations consider the skunk excellent food. Some 8,000 otter pelts are exported to England annually. There is useful discussion about wolves, the characteristics of which are shared by European and American specimens. Captain Lyon is quoted on sledge dogs, trained from the wild packs of their cousins. Arctic foxes can imitate the cry of the brent goose. Canadian lynxes have never been known to attack a human. First Nations and voyageurs are very partial to feasts of beaver, discouraged by the fur companies because the practice ruins the valuable pelts. The scientific name of the tawny marmot is *Arctomys (Spermophilus) Richardsonii*. Discussion of various types of deer is generally about how they taste. Richardson also reports that a Rocky Mountain goat was recently presented to the Zoological Society in Britain. The Rocky Mountain sheep has been described as possessing the hair of the stag and the horns of the ram, or as having the head of a sheep and the body of a deer.[30]

The second volume in the series, 523 pages, is dedicated to birds. The first collections of Hudson Bay birds were published in George Edwards' *Natural History of Birds* (1745) but information about both birds and mammals reached a wider audience with the appearance of Thomas Pennant's *Arctic Zoology* forty years later. Richardson explains that there was not much opportunity for close study of birds on his recent expeditions but the activities of Thomas Drummond had greatly advanced knowledge. William Swainson's contribution is less interesting than Richardson's due to deficiencies in his knowledge and too many other commitments. Richardson states that the golden eagle is regarded by the First Nations as an 'emblem of might and courage', whose genius and energy were characterised by Alexander Wilson, the pioneering American ornithologist expelled from Paisley, Scotland, to the US for his radicalism, as 'fierce, contemplative, daring and tyrannical'. Benjamin Franklin, American sage, for his part, regretted that the bald eagle had been chosen as 'the emblem of our country' because it was a bird of bad moral character, dishonest, lazy, a thief, poor, lousy and cowardly! The Virginian horned owl has a full and nocturnal cry, bearing 'some resemblance to the human voice uttered in a hollow sepulchral tone', which scares travellers, as exemplified by a bunch of superstitious Scottish Highlanders in the service of HBC.[31]

Perhaps the most intriguing of the birds that haunt the Arctic are the ravens, according to Richardson. How on earth do they survive? Each time I have visited the abandoned Royal Canadian Mounted Police post at Dundas Harbour (Talluruti) on the south shore of Devon Island I have been serenaded by a raven who always croaks and crackles incessantly, recounting, as I fancy, the tragedies of Constable Maisonneuve who committed suicide there in 1926 and Constable W. Stephens who accidently shot himself the following year, while hunting walrus. Both men are buried in the tiny cemetery, the most northerly in Canada. I know that the *tuluaq* will still be there if I should ever again have the good fortune to happen by this mournful but stunningly beautiful place.

Richardson was particularly interested in fish. He must have had his own experience in mind when he related that 'no trout affords the young angler more certain amusement than the salmon fry'. A most alluring bait is a worm or a maggot impaled on a hackle. 'We have known a bare-legged truant [himself] kill thirty dozen in one day with the most inartificial tackle.' Richardson's book on game fish contains many references to Scottish rivers and lochs, notably salmon, from the Nith and rivers in Galloway. He quaintly commends Lochenbreck Loch, graced with an attendant spa in Balmaghie parish, but anyone who made the pilgrimage from Canada or America would have undoubtedly been underwhelmed. In Dumfries salmon-trout are sold as 'grilses' and hirlings.

Richardson includes drawings of fish by the late Hood and pays tribute to James Clark Ross, 'an officer who has had the singular fortune of being engaged in five successive expeditions of discovery in the Arctic seas: whose professional skill, exertions and perseverance, are the subjects and contributions of Sir Edward Parry's eulogium, and whose scientific acquirements and contributions to Natural History are so generally known, that any attempt of mine to commend him would be want of taste, were it not allowable for one who has also spent the prime of his life in the same regions and in similar occupations, to add his meed of praise to retiring merit'.[32] The samples were quite a problem. Some were described on the spot but others were sent from Canada or America in different states of preservation and composition. Insects were perhaps the easiest to transport but among the most difficult to capture.

Concerns were raised by the non-return of the John Ross expedition of 1829. Richardson planned to lead a search until it was banned by officialdom, but a public campaign resulted in a venture by George Back, which was abandoned when he received news of Ross's re-appearance in 1833.

Richardson's first wife Mary Stiven and his brother Peter both died in the early 1830s. Richardson's second wife was John Franklin's niece, Mary Booth, with whom he had five children, before she too died. He was knighted in 1846, the same year in which Sir Edward Parry was appointed Captain-Superintendent at Haslar, thus his superior, a happy choice, though Richardson, who was now Inspector of Hospitals, would probably not have tolerated anyone else in the post. Another notable of 1846 was Rear Admiral Francis Beaufort, from Navan, County Meath, who retired that year from the position of Hydrographer of the British Navy. He was the inventor of the Beaufort Wind Scale, a thirteen-point scale from flat calm to hurricane. In February 1836 Richardson had written to him, advocating a further expedition in quest of the Northwest Passage, following unusual movements of ice and whales, of interest not only in scientific circles, but also to the public in general. He believed, as surely Beaufort did too, that a water communication must exist between the two great oceans on the north coast of America, 'so it is no presumption to affirm that the search will not be finally extinguished until it is crowned with success. The lead which England has taken in this enterprise had furnished her with one of the brightest gems in her naval crown.' New discoveries would be 'an act of justice to the various tribes that have a claim on England for protection'. Such would not have included the Inuit at this juncture but Richardson's bow of burning gold was on fire.

Richardson, one of the most culturally comfortable of Scots, chose to invoke England, not Britain. He was impressed that England was a leader in the extension of geographical knowledge at large and the general advancement of science. Recent expeditions had shown the Arctic was rich in minerals, inexhaustible supplies of coal and large numbers of whales. Much of the American coast was already known, leaving a much smaller part to be delineated.

In his letter to Beaufort, he proposed a further survey to the west of the Mackenzie River, followed by a similar quest east of Point Turnagain. Both could be achieved by wintering at the north-east end of Great Bear Lake. He envisaged two officers and sixteen marines or sappers and miners 'accustomed to the oar', who had been brought up as joiners, wheelwrights, sawyers, boat-builders or blacksmiths. He knew that men would be keen to volunteer for such jobs. Bowmen and steersmen 'acquainted with the northern rivers' would be required as would 'two Canadian or Orkney fishermen'. The south end of Boothia might be an additional option. 'The co-operation of HBC is essential since that enlightened body has never failed to lend its powerful and indispensable assistance to an enterprise patronized by Government and having science for its aim'.[33] It would be twelve years before Richardson returned to the Arctic but he was right to stress the role of HBC. Although the relationship between HBC, the British Government and the Navy often appeared to be rocky, all three combined and co-operated, for good or ill, in one of history's notable partnerships.

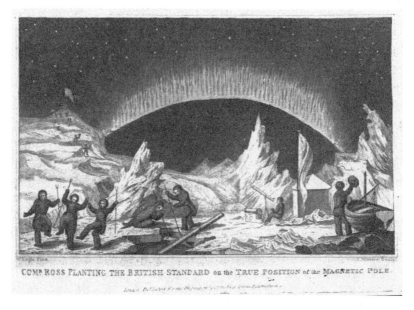

'Commander Ross Planting the British Standard on the True Position of the Magnetic Pole, 1831', from Robert Huish, *The Last Voyage of Capt. Sir John Ross, Knt. R. N. to the Arctic Regions, for the Discovery of the North West Passage* (London, 1835)

'Somerset House', from John Ross, *Narrative of a Second Voyage in Search of the North-West Passage* (London, 1835)

6

THE LONGEST WINTER

The Ross Expedition, 1829–1833

Let us be glad that we have one unspotted place upon this
globe of ours; a Pole that, as it fetches truth out of a needle, so
surely also gets all that is right-headed and right-hearted from
the sailor whom the needle guides.

Henry Morley[1]

It was an older, bolder and more sagacious John Ross who penned the
account of his astounding Arctic voyage of 1829 to 1833, a British record for
over-wintering in the region, and an achievement that captivated the global
imagination for endurance, determination and the triumph of the human
spirit. This was an expedition that travelled to the depths of a Viking Hel –
believed to be a frozen wasteland of snow and ice – to return literally from
the dead. It epitomised the finest aspirations of the seamanship, exploration,
fortitude and ambition, yet ironically it was on one level a failure which was
nonetheless admirable and even heroic. As William Scoresby suggested, it
could be seen as the prototype for the Franklin saga, save for the survival of
almost all the participants.

For John Ross personally it was an opportunity to make amends, to live
down the misunderstandings and errors of 1818, and to establish his reputation as one of the supreme Arctic adventurers, while his nephew, James Clark
Ross, was to emerge as one of the greatest-ever Arctic explorers – possibly *the*
greatest – though even more impressive achievements lay in the future. The
entire venture was unique and in John Ross, assisted by his nephew, it found
a brilliant chronicler who understood well his market and a public hungry for lurid escapades in exotic, even sublime, locations, a writer who had
learned how to capture and communicate something of the polar experience,
combined with an intriguing gift for informative introspection about novel

experiences and the horrendous burden of responsibility entrusted to the captain. All the officers and crew were participating in a spectacular drama in which Ross, rather self-servingly, cast himself as tragic hero, placed firmly in a valiant and world-transforming tradition dating back to the time of the Anglo-Saxons and the Vikings. Indeed his account of the 1818 voyage, for all its faults, provided additional benchmarks and an improved template for the accounts of future explorers. When introducing his second expedition he reiterated his earlier confirmation of the discoveries of William Baffin, who had been traduced like John Ross himself: 'It is not thus that men will be tempted to sacrifice their time, their comforts, their fortunes and their lives, in the service of mankind: but if fame must hereafter be allotted or withheld by any one who may assume the office of a judge, then let the men of ability and enterprise withdraw, unless they are of that better spirit which finds reward in approving conscience'.[2]

On his return from the 1818 expedition, Ross and his wife Christian lived at Balkail House, Glenluce, while he continued the building of his mansion, North West Castle at Stranraer, sometimes known as 'The Observatory', boasting a camera obscura on the roof. Today it is a hotel facing out to Loch Ryan, a fine sheltered harbour that Ross was keen to promote. He became interested in phrenology and the ideas of George Combe, whose society for the study of the subject he joined. It was believed that information about the brain and thus the characteristics of its owner could be revealed by study of the external features, such as bumps on the skull. The topic was bogus but quite popular. Ross arranged for imported Irish skulls to be sent to Combe, who was also the recipient of his 'Essay on Female Character', potentially a truly intriguing subject! Ross also thought that phrenology could be used to screen applicants for the Navy, though James ridiculed the suggestion.

Much more valuable was Ross's profound interest in, and advocacy of, the Navy's adoption of steam power, about which he wrote an impressive treatise, which would have required the much needed revolutionising of the entire Senior Service. He, like others, was initially ignored, the Admiralty Lordships insisting they had a 'duty to discourage to the utmost of their ability the employment of steam vessels, as they consider the introduction of Steam is calculated to strike a fatal blow at the supremacy of the Empire'. Nonetheless, Ross would be the first to take a steamship into the Arctic, admittedly unsuccessfully, the fate of many early experimenters, but he would live to enjoy the satisfaction of steamships taking part in the Franklin search. His *Treatise on Navigation by Steam* was published in 1828, reprinted

1837. His style is plain, no nonsense and very readable. He traces some 416 individuals who had contributed to the steam debate, beginning with no less a figure than Archimedes. We must assume that he considered himself to be the 417th, just as in 1818 he was the most recent of a distinguished line of Arctic explorers. He reckoned that already in 1828 there were over a thousand steamships in existence. Their adoption 'in Scotland in particular' had brought about a great change 'in the activity, commerce, and aspect of the country and in the Highlands, in the very moral character of the people'. Ross was clearly proud that a major contribution to the revolution had come about through the activities of such fellow Scots as James Watt, Patrick Miller, William Symington, Henry Bell and Robert Napier, 'the Father of Clyde Shipbuilding', in developing ships that could defy nature by driving against ebb, flow and, crucially, wind.

John Ross continued to promote an expedition to the Arctic by means of steamship, suffering a number of rebuffs from different quarters, before persuading the gin magnate Felix Booth to donate £10,000 to the project. In Liverpool, Ross puchased *Victory*, an 85-ton, oak-built paddle-steamer for £2,500. She had been employed as a mail-packet for the Isle of Man and occasionally Ireland.

Ross's journal is the main guide to his expedition, supplemented in part by Robert Huish, an anti-Tory writer dismissed by literary criticism as a hack, 'an obscure and unscrupulous scribbler', who was actually an expert on bees and produced books on many other subjects, among them *The Last Voyage of Capt. Sir John Ross, R.N. Knt*. His shipboard informant was William Light, purser's steward on *Victory*, an ideal position for acquiring intimate knowledge of every aspect of the ship and all of its occupants. Ross's *Narrative of a Second Voyage* was published in 1835, Huish's *Last Voyage* followed swiftly. Like other commentators Huish initially engages in the highly popular sport of corpse-kicking as, sixteen years after the event, he mocks the entire Crocker Mountains fiasco. He depicts the captain, 'domiciling amidst his native heather at Stranraer', adding that in public estimation the gallant captain stood, like his thermometer in Lancaster Sound, 20 degrees below zero. Later he becomes much less jovial and much more critical. At the end of the voyage Ross refused to pay him. Politically, Light was Huish's fellow traveller. Both men may have been suborned by someone in the Barrow circle.

The Admiralty eventually donated a decked vessel for supplies and equipment, which Ross named *Krusenstern*, as well as two boats. Seldom did a voyage commence in less propitious circumstances. The expedition departed the Thames on 23 May 1829 but did not reach Port Logan in Galloway until 9 June. Barely a week out, a supply of fish was purchased from a Kinsale boat, fulfilling one of the captain's main concerns, namely the use of fresh foods in staving off disease. Difficult sea and weather conditions were compounded by the failure of the steam technology, 'a cause of hourly torment and vexation to us for many weeks'. It had been Ross's great triumph to implement some of his own ideas concerning steam navigation, but the machinery was put in place in too short a time without proper trial or testing. Some part of the mechanical process seemed to fail on almost every page of his narrative, a courageous admission for such an advocate of steam. Actual progress using steam power was depressingly slow, even before 'the constructors of our execrable machinery quit the ship', after a day at sea. The boilers leaked alarmingly, necessitating the insertion of dung and potatoes to block the leaks, while a forcing pump consumed vast quantities of fresh water in temperatures above 95 degrees in which men could not work for any length of time. In addition *Victory* leaked, requiring the constant use of two pumps, although she proved quite effective under sail. Faulty pistons, loose shafts and broken keys inhibited successful progress. The engine proved completely useless. Repairs at Douglas, Isle of Man, availed little, though modifications were made to the rigging; at best the ship made three miles per hour but usually much less, using steam.[3]

The stoker, William Hardy, 'came up from the engine room unassisted, and alone, and without complaint or exclamation, presented his left arm, shattered, and nearly severed, above the elbow'. Amputation was essential, an operation swiftly and effectively carried out in the absence of either a surgeon or proper saw, by John Ross, though he had to leave the 'broken extremity in a splintery state', to be fixed up by a surgeon on land. He displayed the implacable leadership, courage and decisiveness that he possessed in abundance. 'I should have been much more at my ease in cutting away half a dozen masts in a gale than in thus "doctoring" one arm', said he, 'but I could not but be gratified by the effect which this occurrence, vexatious and painful as it was to me, produced upon the men'.[4]

More machinery crashed and it was reported that the boilers had burst, 'as if it had been predetermined that not a single atom of this machinery should be aught but a source of vexation, obstruction, and evil'. They were forced to tack towards the Irish coast, some further problems with the rigging emerging, as they suffered the ignominy of seeing ships they had already overtaken, re-passing them. Finally they made Port Logan, where Hardy was transferred to a carriage and taken to Stranraer for further treatment.

On reaching Loch Ryan, the *Victory* men learned about an original ploy of Ross's: he had commissioned a ship and her crew as a transport, intending that she would function as a whaler. He hoped to make money out of the 'big fishes' but he planned, at least initially, to keep this information from the rest of the whaling fleet. The whaleship *John* had once been owned by William Scoresby senior, founder of the Greenock Whalefishing Company.[5] Almost inevitably, with Ross's name on it, the scheme went badly wrong. William Thom, who was in charge of *John*, reported that officers and men were near-mutinous. Ross addressed them, regretting their dissatisfaction while dismissing any idea that they acted out of fear, since he knew them well and, as one who had often sailed out of Greenock, he had deliberately requested a crew from that Clydeside port. While the season might seem rather advanced, he spoke, somewhat duplicitously, of the advantage to be enjoyed from steam power, adding that he knew where an abundance of whales could be found. He urged them to return to their duties 'and not proceed in a mode of conduct which would bring disgrace both on themselves and their native port'.

After shuffling hesitation, the boatswain requested a fresh but completely unreasonable agreement. Since Ross was essentially on his home turf, assuming that if they got underway the protest would subside, he hastened back to carry out modifications to the machinery, jettisoning some seven tons of redundant equipment.

A further appeal to the whalers failed, and thirty-eight of the mutineers deserted, selling their possessions in order to buy drink. Although Ross would not recognise the phenomenon, there was a new spirit of labour solidarity in the air in 1829. The whalers had been, and still were, ruthlessly exploited by the owners. Chartism, mention of workers' rights and the promise of reform alike inspired their actions. Ross had little time for such matters. He gleefully reported the moral of the story, for *John* and her crew allegedly came to grief the following year in the throes of 'Baffin Fair' (see page 150).

Ross expressed his gratitude to his officers and men for their support, as was his way, and they accepted his suggestion that they be paid according to their rating, as in previous voyages. Scots aboard *Victory* included James Clark Ross, second-in-command, and William Thom, purser on *Isabella*, third-in-command and keeper of the meteorological journal. Like Ross they served without pay. A majority of most of the company was English but the following were almost certainly Scottish: George MacDiarmid (surgeon), Thomas Abernethy (second mate), who would serve on John Ross's final expedition, Alexander Brunton (first engineer), Allan Macinnes (second engineer), James Dixon (stoker) and George Baxter (stoker), roughly one third of the total crew of four officers and nineteen men.

Off Rathlin a ferocious storm was encountered in which the foremast snapped, fortunately becoming entangled and suspended in rigging and sails, thus avoiding the loss of the ship and two men who were aloft. The crew frapped the broken mast, while releasing other sails, in extremely difficult circumstances. Ross proudly noted that his nephew, James, was among the most active and energetic throughout this exercise. They were barely out of Scottish waters before they began to sample the edibility of various seabirds, 'in case of our coming to short allowance'. It was a simple matter to remove the birds' fishy-tasting oil confined to the fat, leaving the delicious meat. The only exception was the mollemoke or fulmar, the fat of which is rank and all pervasive. It was to the great credit of Ross that he was already intent upon sourcing as much fresh meat as possible. Having left Loch Ryan on 14 June they worked hard to attain their first sighting of Cape Farewell, Greenland, on 1 July.

Two weeks later the first iceberg was encountered and on 14 July they had a fine view of Sugarloaf Mountain in Greenland. After promising trials, the steam mechanisms again caused much trouble, detaining an anxious Ross for long periods in the engine room. In sight of a mountain named Old Woman's Hood, James Ross was sent ashore to look for an anchorage in a creek of Beacon Island; the crew did not seem to realise that they were very close to Holsteinborg (Sisimiut). They had made good progress but irritatingly the accursed boilers began to leak again.

John Ross, like most of us who have visited this part of Greenland, was much taken with the superb scenery – lofty picturesque mountains, magnificent inlets, stunning verdure and abundant wild flowers – so that they were no longer puzzled by the name. The fine weather also encouraged swarms of mosquitoes to attack with a virulence exceeding those of the West Indies. Whales, seals and shearwaters were encouragingly numerous; 453 pounds of cod and halibut were hauled out of the sea, a welcome change of diet for all, 'not less conducive to their health than it was acceptable'. They caught their first sighting of the moon since leaving Scotland but were even more delighted to see a Danish flag, which heralded the arrival of the governor and clergyman of the district of Holsteinborg in the company of numerous

1 *Admiral Sir John Ross*, by Benjamin Rawlinson Faulkner, 1834.
(National Galleries of Scotland. Given by Sir Hew Hamilton Dalrymple 1940 / Purchased 1884 / Presented by Dr J.H. Tallent 1947)

2 *Captain Sir James Clark Ross*, 1800–1862, by Stephen Pearce, 1871.
(© National Maritime Museum, Greenwich, London)

3 *Sir John Richardson*, by Stephen Pearce, 1850.
(© National Portrait Gallery, London)

4 *John Rae, 1813–1893, Arctic explorer*, by Stephen Pearce, 1853.
(National Galleries of Scotland. Given by Sir Hew Hamilton Dalrymple 1940 / Purchased 1884 / Presented by Dr J.H. Tallent 1947)

5 *Landing the Treasures, or Results of the Polar Expedition*, 1819. Engraver: George Cruikshank, artist: Frederick Marryat. This satirical print celebrated John Ross's return from his 1818 expedition.
(© Library of Congress, Prints and Photographs Division, Cartoon Prints, British)

6 'View of the Islands of Wolstenholme Sound', from John Ross, *A Voyage of Discovery* (London, 1819).

7 'A Bear Plunging into the Sea', from John Ross, *A Voyage of Discovery* (London, 1819).

8 'A Remarkable Iceberg', from John Ross, *A Voyage of Discovery* (London, 1819).

9 'Felix Harbour', from John Ross, *Narrative of a Second Voyage in Search of the North-West Passage* (London, 1835). The *Victory* was trapped and abandoned in the ice here in 1832.

10 '1st Communication with the Natives of Boothia Felix', from John Ross, *Narrative of a Second Voyage in Search of the North-West Passage* (London, 1835).

11 'North Hendon, Snow Cottages of the Boothians', from John Ross, *Narrative of a Second Voyage in Search of the North-West Passage* (London, 1835). John Ross and his party visited this Inuit village in January 1830.

12 'Ikmallick and Apelagliu', from John Ross, *Narrative of a Second Voyage in Search of the North-West Passage* (London, 1835).

13 'Shulanina, Tulluahiu and Tirishiu', from John Ross, *Narrative of a Second Voyage in Search of the North-West Passage* (London, 1835).

14 '"Umingmak", Commander J.C. Ross killing a Musk Bull', from John Ross, *Narrative of a Second Voyage in Search of the North-West Passage* (London, 1835). Ross shot this musk-ox bull (*umingmak*) during a hunting trip in 1830.

15 'Kutchin Warrior and his Wife', from
John Richardson, *Arctic Searching Expedition*
(London, 1851).

16 'Kutchin Woman and Children', from
John Richardson, *Arctic Searching Expedition*
(London, 1851).

17 'Dance of the Kutcha-Kutchi', from John Richardson, *Arctic Searching Expedition* (London, 1851).

Greenlanders (Kalaallit). The latter had assumed *Victory* was wrecked since they were unaccustomed to seeing ships in the particular berth they had chosen and they offered a preferable anchorage. Conversing in English, the Rosses were informed that the present season was the mildest in living memory, suggesting that the time was propitious for the discovery of the Northwest Passage, if it existed. They were given a salute on arriving at the community, which comprised two wooden houses for the Danes, a church, a bakehouse, two storehouses and about forty native huts. Ross chatted in Danish with the clergyman's wife; he praised their concern for the spiritual and material welfare of their flock, protesting that it was beyond the power of his pencil to capture the beauty of the surrounding scenery. Supplies were also purchased and items traded with the Kalaallit. James Ross and George MacDiarmid collected plants and other specimens.

The governor's hospitality was bountiful as he dispensed excellent wines. The explorers were informed that some 3,000 reindeer skins were exported annually to Denmark while whales, seals and fish were also taken. Very few cases of immorality were reported, the Greenlanders being 'so mild and pacific as to afford no instances even of common fighting'; they were never the aggressors in conflicts between them and Danish settlers or other Europeans. Ross was delighted to find a garden in which vegetables, scurvy-grass and sorrel, 'so useful to people consuming such quantities of the grossest animal food', were abundant. The main diseases were pulmonary or catarrhal, but he jocularly considered that patients could not suffer too much from medicine since the nearest medic was 200 miles away, 'and even there, his practice is not extensive enough to afford him means of doing much harm'! When a native handed over an oar from one of *Victory's* boats that he had found, he was surprised, as well as delighted, to be rewarded for his honesty, prompting an observation from Ross on 'the natural character of this race' who were 'among the most worthy of all the rude tribes yet known to our voyagers, in whatever part of the world'.

A wrecked whaleship (*Rookwood*) in Holsteinborg harbour provided a replacement mizen mast. The Danes were happy for them to take some of the ship's provisions. They reinforced the point that the present season was the mildest anyone in the community could remember, the winter having generated little frost. The visitors dined on venison, were shown over the settlement and admired the church, which could accommodate 200 people. John Ross acquired six dogs that he obviously intended for sledging.[6] It was almost time to depart. He sketched the mountains, having written a few letters home, to be sent on by the Danes. He attended a church service, greatly appreciating the singing of the women, commending the ability of the Moravians, in particular, to cultivate and encourage this talent for music. There can be little doubt that the sometimes boorish Ross was genuinely impressed by this experience; it was with genuine regret and gratitude that he weighed anchor on 26 July.

En route the company lost a top-mast, and an able seaman, John Wood, broke his leg jumping into *Krusenstern* after its tow-rope broke. The spectacular mountains of Disko were surprisingly snow-free, further suggesting benign warming. Soon they were back at Hare Island and Four Point Island, visited in 1818. Forty icebergs, all apparently melting, were counted. A ship with all sails set was reported to be bearing down on *Victory*. The officer of the watch, Mr Thom, and all on deck identified it as a ship, but it turned out to be an iceberg. Ross, sensitive to mis-sightings, was obviously glad of the corroboration on this occasion. They were now at the point where *Hecla* and *Fury* were beset in 1824, at latitude 73°53' N, but so far they had seen no ice. An unknown bird that flew on board was taken as a good omen by the sailors, whose 'nautical superstitions' Ross was happy to encourage if it boosted their spirits and gave them something to talk about. The temperatures of sea and air at noon and midnight was 40°, the sea and sky 'resembling more what we should have expected in the Mediterranean than in such regions as Baffin's Bay'; at six in the morning the sailors, shoeless and sockless, were out scrubbing the decks. There were still problems with the boilers but even the engine seemed to be working better.

Ross ironically commended as 'great, original and glorious indeed, the idea of ploughing the Arctic fields of ice, by means of steam', but he was also of the opinion that if his experiments with steam power in the Arctic succeeded, he would have silenced a bunch of carping, cavilling wiseacres intent on ridiculing his attempts, though he considered that he had picked the wrong engine for the job.[7] He wrote that 'it was a sight at once exhilarating and flattering to the spirit of the nation, to witness the enthusiasm which appeared to pervade the minds of all the ranks of people', as they cheered the departure of Ross's gallant vessel, which was perhaps destined to carry the flag of Britain 'where no flag ever waved before'. In the later stages of his account Huish became very critical of Ross but at the outset of his lengthy text he was quite supportive in many respects, agreeing with some of Ross's misgivings at the approach of winter, when even the most courageous are influenced by 'the darkness of disappointment closing fast upon them, and the day star of hope is shrouded in the gloomy clouds of despair'.

Ross was a shining example to his men, whether up all night trying to fix a feed pump, or taking possession of an island on an ocean that had never been ploughed by a British keel. When beset in the ice, the captain had the crew make mats, 'an occupation as much in unison with the professional avocations of the sailor, as if they had been placed cross-legged upon a tailor's board, to sew the seams of a flushing jacket', but he approved his attempt to save them from ennui and idleness.[8] Ross was good at inventing jobs that achieved little except distraction. He set up a reading class, featuring the bible. For sheer tenacity, Huish compared him, humorously, to Napoleon, but he had to confide that the crew, debilitated by weather conditions, muttered criticisms of their leader's decisions. Many bickerings and quarrels arose, not attributable to any degeneracy of disposition but to disappointment and anxiety.[9] Such is human nature.

They had now crossed to the west side of Baffin Bay. As they approached Lancaster Sound on 6 August, Ross could not resist reflecting on his previous visit and the uproar that had ensued. He quoted Parry's observation that Lancaster Sound had 'obtained a degree of notoriety beyond what it might otherwise have been considered to possess'. People had assumed that he and Parry must have disagreed in 1818 but the latter's duty as a junior officer was to communicate any difference of opinion to his captain; since he did not do so he obviously did not have one. If he had thought there was a passage through Lancaster Sound he should have spoken up, as should any other officer of that opinion. On that pinpoint of a vast ocean, the decision of eleven years earlier still clearly haunted him. Herein the flaw that characterised John Ross can be clearly detected. He knew himself to be right, but even he was not totally convinced of that right. He was quite correct in asserting that there was no need to recur to 'this history of times long past', so why remind people of it? Why grind their faces in his own mistake? Or was there in John Ross a beautiful honesty? What was it that compelled him to return to the scene of his greatest failure, which yet should have been the place of his greatest triumph, if not to confront himself, in the empty deserts of the Arctic that were as lonely as the burden of command itself?[10] Ross's bouts of introspection are arguably the most interesting parts of his *Narrative*, alongside his accounts of the Inuit.

Having been the first to attempt using steam across Baffin Bay he now tried to power his way through Lancaster Sound with the usual dismal consequences, the engine yet again proving 'a frequent subject of execration', by now affecting the weary reader almost as profoundly as it did the crew. Passing Cape York, where the compasses failed to work, they headed for the west side of Prince Regent Inlet, by-passing Batty Bay (which would later figure in their plans) to make land near Elwin Bay, about ten miles north of where *Fury* was wrecked.[11] In thirty-six hours they had penetrated far beyond the point reached in 1818.

John and James, together with William Thom and MacDiarmid the surgeon, landed on Fury Beach in mid August and the bounty abandoned by Parry. Only the mess tent of *Fury*'s officers was still standing. The polar bears had been there before them. A pocket in the tent near the door, containing James's memorandum book and some bird specimens,[12] had been torn away. However, the preserved meats and vegetables were still intact after four years. The canisters had survived ursine investigation – remarkably given what is now known about the polar bear's incredibly well-developed sense of smell – and the unspoiled contents had not frozen.[13] Wine, sugar, bread, flour and cocoa were also fine, the lime juice and pickles edible. The folded sails were in excellent condition but the spun yarn had been bleached white. Not a shred of *Fury*'s hull was to be seen; it was assumed she had been carried off and ground to atoms by the ice.

The crew jokingly referred to the North Pole Victualling Yard. They had found the Arctic's first superstore, where all the goods were free, but Ross took an enormous gamble since the stores could easily have met with the same fate as the ship. In this regard, at least, his luck held. Thom was busy supervising the transfer of goods and ten tons of coal. Other equipment included a spare mizen top-mast, some anchors and hawsers, with boatswain's and carpenter's stores; boxes of candles had been devoured by mice or ermines; ropes and cables were sound. The carronades were slightly affected by rust. The gunpowder was perfectly dry; as requested by Parry, they took what they needed and then blew up the rest lest it should injure any Inuit. Thus 'somewhat like Robinson Crusoe' they helped themselves to whatever might be of use to them from the wreck, before heading southwards in search of the American continent, following the coastline of the land Ross named Boothia after his wealthy patron.

Next day found them drifting in the ice. Few things are much more boring than a beset ship for there is generally nothing to report. The men were allocated various tasks, such as warping the ship to the north side of the floe to be well placed should the ice open. Ever-present boredom hovered just above the surface of the ice. Distance gained was soon lost in the eternal drift and cycle of rain, wind, fog and snow; 'thus we found use for our patience'. Weeks were spent in literally waiting for clear water, an ever receding possibility as winter advanced. The ship was moved to supposedly more advantageous positions, which proved nothing of the kind; readings and measurements were taken daily and some two-hourly. When weather and topography allowed, vantage points were sought, though as often as not 'the aspect of desolation was indeed extreme'. The captain echoed George Lyon, who in 1824 wrote 'I cannot but be aware that these compass and celestial bearings which are so often repeated, must fatigue many of my readers, and render the narrative of a very dull voyage doubly tedious', but they were a large part of naval experience.[14]

They were liberated when, caught in equinoctial tides, the iceberg to which they had attached the ship was driven through a rocky channel in the midst of masses of ice and a confusion of noise and colliding elements 'which was truly awful', only to place themselves in further danger. John Ross rose to the occasion in a powerful passage of description, which, as a classic of ice-writing, deserves to be quoted once more.

> To those who have not seen a northern ocean in winter – who have not seen it, I should say, in a winter's storm – the term ice, exciting but the recollection of what they only know at rest, in an inland lake or canal, conveys no ideas of what it is the fate of an Arctic navigator to witness and to feel. But let them remember that ice is stone; a floating rock in the stream, a promontory or an island when aground, not less solid than if it were a land of granite. Then let them imagine, if they can, these mountains of crystal hurled through a narrow strait by a rapid tide; meeting, as mountains in motion would meet, with the noise of thunder, breaking from each other's precipices huge fragments, or rending each other asunder, till, losing their former equilibrium, they fall over headlong, lifting the sea around in breakers, and whirling it in eddies; while the flatter fields of ice, forced against these masses, or against the rocks, by the wind and the stream, rise out of the sea till they fall back on themselves, adding to the indescribable commotion and noise which attend these occurrences.[15]

Temporarily escaping the ice, they were propelled by the elements to the mainland, Eclipse Harbour to be precise, from which they sailed south, naming Lax Island, Mary Jones Bay, and Christian's Monument, the latter a tomb-shaped mountain, honouring Ross's late wife. At Cape Verner and Joanna Harbour on 14 September they went through the usual taking-possession ceremony, 'since even that which is nugatory and absurd must be done where custom dictates', a revealing and insightful observation, diminishing the kabloonas.

Ross contributed a few paragraphs on the impact of temperature upon the human body: damp air feels cold and raw, while dry air increases evaporation, a source of cold. Another consideration is fog: 'The power of generating heat varies exceedingly in different individuals'. Ross reveals that he himself does not feel the cold to the same extent as many others. Those with large appetites produce heat, while dyspeptics suffer from cold. Since the Inuit can tolerate low temperatures because they consume vast amounts of food, it is important that sailors are very well fed. Ross criticises the Navy's one-size-fits-all attitude towards diet, and states that supplies must be increased for future Arctic voyages. He shows a most welcome awareness when he notes that it would be very desirable indeed if the men could acquire the taste for Greenland food, since all experience showed that 'the large use of oil and fat meats is the true secret of life in these frozen countries'. Men of sanguine temperament are to be preferred to those who are phlegmatic or melancholic. Another aid to good health is down to the commanding officer, 'to keep up spirits and hopes by any means that he can contrive', an excellent defence, for example, against scurvy. Clothing is obviously another issue but the individual must also generate his own heat, otherwise the effect is 'the attempt to warm a piece of ice by means of a blanket'.[16]

Since the steam technology had proved a massive, time-consuming, frustrating, heart-breaking disappointment, Ross decided to dispense with it; they would revert to sail alone. They were now at a place to be named Felix Harbour, which increasingly looked like becoming their home for a considerable time. John reflected that, while they were busy and active, their perpetual efforts, 'as is usual in life, prevented us from thinking of the future, from seeing that evil which could not forever be protracted, was drawing nearer every hour, that it was coming every minute, that it was come'. He was comparing the onset of frozen darkness to death itself, both of which humankind blindly hoped to somehow resist, prolonging the inevitable, 'when the ship falls asunder on the rock, and the sun fades before the eyes of the dying man'. The prison door was about to close as the long and dreary months loomed ahead. No-one could expect to lead an active life; indeed it was not known if they could find anything useful to do, though it was obviously important to wellbeing to contrive employment, supported by patience and hope. The worry was that the monotonous dreariness of the scenery would affect the men.

> Amid all its brilliancy, this land, the land of ice and snow, has ever been, and will ever be a dull, dreary, heart-sinking, monotonous, waste, under the influence of which the very mind is paralyzed, ceasing to care or think, as it ceases to feel what might, did it occur but once, or last but one day, stimulate us by its novelty; for it is but the view of uniformity and silence and death. Even a poetical imagination would be troubled to extract matter of description from that which offers no variety; where nothing moves and nothing changes, but all is forever the same, cheerless, cold and still.[17]

Ross was grasping at boredom as a literary genre as well as a very real and enervating human experience. It is striking that the man who lived the Arctic saw it as a place of 'frozen darkness' and death, whereas Mary Shelley, who had never been there, imagined a place of everlasting light.

*

Ashore they shot some white hares, found bear tracks and 'a great number of those cairns, or stones, resembling men when at a distance', in other words, *inuksuit*, the purpose of which, according to Ross, was to scare deer, presumably during hunts, though he could not explain the precise function of 'a rude stone of columnar form, erected by the Esquimaux'.[18] By early October the crew were sawing a channel through the quickly thickening ice and hauling *Victory* in to the protection of Felix harbour. Winter preparations progressed, removing steam machinery and stowing unnecessary equipment. An inventory of the stores indicated sufficient food for two years and ten months on full allowance, which must have been a comfort to those who, according to their fanciful leader, had reached the 'tranquillizing conclusion' that they had now become 'a little united and settled family'. On the other hand, men who valued omens, 'were left to speculate on the prophesying of a raven which flew round the ship'.

Krusenstern was secured for the season, and the erection of a roof over *Victory* commenced. As added protection a bank of ice and snow was built

147

up around her. The galley was moved to the centre of the sleeping quarters to distribute the heat more equally. A plate-iron tank was placed on the upper deck above the coppers – the large cooking pots used on shipboard – to trap and condense the steam. At other outlets similar tanks were placed, collecting on average four bushels of ice per week, which was then recycled as water. Ross was immensely proud of the success of these devices. As he observed, without them, the men themselves would have been the condensers, generating much vapour and internal rain. Self-congratulation was, he felt, in order, especially rejoicing, as a parsimonious Scot, that they were contrived 'by means as simple and little expensive as they were rigidly philosophical'. A pipe, really a type of flue, linked the upper deck with the fire, thus making the latter more easily regulated.

Only a small quantity of fuel was required to maintain a comfortable temperature of about 55 °F on the lower deck, which housed the crew's quarters. Violent snowstorms interrupted some of these preparations and haste was made to complete the sail roof as increased protection against the cold. Ross banned the issue of grog (gin), which he considered a pernicious influence contributing to scurvy; only a year's supply remained, to be used for medical and emergency purposes. The captain was gratified that these orders were received 'without remonstrance'.[19] Grog, allegedly liberally consumed by Ross himself, continued to be an issue.

The men slept in hammocks removed at six in the morning, hung up at ten at night, and aired twice a week. The lower deck was covered with sand every day and scrubbed until breakfast at eight. When the upper deck was covered in two feet of snow tramped down, sand was sprinkled on it to create a kind of gravel walk. An ante-chamber was created between the outside upper deck and steerage in which incomers had to disrobe to avoid carrying wet clothes and cold air into their living quarters. All rigging was taken down and stowed. All normal duties continued, weather permitting, while daily exercise – walking round the deck under the roof for a set number of hours – was obligatory.

As winter settled in, there was precious little to report. The armourer, one of the Greenock mutineers, fell sick, the only invalid. Huish praised the excellent health of the men as a result of activity and exercise. Ross enthused about the brief Arctic light.[20] The onboard school was expanded to writing, arithmetic, mathematics and navigation. Out of eighteen who attended, three could not read and write, while most were deficient in arithmetic. The three mates taught astronomy and navigation. Classes ended with bible readings and psalm singing. The men were permitted a dance on Saturday night, the music supplied by the carpenter.

James Clark Ross investigated ashore where the astronomical and magnetic observatories were set up in early December. There he and his uncle spent most of their mornings. Christmas Day 1829 opened with a wonderful display of the Northern Lights, 'occupying the whole vault above'. Similar examples of the Aurora Borealis had been observed in previous weeks. Christmas dinner was Galloway beef, and the grog ban was temporarily rescinded. The crew also enjoyed mince pies as well as iced cherry brandy with fruit retrieved, bizarrely, from the *Fury* stores. Flags were displayed, and planet Venus was in attendance. Ross thought this truly a happy occasion, more appreciated by those who experienced few such days than by people whose lives of luxury rendered them insensible to such hard-won enjoyments.[21]

In summing up the year at the end of December, John Ross rejoiced that no-one had suffered from frostbite. All were in good health save for the armourer, who was dying, but he would have been in the same plight had he remained in Greenock and he was reconciled to the inevitable. So far there had been no need to invent many idle amusements to kill time; those attending school were allegedly enjoying themselves too much to indulge in such frivolity. Both good and evil had been experienced over the past year, but the crew were in a much more advantageous position than they could have expected. Thus far, they had 'pursued the chimera of the Northwest passage', generating hopes that greater results would be forthcoming in finally solving the riddle of the last unknown chunk of American geography. Huish reported that William Light welcomed the extra rations of grog and preserved meats on New Year's Day with singing and dancing at night. As a singer and a musician, Light was probably quite popular with most of the men.

Ross thought that, at home, half of them would have been inebriated, 'that being the exclusive road to happiness in the estimation of our countrymen', who liked to enjoy themselves *bien tristemen* (very sadly). The landscape of New Year presented the dreariest prospect conceivable, 'unaccompanied by a single circumstance of the picturesque, or anything capable of exciting the smallest interest'. The voyager in this 'wretched country' might be a poet or a painter but any descriptive talents would be useless unless 'he has the hardihood to invent what there is not to see'.

The first half of 1830 was to be taken up with welcome and intriguing interaction with Netsilik Inuit, sparing John Ross from recording the trivial and the mundane, while, in addition, his nephew undertook several important exploratory expeditions in and around Boothia peninsula. From 'a most interesting association of natives' the explorers learned the important information that 'we had already seen the continent of America'. About 40 miles to the south-west there were two great seas to the west and east, separated by 'a narrow strait or neck of land'. When JCR investigated with two colleagues and two Inuit, he established that the north land on the Boothia Peninsula was connected to the southern mainland by two ridges of high land 15 miles broad, reduced to 5 miles by a series of freshwater lakes. Further tracing of the coast led to Akulee and Repulse Bay (Naujaat).[22] Huish, informed by Light, considered that the Inuit, 'insulated by nature from the rest of the world', had no idea of other human beings 'and there is more of the true spirit of contentment to be found amongst them than is probably to be met with in any other class of mankind whatsoever'. He greatly applauded the ingenuity of some of their culture but he added that Booth's gin made them merry and familiar, a wounding claim that Ross would have denied, since there is some evidence that the Inuit did not enjoy the taste. Already though, Ross was purchasing items to be displayed in panoramas on his return home. Huish believed that he forbade trade with the Inuit in order that he could acquire items at knock-down prices: dogs, clothing, weapons, furs and sledges, all intended to demonstrate the reality of Felix Harbour, rather than the existence of the Croker Mountains.[23]

As the weather warmed, mosquitoes and melt arrived together. There was a sense of anticipation that liberation must only be a matter of time, as the ships were painted and prepared, tackle stowed and everything made ready, but otherwise there was little to report, save for some spectacular catches of trout. By the end of August they had been anchored to the same spot for eleven months. As Ross ruefully remarked, whatever value Arctic voyages had, they were bought dearly in time if nothing else; they could have circumnavigated the globe in the same period and he thought that in any case no-one was particularly hopeful about future north-west passages even if they should prove successful in their present attempt. They now realised that they had experienced an extraordinarily hard winter, which showed few signs of relenting.[24]

Indeed they had, for 1830 was the year of the notorious 'Baffin Fair' when the whaling fleets from Hull, Whitby and Scotland became trapped in the ice of Melville Bay and thus were unable to proceed northwards. George Laing from Newburgh in Fife, who was serving as a student-surgeon on *Zephyr* of

Hull, just one of thirty-three whaling ships from the town, chronicled his experiences. A ferocious storm during the last week of June and early July hit with such fury that eighteen ships were completely wrecked, crushed in the ice or rendered unserviceable. One thousand men took refuge on the ice along with such supplies as they could salvage, including casks of rum which were consumed by whalers, guzzling what they assumed might be their final intake of grog en route to Fiddlers' Green or Davy Jones Locker. The festivities and frolics inspired the ironic term Baffin Fair, but remarkably only ten men actually died. Laing's ship *Zephyr* was not one of the casualties, but he described how another whaler was caught in the ice, which 'fairly lifted her out of the water . . . as if to give us one last look of her before she parted'. The un-named captain stated that he felt incapable of depicting:

> the magnificent scene which presented itself to my view but it is one that would have suited poet or painter. The first symptoms of destruction appeared among the half-deck planks; then the standing rigging and stays became slackened and nothing was heard but the crashing of the hull as she went to pieces. Her masts meantime slowly bent towards each other, as if to take their final adieu; and when they came in collision, they seemed to say, 'and must we part?'

They then fell with a tremendous crash, and the hull was buried forever beneath a flow of ice 6 feet thick.[25]

September roared in amidst severe gales, snow and dropping temperatures. Ross's crew were back at laborious warping and ice cutting in an attempt to free *Victory*, a dead thing, which essentially remained ice-bound until, attaining clear water on 17 September, it sprang back to life under sail. The crew celebrated, 'the first burst of enjoyment on the recovery of our liberty; but we were not long in finding, as other pursuers of other liberty have found, that it was a freedom that was to bring us no happiness'. They advanced a mere 3 miles. Ice, winds and currents conspired to contain them, as another beset winter became inevitable. Ross's frustration was vented in his unkind suggestion that his nephew was responsible for their predicament in having reassured him, based on his knowledge of the area, that the ice would clear, allowing them to progress without needless risk, but at least he had the grace to admit that one or other possibility would never be known for certain. It remained to cut their way through the ice to a safe haven, which was named Sheriff's Harbour, achieved at the pathetic rate of about 45 feet per day, representing a huge amount of effort for a paltry reward; the whole month yielded an advance of 850 feet. Some of the men tried to calculate the number of centuries required to make a single north-west passage at this rate; 'others speculated on the premiums that might be demanded at Lloyd's on such a voyage'![26]

The terse entries in Ross's journal adequately convey his sense of disappointment and boredom, relating a tale of nothing to tell. Confronted with nothingness the captain resorted to reflection. He actually believed that those who reflected most were the least able to tolerate recurring disappointment. He was painfully aware that it was his responsibility to keep up the spirits of the men and to find them occupations, 'to prevent them thinking too much of the future'. September was a month of 'busy idleness' and despondency. 'He who can hope a second time as he did the first', he wrote, 'is of a more fortunate constitution than some of our people seemed to be. The despondent could not conceal their feelings; though, of the greater number, I am bound to say that their contentedness, or rather resignation, exceeded what I had anticipated'. It was his responsibility to draw the brightest possible picture by talking up their successes so far – the fine condition of the ship, the comfort it offered, the ample provisions, their peace and good health, and a safe harbour. But Ross was a true Scottish pessimist, as well as a realist: 'the bright side of life is not easily seen through the dark one'.

The ship was further prepared to over-winter at Sheriff Harbour, the observatory set up on a rock, and the school resumed. But Ross mused that the whole of life was curtailed in this region: 'sea and land, summer and winter, it is difficult to say which is worst'. The Inuit alone understood the true secret of happiness and the art of living in such desolate surroundings. A philosopher would have to admit that in this environment 'nature is not always the stepmother she has been termed'. If the Europeans had been wiser they might have imitated the natives in finding happiness in cycles of sleeping and eating, 'but we were here out of our element, as much in philosophy of life as in the geography of it'.[27]

He lamented the keeping of records and the taking of readings as nothing but the 'registries of labour', which revealed little of interest. Time went by, the men tracking animals they did not see, carrying guns they did not fire, seeking an invisible sun, and welcoming the end of a day that was actually night. Yet, thought Ross, the larger burden rested upon the captain, not because he was any more optimistic or resilient than those who obeyed, but because he had to keep objectives in view that subordinates could barely comprehend. Driven as he was by ambition or vanity, or whatever, he could contemplate gratification denied to others, who would share in the labour if not the fame, while, as some compensation, remaining free of anxiety and of any responsibility. Once again John Ross displayed perhaps the most courageous side of his character in laying bare his private thoughts on the undertaking that command represented.

Ross managed to fit the first three dreary months of 1831 into a single chapter of his journal. On 18 January the sun returned. In both January and March the temperature fell to 52 degrees below; when it hit 11 degrees below, the weather felt warm. There were considerable snowfalls. Numerous foxes were trapped for stud purposes and as food for the dogs, two of the poor beasts losing their tongues to the frozen iron of the traps. A ball of frozen mercury was fired through a plank; a similar missile made from oil of almonds remained intact when it split its target, but a ball of ice had no effect. A few birds fell to conventional shot. The men remained in good health albeit with dampened spirits. The monotony of the passing ice-bound months was lifted that summer with JCR's discovery of the Magnetic North Pole.

*

Arguably, the supreme accomplishment of the Rosses' four-year confinement in the Arctic was James Clark Ross's discovery of the Magnetic North Pole on 1 June 1831. With five companions James began his exploratory mission on 20 April. By now he had a shrewd suspicion of the location of the pole but he was unable to recruit the aid of the Inuit, as his small party crossed to the opposite shore of 'the inlet into which the Stanley river flows'. Thick fog hindered their progress but by the afternoon of the second day the sun was a cause of snow blindness, leading them to travel at night. The weather had cleared by the time they reached Lake Awatutyak. Having climbed a hill to scout their surroundings, James and Thomas Abernethy moved on to survey the inlet, and to discover that the Inuit had taken some coins from the 'monuments' the Brits had constructed two years earlier. James now knew where the pole was as he approached, marching rapidly with mounting excitement and anticipation, the site on Boothia Felix (Peninsula) about 60 miles west of Victoria Harbour:

> I believe I must leave it to others to imagine the elation of mind
> with which we found ourselves now at length arrived at this great

object of our ambition: it almost seemed as if we had accomplished everything that we had come so far to see and to do; as if our voyage and its labours were at an end, and that nothing now remained for us but to return home and be happy for the rest of our days. They were after-thoughts which told us that we had much yet to endure and much to perform, and they were thoughts which did not then intrude; could they have done so, we should have cast them aside, under our present excitement; we were happy, and desired to remain so as long as we could.[28]

James admitted that he might have wished 'a place so important had possessed more of mark or note'. After all, at the pole, 'he would shortly set his foot so that it lay between him and the centre of the earth'.[29] There was no mountain such as that of Sinbad, no towering mass of iron, 'or a magnet as large as Mont Blanc' to indicate the spot. Nature had not chosen to place any kind of monument 'as the centre of one of her great and dark powers'. It was up to the scientists to describe 'by mathematical numbers and signs . . . what they could but ill distinguish in any other manner'. The party made use of some abandoned Inuit huts as they took measurements during the next two days. The amount of the dip was 89.59°, 'being thus within one minute of the vertical'. The latitude was 70°5'17' N, longitude 96°46'45' W. Ross reported his awareness that the pole was moving as he attempted to locate it. The flag was raised, possession taken in the name of Britain and William IV, and a sizeable cairn was built. Ross rightly stated (more than once) that the subject of the magnetic pole was 'somewhat too abstruse for popular readers'.

He makes much the same point in his Royal Society lecture. The position of the Magnetic Poles had long been considered 'a desideratum in the science of magnetism of the highest importance', which has attracted the observations and experiments of the most ingenious and learned philosophers to solving 'this difficult and perplexing problem'. The main cause of magnetic phenomena remains 'one of the secrets of nature'. He acknowledges the contributions of Franklin, Sabine, Parry and Fisher. In his own search he had proposed advancing further westwards, 'guided by some Esquimaux'. It is much to JCR's credit that he envisaged a prominent role for the Inuit, a partnership in the discovery of the Pole, an event of world significance, even though they were not actually present. The print showing them celebrating the momentous occasion (see page 134) is highly appropriate but misleading.

James would have achieved more, he claimed, with better instruments and a team of men placed at strategic points to make as many measurements as possible in the quest for accuracy. Since the position of the pole was so nearly known, and in a place reasonably accessible, 'it only remains to be considered whether those who have the power to promote such an undertaking may attach sufficient importance to the subject to direct its being carried into execution'. He regards magnetic science as 'eminently British' for 'there is no other country in the world whose interests are so deeply connected with it as a maritime nation, or whose glory as such is so intimately associated with it as Great Britain'. He warmly acknowledges Felix Booth's contribution in enabling 'a few British seamen to plant the flag of their country upon the Northern Magnetic Pole of the earth'.[30] In his contribution to his uncle's *Narrative* he expresses the hope that Britain, having established its supremacy in scientific and geographical researches, will not now desert them, 'leaving others to reap the crop of which it has in this case sown the seeds'.[31]

JCR seemed incapable of rest. He and Abernethy (known as Aby) expended considerable energy in four hours of 'very quick walking' northwards to conclude that the way beyond led to Cape Walker. They erected a cairn to mark their furthest point, returning by eight in the morning. During his residence at Gjoa Haven (1903–5) Roald Amundsen was to confirm that the Magnetic Pole had an annual drift of almost 7 kilometres.[32]

*

On 25 August 1831 a whale boat was jammed between the ship and the ice to protect *Victory* as the pack moved. John Ross described the bergs as 'never-ending rocks', which were replaced as soon as they floated away, since the 'storehouse which supplied them was inexhaustible'. Ross went on to make reference to Robert Burns's immortal song 'A Red, Red Rose', and rocks melting with the sun, considered an impossible event: 'in one of the songs of my native land, to which some swain compares the durability of his affection for his beloved'. The ice-bound were beginning to think their particular rocks never *would* melt. The task of warping into an advantageous position was again commenced but with little result for the weather was just not minded to co-operate. They made precisely 4 miles finding shelter at Mundy Harbour, which Ross had named in 1829. When clear water seemed to offer escape, the wind would be against them; ice would appear almost instantaneously; or gales and currents would conspire to confuse. In early October there was a brief shifting of the ice northwards which allowed them to cut the vessel into a better berth but then the ice quickly closed in again. And that, effectively, was that. It was obvious there was no way out during the present season. As Ross observed, 'The hopeful did not hope for more, and the despondent continued to despair'.[33]

To convey a rough impression of what he was experiencing perhaps required a postmodern novel about boredom that almost nobody would read. History, like life, cannot succeed as a subject without action; the non-eventual is the opposite of historiography, impossible if nothing is happening, as is literary description of an indescribable scene, which perhaps requires an example of modern art to replicate white light or Arctic darkness. John Ross, who lived through the dismal reality, as usual, communicated the experience and the mental anguish rather effectively:

> We were weary for want of occupation, for want of variety, for want of the means of mental exertion, for want of thought, and (why should I not say it?) for want of society. Today was as yesterday, and as was today, so would be tomorrow: while if there was no variety, as no hope of better, is it wonderful that even the visits of barbarians [the Inuit] were welcome, or can anything more strongly show the nature of our pleasures, the confession that these were delightful; even as the society of London might be amid the business of London?[34]

Ross further reflected on the dullness of daily experience and the environment, which his journal adequately recorded. 'But what can the journalist do more than the navigator?' The sameness of everything was acutely depressing, and the mind was numbed by the lack of excitement. All was a weary iteration of what had gone before. The picturesque was absent, lochs and rivers displayed no beauty, and vegetation was completely lacking: 'everything was suffocated and deformed by the endless wearisome, heart-sinking, uniform, cold load of ice and snow'. How could anyone produce a book of interest and amusement out of such materials? Ice is greatly valued in Europe for recreational purposes such as skating, or in viewing glaciers or mountains. Ross had climbed Mont Blanc: 'I the fearless and enterprising, have ascended the father of mountains, yea, even when the guides hung back in fear.' Yet he commented that snow deforms landscapes and renders colour as black and white. For ten months of the year snow penetrates everything, including human bodies, in the Arctic. He admired glaciers and icebergs: 'Have I too not sought amid the crashing and the splitting and the thundering roarings of a sea of moving mountains, for the sublime, and felt nature could do no more? In all of this there has been beauty, horror, danger, every-thing ... that would have excited a poet even to the verge of madness'. To live with snow day-in and out all year is a very different matter.[35]

On Christmas Day 1831 the men dined on beef and veal, taken from *Fury*'s stores, as good as the day it was cooked some eight years past. Ross later claimed that similar cans that he had taken back with him to Scotland were just as edible in 1835 as they had been when they were processed in 1823. He mused, had such a technology been around at the time it might have been possible to dine on exotic dishes made at Herculaneum or Pompeii. Thus it could be envisaged that in a thousand years' time the enduring frost of Boothia Felix (Boothia Peninsula) might preserve the durable cans of *Fury* and 'thus deliver down to posterity the dinners cooked in London during the reign of George IV'.[36] Some of the cans which Ross took back to Stranraer are on display in the town's museum. In those that were opened, the meat was judged good. It almost beggars belief that Ross could have thought that it was worthwhile repatriating these supplies but once again he certainly showed himself the very essence of the canny Scot.

New Year brought a spectacular meteor as large as the moon. James Dixon, the stoker, died in January; it took a week to dig his grave out of the freeze. Storms raged for three weeks. Observations were impossible. Many of the crew were in an enfeebled state, suffering from ailments, if not from disease. An old wound of Ross's broke out, which he knew to be scurvy: 'he on whom all the responsibility fell was not the least victim of anxiety'. Weather patterns were repeated in February. A 'glutton' (wolverine) came on board to devour the dogs' food. It seemed inhospitable to kill it but this was the first specimen they had been able to obtain. 'Are the life and happiness of an animal to be compared with our own pleasure in seeing its skin stuffed with straw and exhibited in a glass case?' On 7 April the temperature suddenly rose to 7 degrees above, passing zero for the first time in 136 days. With the diminishing state of provisions and declining health of crew members, preparations to abandon the ship were put into action. The initial plan was to move to Fury Beach to take advantage of the remaining supplies and boats there. Over the months of April and early May the sledge boats were to transport materials and stores part way, and return, in order to facilitate advancement later. This involved the negotiation of very difficult terrain, while camping out in atrocious weather conditions, at incredibly low temperatures. Supplies were stowed in *Krusenstern* in case they had to return, while the men with their sledges went ahead, unloaded their cargoes, and returned for the next load. Humour seemed out of place but their predicament reminded some of the algebraic equation in which a person had to carry eggs to a certain point, one at a time. Snow and gales continued to plague them.[37]

*

James Clark Ross is often overshadowed in his uncle's account of the entire *Second Voyage* though he enhanced the volume by contributing a number of chapters about his own activities. Fortunately, JCR's journal has survived for the period 4 May to 14 October 1832.[38] Although somewhat repetitive, it adequately conveys the flavour of the difficult period as the crew made preparations to abandon the ship at what his uncle now called 'Victory Harbour' en route by sledge to Somerset Island to what they hoped would be salvation. His journal begins with a broken sledge and throughout, as might be expected, contains much detail on weather conditions. Much of it is tantalisingly brief, for example, 'Row about smoking'. Seven or eight men, out of ten, suffered from eye problems, forcing all to switch to night travelling. David Wood had a 'nervous fit'. JCR felt giddy and sick after hurting his back. Many hares were spotted; James indulged his scientific interest in wildlife wherever possible.

John Ross reckoned that in five weeks they had cumulatively, back and forth, traversed 320 miles in order to gain about thirty. The work was extremely painful, and the crew was starving. In this process of relocation the captain was regarded as a major liability since he had to be carried and manhandled along the route. According to Huish, it was thought by the crew that the operation would have been much shorter if James had taken over, but John and James were often at loggerheads. John was not required at all because he was seen as a drawback, more of a 'dead weight than an acquisition', a nuisance rather than a co-operative member. Dragging his 'ponderous frame' over hills and hummocks resulted in the complete exhaustion of the bearers. And so the criticisms continued; it was admitted that John Ross was a very good draughtsman but when drawing a sledge he was the very type of old mule that the nuns thumped in Sterne's *Sentimental Journey*![39]

Victory was abandoned at 10pm on 29 May 1832, along with *Krusenstern* and the masts, sails and rigging that might be of use to returning sailors or 'the natives'. All drank a parting glass of Booth's cordial to *Victory*, which sad sight Ross sketched. This was the first time that he had abandoned a ship, having sailed on thirty-six of them during a period of forty-two years. It was like parting with an old friend 'rendered even more melancholy by the abandoned, helpless home of our past years, fixed in immovable ice, till time should perform on her his usual work'.[40]

Allegedly Ross told the men to wear no more than regular apparel as they moved on, while he reserved blankets and wood for himself. He also commandeered a box of extra provisions and cordial, while hiding biscuits in his bedclothes, thus 'alienating the esteem of his men and rendering him so contemptible in their eyes'.[41] There can be little doubt that Ross reserved some supplies for his private use because Navy rules allowed for exactly that. Rank and food levels were carefully equated; the captain's table was a much grander affair than the provision for those below decks. However, it is also likely that men compared and complained for such is human nature, especially in the uncomfortable conditions in which they existed and the persistent rumour that they were on the verge of starving to death. But it is impossible to tell whether, as Huish asserted, Ross attempted to deny the party sustenance once it had reached *Fury*, for even he admits that, from then on, a recalcitrant captain allowed everyone three meals per day.

Once again Ross reflected on the particular burden of command. The public had rather a romantic view of the sailor's life, which belied reality. Anything that went wrong was 'the captain's business', be it supplies, hurricanes, accidents or the loss of sails. The men obey but, when work is done, responsibility reverts solely to the captain. Yet the crew have learned enough to disagree with the captain at times. All developments, novelties, and problems fall within 'the captain's business, a happy reponsibility on his part it cannot be denied; yet is it not one under which he deserves the praise which he does not always attain?'[42] No captain in the British Navy before Ross had ever confided the burden of command in quite this fashion, a circumstance made possible because his private expedition freed him from the restraints of the service, resulting in possibly the most compelling and revealing Arctic journal ever produced. The sailor ridiculed as the clown of Lancaster Sound was actually an incomparable sage of the sea.

The plan was to take both remaining boats to Elizabeth Harbour with supplies for six weeks. There the boats and half the provisions would be deposited while the sledges and the remainder of the stores would proceed to latitude 71° N, from where a 'light' party of five would check out the state of play at Fury Beach. Some of the men now exhibited the rebellion of fatigue. Chief mate Blanky was deputed to inform the captain that they wished to abandon the boats and provisions and head straight for Fury Beach. Ross took a hard line since they planned to leave resources at a point to which it would be impossible to return. He was emphatic that they obey orders, refusing to accept any arguments, while tearing several strips off Blanky, in order to nip this first near-mutiny in the bud. Why Ross felt compelled to include this episode in his *Narrative* is far from clear. It cannot have done Blanky any good to be advertised as a mutineer. Ross was satisfied that these difficulties were surmounted and he brought the party safely home: 'if I have not experienced the gratitude that I deserved, for this and more, I am too well experienced in mankind to be surprised, or to entertain enmity against those who only acted according to their evil natures' – strong words from a strong man. And so the plan was executed.

Predictably James Clark Ross was chosen for the descent on Fury Beach. He was ordered to leave messages daily in cairns that would be consulted by the following party, proceeding at half his rate. His target was 150 miles away via Port Logan, Possession Island, at the mouth of the Bellot Strait, unknown at the time but probably suspected by JCR to exist, where they visited the monument they had built in 1829, continuing to Cape Garry and across Creswell Bay, becoming weaker and wearier as they approached their destination in a violent gale. Arrival at Fury Beach proved therapeutic: 'joy now overcame every other sentiment and gratitude threw us prostrate on our kness to bless the name of the Power who had again saved us from ourselves'.[43] They experienced burning thirst, freezing fog, painful glare and frequent falls. JCR stated that a long rest was necessary but next day they were off again, though forced to stop because of knee pain experienced by Abernethy. John Ross having deposited provisions at pre-determined sites, and suffering conditions and fatigue that made it difficult to keep to schedule, met up with James five days later, returning from Fury, which they all reached by the beginning of July 1832. There is an indication in Ross's account that some of the men were out of control as, half-starved, they guzzled some of *Fury*'s stores and made themselves unwell. A building, 31 by 16 feet in ground area and 7 feet in height, was constructed and given the name Somerset House, since this district had been known as North Somerset. The house was divided into one room for officers and another for the men (see page 134 and Plate 21).

Carpentry work on the boats occupied the whole of July. The two Rosses agreed to disagree about the best type of sails to be used, each preferring their own. James became increasingly frustrated when John flatly refused to allow him to increase the capacity of his boat. 'When will this system of persecution end? God be praised it cannot last much longer'. After three years it is surprising that there were not more eruptions. Blanky was stricken with joint pain; Thom regularly shot dovekies for food, thereby almost eradicating scurvy. A cairn was built. The plan was to depart Fury Beach in the hope of reaching Baffin Bay before the whaling ships made for home. John and James exchanged copies of their journals and charts in case they became separated, and a bottle was buried in Somerset House giving some account of their movements. In 1843 the Hull whaler *Traveller* retrieved the bottle left by John Ross containing a summary of the expedition's achievements. It recorded their departure, the abandonment of *Victory* and their full survey of the coast, ascertaining that there was no passage between America and Asia to the south of latitude 70° N. In addition,

> they discovered the Gulf, the Land of Boothia E & W of the Isthmus of Boothia and the Peninsula of Boothia north of it – the Isthmus which divides the Gulf from the Magnitic [*sic*] Polar Sea is only fifteen miles Wide and Westward the coast was surveyed to the 100th degree of west Longitude – the Expedition having since travelled to the Northward along the coast being frozen in 3 years, Fury beach in the *Fury*'s boats on the First of August 1832.[44]

JCR packed up the magnetic instruments. Conditions for sailing were excellent but Ross favoured waiting for the third boat to be ready, his nephew lamenting the loss of a fine opportunity: 'We did not deserve to succeed when such precious moments are thrown away'. Ice, as might have been anticipated, impeded their progress making rowing difficult. After five hours they halted right below the cliff where *Fury* had foundered in 1825. The boats were hauled up on the beach just before a floe of ice crashed against the shore. They had a narrow escape, as Ross noted, not only at the spot where *Fury* came to grief, but on the same day that she was lost eight years earlier. They were still in peril, however, because as temperatures rose, stones from the cliff rained down on the boats. Falling debris from the 500-foot precipice remained a constant menace. Ross decided to move to a safer place, and this they did, only to encounter the same problem with tumbling rocks. Snow, wind and ice also remained a problem. William Thom was sent back to *Fury* to secure additional supplies but ice detained him there for some days. The weather remained exceedingly harsh with snowstorms and low temperatures combining with high winds. The men built a lookout post on some cliffs and anxiously scanned the horizon for signs of a break in the ice but to no avail. Ross himself viewed the surrounding ice fields only to reach the depressing conclusion that they were probably impassable. Lancaster Sound, Barrow Strait and Prince Regent Inlet were covered in ice. At night the men almost froze in their tents. Once again they attempted to break through to the north and once more they were defeated by the ice. There was nothing for it except to return to Fury Beach. Once again they suffered the anxiety of being detained beneath hazardous cliffs, while large blocks of floe were thrown up on the beach.

Both Rosses became convinced (the younger less so) that they had no alternative but to over-winter yet again. John revealed much about himself in a passage which harped back to the Croker Mountains identification of 1818. He realised, or convinced himself, that he was standing on Hope's Monument, which he had named at that time. Barrow Strait was now frozen exactly as it had been in 1818, rendering sea and land indistinguishable from one another. The Monument had since been designated Leopold Island, which he wished to rescind in returning to his own nomenclature, applied when he took possession: 'Since this spot is also a portion of the mainland . . . it is equally my duty to point out that the discovery of the north-east cape of the American continent thus belongs to myself, and to the original voyage I made to these northern seas.' In making these claims he rejected any charges of egotism or 'ambition for insignificant fame', for he was defending the rights of all discoverers, while, as the text fully relates, once again highlighting his personal drama: 'It is but a small reward which ever falls to their share, in recompense for all their hardships and hazards; and if they are thus to be robbed of the only name and fame they can ever hope to obtain, the effect will be to check their ardour, in addition to the injustice thus committed.' Ross then stated that Columbus was shamefully treated by his contemporaries and, while no achievement could match his, it should be remembered that 'the fame of every man, however small, is equally his right' and no less precious than that of greater achievers. Furthermore, he was convinced the sea had remained solid during the past ten years, implying that he would have made the same call at any point in the decade. He remained haunted by the memory of the abyss that the Croker Mountains represented.[45]

On 1 September Ross climbed the mountain that marked the north-east point of America (Cape Clarence on Somerset Island) to view Cape Warrender,

Cape York and Barrow Strait. There was not the smallest pool of water to be seen. Everything was precisely the same as it had been on 31 August 1818, a prospect that suggested they would have to return to Fury Beach. The records showed that the September they were experiencing was the coldest ever known, resulting in the diminution of hope, matched by the dissipation of energy. The result was enervating misery. Since the middle of August, winter had seized everything in its grip. By the end of September they found themselves occupying a beach 6 feet wide, beneath cliffs 500 feet high. Before departing, JCR visited Cape Clarence twice, on the first occasion erecting a cairn, hoisting their colours and completing their survey. On the second he was accompanied by Abernethy but had no other comment. The boats were now useless so they were stowed at Batty Bay at the end of September, while the party carried on overland with the sledges to Fury. Taylor, the amputee, was transported like a piece of cargo since he was helpless in the icy conditions; he obviously could not use his crutches, but also the sledges kept overturning on the hummocky ice. All made it safely, however, to Somerset House, though two men were suffering from frostbite and Ross had a deep cut in one of his legs.

Winter set in with a vengeance. The storms lasted three weeks; temperatures continued to fall as they reached Cape Seppings and Elwin Bay. The company's mettle was seriously challenged. Some distraction was provided by what Ross tactfully described as 'discussion', often fairly fierce, which became more 'persistent and energetic', some magnifying the team's chances of success, thus conferring some hope and courage upon the timid and desponding. He explained how each of their three tents became like separate little deliberative societies in which the leader's view encapsulated those of the men who supported him. James Ross was in charge of the most hopeful group: 'much violent contention about the propriety of returning to Fury Beach . . . All our tent are unanimous in the wish to persevere to the last'.[46] William Thom was much more of a pessimist. John Ross presided over a tent of divided opinions. He, however, kept his own counsel, deliberately removing himself from the debates, which, if true, was sensible.

On arriving at Fury some effort went into trying to improve the house, with additional heating for the officers, of whom there were four: the two Rosses, George M'Diarmid (surgeon) and William Thom RN. Each had their own room. There were eight seamen's beds, each accommodating two persons, in a very poorly heated room. A valve in the roof was designed to allow the escape of bad air and vapour. The whole building was sheathed in ice, a perfect sheen of which was created when fresh water was thrown against the walls; according to Huish, since all water was frozen, the sailors donated their urine.

As their fourth Arctic winter dragged on, 1833 brought no respite, but Ross's journal entries were much shorter. Perfect storms, gales, drifting snow, moving ice and darkness produced little to relieve the tedium and monotony of existence. The men obviously experienced much more cold than they had on *Victory*. The carpenter, Chimham Thomas, died, missed by everyone, the first death that could be attributed to the climate and circumstances of the expedition. He was by all accounts an excellent character, forty-eight years old when he died, at that time of life when a seaman with his service was an aged man, if not totally worn out, as Ross noted. Several of Ross's own wounds were opening, raising recurrent fears of incipient scurvy, and he began to contemplate the possibility of his own death, though he claimed his major concern was how the men might fare in his absence.

One problem was that the harshness of the weather prevented the men from exercising outside. Ross thought that poetry might just once be able to describe the miserable conditions, 'which neither poetry nor prose can repeat forever, with the hope that any one can listen, and understand, and feel'. Also, they were on reduced rations and 'the inevitable lowness of spirits produced by the unbroken sight of this dull, melancholy, uniform, waste of snow and ice, combined to reduce us all to a state of very indifferent health'. One bonus was that reindeer and dovekies appeared unseasonably early. Thom was now ill and two of the seamen were suffering very badly from scurvy. Ross eloquently reflected on how weary they had become of Somerset House, which a few months earlier they had been so relieved to reach. Days lacked variety, one storm much like another in the 'eternal sameness of snow and ice'. He apologised for his journal with its 'unavoidable repetition of similar occurrences'.

The most fortunate among them were those who 'dozed away their time in waking stupefaction', he thought, promptly contradicting himself by suggesting that on the other hand those who had responsibilities and minds filled with prospects and schemes probably fared better.

> Let him who reads to condemn what is so meagre, have some com-
> passion on the writer who had nothing better than this meagreness,
> this repetition, this reiteration of the ever-resembling, everyday
> dullness to record, and what was infinitely worse, to endure. I
> might have seen more, it has been said: it may be; but I only saw

ice and snow, cloud and drift and storm. Still I might have seen what I did not; seen as a painter, and felt as a poet; and then, like painter and poet, have written. That also may be, but let painter and poet come hither and try: try how far cold and hunger, misery and depression, aid those faculties which seem always best developed under the comforts of life, and under that tranquillity at least, of mind, if not much more, which the poet and writer require to bring their faculties into action . . .[47]

In mid April they began to make preparations for a new attempt at Baffin Bay. Under the command of JCR, supplies were conveyed to depot points on the route. This was an example of acute forward planning since they did not expect to man the boats until the beginning of July. The thoroughly exhausting, and above all tedious, work continued through May and June: 'To us it was so: it cannot be otherwise to a reader'. The boats stowed the previous September at Batty Bay were recovered in late May. Ross was resting in the hut there when around midnight a bear removed the stones supporting the canvas roof and the creature fell into the structure, almost landing on Ross himself. Not realising the nature of his visitor he called out who was there and then fired as *Ursus maritimus* took off.[48] Huish was able to demonstrate that he had read *Tristram Shandy*; he also introduced a very rare word, meaning an alternative or a substitute: when the foxes had consumed all the pork and beef, they ate the tops off the steward's sea-boots, by way of a *succedaneum*.

One advantage of the return of the Arctic summer was the accompaniment of game birds: ducks and auks accounted for some very welcome variety in the diet. The time had now come to abandon Somerset House. An acute problem was the number of the sick, who quite simply could not fend for themselves. The three heaviest men in the crew could not walk. Others were just barely mobile but were of no help in hauling any of the gear. Apparently Ross received some criticism on his return to England for his failure to abandon the sick, thus jeopardising the wellbeing of the healthy, but he claimed that such a possibility never occurred to him. His claim is perfectly believable because he took pride, in all of his expeditions, in reporting minimium numbers of deaths, or preferably none at all. Much more serious was an assertion, presumably originating with steward William Light, that Ross considered abandoning the dying mate, George Taylor, to his fate. The latter had lost half of a foot to frostbite, had to use crutches and could not walk.[49] In an indiscreet moment Ross may well have questioned aloud whether a dying man should be abandoned, and as a commander responsible for the wellbeing and safety of his entire crew he would have been within his rights to do so, but he records that in fact he supplied a sledge for Taylor. Just before final departure there was a spectacular ice avalanche from the cliffs. The shooting of fifty little auks provided a tasty Sunday dinner but on Monday 8 July the entire company departed in some apprehension. Most shared hopes and fears in equal number, worried lest they be forced to return to despair and possibly death. They were abandoning the known, however miserable and dreary, for the completely unknown, leaving a home of a kind, for the trackless wilderness.

The scheme adopted was to take forward the baggage and then return for the sick, struggling through heat and meltwater, to reach Batty Bay after four days, where, although the ice began to move, they were trapped by incessant rain for some time. The boats were repaired and caulked. A steady supply of dovekies fed the crew and nurtured the sick, while the entire party was rendered static by dense ice. As ever, the waiting was painful, so Ross encouraged the men to explore the shore for a possible way through, a futile activity, but nonetheless valuable because 'to do even what was useless was to keep up the spirits and hopes of the people, as it also interrupted that uniformity of idle wakefulness which led them to brood over their present condition, and to indulge in evil anticipations'. He added that 'the Highland squire who makes Boswell haul on the backstay in a gale of wind, displays more knowledge than a landsman has any right to possess', an allusion to James Boswell's famed tour of the Hebrides with Dr Samuel Johnson in 1773. When crossing from Skye to Coll in a fierce storm the skipper thrust into Boswell's hand a rope fixed to the top of one of the masts and bade him pull. 'I might have seen that this could not have been of the least service but his object was to keep me out of the way of those busily working with the vessel, and at the same time to divert my fear, by employing me, and making me think I was of use. Thus did I stand firm to my post, while the wind and rain beat upon me, always expecting a call to pull my rope.'[50] Such make-work Ross considered essential. He insisted that the men were not much given to thinking, 'though seamen of the present day (and I am sorry to say it), think much more than they did in my days of junior service, and, most assuredly and certainly, are "all the worse" for it'. The elderly reactionary continued, 'Let my fraternity in command say whether this be true or not; and they are bold men who will so say, despite of the paltry, fantastical, and pretending, ultra philosophy of these days of ruinous folly'. Endless scanning of the horizon looking for a break in the ice brought thoughts of Bering's doomed crew and a quotation from James Thomson's *Castle of Indolence*, 'Thank God, the day is done.'[51]

After spending a month at Batty Bay, they departed in the boats, finally reaching Port Leopold on 16 August. Next day they crossed Prince Regent Inlet. A week later detaining gales and fog enabled essential boat repairs. On 26 August they spotted a ship, dismissed by the doubters as an iceberg but, despite signalling with wet powder, they were unable to attract or reach it. It appeared they would suffer the same frustrating, not to say alarming, experience with a second ship, but in the event they were spotted and a boat was lowered which rowed towards them. The mate assumed they had lost their ship, which Ross, of course, affirmed, requesting the name of the vessel and asking to be taken aboard. '*Isabella* of Hull, once commanded by Captain Ross' was the unbelievable reply, 'on which I stated that I was the identical man in question, and my people the crew of *Victory*. That the mate who commanded this boat, was as much astonished at this information as he appeared to be, I do not doubt; while with the usual blunderheadedness of men on such occasions, he assured me that I had been dead for two years', given up for lost not by them alone but by the whole country.

Ross's motley crew received a sincere welcome from Captain Humphreys of *Isabella* and a rousing three cheers from his men as they climbed aboard. It would have been interesting to know the response of the Inuit to these filthy scruffs who had so often traduced the people of the north without whose aid they would almost certainly have perished (see Chapter 7).

> Unshaven since I know not when, dirty, dressed in the rags of wild beasts instead of the tatters of civilization, and starved to the very bones, our gaunt and grim looks, when contrasted with those of the well-dressed and well-fed men around us, made us all feel, I believe for the first time, what we really were, as well as what now seemed to others. Poverty is without half its mark, unless it be contrasted with wealth: and what we might have known to be true in the past days, we had fogotten to think of, till we were thus reminded of what we truly were, as well as seemed to be.[52]

It transpired that Humphreys had actually been looking for some remains of *Victory*'s expedition. He was, of course, a whaler, who had taken twenty-seven 'fish', and who intended to remain at sea to fill, if possible, the remaining one third of *Isabella*'s cargo with his catch. The first vessel they had spotted was another whaleship, *William Lee*, trailing *Isabella* up Prince Regent's inlet, and to which some of the rescued crew were transferred. Ross buried a message-bottle detailing some account of their adventures in the cairn he had built in 1818 at Possession Bay. He was incensed that the 'Isabella and Alexander Banks', named on his previous voyage, had been 'unwarrantably expunged' from the charts. He therefore reconfirmed his earlier observations and resurveyed the coast, 'with the intention of publishing a special chart of a place rendered so important by its abundant fishery'. On the Banks he was visited by a procession of whaling masters bringing gifts and congratulations. They left the Davis Strait on 30 September, landing at Stromness in Orkney on 12 October. Delayed for two days at Long Hope on Hoy, they sailed to the Humber and on to Hull, to be feted by all and sundry. From Hull, Ross travelled to London, arriving by steamboat, as he had left it four years, four months, three weeks and four days previously, 'having lost his ship, and won his reputation'.[53]

*

The saddest of the many painful relationships in which the Rosses were involved was their on-going feud with each other, first surfacing on their return from the voyage of 1818, as tiresome to posterity as it must have been to them. James was a reasonable individual on the whole; John was not. We have already noted the ruckus about who was responsible for the magnetic observations that first summer, the captain initially accusing his nephew of disloyalty but eventually withdrawing (see Chapters 2 and 3). James presumably had a happier time with Parry but he was persuaded to re-join his uncle on the 1829 expedition. The carrot on this occasion seems to have been some sort of arrangement hitherto unknown in the Navy, whereby James and John were regarded as joint captains, in practice if not in fact, or so James believed but John denied. What turned out to be a particularly grim and difficult voyage was rendered much more fraught by William Light, purser's steward, who was perfectly positioned in occupation and placement to acquire all sorts of information about everyone from the captain to the humblest sailor. His litany of complaints against Capt. Ross were captured by Robert Huish. At more than 700 pages, some of which appear to be adorned by his own unremarkable poetry, *The Last Voyage of Capt. Sir John Ross* is too detailed for any kind of full scrutiny here. Light, a sympathiser of the men abandoned by Ross at Greenock in 1829, was the author's main source. The book's main value is to present, alongside Ross's *Narrative*, the most complete reconstruction we have of the tensions between members of the contingent who depended upon their small ship in one of the world's most unsympathetic environments. The associated stress is unimaginable, even when the men were reasonably civil towards one another, and they must be seen as worthy of the highest regard. Confinement with companions can prove, in certain circumstances, as attractive as incarceration. For these men it must have seemed that the only rest they could look forward to was the Big Sleep.

It is impossible to check all of Light's assertions; he succeeded in maintaining a barrage of complaints and criticisms concerning Ross personally for over four years. It is possible that the animosity between the two men stemmed from an incident in which Light's dog killed Ross's heavily pregnant canine.[54] Huish obviously did a fair amount of research in order to supplement, and in some cases to moderate, Light's input. The writer included much detail and reflection about the Arctic that, so far as we know, he experienced vicariously. When *Victory* grounded leaving Felix Harbour, she had to be completely cleared of everything. All feared the worst: 'It was one of those trying moments of human life, which description cannot reach, and which imagination in the wildest of her flights, can scarcely approach. It was the moment of decision, perhaps, between life and death – between a long and dreary period of misery and want, in the utmost extreme of human suffering, and a safe return to their country and their home.'[55]

Some of the complaints that Light promoted included embedment in the ice due to poor management, and ice-cutting for exercise rather than eventual escape. The steam engine was a hindrance, a view that Ross would have shared. The school for the crew was protestant and sectarian. Light accused Ross of collecting and hoarding Inuit artefacts for exhibition in panoramas on his return, creating excessive baggage. The favours of Inuit women could be purchased very cheaply; they signified their willingness by the word *koonig* (kissing).[56] There were many disagreements between the two Rosses concerning the Northwest Passage, doubtless intensified by the crushing limitations of their immediate shipboard surroundings and the greater environment. There were several references to the captain's fondness for gin, though he claimed to prefer Ferintosh Whisky. On the second voyage there was no replacement for Sacheuse. The sailors were not properly fed (less than convicts in the hulks), unlike the officers, who enjoyed lavish food and drink. The discovery of the Magnetic Pole was kept secret until the panorama exhibition in London. There is good evidence for the very serious claim that John Ross was withholding the crew's wages, due for three years of service. It seemed that he attempted to hold on to the bounty for himself; he was actually forced to pay the men but the amounts allegedly remained grossly inadequate.

Light constantly claimed Ross was unloved by his men. Among his assertions were that Ross had an Inuit boy flogged (though gently). JCR was a hero; John Ross was not. Ross monopolised all the shot game; the men were sick of eating fish. He was not communicative. He promoted food poisoning. He considered leaving a man behind to die. Ross was not religious. He invented useless tasks. He gave the Inuit rum. Ross was unfit to lead since he was fat, unfit and old. In his list of financial rewards for the crew when they were finally paid, Ross wrote 'nil' against Light's name.

*

While John Ross may have had his detractors, in the form, for instance, of William Light, he was regarded as somewhat of a national hero when he returned from his second Arctic expedition to triumph in 1833, and the publicity did not damage his nephew, James, though the latter's light was more than a little eclipsed by John's. A recent novelty was the development of panoramas, for which the Ross expedition was a perfect fit for a collaboration with Robert Burford and Henry Selous. The whole story was told in a large-scale circular installation of images that began with *Victory* and ended with the magnetic observatory, taking in the Inuit, the Magnetic Pole, the aurora and the imprisoning ice. The phenomenon of visual representations of the Arctic has been sympathetically researched by Russell Potter, and he describes the creation of this one in entertaining detail. Predictably Ross was not the easiest collaborator but it was, after all, his story. Selous, who painted most of the show, divulged in his diary his fears that Ross would 'destroy a great many flights of fancy of ours'. Next day he 'did us the favour of obliterating nearly half our sketch and we shall have to commence our work over again'. Ross clearly put his heart into the project, displaying considerable artistic sensibility, particularly respecting the sky and the astounding light of the region.

There were several other 'Ross Shows'. A father and son team, the Marshalls, who seem to have been Scots, devised panoramas that moved. At least one of their shows paired Boothia and Bannockburn. Another Scot,

J.B. Laidlaw, married into the family. As Professor Potter has indicated, when Laidlaw mounted a panorama in Dublin, John Ross was attending a meeting of the British Association for the Advancement of Science and so may have attended the exhibition. Indeed, we may think he would not have foregone the opportunity to make an appearance.[57] In the end, Ross's four hellish years of Arctic agony were reduced to an Arctic sideshow.

'Marshuick and Meigack', from John Ross,
A Voyage of Discovery (London, 1819)

7

THE SCOTS AND THE INUIT

... there is only
One great thing,
The only thing:
To live to see in huts and on journeys
The great day that dawns,
And the little light that fills the world.

Inuit Poem[1]

First sustained contact between Inuit and Scots was probably a result of whaling.[2] The relationship during the first half of the nineteenth century was, in the main, positive, differing spectacularly from the usual concomitants of British imperial excess. Apart from whaling there seemed little in the Arctic that was exploitable. Since the environment was, to European eyes, desolate and unproductive, initially offering no obvious access to precious metals, while the people were few and dispersed, 'there was no incentive to rob, dispossess and enslave them'. It is as remarkable as it is inspiring that in numerous accounts the word most associated with the Inuit is 'laughter', in all its forms.[3]

John Ross was not alone in assuming that humans could not sustain life so far north. On 9 August 1818, his crew on *Alexander* saw several individuals on the ice and assumed them to be shipwrecked sailors, but they proved to be Greenlanders, driving their sledges back and forth 'with wonderful rapidity'. After the ship stopped, about a mile away, Ross's interpreter, John Sacheuse, attempted, unsuccessfully, to communicate with them. Ross then sent over a boat that deposited various gifts on the ice, such as knives, clothing and a dog decorated with strings of blue beads. Ten hours later the dog was sleeping and the presents remained untouched.

Having spied a lone sledge in the distance, Ross ordered the hoisting of a flag on which was painted the sun and the moon above a hand-held sprig of heather. It was placed mid way between ship and shore, together with a bag containing gifts, and a sign displaying a hand pointing towards the ship. There was an opportunity for some auk-shooting as the adventurers anticipated their meeting with a people hitherto unknown to, and unimagined by, Ross, but probably familiar to whalers.

On 10 August, eight sledges were seen advancing circuitously towards the ships, halting some distance away. Four moved towards, but stopped short of, the flagstaff. Both ships hoisted white flags; Sacheuse carried a similar banner in an attempt to parley. A canal or small chasm in the ice, 'not passable without a plank', separated the two parties, lending each some security from possible attack. The Greenlanders (Inughuit) approached hesitantly, dog-whips in hand. Removing his hat, Sacheuse signed them to advance. Having satisfied themselves that the canal was impassable they gained some confidence. Shouts and gestures were exchanged as Sacheuse realised the visitors spoke the Humooke dialect, learned from his childhood nurse who came from Upernavik, so he employed this language to offer them gifts. 'Kahkeite', said he, 'Come on', to which they replied, 'Naakrie, naakrie', 'No, go away'. The bravest then stood at the edge of the canal where, drawing a knife from his boot, he repeated, 'Go away. I will kill you.' The bold John was not intimidated, telling them he was a friend, while he threw across some strings of beads and a chequered shirt, which were regarded with suspicion: 'Don't kill us!' He then tossed them an English knife, and this successfully cut the tension, so to speak, as they cautiously picked it up, and then started to shout, pulling their noses, actions he imitated, calling out Heigh, yaw! explained as 'an expression of surprise and pleasure'. They enquired what skin the shirt was made of: 'from an animal they had never seen'. And then the questions came fast and furious. What kind of creatures were these, they asked, pointing at the ships. 'Do they come from the sun or the moon?' John explained that he was a man with a father and mother like themselves and he came from a distant country to the south. 'That cannot be, there is nothing but ice there'. Asking again about the ships, they were told these were 'houses made of wood'. 'No, they are alive, we have seen them move their wings'. When John then asked who they were, they replied they were men from that direction, pointing to the north. There was much water there and they had come to fish for narwhal. It was then agreed that Sacheuse should cross over the canal, so he returned to the ship to collect a plank, and to report on his findings.

'The hope of getting some important information, as well as the interest naturally felt for these poor creatures, made me impatient to communicate with them myself', wrote Ross. Armed with additional gifts, he and Parry met up with a total of eight Greenlanders and fifty dogs, two sailors and Sacheuse, who advised the officers to win over the still nervous inhabitants by pulling their noses and shouting *Heigh, yaw!* The Inughuit leader was given a knife and a mirror, which occasioned in turn astonishment, puzzlement, shouting, laughter and surprise, noisy exhilaration in which the Brits joined. Knives, narwhal tusks and seahorse (walrus) teeth were gifted in return. The invaluable Sacheuse persuaded the natives to uncover their heads as a mark of respect and thus friendship was secured, a convention that seems more British than Greenlandic. Displaying his artistic talents, Sacheuse later painted a picture of the scene. He had been tutored in art by the Scottish painter Alexander Nasmyth, famous for his landscapes and portraits, especially that of Robert Burns. His picture is entitled *First Communication with the natives of Prince Regent Bay as drawn by John Sacheuse and Presented to Capt. Ross, Aug. 1818.* The artist depicts himself addressing two Inughuit who are examining a mirror as he prepares to give them a shirt, while in the foreground Ross and Parry, both unarmed, meet two others holding their narwhal lances. Ross was clearly happy to own the scene since he included it in his *Voyage of Discovery*. It is interesting also to consider an etching from the Boothia expedition 1829–33, 'First Communication', which shows the explorers meeting the Inuit, having placed their weapons on the ice (Plate 10). Another illustration depicts an Inuk with dogs driving a musk-ox towards JCR, who fires at it from behind a rock (Plate 14). What is interesting is the absence of heroism or derring-do as exhibited, for example, in the lithographs of David Livingstone, attacked by a lion as the natives flee in terror.

Sacheuse invited their new contacts on board ship, laughing as Ross and Parry were hauled on their sledge by two sailors. A sailor-driven Navy boat was then launched, stimulating further clamour. Attempts to lift the ice-anchor prompted questions about the 'skins' it was made from. More officers were now on the ice, while the crew crowded the bow to view the ethnics amid much shouting, laughter and *Heigh, yaw* cries. The Greenlanders were intrigued as a sailor climbed to the mast-head, supposing the sails to be skins. They were finally persuaded on to the ship by climbing a rope ladder, not the easiest of tasks for novices. Various objects on the ship were greeted with amazement, joy, fear and, again, much laughter.

Ross's first thought was to trade, and he was gratified to find the people of Kalaallit Nunaat trustworthy, a quality he frequently complained was in short supply in later dealings: 'Being desirous of procuring a sledge and dogs,

I offered them a rifle musket for one completely fitted, which they promised to fetch; with much honesty of principle, however, refusing to accept the rifle till they had brought the sledge.' He was clearly interested in sledges for exploration purposes. Naval personnel were later to be heavily criticised for their failure to use dogs, preferring man-hauling, which lasted until Scott's Antarctic expeditions, but there were good reasons for this. It was thought the practice would keep the men fit. On the debit side there were difficulties in training men to use dogs. Sailors had a hard time attempting to quickly master the skills acquired by the Inuit over generations. The latter understood the best routes and the best conditions for dog-travel; the visitors did not. Sometimes dogs were exhausted as quickly as the men by horrendous ice conditions that cut their paws. Nonetheless Ross should be given credit for at least considering the Inuit example.

Ross was convinced these Inuit knew no more of timber than the stunted heather defying the surrounding stones, nor did they have any idea of its weight. They scorned a terrier dog on board but were terrified by a Shetland pig. They were intrigued by mirrors, looking behind the frame to seek the source of the reflection; they asked if a watch was good to eat, and enquired as to the kind of ice used in the skylight and binnacle glass. Both groups were mutually fascinated by the others' clothing. The Inughuit had no concept of furniture. They tried to grasp at illustrations in books. They were unimpressed by fiddle music but responded to a flute. They spat out biscuit and salt meat. They were unsettled by the 'Jugglers' tricks' of Mr Beverley, Ross's surgeon. It appeared they could count no higher than five or ten.

The Inughuit were invited aboard for coffee and biscuits. Their portraits were painted, after which 'they danced Scotch reels on the deck with our sailors, to the animating strains of our musician', the Shetland fiddler. Sacheuse now came into his own as, 'with a good-humoured officiousness', he took on the role of Master of Ceremonies at a ball, as Ross called it, on one of the king's ships in the icy seas of Greenland. His talents outdid those of Beau Nash, the famous Master of Ceremonies at Bath, for John Sacheuse combined in his person 'the discordant qualifications' of seaman, interpreter, draughtsman, painter and hunter of seals and polar bears; he also exchanged gifts with an eighteen-year-old lass who took his fancy. He escorted the party as they left the ship, promising to return with a skin-boat, which Ross thought might be useful on the ice. Sacheuse was charged with collecting natural history specimens but there was some alarm when, presumably distracted by his new girlfriend, he did not return next morning. It transpired that he had broken his collar-bone firing an overloaded gun, doubtless thinking 'Plenty powder, plenty kill'! Unstated was plenty chance to impress girlfriend!

On departure of the Inughuit there were further gifts of clothing, biscuits and pieces of wood. Mounting their sledges they 'drove off in a body, hallooing, apparently, in great glee'. Thus ended the first encounter with a people that Ross believed to be hitherto unknown to Europeans. It is striking that the sorts of information and responses solicited by the Scots were as insensitive as the native response was supposedly barbaric. There was great need for haste, to learn as much as possible in a very short period of time before the weather closed in or the Greenlanders disappeared as suddenly as they had arrived. Furthermore, the information was transmitted through the somewhat imperfect transit of Sacheuse's well-meaning, but possibly misleading, translations, encumbered with the cultural and relativist assumptions of the explorers, who had already read numerous accounts of contact with indigenous peoples. For John Ross these contacts clearly represented the high point of the voyage and he devoted many pages of his narratives to the experience, often recounting their influences and impacts upon himself.

Shifting weather conditions necessitated the ship's departure and generated further adventures in, and on, the ice, a collapsing berg, ice-lock and heavy snow, compensated by numerous whale sightings, some sea-unicorns (narwhal) and the daily shooting of hundreds of auks. When the ship was ice-bound, three Inughuit appeared on sledges; they had obviously been in contact with the earlier visitors and knew what to expect. Ross was afforded the chance for a close inspection of the sledge and dogs but his disappointment at discovering that he, his companions and their possessions were no longer regarded as exotica was almost palpable. He received a spear made from narwhal tusk – the cetacean's ivory tooth. He 'purchased' a dog, a reluctant sale, but at what price he did not reveal. Three of the sledge dogs had lost an eye to the whips. The Inuk was named Meigack, aged about forty, who, with his two sons, was invited on to the ship. They came from a place named Petowack (Wolstenholme Sound) and were visiting their present location, 'Ackullowissick' (Akuliaruseq), to hunt seals and narwhal, as well as to collect some iron from a mountain at Sowallick 25 miles away. Meigack promised to bring samples of the iron to the fascinated explorers, who had already noticed that his knife was edged with iron, samples of which Ross was given.

More Greenlanders joined them on the ice, initiating a game of football using a harpoon buoy, or float, made of sealskin, the first recorded Arctic international between the Kalaallit and the Scots! The betting is that the

Greenlanders won! Ross acquired a second sledge but no dog. One Inuk ate an auk raw. Some of the locals endured a ride in a small boat after Ross had personally demonstrated its safety. Portraits were painted of Meigack. The guests disliked bread and wine, though Meigack was pleased to receive a wine-glass that he said he would give to his wife. Meigack purloined Ross's best telescope, a case of razors and a pair of scissors, but immediately surrendered them when challenged by Ross's attentive steward. The captain showed their guests a miniature of his wife when asked if the British consisted only of men. Seized by the idea that the ship might contain females, they went off to find them. To the Inuit there was something anomalous about men without women.

It was later proved, as Ross suspected, that Inuit iron was meteoric in origin. It came from 'Iron Mountain' or Savissivik, a site near Cape York in western Greenland, later shamefully plundered by the American explorer Robert E. Peary and placed in the Smithsonian. As he was forced to resume his quest, Ross must have reflected on the paradox that the 'Arctic Highlanders', a notably primitive people, had access to iron.[4]

In 1902 the inhabitants of the region apparently had no name for it, but to those further south in Greenland it was Avanersuaq, meaning 'the place in the farthest north', a name applied in the later twentieth century. The nomenclature of Highlands and Arctic Highlanders had, for Ross, a personal cultural resonance. He belonged to the Ayrshire and Wigtownshire side of his family, in south-west Scotland, but another branch took its name from the beautiful, mountainous county of Ross, north of Inverness, extending from the east coast to the Minch, and in Ross's day including the island of Lewis in the Outer Hebrides. The inhabitants spoke Gaelic, a totally different language from Lowland Scots, and were perceived by outsiders as poor, primitive, economically backward, dirty and doomed, yet loyal, militaristic, hardy, noble and sentimentalised. It was widely believed that the Highland, or Gaelic, way of life had come to an end at the Battle of Culloden (1746). James Macpherson's translations of Ossianic poetry (1760) took Scotland, the English-speaking and the literary world, by storm, memorialising as it did an ancient culture, hitherto unsuspected but now irrevocably finished, a theme taken up by Walter Scott in numerous poems and stories. Highland emigration was generally opposed by the landlords up until the end of the Napoleonic War but the first 'Highland Clearances', by clan chiefs turned commercial landlords, had been experienced in 1807. After Waterloo and the postwar economic depression, emigration became more common. As a Lowlander, John Ross undoubtedly considered himself superior to the Gaels, but his cultural baggage also included certain racial assumptions as well, inevitably informing some of his preconceptions concerning the Greenlanders and Inuit, though he was, in some respects, surprisingly open-minded, and there is no doubt that his curiosity about other peoples and cultures was genuine.

One such assumption was that the Inuit exhibited the 'desire of possessing what they admired, which is so universal among savages', in other words thievery. Scots supposedly were not similarly motivated though, as Ross's own actions show, he had no hesitation whatsoever in exploiting the Inuit whenever possible, essentially exchanging junk for valuable commodities within Arctic culture, while pretending that such barter constituted legitimate trade. Thus one man, having failed to carry off the ship's anvil, took a hammer and hid it in the snow to be collected later; his features were described, tellingly, as 'savage and dishonest', two words that, in Ross's mind, 'ganged thegither'. Of a prominent Greenlander named Ervick, he noted that 'though good humour was fully expressed in his countenance, it also bore the indescribable mixed appearance of ignorance and wildness, which characterises all uncivilised people'.[5]

When a second party of Greenlanders went on board they immediately began to beg and steal, 'laying hands on every small piece of wood they met with, and pocketing every nail they could find about the ship'. They helped themselves to whatever appeared portable, often laughing as they did so, an obvious give-away. Meigack was one example, like his fellows showing 'a propensity to pilfering'. Respect for the rights of property could not exist in a culture that had little or no sense of either possession or ownership, but believed in use based on need, and a communitarian sharing of available resources. When those accused claimed that items taken or begged were for their wives they were probably telling the truth, but they also laughed when they were caught in the act and forced to return the booty.[6]

Other signs of so-called primitivism (also levelled against the Gaels) included personal uncleanliness. Inuit skin was said to be dirty in colour, their habits 'filthy in the extreme; their faces, hands and bodies, covered in oil and dirt, and they never seem to have washed since they were born, their hair matted with filth . . .'[7] One further similarity was that none of them were willing to leave their country, seeming perfectly happy and contented, bewilderingly so, to outsiders. At this time, however, Ross's comparators were Greenlanders, familiar because they had been written about by

Moravian missionaries, and considered superior to the Canadian Inuit, and this remained the case for many years. Christians were considered somehow cleaner, their houses better built, their culture more developed than that of the Canadian Inuit.

Scottish Highland dancing is often regarded as wild, but it is tame compared with Inuit performance. Ross was convinced that one performer was suffering an epileptic attack, as he prepared for his demonstration, distorting his face and turning up his eyes. He then demonstrated 'a variety of extraordinary gestures and attitudes, accompanied by the most hideous distortions of countenance'. It was the Scottish puritan in Ross which inspired the observation that, 'like the similar amusements of very different climates, these contained the indecent allusions which are well known to form an essential feature in the dances of many nations, in other respects far advanced in civilisation'.[8] There is a shadow of veracity in the old witticism that presbyterians disapproved of sexual relations because they might lead to dancing!

The greatest mystery was that this small number of people were apparently cut off from the rest of the world since Time Immemorial:

> The origin of the Arctic Highlanders is a question as yet involved in peculiar obscurity. They exist in a corner of the world among the most secluded which has yet been discovered, and have no knowledge of any thing beyond the boundary of their own country: nor have they any tradition of whence they came; appearing, until the moment of our arrival, to have believed themselves to be the only inhabitants of the universe, and to have considered all the rest of the world as a mass of ice.[9]

This was Ross in ethnological mode, though the word 'ethnology' would not be invented for a further twelve years. He pointed out that the south Greenlanders believed themselves to be descended from a nation in the north. In the view of Sacheuse they were '*right* Eskimaux, these are *our* fathers!' His use of 'right' in the sense of 'true' is a genuine Scoticism that he presumably picked up in Leith. It is the same adjective that describes the 'right whale'. Ross was greatly exercised by the apparent absence of boats. That the Greenlanders had no canoes was understandable, since timber was so scarce, and in any case canoes could only be used for a few short summer weeks, 'but it is at the same time, not easy to understand how they should be so ignorant, even traditionally, of the existence of a boat'. He thought they represented a solitary and singular instance 'of a maritime and fishing tribe unacquainted with any means of floating on the water'. On this issue Ross was undoubtedly somewhat confused, claiming that in the absence of wood they could easily have constructed boats out of the same materials as they used for sledges – bones and skins. He contradicted himself by noting the appearance of five deerskin-clad women with a sledge and dogs in an umiak or 'woman's boat' that they rowed standing up. These ingenious skin-boats, built by the women and designed for passengers and/or cargo, were often regarded by European commentators as somewhat fragile for Arctic conditions but in fact they were highly flexible with prows able to absorb the shock of collision with ice, over which, when circumstances dictated, these lightly structured vessels could be dragged. Perhaps Ross disregarded the craft because it was associated with women; there was nothing whatsoever in his own culture that suggested women-only boats. However, it should be emphasised that the Scots spent exactly one week with these people, a hopelessly inadequate time for the most basic of ethnographies.

Some further aspects of Ross's information or assumptions about the Etah Inughuit (Arctic Highlanders) were incorrect. Tulloowak, the 'king', was in actuality a shaman called Tuluvaq who left Upernavik in West Greenland about 1800 to escape an epidemic, travelling with his family in an umiak (*umiaq*, open boat). This strongly suggests that they did not believe that they were the only people in the universe, and indeed they had a name for the folk around Upernavik, as they did for people from the other side of Smith Sound. They may well have forgotten about sea-going craft: legends suggest that they once had kayaks but they may no longer have had a need for them. Another consideration is that since the polar peoples migrated from time to time, there may have been very little human activity on either side of northern Baffin Bay during the seventeenth and eighteenth centuries. The total Etah population may have been between 100 and 200; they were a people who were wholly self-sufficient, who did not fish or hunt caribou, but who used meteoric iron to tip their knives and harpoons. After Ross wrote about these people they were to be visited by many other explorers in the course of the nineteenth and twentieth centuries.[10] That much more is known about them today than he could possibly have learned should not detract from the sense of wonder and discovery that his account conveys.

Several of the misunderstandings between the two peoples arose from Ross's own imposed cultural assumptions and dafter notions. The device of the sun and moon, and the hand pointing towards the ship, not surprisingly, led the Greenlanders to believe that 'the ships would fly to the sun and the moon from which they concluded we must have come'. The Greenlanders had sent their women away to the mountains for safety and they had originally approached the ships intending to request their departure, in preference to any attempt at destroying them.[11] One man had been so worried that he had run off to the mountains and had not returned, and no wonder, since living creatures descending from the heavens were likely to be about as appealing then as the approach of UFOs would be today. Since even small sprigs of heather were valuable in a culture sometimes lacking an abundance of flora, the one held in the flag's hand could have been interpreted as offering unlimited bounty, some of which might conceivably be there for the taking. Arguably Ross confused concepts originating in his own mind with the *mentalité* of the Inuit.

Similarly it was Ross who introduced the misunderstandings about 'king' Tulloowak for whom he made up a parcel containing clothing, mirrors, scissors and 'a snuff-box, on which was a portrait of His Royal Highness the Prince Regent'. Sacheuse must have known perfectly well that kings were alien to Inuit culture but he played along until he found a match for Ross's own preconceptions. The Greenlanders apparently did not understand words meaning 'a person in authority', or 'a strong, respected or dreaded man who kills more seals', but when Sacheuse remembered the word *pisarsuak* for a chief, they recognised it and said his name was Tuluvaq.[12] He was satisfied that all acknowledged the king Tulloowak, in reality a shaman and a neat example of euhemerism. He lived, Ross believed, in a large stone-built house, 'nearly as large as a ship', on Wolstenholme Island where the mass of the natives fancifully subsisted in the position of feudatories, allegedly paying him a portion of all they caught, returning there over the winter. This was sheer nonsense, the wishful thinking of a Scottish patrician who was engaged in building himself a fine new mansion in Stranraer. However, Ross had to relinquish any idea of 'communicating with the King of the Arctic Highlanders', due to the lateness of the season and because he anticipated that he was on the verge of solving the issue of the Northwest Passage.

Ross had a related problem with his questioning about a Supreme Being, a topic in which Sacheuse, a man of faith, might have been expected to intervene since he had, after all, converted to Christianity and it was his avowed intent to return to Greenland, once he had received further instruction, as a missionary to the 'wild people'.[13] Sacheuse presumably could have, at the very least, advised Ross on the drift of his questioning. Communication totally failed, for Ervick could not comprehend what Ross was asking about since he did not worship the sun, moon or stars, any image or any living thing. When pushed by Ross, he stated that the purpose of the sun and moon was to give light. According to Ross, Ervick 'appeared to have no idea respecting his origin, and no conception of a future state'; when he died he would be put in the ground. Ross had no better luck with his questions about an evil spirit, which yielded a short dissertation on the spiritual figure of the angakok: variously interpreted as a sorcerer or shaman, doctor or priest. When told of 'an omnipotent, omnipresent, and invisible Being, who had created the sea and land, and all therein, he showed much surprise and eagerly asked where he lived'. When informed that he was everywhere Ervick became alarmed and sought the comforting breathing space of the ship's deck. When told of the Christian belief about the hereafter, he said that a wise man had once said his people were to go to the moon. This was no longer credited, though birds and other creatures did have lunar origins. Such notions, thought Ross, indicated that the people did have some religious ideas, 'however barbarous', and that the unsatisfactory information obtained derived from problems of language and communication.[14] The mischievous Sacheuse was more than partly responsible since he held all the linguistic cards and could interpret as liberally as he wished; there was no one to confirm, corroborate or challenge his translations.

One of the most interesting of Ross's discoveries about these Greenlanders was that he could not communicate to them what was meant by war; they even lacked warlike weapons. All credit, however, to the captain, who had spent most of his life in hostile engagement, for his response: 'I therefore gave strict and positive orders that no fire-arms, or other warlike weapons, should be shown them, or given to them on any account, and, when they were with us, all shooting-parties were called in'.[15] It was easy for the know-it-alls back home to scoff but Ross at least demonstrated that he was much more open-minded than they might have expected and more sensitive to novel experiences than a majority of his traducers.

*

Eleven years later, in 1829, the Rosses and their men had a further opportunity to find out more about Arctic folk during their extended entrapment in Boothia on the ship *Victory*. En route they sailed up the coast of Greenland and visited the Moravian settlement at Holsteinborg (Sisimiut), the inhabitants of which John Ross characterised as 'among the most worthy of all the rude tribes yet known to our voyagers, in whatever part of the world'.[16] In January 1830 the explorers, now icebound in Felix Harbour, encountered a group of Inuit whom they greeted by shouting *Tima, tima*, which Ross claimed was a 'salutation between meeting tribes'. Both sides threw down their weapons and the Rosses approached, with JCR's prompting and advice, to embrace them, smoothing down their clothing, in traditional greeting, which was reciprocated with laughter, clamour and strange gesticulation. When told that their visitors were Europeans they responded that they were 'men Inuit' of whom there were thirty-one in all, one of whom, Illicta, was aged 65, six were aged between 40 and 50, and twenty between the ages of 20 and 40, as well as four boys. Two were lame, hauled in a sledge with Illicta; one had an injured limb, another had lost a leg to a bear. Their clothing, meticulously described by Ross, made them appear larger than they actually were. Their spears bore a resemblance to walking sticks and were made up of small pieces of wood and bone skilfully joined together. They had bone and horn knives, as well as others pointed or edged with iron. One had a dagger made from an English clasp-knife with the maker's mark on it.[17]

JCR mentioned some place-names which the Inuit recognised. They were invited on board ship to be presented with hoops of iron, though reciprocal objects were refused. Ross does not say why, but the refusal may have been intended to indicate a degree of European superiority. He found their appearance to be superior to that of his crew, as well as more efficiently dressed for cold, and they looked better fed. They seemed altogether neater and cleaner, with tidier hair-cuts than the people he had encountered in 1818, and they were not as greatly impressed by the ships as previously. But when three of the men were invited into the cabin they 'showed abundant signs of wonder', particularly with reference to Inuit portraits and the mirrors, lamps and candles, but they did not attempt to steal anything. They seemed to accept preserved meat out of politeness, saying it was good, but on closer interrogation by JCR they admitted they threw it away. One man who was questioned was then given some oil to drink which he claimed to enjoy. This little experiment prompted John to reflect that all tastes are governed by regular diets, and these men, 'amidst their blubber and their oil, their dirty diet and villainous smells', had no reason to envy the refined tables of the south, at which 'they would not only have experienced disgust, but felt pity for our barbarism and ignorance'; only starvation would have forced them to partake.

A short race was run between an Inuk and an officer, 'but with so much and such equal politeness on both sides, that there was no victor to be declared', thus pioneering, we may suspect, the Canadian approach to competitiveness! All joined in some dancing, as the carpenter, Chimham Thomas, produced his fiddle. When the visitors departed, the Rosses accompanied them two miles out on the ice. Seal-hunting techniques were explained but the natives did not seem to understand questions about the direction in which open water would be found. A meeting point for the next day was marked on the ice, when the Brits would visit the Inuit. John Ross sensibly reflected on the circumstance that a group so small and secluded could subsist in 'so apparently hopeless a country, so barren, so wild, and so repulsive', a genuinely interesting topic which he then squandered with pious prattling about 'the Hand which under the most apparently hopeless circumstances, thus spreads for His creatures, a table in the wilderness', though not one at which Ross wished to dine since he was no great admirer of Inuit country foods.[18]

On visiting a village of twelve snow huts, Ross commented on the building techniques and the clutter within. He was delighted to discover that these people caught salmon, a productive activity in which his men could share. He accepted some gifts and was intrigued to note that the igloos were lit by a large piece of clear ice on the roof. He remarked on the women, finding them less presentable than the men, noting their facial tattoos. He and his associates learned about Inuit hunting skills, but information about geography proved elusive. Eight men returned to the ship, the two leaders being invited to dinner while the others joined the crew for more dancing. The dinner guests quickly learned how to use cutlery. They liked the soup and, on this occasion, the preserved meat, but did not take to salt meat, pudding, rice or cheese. Later, when Ross and his men accompanied the Inuit part-way across the ice, a blast of wind struck the party, frosting Ross's face. An Inuk made a snowball and rubbed it on the captain's cheek to prevent a sore, thereafter keeping an eye on his injury.

The man who had lost a leg, Tulluahiu, arrived with another 'very intelligent native', Tiagashu, who hauled him on a sledge. The carpenter examined the stump and, finding it sound, set about manufacturing a wooden leg. The Rosses then produced a chart and questioned their guests about certain features. Tiagashu drew a line to the west, and then traced it north, to indicate the way they should travel in the autumn. He indicated rivers, lochs and good spots for salmon fishing. The Inuit promised to bring someone else more knowledgeable than themselves on a later visit to clarify some of these matters. JCR tried them on the names of folk he had met earlier, some of which his uncle thought they recognised, or had heard of, eliciting the observation: 'had we known their language better, we should doubtless have found that the science of being acquainted with whatever may discredit one's neighbours is as well understood here as in an English country town; and that it is not even necessary to be very near neighbours to be very intermeddling, and as malicious as possible'. He was gratified at the native response to candle snuffers and a large reading glass that magnified objects and faces. 'Such are the delights of novelty', he wrote, 'and thus does the curiosity of pure ignorance ever find new gratifications.' He contrasted them with himself and his fellows; 'we, who know every thing, knowing even what we have not seen or learned' and consequently have lost their sense of wonder.[19] The Inuit did not like plum pudding or brandy, the former unfortunate, the latter a boon, since they had so far avoided the ruination of morals which had hastened the 'extermination' of their North American neighbours.

The inevitability of the eventual disappearance of indigenous peoples was a widely held view at this time, shared by such luminaries as Sir Walter Scott. The 'savage' and the 'uncivilised' must inevitably give way to 'knowledge' and 'civilisation'. Matthew Macfie, in 1865, commented on the mixed population of Victoria on Vancouver Island – Russians, Scandinavians, Italians, French, Germans, Spanish and British; Blacks from the US and the West Indies; Chinese; Yankees, Native Peoples, Mexicans and Chilanos; and Polynesians, conspicuously from Hawai'i. Macfie was not racist; he believed that 'the prejudice which characterises race or colour as a disqualification for the exercise of civil rights reflects dishonour upon the civilised community that indulges it'. But, like most of his peers, and Washington Irving before him, he was concerned about the mixed bloods, and he feared, in particular, for the inevitable extinction of American indigenous peoples and those of Polynesia, a demise he ascribed to the influence of the Europeans – 'the evil practices of the white man have ever been more potent to ruin the aborigines than his gospel is to save them'.[20] Such was 'the order of the world', but John Ross opined that it was the duty of people like himself to ensure that the process was 'not hastened by oppression and wrong, that it may not be attended by the suffering of individuals'. Personally, he considered that gradual death through rum was preferable to Spanish-style extermination.[21]

On visits to the ship some items were put away 'lest they should tempt these hitherto honest people, and thus make us guilty of teaching them a vice to which they appeared strangers: a vice common among all savages and too much so', even among the Inuit, as previous navigators had attested. Ross, however, noted that the temptation was greater than retention; stolen items were returned without complaint.

> Their opinion seemed to be, that although it was wrong to steal, no harm was done if the owner did not miss the property; an argument not uncommon, I am sorry to say, among their betters in our own country, but not more desirable because it has an apologist in Shakespeare: 'The robb'd that smiles, steals something from the thief; he robs himself that spends a bootless grief' [*Othello*].

In Ross's mellowing view the Inuit seemed to regard theft as a 'good joke'.[22]

*

If Scots are traditionally dour, the Inuit are, and were, noted for the laughter that seems to accompany everything that they do, not least at the expense of some of the idiotic antics of the kabloona (European foreigner). When we visited Grise Fiord, on Ellesmere Island, an Elder told us of his plans to introduce T-shirts imprinted 'Gateway to the South'. On another occasion, when we were travelling with actor and drum dancer Pakak Innuksuk and were attacked by hordes of insects, he was asked by a tourist 'Do you people eat these things?' to be told with a straight face 'Only when my mouth is open'! The girls and women engage in throat-singing, the loser being the one who first laughs so infectiously that everyone in the audience does too. Ross was similarly rather taken with the singers as the women arranged themselves in a semi-circle, shutting their eyes and opening their mouths singing with all the power of their throats and lungs.[23] The explorer's journals are full of examples of Inuit laughing off horrendous weather conditions, starvation, accidents, and hazards which boggle the minds of the rest of us. One young Elder, for they need not be ancient, told me that his children, by three different women, earned him great prestige in his community. Like many of his peers he is politically articulate, keen to improve the situation of his people, and well able to take on the arguments and criticisms of outsiders, whether Canadian or otherwise, who are often oppositional. Yet he can turn on the charm in a moment, joking, teasing and laughing. People such as him, and they are numerous, make for very good company. This is not to deny the Inuit sharing of other, more serious problems that are common to all of us worldwide. One of the attractive aspects of the Ross era is that Scots and Inuit shared an essential mutual dependency. Of course there were undeniably innumerable problems, misunderstandings and unfortunate occurrences between the two peoples, for example, when both thought they were exploiting the other, but there was also much shared experience, mutual support and co-operation. This was not a part of the Empire seized and defended by guns and war.

*

Ikmallik, a man knowledgeable in geography, arrived with Tiagashu in 1830, to be presented by the explorers with a sketch map that was marked with various places he apparently recognised (Plate 12). Like his companion he traced a line westwards but instead of indicating a turn north he pushed out to the north-west. In truth he was not very helpful to the explorers since he did not insert the islands, nor did he estimate the time required to cover the distance.

Ross and his men had been invited on a seal hunt but instead they revisited the village, where the captain was presented with a complete female outfit. In return, this generous Scot presented the clothes maker, a woman called Tiriksiu, with one silk handkerchief! It transpired that she perfectly understood the sketch map prepared by Ikmallik and she drew her own version, adding islands, as well as, invaluably, places good for sleeping and other spots where food could be found. On the return journey to the ship, the freezing atmosphere claimed some more skin from Ross's cheek.

Next day Tulluahiu had his wooden leg fitted; it was a great success and its owner strutted around 'in apparent ecstasy'. Two days later a foot was attached to the leg, the recipient arriving with a large group of spectators, including a number of boys. Ross was sure that 'the simple contrivance of this wooden leg, raised us higher in the estimation of this people, than all the wonders we had shown them'. As a mark of gratitude, the village anga-kok (shaman), Otookiu, offered to cure the ship's armourer, James Maslin, who was dying, a proposition conveniently ignored by Ross, who did not approve; Maslin died on 20 January of tubercular consumption. Meanwhile, the ship's mate persuaded one of the visiting women to have her hair cut, thus inspiring others to follow her example, causing Ross to regret that he had not included combs among his gifts.

JCR, throughout, took a particular interest in the Inuit dialects. He also enjoyed an exhibition of singing and dancing at the village, as other visitors

188

continued to cross the ice to the ship. When he shot three willow partridges, the Inuit closely examined them to discover how they had been killed. Ross, unwilling to indicate the power of their weapons, carefully fudged his answers. However, next day, a pistol was demonstrated to show the superiority of British weaponry. The Inuit stayed away during Maslin's funeral but thereafter regular visits resumed. John Ross mused on the shooting of the raven that had stayed with them all winter and, in his view, should have been spared: 'in other days, or in minds more deeply tinctured with poetry or superstition, I know not what mental misery might not have followed an act so sacrilegious': killing a raven brought bad luck.

Thus the first month of 1830 passed 'like a dream'. All had enjoyed the interaction and exchanges with the Inuit and much had been learned about their culture, their ideas of geographical space and their great interest in the wonders displayed by *Victory*'s crew. This bright picture was soon marred by incidences of theft to the extent that Ross had to communicate the idea that future pilfering would debar all visitors from the ship. When some of the guns were fired in connection with sound experiments, James Ross was asked what the guns were saying. He replied that they were naming those who had stolen property from the ship. Following a discussion among themselves, the Inuit decided to return everything.

The Inuit traded prey and skins. One woman astonished the sailors by exposing her naked baby while she breastfed at a temperature of minus 40 degrees. Ikmallik returned one day with some twenty others to perform a dance, followed by women singing, but their efforts were not greatly appreciated by the sailors. Ross calculated that in one month the denizens had killed two bears, three gluttons (wolverine), a dozen foxes and fifty seals; his own company had killed or taken five foxes with some hares, ptarmigan and partridges, and so clearly were much less adept, despite their superior weapons.

Most importantly of all, however, communication between the two peoples was steadily improving. Both Rosses took care to learn and memorise the names of individual Inuit women, men and children. The informants were asked to identify many of nature's creatures including animals, birds and plants. James, especially, worked hard at learning the language and discovering place-names. They gathered information about Inuit culture and ideas, valuing whatever they were told, even when they did not actually believe all of it, thereby gaining the confidence of their informants, despite severe disagreements over issues like pilfering. Relations had now settled into a pattern. Ross bought a dog from an Inuk; purchasing another the next day, he completed his team.

The partnership between the races was not only inspirational but essential so far as the explorers were concerned. Few British naval officers would have immersed themselves in this common-sense fashion. John's idea of commerce was revealed when an Inuk approached him for a new spear shaft since the old one was broken; the request was refused. 'To give lightly, was to deprive ourselves of the power of rewarding; even had it not been absolutely necessary to keep up the price of our commodities, lest they should fall to no value, and deprive us of the future means of purchasing what was indispensable'.[24]

In March, the oldest man, Illictu, had died, or as his fellows put it, was asleep in a hut, the entrances to which were gradually demolished and the ice-windows removed. When the corpse was examined it remained in the posture in which he died; an incision was made in the abdomen.

The Inuit continued to visit the ship with such presents as salmon, two seals and a dog. When two individuals stayed over for a night, one slept while the other watched, though Ross was unable to decide whether such behaviour derived from suspicion or ceremony. For breakfast, each consumed five or six pounds of seal meat. In return, they built a snow hut for the observatory to house the crew's instruments. James Ross went off to explore with Ikmallik. One Inuk was terrified when he picked up a loaded gun that went off in his hands, though he was uninjured. A nephew of Ikmallik, an orphan, joined the crew's school. He was the individual that Ross had already picked out as the most likely to be trainable as an interpreter after he had learnt English, but he soon lost interest and no substitute was forthcoming.

John Ross acquired sufficient dogs to form a second dog team while his nephew set off with a dog-sled to explore. The dogs kept returning to their original owners but the Inuit brought them back to the ship. Ross and his associates had the opportunity of observing the building of a snow house and were very impressed that a tent could scarcely be pitched faster than such a house was constructed. The sailors were given further information about a possible westward passage, in the direction of a place called Neitchilee.[25]

Early April 1830 brought severe gales and snowstorms during which, much to the concern of his uncle, JCR was off exploring. In mid month 'the temperature rose so much, as nearly to reach the freezing point'. Snow was removed from the ship, and the wall around it was demolished. The Inuit had long been convinced that the Navy men took observations in order to discover the possible whereabouts of prey. When asked where seals might be found, John Ross pointed at random, but when three were subsequently caught, he was in danger of becoming a seer in Inuit eyes. They rewarded him with one of the animals, though in Ross's view 'prognostication was a trade far too dangerous to our reputation to be indulged in'. He need not have worried for long because it was time for their new friends to move on with affectionate farewells. St George's Day was celebrated with a naval salute witnessed by none but the crew; 1 May was 'not the May-day of the poets', but shortly afterwards JCR returned from one of his more exhausting forays, bringing with him welcome musk-ox meat.

A passing party of natives taught John Ross something about Inuit kinship. An old man was the fourth husband of a young wife, though he had another, and his two sons shared one wife between them. An old woman had two husbands. Ross admitted his imperfect understanding, remarking only that Caesar's descriptions of the matrimonial arrangements of the ancient Britons were probably not so far-fetched as had sometimes been alleged. JCR set off again shortly before his uncle celebrated the anniversary of their departure from England. Several birds were shot as temperatures gradually warmed.

At the end of May both Rosses were off on independent but related expeditions. Some two weeks behind his nephew, John headed south-west along the coast observing a feature that reminded him of the Bass Rock in the Firth of Forth, to reach a village 17 miles from the ship, and another 5 miles further on, encountering a few Inuit. He later named the rock 'Adolphus Dalrymple' because of its similarity to the Galloway family's crest. John's party found their journey gruelling but were cheered to find another rock inscribed by the advance party, 'twenty miles from *Victory*'. However, an axe buried by MacDiarmid and Blanky on a previous expedition could not be recovered. Ross's party had been overtaken by an aged female nicknamed 'Old Greedy', who had a sledge full of blubber drawn by three dogs. On subsequently returning, having deposited her cargo, she confessed to having been party to the borrowing of the axe, which was now in the possession of two men. At another camp they were told the woman still had the axe. Deviating from James Ross's trail, they received local help in acquiring a haunch of venison and advice about where to fish. They also deposited supplies on an island to be picked up by James's returning party. According to John, he was the only one among his men who did not suffer snow-blindness. The Inuit seal hunt was going badly; one Inuk, in tears, asked Ross where he would find one.

191

Again Ross pointed at random to a place to give them hope and occupy their time, recording that 'it was not a very profound jest, to say that they would certainly take some if they would wait till the animals came'. Pushing on down the Amitioke River they reached the great lake of Neitchilee, the name also applied to the land, the river, a mountain and the settlements, comprising some twenty-one snow huts and thirty summer dwellings. Accompanied by his Inuit guides, a highly impressed John Ross ascended a mountain and took possession, allegedly, but misleadingly, 'with the consent of the natives':

> The termination of the extensive piece of water beneath us, towards the south-west, was invisible; but it was bounded by flat land on each side, on which I could count hundreds of reindeer. To the northward, the river Amitioke was seen for a long space towards its source, when it was lost in the distant mountains. The land in that direction was higher than that on which we stood; and a stream, running from it through a ravine, formed a cascade, which, presenting nothing but its complicated pendants of icicles instead of falling water, produced a very singular effect.[26]

Neitchilee, as even Ross must have understood, was a highly important hunting, fishing – and probably ritual – site, yet with gross insensitivity, he unimaginatively named it Lady Melville's Lake. He suffered some slight retribution since, having lost his percussion caps, he was unable to take advantage of the numerous birds and available deer that he might have shot, much to the surprise and disappointment of the Inuit. He excused himself by pleading snow-blindness, 'not wishing them to suppose that our fire-arms could ever be disabled or useless'. After descending the hill, they left a note for James under a cairn. To ensure that he knew where the provisions were cached, John sent a message to his nephew with an Inuk. They met a man who some months before had been given a phial of medicine by surgeon George MacDiarmid as treatment for a sore throat, which was hung around his neck, intact and unopened. Noticing that the doctor's face was swollen due to a painful toothache, the sometime patient tapped the phial three times, while blowing on it. Ross reported, 'that the doctor shortly recovered is certain; and if it was by means of the charm, it is not the first time that toothache has been cured in the same manner'.[27]

The party then proceeded by way of Lake Teijgriak to the gulf of Shag-a-voke, on the eastern side of the Boothian Isthmus, a stretch of land about five miles wide separating the eastern and western seas. After a laborious trek they reached Cape Keppel. In the distance they could see a flag marking some supplies left by William Thom and a search party from the ship. As it happened they were not required since Ross was well stocked with fish and venison, and it was a rather smug captain who returned to his ship after an absence of eight and a half eventful days exploring a small part of the Boothia peninsula.

Meanwhile Tulluahiu arrived to get his wooden leg fixed since he had broken it, and the carpenter obliged. William Thom, who had been left in charge, rather bizarrely noted in the log that 'the wooden-legged man, who, having broken his new leg, was drawn by dogs, on a seal-skin, their fish sledges having been eaten', a reference to the sledge runners that were made from frozen fish and were actually consumed after they had been thawed out. In mid June the other expedition returned, having reached a point a hundred miles west of Neitchillee.

John Ross was concerned because at least four men had been disporting some signs of mild scurvy for several weeks; others complained of rheumatism. He had already shown himself, on the previous expedition, to be a leader very attentive to the health of his crew. Geese, ducks and other wildfowl regularly supplemented their diet, but Ross determined on a fishing expedition. Gazing down on a bay they saw a lone figure crossing. They fired a rifle to attract attention, and it turned out to be an Inuk named Awack, whom they had already encountered. He accepted an invitation to eat and was no doubt flattered when he was given a rifle to carry as a sign of trust. He reported that his uncle Ikmallik with his group was camped ten miles away and was delighted when the explorers decided to visit, passing several islands and points, to be greeted with open arms. Ikmallick was about to depart since fishing at this spot was over for the season, but he agreed to stay another day if Ross's men would join them. Of course Ross was happy to do so and camp was pitched. The Inuit had to re-erect their tents that they had partially demolished and were joyful when Ross flew his flag above Ikmallik's tent rather than his own. These means of flattering their friends seem to have been an innovation on Ross's part, designed to cement the relationship between the two peoples. His reward was a present of fish including two fine salmon, which were promptly cooked. The twelve Inuit were invited into the tent though the Brits were at a loss as to how to cook for such a large party of seventeen in all. The problem was solved when it was discovered that the guests preferred their fish raw. Ross was horrified by how much they

193

consumed. While one and a half salmon sufficed for five 'English', the Inuit ate two apiece, so that each of those 'voracious animals' consumed fourteen pounds of fish: 'The glutton bear (or wolverine), scandalized as it may be by its name, might even be deemed a creature of moderate appetite in the comparison: with their human reason in addition, these people, could they always command the means, would doubtless outrival a glutton and a boa constrictor together.'[28]

Ross was not surprised that the Inuit often suffered from famine since they never appeared to store food for the future, but he was more puzzled as to why they needed to eat so much compared with peoples elsewhere: in his own observations the inhabitants of Iceland, Norway and Lapland never consumed such vast amounts. He wondered how their stomachs coped with such huge intakes, concluding that 'the Esquimaux is an animal of prey, with no other enjoyment than eating; and, guided by no principle and no reason, he devours as long as he can, and all that he can procure, like the vulture and the tiger'. He described how the raw fish were consumed: head and back-bone were removed and the fish equally cut in two, lengthwise, and then halved again. Each piece was then rolled into a cylinder 2 inches in diameter, which was placed as far into the mouth as possible, and cut off by the knife, 'so close as to endanger the end of the nose'; the severed piece (known as a *sipak*) was then handed to a buddy. One diner, lifting scraps off naval plates, inadvertently scooped up some lemon juice, his wry face affording his fellows great amusement. 'Man seems a laughing animal', remarked Ross dryly, if cruelly, 'even when he approaches as nearly as he can to his inferiors of four legs'. Earlier he had described two Inuit couples, in their respective beds, eating a trough of boiled fish and oil between them, 'much like swine, their faces and hands being bedaubed with this odorous compound'.[29] For Ross such contact reinforced his sense of his own civility and manners, just as to this day suspicion of exotic foreign foods and the mode of consuming them remains one of the basic expressions of racism.

When the Brits attempted to fish, however, the Inuit generally had some revenge by ridiculing their futile efforts, though on at least one occasion a gift of a gull and a goose shot on the wing restored naval credibility. Ross was able to purchase three caches of salmon from the Inuit in return for three knives, a total of one ton of fish to be taken back to the ship with the greatest difficulty and fatigue, but this was ideal food for those prone to scurvy, for whom it proved a medicine 'which all the drugs on the ship could not replace'. Ross was sad to learn of the death of the geographer Tiagashu, who had always shown great kindness, though his one-line obituary, while laudatory, seems grudgingly callous: 'whatever he might be as an Esquimaux, he at least died an amiable and an exemplary man'. Ross wondered whether British medicine could have done anything to save the deceased but, heartened by news of the fish purchase that would benefit the crew's health, he set off to collect it.

The Inuit built a new house to accommodate Ross's party on their visits, and the doctor was able to treat the 'woman of many husbands', who repaid him with her strike-a-light, the stone she used in making fire, a valuable gift. It was obvious that the residents had enjoyed a good hunting season with a take of at least fifty seals, two musk-oxen and two bears, while a third cache of fish was brought and their hosts assisted in transporting the supply back to the ship.

Again Ross indulged in some Inuit ethnology. A recently born child had been named Aglugga, as a compliment to James Ross, for his uncle believed this was James's Inuit patronymic: the same title 'Aglooka' – 'the long strider' – later conferred upon John Rae. Francis Crozier, second-in-command of the Franklin expedition, earned the same accolade while over-wintering at Igloolik during William Parry's voyage of 1821–3.[30] Could this accolade suggest the sense of 'one who comes from far away to travel he knows not where'? James Clark Ross was the Brits' greatest authority on Inuit language, life and culture, working with the populace, sharing their accommodation, fishing and hunting trips, and of course their food, but much as he admired them he was no starry-eyed romantic where they were concerned:

> There have been two hypotheses, and two errors, among travellers who have visited the rude and savage tribes of the world. The one sees virtues everywhere, and even finds it disguised under the garb of vice: the other is the direct reverse. I cannot help sometimes suspecting that we ourselves have been somewhat too much inclined to look at our Esquimaux friends through a sunny coloured glass: but at any rate, that is the most comfortable view which preserves ourselves in the best humour.[31]

The widow of Tiagashu had acquired a new husband because she had five children. Ross remarked that in Britain a ready-made family was not often welcome, whereas in contrast, the Arctic children were regarded as a source of profit rather than loss, and of 'happiness instead of vexation and torment'. This is perhaps as revelatory of Ross's attitudes as of those of the Inuit. He was more troubled by wife-exchange – indefensibly practised, for example, by the Romans – but he thought that the Inuit might be 'physiologically philosophical', because of the need and desire to produce more children; 'it is a good thing to have good reasons for doing what may not be very right'.[32]

James Ross ascertained that there was no route to the western sea from the area he had explored around the Agnew River. His men had suffered from snow-blindness and, in early May 1831, the mate George Taylor later had to have his frost-bitten foot partially amputated. The cold remained intense. An expedition was then undertaken to explore the west coast of Boothia. John Ross would lead the first party, and James would lead the second, each with three weeks' provisions, both accompanied by Inuit guides. Ross's men would return for further supplies while James would continue his advance. They also hoped to find out more geographical information from the *indigines*. This was a genuine Inuit–Scot collaborative venture: the line was led by a native woman, the mother of the two guides, followed by John Ross's sledge, with the dogs conveying a child and some native goods, guided by a woman with a child on her back. Behind was James sandwiched between two sledges. An Inuk hauling two skins of oil brought up the rear, along with John Ross and the Brits.

The whole appearance was very nomadic, according to John. They crossed the mouth of the Lindsay River on 18 May in a snowstorm, travelling 16 miles to the south. James climbed Mount Kakoloktok for surveying purposes, rejoining the main party at the River Saumarez, confined in a narrow gorge 80 feet deep, where all were surprised to find the stream open, as it had been all winter. One of the Inuit guides, who had gone ahead, suffered frostbite and was of little further help: 'he had concealed the injury so long that we could do little good'. The party passed several fishing stations before reaching the great lake, which Ross named after Krusenstern. Indeed, quite a bit of the imposed nomenclature recalled the captain's glory days in Sweden during the Napoleonic War and so represented self-commemoration.

The weather, however, was fairly brutal: gales, snow and freezing temperatures rendered them immobile. Nonetheless they struggled through blowing snow, when permitted, and, on 26 May, reached Padliak where they purchased trousers, deer skins and 'a skin of oil for fuel' from the Inuit. The following day the two parties separated, James heading west and John east to the valley of Shag-a-voke (Sagvac), which was of great importance because it provided a link, on the Boothia Isthmus, between the eastern and western seas, and John thought it might have formed a Northwest Passage, had it been 30 degrees further south, and where, in time, a canal might possibly be constructed. The concept of a canal in the Arctic may seem bizarre but the British canal craze was well and truly established before Ross left home. John's party reached a point 26 miles from the ship, close to where they had camped the previous year. The atrocious weather was sapping the strength of everyone. Ross could not help noticing that the present season was much colder than the last, when pools of water and significant snow-melt were much in evidence, unlike the conditions they were now experiencing. As ever, John displayed his superior stamina by leading the way home ahead of his exhausted followers. He was soon back out in the field, however, once again in atrocious weather, delivering supplies and a note with instructions, secured under a cairn, for when James's party would return from their western explorations and pass through Shag-a-voke.

Returning to the ship in early June, John conducted divine service for their Netsilingmiut Inuit friends using a bible he had been given at Holsteinborg in 1818, as well as the Danish–Norwegian missionary Hans Egede's translations of the creed and the Lord's prayer. The Inuit seemed to understand the words, though Ross admitted that his own linguistic skills were not sufficient to gauge what they thought of what they heard. The Netsilik Inuit brought the ship welcome supplies consisting of ninety-seven pounds of fish, some clothing and a bear skin, before returning to Neitchillee to fish for more. On 13 June, James Ross returned with the news that he had discovered the location of the Magnetic North Pole, the greatest single achievement of the entire expedition (see Chapter 6).[33]

As the summer solstice approached and passed, the weather proved relentless. Ross remarked that the British winter solstice seldom resembled the summer one 'in this most miserable region and abominable climate'. The irony of boiling snow for a drink of water in mid summer prompted thoughts of other Arctic paradoxes where the traveller smells no flowers because there are none and so he prefers the odour of train oil (extracted from whales or seals), which doubles as soup or seasoning in the absence of carrots or herbs, the only salad obtainable being that in a reindeer's stomach. Though the traveller never sees a tree, he can construct coaches of fish and sledges of crystal out of nothing but ice. He can build his own marble house in an hour, which can be renewed, like that of Aladdin, any time, anywhere, he wishes. Could anyone else except a 'Boothian Esquimaux' 'that could do all this, endure all this, contrive all this, conform to all this, to all this and more, and still be happy: happy if he is in Naples, happy too in Boothia Felix?'[34]

James Ross met five native families while out shooting, bringing the men back to the ship for the familiar introduction to naval, and British, culture. They knew of the peoples further north but, with the exception of one individual who had visited before, they had never seen a ship. They returned next day with wives and children, prompting Ross to reflect on the gender relations of the Inuit. He detected a 'gallantry' towards women among them that he thought was unexpected in a 'savage' people. In a failure of his own imagination he reflected that chivalry was associated with monarchical or despotic governments but the Inuit had neither aristocracies or governments and so he could not explain male attitudes towards females.[35] It is certain that the inclusion of women in Ross's expedition would have greatly deepened British understanding of Inuit culture.

James, with eight men and the surgeon, went off with two Inuit who had fish to trade and they ended up catching thousands, which were preserved in vinegar, pickled, salted, dried on rocks or consumed immediately. Transport was difficult as the ice was finally breaking up. The curing process was also exhausting, leading to consequent ailments, but all recovered, including an amputee, the only real casualty being one, Buck, who suffered from epilepsy. Many game birds supplemented the diet. The natives had immediately realised the efficacy of the net that James Ross used, so he showed them how to make one, even though he was unsure if they could find materials locally to manufacture another. The Scot thus taught the Inuit a 'valuable art, in making a present of knowledge which, to them, was of the first importance', thus improving their condition to a greater extent than by all the other objects they sold or traded to them.

John was proud that in their dealings with the Inuit they had traded no rum, spread no diseases, had done nothing to corrupt their morals, or to make them less happy than they had found them. 'Nor had they learned anything from us, to make them discontented with their present and almost inevitable condition . . . we can reflect with pleasure on what we have avoided to do, and even on what we did; indulging too at times in the dream, that should they ever again be visited by an European people, our memory may be handed down to a remote posterity, with, possibly, as mysterious a fame as that which gilds the name of Manco Capac', the legendary Inca ruler and sun-god.

He was, of course, deluding himself. He and his men had affected the *indigines* in ways that he could not even guess, but arguably he was allowed to dream. Cultural contamination, as he knew full well, was unavoidable, but one of Ross's remarkable characteristics was that he was aware of what the Inuit gave in return. He could not help his innate assumptions about 'savages', and some Inuit activities disgusted him, but he sincerely conceded that 'they were not only kind, but as Falstaff says of wit, they were the cause of kindness in those around them, including ourselves; and perhaps among ourselves, in one or two, who, with a different people, would have displayed a far other character than they did'.

The man with the wooden leg required more repairs. Natives went aboard to apologise for their dogs, who had stolen some fish, an action for which they had been severely punished. Ross, like several others, deplored the way the Inuit treated their dogs, which were 'hardly used and worse fed', and certainly not loved. Yet he mused that the English did not treat their horses much better and he commented that a comparison between a pack of British fox-hounds and a team of Esquimaux dogs 'would not leave much to boast of on the part of our own countrymen'. In fact, animals were often treated cruelly and unsentimentally in nineteenth-century Britain. There were, as now, specially favoured animals, but overall they did not receive much sympathy.

*

Captain William Penny of Peterhead (1809–1892) was one of the most remarkable whalers of his generation. In his travels he had often encountered the Inuit, one of whom, Eenoolooapik (c. 1820–1847) (known to the Scots as Eenoo, with a Sunday name of 'Bobbie'), he took back to Aberdeen with him in 1839, to help publicise and raise support for exploring new possibilities for whale hunting, an industry in decline at that time. As a boy Eenoo travelled with his family from Kingmikksoke, Cumberland Sound, to Durban in the north-east of Baffin Island, where he became fascinated by the exploits of the whalers, longing to visit their homelands. His chance eventually came when he met Penny, who was attracted by Eenoo's knowledge of Tenudiackbeek (Cumberland Sound), reportedly well stocked with whales. In Scotland Eenoo became something of a celebrity, having his portrait painted, and a book written about him by Alexander McDonald, a medical student who paid for his training by working on whaleships and by borrowing money from Penny, who was generous.[36] McDonald graduated from Edinburgh University in 1840 to become a doctor at Laurencekirk, Kincardineshire. At age 23 he was appointed to Franklin's crew for his final failed expedition.

McDonald was first introduced to Eenoo in Scotland in 1839 and became his tutor, and his doctor after the Inuk contracted a respiratory infection. Both men returned to the Arctic with Penny in April 1840 and McDonald was inspired to write a biography of Eenoolooapik and an account of the voyage. McDonald's *Narrative* concerning Eenoolooapik is full of interest, though it begins by publishing an excellent picture of the subject, and then stating that with Scottish tutelage he soon 'acquired habits of extreme personal cleanliness – a circumstance the more surprising, [because] the Esquimaux are generally very inattentive in that respect'. He also relates that Eenoo's mother, hating the suggestion that he leave with Penny, mounted displays of grief until, 'in accordance with the peculiar customs of her country on such occasions, she laid bare her bosom, and invited him by an appeal which, though silent, was irresistible, to kiss the warm breast which in infancy had suckled him'. Unsurprisingly, at this point Eenoo almost relented but managed to resist maternal pleading due to Penny's guarantee of his safety. Unfortunately for the Inuk, he was ill for almost three months in Aberdeen, during which time Penny tended and cared 'all the same to him as a mother'.[37]

Eenoo was taught the alphabet but showed little interest in reading. Carpentry was more interesting; he was fascinated by trees as these were non-existent at home. As McDonald observed, Eenoo followed the 'prospective principle', concentrating on subjects and objects that he thought might be of 'future utility'. He visited a cotton factory, since he was usually rather intrigued by machinery, but found it rather boring. He loved drawing, displaying considerable artistic talent, and he greatly enjoyed the theatre. He was also an accomplished mimic and imitator, observing and copying actions and gestures of others and such matters as table manners. He visited the Castle of Mey in Caithness and Inchkeith in the Firth of Forth. It says as much about McDonald as it does about Eenoo that 'he was equally at home with every person, knowing none of the ordinary distinctions of society'. He was, unusually for an Inuk, a modest eater. 'He showed none of those fierce and ungovernable passions which characterise man in his savage condition, but, on the contrary, he was mild and gentle in his nature, and modest, and even delicate, in his intercourse with female society'. He left Scotland on 1 April 1840 on Penny's ship *Bon Accord*, and was dropped off at Tenudiakbeek to be reunited with his mother and siblings. He married Amitak and they had a son called Angalook. Over the following years Parry continued to visit to trade baleen whale but unfortunately Eenoo contracted consumption and died in 1847.[38]

There is much to ponder in McDonald's small book. Some wondered why Eenoo was so keen to return to his barren homeland but McDonald supplied an explanation, a very obvious one understood by every Scot.

> We may be apt to think that he shewed a strange and unnatural predilection in thus choosing to forego the advantages of civilized life, and return to the barren haunts of his early childhood; but let us only think of the deep and uneradicable associations that cluster and cling round the home of our own early years, and our surprise at Eenoolooapik's resolution will be qualified. It was Nature's earnest promptings that urged him to return to the land of his birth; for, dreary and desolate though it might appear to others, its snow-clad hills and craggy cliffs were to him as the faces of familiar friends; and, besides, there were the strong and enduring claims of maternal relationship binding him to home – principles which, we have seen, reigned paramount in his ingenuous nature when laid on a bed of languishing and apparent death.[39]

Some thought of dispersing the alleged mists of superstition that clouded his mind but mercifully there was not enough time for revelation. McDonald superciliously hoped that the Inuk's visit had softened the remaining barbarity of his nature, and 'in the evolution of Time's dark mysteries, become subservient to the good of the hyperborean races'.

Perhaps the most whole-hearted assessment of the Inuit came from the remarkable John Hepburn, the Scottish 'Hero of the Barrens' during Richardson's and Franklin's expedition of 1819–22. He once confided that in situations of the greatest straits he should have considered it a great privilege to have been allowed to settle down among the Inuit for life. Had he been permitted, he would have considered his chances of life greater by adopting their habits than by remaining with his own people.

Thomas Simpson, 1845
(Public domain, via Wikipedia Commons)

8

THOMAS SIMPSON:
UNITING THE ARCTIC WITH
THE GREAT WESTERN OCEAN

The Dease and Simpson HBC Expedition of 1836–1839

Fame I will have, but it must be *alone*.

Thomas Simpson[1]

When George Back learned that John Ross and his crew were overdue in returning from their 1829 expedition (see Chapter 6), he hastened from Italy in 1832 to offer his services in leading a search. John Richardson had already made a similar suggestion, which was refused, but his plan was followed up by George Ross, brother of John, who, seeking someone to take on the task, was planning to petition the king. After Back was proposed as leader, the Government supplied £2,000 to be supplemented by £3,000 donated by Ross's friends, as well as supplies and canoes contributed by HBC. George Ross resigned as Honorary Secretary of the scheme to pursue an abortive initiative of his own, Robert McCulloch, a cousin of the Rosses, taking over the office. HBC issued a seal giving special protection to Back as commander, as well as 120 bags of pemmican, two boats and two canoes. Two officers and eighteen men were to be involved, and the expedition would explore the area around the Great Fish River (Slavey, *Thlew-ee-choh-dezeth*; Dogrib, *Thlewechodyeth*; Inuktitut, *Haningayok*), the mouth of which was thought to be less than 300 miles from the wreck of *Fury* in Prince Regent Inlet, which Ross had planned to visit. It was not known where precisely the river reached the sea but First Nations testimony placed it to the east of Great Slave Lake 'and might be approached by an intervening chain of smaller lakes and portages'.[2] At the very least the expedition would lead to new geographical discoveries and would add to knowledge of the Magnetic Pole. Furthermore, new information would be discovered about the northern limits of America, specifically the coast to the east of Point Turnagain, which Back was ordered to map. His instructions were almost painfully obvious and common-sensical. In his *Narrative of the Arctic Land Expedition*, Back explained that, since so many modern travellers had by now described the route to Great Slave Lake, 'a minute detail of our progress seems unnecessary'.[3] In the event he was advised within a year that Ross had returned safely. The new plan involved finding the obelisk that marked Ross's furthest point, at about 69°37' N and 98°4' W, thereafter exploring east or west, both of which objectives the puppeteers in London thought should be possible in one season.

Back was particularly grateful to Governor George Simpson and Dr John Richardson for help with the expedition. He met Consul James Buchanan again at New York (as he had done during Franklin's 1825 expedition), survived a fire in his Montreal hotel, thereafter facing a phalanx of Scots as he embarked on the long journey to the Barrens. His second-in-command was Richard King, a Londoner who claimed to have graduated in medicine from St Andrews. Like Back, he was thought by some to be a troublesome individual and it seems that the two men tried to avoid each other. George Simpson was off to Britain for medical treatment and could not meet Back in Canada but he wrote to extol the humane and philanthropic views of the enterprise, such that 'they cannot fail to excite and command the sympathies of all with whom you may come in contact'. En route Back recruited Highlander James McKay, 'a powerful fellow, one of the best steersmen in the country'. Another acquisition was the talented steersman George Sinclair, born in Canada but with an Orcadian name. Other Scots in his party were artilleryman John Ross, Donald McDonald, Morrison Morrison and James Spence. On one of his own excursions, Back's motley crew consisted of an Englishman, a man from Stornoway, two Canadians, two Métis and three Iroquois; 'Babel could not have produced a worse confusion of unharmonious sounds than was the conversation they kept up'. At Pine Portage, Back was relieved and delighted to recruit an old acquaintance, Alexander Roderick McLeod of HBC, a physically powerful and controversial figure. Born in Quebec, McLeod joined NWC and became Chief Trader of the HBC's Athabasca region. Contemporaries and historians have given him a rather mixed assessment but there is no doubt he provided stalwart and essential service for Back.

Having reached Fort Resolution on Great Slave Lake, Back divided his men; there were no Scots in his section. In late August he set out on his own to look for the men he had sent ahead to scope the great river that was the goal of the expedition. He climbed a hill to behold rapids, encouraging him to cross two rivulets that he correctly identified as tributaries of Thlew-ee-choh. His forward group had encountered the same river the day before. When they turned up, all shared 'a little grog', to celebrate the occasion. Returning to Slave Lake they re-joined the invaluable McLeod. The rumour-mill was once again operating. William McTavish at Norway House unkindly described Back's expedition as a 'bungle' as it had achieved very little. He assured his sister that Back and his crew would take none of the blame for its failings themselves, 'like all other expeditions [they] will do little & speak a great deal'. Another commentator stated that Back had not added much to science and geography, while an interview with the 'Eskquimaux' on the coast 'bodes no great things'.[4] Bad-mouthing expeditionaries was one of the great recreations of HBC employees, who always seemed to greet newcomers with disdain.

Throughout his *Narrative*, Back makes mention of the crucial contribution of the First Nations to the expedition and its eventual successful outcome. He also includes much of interest concerning their culture, activities and attitudes. Some of his most impressive writing describes the aftermath of discovering the river as he captures scenery and weather, the vastness of the landscape and the power of the water. He ordered the building of what became known as Fort Reliance, complete with an observatory. As winter advanced, many starving First Nations people arrived or passed through. Expedition members also suffered but were saved from extreme hunger thanks to the hunting abilities of Akaicho, veteran of Franklin and Richardson's venture of 1820 to 1822. McLeod had his own problems trying to feed employees and servants of HBC. One victim was Augustus, the faithful interpreter, who died of hunger or cold or both.

McLeod left the expedition as he was now surplus to requirements. Back pushed on with his second-in-command Richard King (surgeon and natural scientist), James McKay (steersman), George Sinclair ('half-breed', steersman and bowman), Charles MacKenzie (Highlander, bowman), James Spence (Orkney, middleman), John Ross (Highlander, middleman) and Peter Taylor ('half-breed', middleman): a complement of eight. King is often written off in Arctic literature as a sour and disagreeable character but, whatever his personality, he was undoubtedly a high-powered individual and a founder of the Aboriginal Protection Society, as well as a pioneer ethnologist.[5] All now ventured down-river, often in rapids and extremely rough water, plagued by rain, fog and wind. This was classic, hair-raising, brilliant canoeing evocatively described: 'Still widening, the river rolled on without obstruction, being here large enough to remind me of the Mackenzie.' Ahead there was something in the water that was taken to be a fawn. The bowman, almost without looking, reached into the water to grasp it but withdrew as quick as lightning shouting 'Damn it, it has bit me! It's a fox'!

Back had the sensitivity to consult his steersmen from time to time:

> The success of an expedition depends materially on the temper and disposition of the leading men, who must sometimes be reasoned with, and at other times kept in check as circumstances may direct. It is necessary that they should feel a confidence in, and an attachment to their leader, not paying a mere sulky obedience to his orders; and what they do will thus be done heartily and with good will, not as the cold fulfilment of a contract.[6]

The men generally responded to Back as he would have wished. In one confrontation with a 'frightful abyss' of raging water a crewman began to cry aloud to heaven for aid. McKay in a louder voice yelled 'Is this a time for praying? Pull your starboard oar!'[7] Spectacular cliffs were reminiscent of Orkney. 'Here's Hoy Head – give way boys we are not far from the sea!' The steersman climbed a rocky hill 'to get a good look at the river'; it was instantly named McKay's Peak. They continued to cross lakes and rapids that seemed to be endless. A group of Inuit met them at a fall in the river, round which they decided to portage, worried that their new acquaintances might attack. When portaging proved impossible the Inuit were asked to help and they gladly did, yet another example of co-operation between Inuit and incomers. One Inuk climbed a rock with Back to indicate the trending of the land and the direction of the sea. He knew of the lands of Akkoolee (in the Fury and Hecla Strait), thus confirming a continuous coastline beyond the Melville Peninsula. After 'a violent and tortuous course of five hundred and thirty geographical miles, and the conquest of eighty-three rapids', they had reached the sea. They named Victoria Headland and Cockburn's Bay since the nominee, first Chairman of the Arctic Committee, had supported the expedition. An island was named for 'my intrepid friend Captain James Ross'. Back honoured Richardson with a headland at the end of a mountain range, since Richardson's ideas about the Great Fish River and its relationship to the sea had been verified. There was a distressing and totally frustrating amount of ice around, such that they feared they might be trapped. The speed of the river was becoming a distant memory.

> I shall not attempt to describe what were my feelings at finding my endeavours baffled in every quarter . . . When the mind has been made up to encounter disasters and reverses, and has fixed a point as the zero of its scale, however for a time it may be depressed by doubts and difficulties, it will mount up again with the first gleam of hope for the future; but in this instance, there was no expedient by which we could overcome the obstacles before us; every resource was exhausted, and it was vain to expect that any efforts, however strenuous, could avail against the close-wedged ice, and the constant fogs which enveloped everything in impenetrable obscurity.[8]

Finally, the ice released them. It was time to return, but not before taking possession. The Union Jack was unfurled and saluted with three cheers, while naming this portion of America William the Fourth's Land, at latitude 68°1'57' N, longitude 94°58'1' W. They were 4 miles south of the latitude of Point Turnagain, which was almost due west of the ceremony site. Small amounts of spirits were provided. To cheer up his men Back sent them on a hunting expedition. They needed it because most would be reflecting on the sodden, back-breaking prospect of returning the way they had come. At the first portage they were met by the reliable Alexander Roderick McLeod with six men. He had been managing the expedition on behalf of HBC during Back's absence.

Back had travelled 7,500 miles since leaving and returning to La Chine, Quebec. He had been on the American continent for two years and almost seven months. He sailed from New York on 17 August 1835, arriving at Liverpool on 8 September. The king gave him an audience at which he expressed his 'approbation of my humble efforts, first in the cause of humanity, and next in that of geographical and scientific research'.[9]

Within a year Back had returned to the Arctic in *Terror*, a bomb-ship. One party was to approach Wager River or Repulse Bay, supplied with light boats that could be carried overland to trace the eastern coast of the Gulf of Boothia, the haunt of the Rosses' expedition. Another was to follow the American coast to Point Turnagain (Ross's Extreme). It was anticipated that the surveys could be carried out in the course of a single season (1836), demonstrating promptitude of execution while escaping 'the gloomy and unprofitable waste of eight months' detention', an overly ambitious expectation. Alexander Simpson mocked the geographical societies and Lords of Admiralty, who produced plans incompatible with the capriciousness of the Hyperborean Sea.[10] In the event, Back and his crew were icebound in Hudson Bay until the summer of 1837. What was still required was an HBC expedition to explore the blank between Franklin's Extreme West (beyond the MacKenzie River) and Point Barrow (Nuvuk). Also, a survey was needed of the coast between Franklin's Eastern Extreme and Prince Regent's Inlet (Qikiqtaaluk Region). The resulting expedition was to be undertaken by Thomas Simpson and Peter Warren Dease.

*

According to his brother Alexander, Thomas Simpson was fond of a quote from Horace, *Odi profanum vulgus et arceo* ('I hate the common masses and avoid them'), which can be interpreted as a disappointing example of self-exceptionalism and superiority with anti-social tendencies, or simply a determination to rise above the crowd. It is difficult to be sure one way or the other from the surviving evidence, which consists of his *Narrative of the Discoveries on the North Coast of America* and a biography written by his brother Alexander.

Thomas was born in 1808. His father, the son of a farmer, studied for the ministry but became a schoolmaster in Dingwall. His mother Mary was the daughter of the minister of Avoch, the village that is the burial place of the explorer Sir Alexander Mackenzie. Young Thomas was brought up in a happy Christian household with loving, liberal parents. He was rather a fragile child who, because of health problems, avoided rough games. He went on to Aberdeen University where the professors were allegedly as interested in the wellbeing of their students as they were in their education. The institution offered a range of bursaries and, according to Simpson (a canny Scot), Aberdeen was a cheap place to study such subjects as Latin, Greek, mathematics, natural history, chemistry, moral philosophy and logic. Fellow students consulted him on mathematical problems. The university debating society was split between the Highland party, favoured by Simpson, and the Lowland or 'Saxon' group. His summers were spent visiting relatives in the wild mountainous country of Wester Ross, convincing him that Highlanders were inspired by the magnificent scenery in contrast to 'the plodding stolidity of the inhabitants of the lowland'. In his final year he was awarded the Huttonian prize for best student.

He supposedly had a rather priggish view of women, who fascinated him and whom he tended to idealise. To him a beautiful woman was 'too ethereal a being to allow of a sensual thought being raised by the contemplation of her', although, in keeping with the sexism of his era, he was pained that such a beauty should indulge in the 'sublunary enjoyment of eating and drinking, still worse of gossiping'. However, during his Canadian travels, one source states that he had a female companion, Miss Armstrong, probably resident in Red River, but we have no further information.[11] According to his brother, Thomas remained devout and committed to Providence, whose aid was invoked throughout his travels, though noticeably less so with the passage of time.

Thomas's maternal cousin was Sir George Simpson, who became a governor of HBC; he was a fascinating character, a ruthless economist with a Richelieu-like dedication to the company, a proud Scot with a great love of, and flair for, ostentation, and a physical courage that was outmatched by no-one. A contemporary, chief trader John McLean, observed that 'his caprice, his favouritism, his disregard of merit in granting promotions could not have a favourable effect on the company's interests', while a more recent authority has distinguished among his characteristics 'a strange mixture of obsequiousness and assertiveness which made him acceptable to his masters and to his followers alike'.[12] Governor Simpson's experience of western Canada rapidly convinced him that many of HBC's difficulties could be attributed to sheer waste and inefficiency. While visiting back home in Dingwall he offered cousin Thomas a position as his secretary. Thomas initially declined but on graduating from Aberdeen he decided upon a kind of extended 'gap year' of twenty-four months before returning home and settling into the ministry. So it was that Thomas arrived at Lachine, Quebec, now a borough of Montreal, in April 1829, joining George Simpson at Norway House, at the north end of Lake Winnipeg, two months later. He was paid twice the normal rate for his employment, surely a family favour.

Less than a year after his arrival, Thomas was ordered to lead the first Western Brigade (brigades were hunting parties in the fur trade), comprising almost 100 people, to the head of Lake Superior, a remarkable commission. Yet he was soon complaining about cousin George, the long hours he was expected to work and the variety of tasks he was expected to master.[13] He quickly discovered a bonus in the exhilaration of travel by canoe, especially when accompanied by the songs of the voyageurs. One drawback was that his reputation as a scholar and a gentleman rendered his life a misery because of the hostile attitudes of other members of the workforce. The old lags warned him that he had been in paradise and would soon be in purgatory when he reached the wilderness. Simpson spent most of his time travelling on HBC business with spells at York Factory and Red River. In February 1831 he made a journey of 700 miles. He had an excellent set of dogs but he claimed that he 'never took refuge in his vehicle' (his sledge), preferring to use his snow-shoes. No longer the frail child, he claimed that he was not troubled by the cold and was not affected by 'arctic change'. During the march he claimed he 'never wore anything warmer than a cloth capot'.[14] Some thought he was foolishly exposing himself to fatigue but he had no wish to emulate the officer who crossed from Hudson Bay to the Pacific without once wetting his feet! He was heart-broken when his half-cousin Aemilius Simpson died of an old complaint. Aemilius and George Simpson had grown up together, the former escaping redundancy in the Navy by joining HBC as a surveyor and hydrographer. Thomas told his brother Alexander, who was also an HBC employee, that, following Aemelius's death, the two of them must love each other even more than before: 'I am much harassed with business and my own feelings which I must suppress.' He had reached the conclusion that the surname Simpson was a disadvantage.

He was becoming very critical of George the more he learned about how he operated. When the Governor was in England there was 'far less bustle' and just as much excellent work as when he was present. Thomas considered that his cousin miscalculated when he depended upon 'sheer driving', since it made everyone bad tempered and resentful. In his absence there was much cheerfulness but 'he has been to me a severe and most repulsive master'. Thomas had been forced to teach his fellow-workers to respect him, so that he was now treated by everyone as more *en bourgeois* than *en commis* (meaning of high rather than low rank). He was much happier under the governance of Chief Factor Alexander Christie from Glasgow, Governor of Red River.

> I feel particularly happy in acting under him; in fact, he is the only man whom I have yet seen in the country whom I could now respect and esteem as my immediate superior. His sound judge-ment, his integrity, his liberal and enlarged views, entitle him to the former, while his genuine kindness of heart and manner, ensure the latter.[15]

Governor George had often told his cousin that manners – meaning a way of behaving with respect to others – was more than half the battle but Thomas believed he should have set an example.

> By assuming such a harsh manner towards me, he should have known – he who lays claim to so much tact and knowledge of human nature – that the necessary effect on a young and generous mind would be a reciprocal repulsiveness, perhaps hatred; but I know his real sentiment, and forgive his apparent, though unnecessary unkindness . . . in every peaceful service, he who does not endeavour to make himself agreeable to his fellowmen acts in opposition to the first social principle, and cannot expect that his fellowmen should step out of their path to benefit or advance him.

Thomas lost much of the respect he once had for George whose 'firmness and decision of mind are much impaired'; George had become wavering, capricious and changeable, painfully nervous and crabbed. Furthermore, he was 'guilty of many little meannesses at table that are quite beneath a gentleman, and I might add, are indicative of his birth', a needlessly spiteful reference to George's illegitimate origins, unworthy of both men. He condemned the Governor's general management, stating that he was too much under the influence of the clergy and 'was at the beck of every beggarly long-winded Scot who came with a pitiful story, to ask a pound of tea or tobacco'.[16] Ironically some of the qualities that Thomas condemned in George were also detectable in himself. In exposing his cousin's supposed flaws he revealed his own mean spiritedness. He was sounding like a man in a hurry who was never satisfied, who enjoyed demolishing the achievements of others and who whinged excessively when given the opportunity. He told brother Alexander that there was so little talent among the HBC officers that both of them must 'soon become conspicuous' (for promotion).

Thomas listed the chief factors of HBC of whom he approved. These included John Dugald Cameron, 'an excellent and truly upright Canadian Highlander'; John Rowand, an English Canadian, 'brave as a lion and fiery as gunpowder'; Chief Trader Miles, 'a good-hearted Englishman, very able at the desk but eternally grumbling'; James Hargrave, store manager, 'a good, able, deep-thinking and deeply-read, Scotchman from the banks of the Tweed, my most intimate friend in the country, and likely to become a very leading man'; John Tod, a good Lowland Scot, and a very experienced trader, 'having been many years in that starving but valuable district, New Caledonia, was a man of excellent principle but vulgar manners'; James Douglas, 'of highly respectable English extraction' (actually the son of a Glasgow merchant, John Douglas, and Martha Ann, a 'creole' from Barbados). Douglas was born in the West Indies and educated in Lanark, Scotland, and would later become Governor of Vancouver Island and British Columbia. As usual the list was somewhat self-serving. Thomas considered himself 'perfectly confident' of becoming Governor of HBC in succession to George – the sooner the better – but he continued to fulminate about the unsatisfactory administration of the Red River Colony.

*

In 1836 Thomas Simpson began planning for the HBC expedition to chart the Arctic coast of Canada, filling two gaps left by earlier Royal Navy expeditions in search of the Northwest Passage. But, much to his annoyance, the nominal chief command was given to Peter Warren Dease, born at Michilimackinac (Mackinac Island between Lakes Michigan and Huron), who had been with Franklin on his two land expeditions. It was thought that appointing Thomas in command would have bred jealousies among older members of HBC, leading them to create as many obstacles as possible to success. It is also likely that Dease, who had been involved in the fur trade since 1801, was given command due to Thomas's somewhat adventurous reputation, volatility and lack of experience. He was extremely fortunate to have been considered at all, a circumstance that required the backing of his much-despised cousin, George. Another reason for Thomas's imagined slight, according to Alexander, was George Simpson's unwillingness, for personal and political reasons, to permit Thomas to 'attain a position so prominent and independent', should the voyage be successful. This is not convincing but it may explain why Simpson felt compelled to stress his own achievements during the expedition at the expense of poor Dease, whom he damned with faint praise and sometimes outright humiliation. While Dease was at Fort St James in New Caledonia, 1830 to 1835, he made handsome profits for the company and was appreciated as a 'most amiable, warm hearted sociable' individual. A talented musician, he organised feasts and games. The detailed journals of his expeditions with Thomas Simpson reveal him as a truly admirable individual and a conscientious servant of HBC.[17]

The Governor supplied comprehensive expedition instructions in July 1836. The purpose was to complete the discovery and survey of the coast of North America. HBC aimed to succeed where others had failed. Those selected for the important task were men whose abilities and qualifications were highly valued. With twelve men, Simpson and Dease were to spend the winter of 1836 at Fort Chipewyan (on Lake Athabasca) or preferably at Great Slave Lake. When conditions allowed, they were to proceed down the Mackenzie River to Fort Norman (situated on the south-western extremity of Great Bear Lake) leaving four men there who were to erect buildings and create fisheries at the north-east end of the lake. The remaining eight men were to travel down the Mackenzie towards the sea, tracing the coast westwards, making observations and surveys to the point where Beechey's barge was wrecked in 1827 on the watch of Lt Belcher who, as Admiral, would later achieve the distinction of losing four ships during the Franklin search.[18] At furthest west they were to raise a pillar or mound with a message in a hermetically sealed bottle at its base, giving details of their voyage. Two small canoes were to be constructed for emergencies. The leaders were to use their own discretion regarding the First Nations and the Inuit. Return to Great Bear Lake before winter was essential to prepare for another voyage in 1838 to trace the coast from Franklin's Point Turnagain to the mouth of Back's Great Fish River. Provisions such as ammunition, fishing tackle, babiche (rawhide) for snow-shoe lacing, along with other implements and other food, like pemmican and flour, were to be cached at Lake Beechey (part of the Back River), and some other point, or points, on the route. Other instructions directed them to keep journals, to name geographical features, to collect natural history specimens, to use any HBC facilities they may require and to appoint a substitute if an accident should afflict either of the principals.[19]

Thomas Simpson took a refresher course in maths and astronomy at Red River but he was not supplied with a proper set of measuring instruments until the voyage of 1839. While he commended Dease as a good, honourable man who accepted his advice in everything, including the route of their journey, so that, 'while the whole onus of the duty thus rests on me, I cannot help feeling sore that you [cousin George] should have considered it necessary to entrust another with the command'. He mentioned that he had received the printed copy of Back's journal, which in his opinion contained little in the way of thought, 'with no small portion of French sentimentality and self-admiration'. He would later dismiss it as 'a painted bauble, all ornament and conceit, and no substance'.[20] He received reassurance from Chief Trader Christie that Back's current voyage would not interfere with the plans of Dease and himself. Back had departed for Fort Chipewyan in July 1836.

Simpson and his men set off from the Red River colony towards Athabasca on 1 December 1836. The cuisine was not of the finest, prompting the remark, 'Tis not alone in Scotland that the complaint might be made that "God sends the meat but the devil the cooks"'! At Ile-à-la-Crosse in Saskatchewan he was hosted by Roderick MacKenzie, 'a hale highlander', a petulant but worthy veteran of the fur trade, who was told by the local Chipewyans that 'he is too old – it's time for him to go and die in his own country'. Simpson clearly displayed an occasional flash of humour but also seemed to enjoy his capacity for recording trivial irritants: things that went wrong, folk that annoyed him and so on. There is something retentive too, about informing the reader that the distance from Ile-à-la-Crosse to Fort Chipewyan, Athabasca, was 1,277 miles, a daily average of 28 miles, and his pride at arriving at Fort Chipewyan on the very day he had predicted was evident. There was no-one to challenge or verify his claim that this achievement represented 'the longest continuous journey ever performed by the same (sledge) dogs'. As time went by, he became more resentful of Dease, whom he characterised as 'a worthy, indolent, illiterate soul, and moves just as I give the impulse'.[21] By the end of their last season together Simpson cruelly opined, 'Had I not been, like Sinbad the Sailor, hampered with an old man on my back I should immediately have turned eastwards with both boats but the apprehensions of my useless senior and of the crews overpowered my single voice.'[22]

Thomas used two small boats, reserving a single large one for river and lake duties. (Richardson and Franklin had already demonstrated the potential and effectiveness of deploying smaller vessels.) These vessels were versions of York boats, named for York Factory in Hudson Bay, which were gradually replacing or complementing canoes in HBC because they were more robust and provided a much larger cargo space. There was and is no finer water transport than the canoe, but change was dictated by economics. York boats bore a resemblance to Viking ships, and indeed the early examples were often built by Orcadians.[23] Thomas's boat and fort builder, Orcadian John Ritch, constructed two shallow-draught sea-going boats, named *Castor* and *Pollux*, described as identical light clinker-built craft with a 24-foot keel and 6-foot beam, furnished with wash-boards and carrying two lug-sails. They were painted with clear pine resin and coloured paints made from natural materials. The steersmen were late of Back's Great Fish River adventure of 1834. The larger boat, *Goliah*, was retained on Great Bear Lake, Ritch diverting to work on Fort Confidence, partly designed by Thomas, in the lake's north-east. Thomas was soon complaining again to George Simpson that he had been deprived of the command after it had first been held out to him, 'and was, I think, my due', but he was confident about, and dedicated to, the venture. Alexander described his adored brother, Thomas, as possessed of a cheerful expression and twinkling eyes, while the expression of his mouth signalled stern decision. In addition, in his view, he was brave, judicious, enthusiastic and persevering.

With their supporters and three hearty cheers, Dease and Simpson left Fort Chipewyan on 1 June 1837, making for the western mouth of the Mackenzie, with high hopes of 'achieving what far more distinguished names had left undone'. They covered between 30 and 40 miles per day on Slave River, negotiating Pelican Portage and the Rapids of the Drowned, named for a canoe-load of voyageurs who perished there. 'Chipewyans squatted, like so many beavers on the muddy banks of the Salt River.' Thirty bags of salt were collected from a single mound on the plain, and hunting, especially of geese, was good. Entering Great Slave Lake they were halted by ice at Fort Resolution for ten days. They enjoyed a dance at which tea was served, 'all intoxicating liquors being excluded from this sober land', thanks to HBC's sensible policy. Games and sports passed the midnight hour. Dease vaccinated all the young people in and around the fort. Magnetic variation was measured. They caught fish, which they consumed with wild onions. Twenty-one dogs, brought from Red River, intended for hauling seven sledges, were placed in *Goliah*. Ice remained a problem, and the going was tough until they reached the Mackenzie, where they had better weather conditions, and the Athabascan-speaking Dogribs had learned to say '*merci*' when receiving gifts. At two in the morning Simpson was moved by views of the Rockies: 'The Day was lovely, and I fed my eyes with gazing on scenery so novel and romantic, that forcibly recalled to mind my native highlands', appropriate sentiments, for they were now following the passage of Alexander Mackenzie.

The crews for the sea included McKay and Sinclair from Back's expedition, and a group of individuals listed as middlemen: George Flett (Orkney, sailor), Charles Begg (Orkney, sailor), William McDonald (Highlander), Hector Morrison (Highlander), and John McKey (Canadian, Highlander). François Felix and Pierre Morin were both Canadians and bowmen. Peter Taylor, who had worked with Back, was bowman. He was also Métis, as were teenagers François Boucher and Ferdinand Wentzel. All went down the Mackenzie past the burning cliffs earlier described by Richardson, to Fort Good Hope where they were welcomed by Dease's son-in-law. The fort was on a new site on the other side of the river, the original having been wiped out by a fearsome ice-quake that destroyed all in its path though luckily the human inhabitants escaped. They were now following a more westerly branch of the river than that used by Franklin. Simpson was deeply impressed by the First Nations Loucheux people, who were not violent towards whites but who had a feud with the Inuit, which Dease had attempted to end by negotiating a peace in 1817–19. Wherever the party stopped, the Loucheux placed logs at the water's edge so that the visitors might enjoy a dry landing. The explorers exchanged gifts with them, mainly tobacco for fish, but the crewmen were each given a gun and ammunition just in case of possible trouble from the Inuit with whom they hoped to communicate using an 'Esquimaux vocabulary' they had brought along; the inhabitants of another Inuit village were convinced that the book 'spoke' to its users. They came across an umiak (open skin-boat) containing four women and two dogs, all of whom fled. Then a single kayaker appeared with whom they exchanged gifts, but he played the Inuit game of helping himself to whatever he fancied, on this occasion a knife and fork, which he good-naturedly returned when he was detected. He claimed to be the chief who had stopped the plunder of the Franklin party at Pillage Point in 1826.[24] Shortly after he left, the Arctic Ocean 'burst into view'.

Moving west along the coast, more Inuit followed, seeking to trade and indeed camp with the newcomers, an idea of which they were swiftly disabused when the sailors fired a couple of blanks. At Shingle Point a 24-foot-long umiak was discovered and a large sledge so well made that the Canadians described it as *comme à Montréal*. As Simpson observed, French vanity still thrived in the New World: for example, the largest ducks were called *canards de France*, all whites were *les François* and one old man believed that HBC's merchandise came from *la vieille France de Londres!*[25] Thomas took the opportunity to attempt the unspoken, but insistent, requirement that all Arctic explorers must describe icebergs: 'We twisted and poled our way through [the ice]: the transparent masses exhibiting every variety of fantastic shapes – altars, caverns, turrets, ships, crystal fabrics – which changed as we gazed upon them; and often rolling over or breaking down, with a thundering noise, tossed our little boats on the swell caused by their fall.' They viewed a reindeer trap designed to drive the animals into the sea, where kayakers gave them a deadly welcome.

There were other Inuit visits on their way to Herschel Island. Both Inuit and kabloonas had valuable trade, the former receiving the usual items while the sailors coveted pairs of waterproof boots, 'an invaluable acquisition', as well as lip ornaments intended as souvenirs rather than personal adornment. When Inuit names were written down, the men and some older women lined up to have theirs recorded. The Highlander's name, Eachin (Hector) caused great hilarity because it resembled a word in Inuktitut. Demonstrations of singing, dancing and leaping were greatly enjoyed. The Scots reciprocated with a reel that delighted the audience. The crew noted some evidence of Inuit trading with the Russians.

Moving on, the travellers battled ice that squeezed the boats, forcing Thomas Simpson to throw everything overboard. 'By means of portages made from one fragment [of ice] to another – the oars forming the perilous bridges – and after repeated risks of boats, men and baggage being separated by the motion of the ice, we at length succeeded, with infinite labour', in landing on a small floe, but remained cursed with fog and fierce winds.[26] They named a mountain range for Franklin as they approached Return Reef, offering thanks to the Omnipotent Being for his gracious protection.

Bad weather impeded progress, persuading Simpson it would be more efficient to proceed on foot with five men, including McKay and Morrison, departing on 1 August; both were subsequently honoured by having their names attached to inlets. Weather conditions were dismal, the sodden ground giving way to marsh and streams, clothes encrusted with hoar-frost, beaches muddy, creeks salty, all contributing to the naming of Fatigue Bay. They spotted Inuit who, much to their disappointment, seemed to be fleeing them, in a kind of role reversal compared with earlier encounters, until Thomas yelled that they were friendly whites. The Inuit men were absent from the camp, hunting. Initially suspicious of the newcomers, the Inuit women gradually came round offering fresh venison, which the sailors relished, and a mess of 'choice pieces steeped in seal-oil' that they thought was disgusting. Simpson exchanged his tin pan for a platter made out of a mammoth tusk. The explorers found a collection of large wooden sledges joined with whalebone and shod with horn. The Inuit gladly agreed to lend Simpson an umiak for two or three days (or 'sleeps' as their hosts called them). These ingenious vessels could float in 6 inches of water. According to Simpson they were so efficient in preparing for the voyage that the Inuit women declared 'us to be genuine Esquimaux, and not poor white men'. One of the women made a sketch of the inlet where they had landed, advising that it was very deep. She also drew a representation of a bay to the west to which an old man added a long narrow projection covered with tents that Simpson assumed to be Point Barrow. Just as they were leaving, the hunters returned. Despite further difficulties, such as dense fog, wild waves, wind, bitter cold and swells that soaked them to the skin, they reached Point Barrow, the climax to the journey from the Mackenzie, 'with indescribable emotions'. Thomas 'poured forth [his] grateful orisons to the Father of Light, who had guided our steps securely through every difficulty and danger'.

Spirits rose: 'Seeing the ocean spreading far and wide to the south-west, we unfurled our flag, and with three enthusiastic cheers took possession of our discoveries' in the name of the king. On landing they found a large cemetery with bodies scattered around in a state of decomposition. The Inuit assured them that these were not the result of cholera, the dreaded disease that had recently broken out in India, Britain, America and Canada. Simpson later surmised, correctly, that the cold temperature greatly slowed corpse decay. The local Inuit were keen to trade. Dancing displays were rewarded with tobacco, to which they were more or less addicted. Inevitably Simpson was moved to an outburst of racist arrogance. The women, indefatigable in their blandishments, were 'whores' without exception. The men are 'a set of lousy, good-humoured, thievish, pimping rogues. Without fire-arms I should be sorry to trust to their tender mercies, notwithstanding their smiling physogs.' This quotation is from a letter Thomas wrote to his brother but omitted from the *Narrative*.[27] 'While all were thus pleasantly occupied', reported Simpson, 'I walked across the point, to obtain the requisite bearings'. The enticing prospect of fine weather and seascape in the beauty of the moment was such that he would not have hesitated to paddle to Bering Strait in his canoe. Instead, he penned a brief discussion of the First Nations, mentioning William Robertson's theory that the American peoples had come from Asia via the Straits.[28]

While visiting Boat Extreme (to the east of Point Barrow) a few Inuit were treated to a medley of French and Highland boat-songs that, 'probably for the first time resounded from an Esquimaux *baidar*' (Russian word for an Alaskan kayak). The small audience responded with harmonies, bending their heads down over the water and pounding their chests. The travellers left Boat Extreme on 6 August and reached Beaufort Bay and the mouth of the great Mackenzie on the morning of the 11th; overall, apart from the Inuit presence, it had proved rather a depressing experience. One achievement was the discovery of the Colville River, which Augustus the interpreter had informed Franklin about in 1826, more proof, wrote Simpson, of the accurate information supplied by the Inuit. Robert Campbell had recently been commissioned by HBC to set up a post on the Liard River in the largely uncharted Rocky Mountains; he was soon driven out by First Nations Nahanies who were allies of the Russians.

At Demarcation Point, the local Inuit knew by the explorers' boots that they had come from the far west. All enjoyed a leaping match, and the home-team triumphed. The Inuit were fascinated when the sailors read out names of recent acquaintances from their notebooks. Deer meat was plentiful. It appeared to Simpson that the arrogance of the Inuit increased in proportion to their numbers, hardly a surprising observation. He asserted that in their minds they ascribed 'the moderation and forbearance of the whites to weak-ness and pusillanimity', warning of how dangerous the Inuit might become if they ever acquired fire-arms. Having reached the Mackenzie, the team advanced by towing. A family of Loucheux was descending the river 'on rafts formed by two large logs joined by a cross bar' (in the shape of capital 'A'), a simple but clever vessel that impressed Simpson. There was a raised platform on the forepart for passengers. Escorting them were canoes that could be secured between the projecting arms of the raft's afterpart. Thomas made some remarks on such practices as infanticide and cannibalism that the HBC was attempting to eradicate but pointed out that these atrocities had occurred at one time in British history as well, citing Gibbon's *Decline and Fall* as his authority. There is no doubt that Simpson was quite interested in the ethnologies of the north-west peoples. Pausing at Fort Good Hope, he noted that the Loucheux used cowrie shells as currency. On departure, the group was joined by Dease's wife, niece and grand-daughter. They enjoyed a 'profusion' of raspberries and gooseberries as well as the excellent flesh of a large black bear shot by McKay. They edged their way up the river, alongside rocky, life-endangering cliffs. Drowning accidents were now less frequent since boats had replaced canoes but Dease's boat had to be rescued when it sprung a leak. At Great Bear Lake they netted satisfying quantities of fish. The company was detained for four days by severe winter conditions. Lots of ice had accumulated on the lake shores. As they headed for their winter quar-ters at Fort Confidence, at the north-east end of the lake, 'a solitary Canada goose, the very last straggler of the rear guard, flew past to the southward'.

The difficult winter weather had caused the fort builder John Ritch much trouble as well. Many at the fort needed help as they were suffering from influenza; a diet of fish brought some relief but became scarcer as the temperature dropped. Reindeer were hunted. Middleman Peter Taylor died of an incurable pulmonary disease. A flattering complimentary letter of congratulation was received from Governor Simpson, who urged Thomas to take another year if required to complete his mission. In the dismal dark days of winter from 30 November 1837 to 12 January 1838 the sun did not rise and nature slept, with the exception of the raven and 'whisky-john' (Canadian jay).

The people of the Arctic and the subarctic still look forward to winter as their favourite time of year. It is a period for hunting though nowadays perhaps more for recreation than food. Those born in kinder climes do not look forward to the season of cold and darkness. So it was with Thomas Simpson, who took comfort from an 'excellent' little library at Fort Confidence when 'fatigued with writing, chart-drawing and astronomy'. There was a fair collection of books on science and northern travels but also available were Plutarch, Shakespeare and Gibbon's *Decline and Fall*. He also mentioned Scottish writers – David Hume, William Robertson, Tobias Smollett and Sir Walter Scott. 'It was well that we came so provided for our friends have not thought fit to send us any publications of the day'.

At Christmas and New Year's Day the entire populace celebrated. Folk on the Arctic frontier were big eaters when they had the chance. Dease remembered employees who negotiated a daily allowance of 14 pounds of moose or buffalo meat. Another man allegedly required 20 pounds of animal food per day. Highlanders and Orkneymen found food for the brain in the contents of the small library at the fort, but the Canadians – the voyageurs – were illiterate. HBC officers ate, smoked and chatted with First Nations folk, who also slept in their hall at night, generating a 'kindly familiar intercourse' that was reciprocated by loyalty to the company. Attempts to transform hunters into pastoralists were doomed since the latter's attitude was: 'Why should we be bound like slaves to follow the motions of a band of tame animals, when our woods and barren grounds afford us moose, red-deer, buffalo, caribou and musk-cattle; when our lakes and rivers supply us with fish, for the mere trouble of killing them?'

In preparing for his next expedition Simpson announced he would need two summers for the investigation of the eastern seaboard, as well as additional supplies of pemmican, dogs, birchwood for sledges, and ammunition; 'as for everything else we resolved to live like the natives'.[29] Simpson wrote eloquently about the intensity of winter cold in the Barrens. The First Nations were circulating stories about 'an approaching change in the order of nature', signified by men on the west side of Great Slave Lake, sprung from the earth, whose eyes and mouths were reportedly situated in their chests. They offered 'unbounded hospitality' in the shape of a great cauldron containing five moose-deer. Simpson dismissed the whole episode as originating in a dream but this cry of starving warriors could have been a message to HBC, with the potential to grow into some kind of cultic or apocalyptic event. News was coming in also of serious outbreaks of smallpox that would later spread to the Rockies and the north-west coast.

Towards the end of March and early April 1838 Simpson set off to explore the Barrens between Dease River and the Coppermine, writing evocatively about the misery of the experience and enduring temperatures regularly below minus 30 degrees. They were out for only seven days but in that time two of his dogs froze to death and several of his men suffered snow-blindness, inspiring Simpson to provide protection in future, with shades and laudanum eye-drops. Simpson went off again in May with two men for twelve days of exploring. He was cheered that the First Nations were showing some signs of more 'civilised' behaviour but could not resist adding that he wished he could 'speak as favourably of their honesty and veracity'. It would be interesting to know what they thought of him but there are almost no witnesses whose impressions have survived, save for those of mixed-race people, who were emphatically negative.

The news of Simpson achieving his first objective, of surveying the western coastal route to Point Barrow, did not reach Britain until the following year, in April 1838. Thomas celebrated this triumphant moment in a letter to Alexander:

> Fortune and its great Disposer have this season smiled upon my undertakings, and shed the first bright beams upon the dark prospect of a North American life. Yes, my dearest brother, congratulate me, for I, and I *alone*, have the well-earned honour of uniting the Arctic to the great Western ocean, and of unfurling the British flag on Point Barrow.[30]

He later referred to 'our first glorious campaign; I should say *mine*, for mine alone was the victory'.[31] He also wrote to George Simpson enquiring about any 'pecuniary reward that might be forthcoming'. When working as George's Secretary at Red River he had earned a chief-tradership, so he believed that he now qualified for a second step. He had solved an important geographical problem that had baffled many able officers who nonetheless received rewards for what they had done; 'Do not reject my just claims, although I am one of your own relatives'. At least one newspaper agreed with him; 'the north-west passage around the continent of America is at length determined'.[32] In 1827 Beechey had reported that 'the extent of land left unexplored between Point Turnagain and Icy Cape is comparatively so insignificant that, as regards the question of the northwest passage, it may be considered to be known'.[33]

*

The conquest of the eastern section was to prove more elusive. The expedition set off on 6 June 1838, 'the first flush of water having passed off and the ice descending'. Simpson's *Narrative* contains a great deal of detail, which, while undoubtedly fascinating, must be set to one side in the present account of his adventures and those of his followers. The first challenge was the ascent of the Dease River choked with rapids and embanked by willows that impeded tracking. A rock in the middle of a river chasm was named 'the Old Man of Hoy' by the Orcadians. Snow and ice blocked their progress as they dragged themselves through water waist-deep. The Loucheux invited them to a feast of musk-ox; another bull proved highly palatable while geese and deer were also shot for the pot. Six of the young warriors were recruited to join a short part of the expedition, receiving European names. Thomas acquired four brindled wolf pups that he intended to train for sledging; they shared his night blankets.

On 20 June the party reached the same spot that Simpson had explored in April. 'We had now achieved what the men had long regarded as one of the most dubious and difficult portions of our enterprise'.[34] The Coppermine, well supplied with large blocks of detached ice, was in full flood. On some days the river had to be avoided due to force and turbulence. The intrepid Simpson, like a character in a *Boy's Own* type magazine, accompanied by the experienced and highly skilled Sinclair, negotiated a pass only 8 feet wide, as their boat 'shot safely through those jaws of death'. At Bloody Fall some detritus remained scattered around, a legacy of the visit by Richardson, who was honoured in the naming of another powerful river. Thanks to the diplomatic skills of Dease, they made friends with an Inuit family.

On 1 July they pitched their tents at the mouth of the Coppermine but the ice did not open until 17 July. At the end of the month they sailed around Cape Barrow. But the ice persisted, necessitating a 140-mile circuit to reach Point Turnagain, worsening conditions leading Simpson to decide on a foot expedition portaging a wooden-framed canvas canoe, with two

First Nations and five servants each carrying half a hundredweight and averaging 20 miles per day. Simpson named Cape Franklin, where the captain had visited in 1821, and similarly honoured his own cousin with Mount George. He claimed to have covered 100 miles of the coast and to have distantly seen a further thirty. An extensive stretch northwards, of *terra incognita et nivea* ('land unknown and snowy'), was dubbed Victoria Land, in honour of the young queen who succeeded on 20 June 1837. It was a right royal sight! 'The ocean, as if transformed by enchantment rolled its free waves beneath and beyond the reach of vision to the eastward . . . In fact I stood on a remarkable headland at the eastern entrance of an ice-obstructed strait'. A promontory was named Cape Alexander for his brother, who would have been very keen on sharing his journeys. After five days the men were already showing signs of stress due to the difficulties of travel. A pillar of stones was erected, Thomas taking possession of the country in the usual way in the name of HBC and the queen. Whether there might be a seaway through to the south of Victoria Land and surrounding islands, as well as a route to Ross Pillar and the estuary of the Great Fish River, he could not conjecture, though the trending 'of the most distant land in view should rather seem to favour the latter conclusion'.

However, he regarded his attempt overall as a failure. 'All that has been done is the fruit of my own personal exertions, achieved under circumstances of peculiar difficulty. I was not altogether free to follow my own designs'. Dease was allegedly nervous about storms, snow, frost and ice, a family man prepared to risk nothing and 'therefore the last man in the world for a discoverer . . . I cannot help regarding him and his followers as a dead weight upon the expedition'. This comment in a letter to George Simpson was unforgivable. The Arctic was absolutely the last place to be explicitly condemning the activities of a colleague, especially one well regarded by others and whom he had himself occasionally commended. At Bloody Falls he had proved that earlier explorers (including Franklin, Richardson, McKay and Sinclair) had been wrong to assert that further ascent of the Coppermine was impossible. Thomas believed he had demonstrated that 'ten years experience well applied may be more valuable than that of a life-time'. Nonetheless his authority was beginning to slip. The men started to argue about everything, shattering the camaraderie and cohesion of the group. He and Dease led their followers back to Fort Confidence, arriving on 14 September.

Though he had joined the ranks of northern discoverers, Thomas still expected to be snubbed. Finding three white wolf cubs he intended to train to the sledge was not adequate compensation, though there was some 'balm for a wounded spirit' when news arrived in late December that his despatches had been very well received by readers of *The Times* and other newspapers worldwide. The Geographical Society had awarded him a gold medal presented by the king.

Simpson spent a miserable winter at Fort Confidence. Others enjoyed few comforts of any kind throughout the season of 'care, anxiety and privation':

> A winter of intense anxiety is nearly over without mortality. But for our aid many of the natives must have perished from hunger; for a murder among themselves, last fall, paralysed their energies, and, to add to this calamity, the reindeer forsook their lands. We have saved them through great sacrifices, and greater exertions.[35]

He made arrangements for the men who would remain behind while he embarked on another expedition in 1839. Alexander Simpson might be thought guilty of exaggeration when he refers to his brother's 'determination to succeed or perish', invoking the example of Wellington with whom he supposedly shared 'daring courage, enthusiastic ardour, a sedulous attention to minute details', careful preparation and cautious judgement, but Thomas later made a similar claim. He also prepared his will before setting out. HBC held £500 of his money with a revisionary share as a chief trader of 'at the utmost fifteen hundred pounds sterling'. In October he was able to report that all of the expedition's objectives had been realised. He spent a week exploring Richardson's River having been unable to advance beyond Bloody Fall because of ice conditions. When they reached Cape Barrow they enjoyed a spectacular view of Coronation Gulf, ice-free in parts. They landed at Cape Franklin (on the Kiillinnguyaq peninsula) but experienced great difficulties in sailing around Cape Alexander (Hiiqtinniq). Much of their route consisted of labyrinthine ice, bays, headlands and numerous islands, features that the two leaders considered would deter future ships. They expected the currents would carry them round James Ross's Cape Felix but instead they found a strait 10 miles long, where 'the rapid rush of the tide scarcely left a doubt of the existence of an open sea leading to the mouth of Back's Great Fish River'. Now in mid August they were hit by the fiercest thunder storm any of them had seen in the Arctic. They made for Montreal Island where McKay and his cronies found some rotten food left by Back's contingent.

Simpson decided, and his men agreed, they should try to find more information about what lay beyond, so that they might 'speak with greater precision of that land on which stands Cape Felix of Captain John Ross'. He slightly miscalculated since what he thought was the southern shore of Boothia was actually King William Island. They sailed across Chantrey Inlet where Simpson climbed and named Cape Britannia. From there he detected the easterly trend of the coast, the view to the north-west showing an ice-free sea and distant islands. Dease and Simpson named their furthest point Castor and Pollux River after their remarkably resilient boats. High land to the north was dubbed Cape Sir John Ross and there they took possession. Dease and Simpson expressed their admiration for John Ross's 'extraordinary escape from this neighbourhood after the protracted endurance of hardships unparalleled in Arctic story'. In mid September they returned to the Coppermine having achieved 'by far the longest voyage ever performed by boats on the Polar Sea'. Thomas definitely had no notion of hiding his lights under a bushel or a winter's worth of snow. The final leg of the journey involved ice, wind and intense cold such that many of the men suffered acute pains and swollen limbs. Twenty miles off Victoria Land he captured something of what the Arctic meant to him.

> We have never seen anything more brilliant than the phosphoric gleaming of the waves when darkness set in. The boats seemed to cleave a flood of molten silver, and the spray, dashed from their bows before a fresh breeze, fell back like showers of diamonds into the deep. It was a cold night, and when we at last made the land, cliffs, faced with eternal ice, obliged us to run on for a couple of leagues before we could take the shore with safety. The coast of Victoria Land, which we explored for upwards of one hundred and fifty miles, is incomparably the boldest we have met with in these seas. Often near the shore no bottom could be found with thirty-five fathoms of line, and the cerulean blue colour of the water everywhere indicated a profound depth.[36]

He could not know that this was his farewell to the Arctic. He wrote to the directors of HBC in London, noting that since Dease had handed his command over to him he was making plans for the exploration of the Gulf of Boothia with a recommendation that Fort Reliance should become the wintering ground for attacking the Great Fish River. He favoured two seasons, if

225

necessary, for a thorough search and survey. London's initial response was to offer him a winter's leave of absence, to which he responded that he had no interest in such leave, 'so kindly offered unasked'. He supplied an embryonic plan for exploring the Gulf of Boothia and the Great Fish River, 'the only section of the Arctic coast of America now unknown'. McKay and Sinclair were willing to serve, as the only steersmen with experience of the river. He would require thirteen men; his intention involved pushing through the Fury and Hecla Strait and on to York Factory. The final flourish of his missive stated that he was ready and willing to devote 'not only my life but my means to the achievement of an enterprise that cannot fail to confer new lustre on the Honourable Company's name'. He was prepared to offer £500 of his own money to the venture. This time his proposals were accepted in a letter of 3 June 1840. It never reached him. Two weeks earlier Thomas had written to Alexander envisioning 'a comfortable retreat together in our native land, having but one heart, one soul and one united family. The friendship of the world I know and feel to be vain and worthless; ours will endure fresh and unchangeable till death.' He observed that for those who remained too long in HBC service the reward was wretchedness. On 5 June 1840 Thomas wrote to Alexander for the last time. He was on his way to England via the United States presumably to consult the Company directors, following a route recently adopted by Red River merchants seeking a more promising market than the long exhausting haul through Hudson Bay, trekking instead through the US by way of St Peters and the Mississippi.

Alexander first learned of Thomas's death in a New York newspaper report with the headline 'Murder and Suicide', which he read in Hawai'i. He believed that his brother 'fell a victim either to the malice and cupidity of his companions or to a sudden and unpremeditated quarrel'. A great deal of confusion surrounds the death of Simpson. His last words to Alexander were to the effect that he was departing with two well-armed companions since they expected to encounter the Sioux on the Prairies. To judge from his *Arctic Narrative* he was hostile towards the Bois-Brûlés soon after he arrived on the continent. He opined that, while the children of native women and Orkneymen 'inherit the plodding careful disposition of their fathers, the half-breed descendants of the French Canadians are, with rare exceptions, characterised by the paternal levity and extravagance, superadded to the uncontrollable passions of the Indian blood'. On the other hand, industrious Scots who had saved some money, 'dreading the predominance of the half-breeds, with whom they avoided intermarrying, have converted their property into money' and moved to the USA.[37] His animosity towards mixed-race folk never left him.

*

Alexander Simpson has been accused of blindly hero-worshipping his brother Thomas, comparing his organisational skills to those of Wellington. He felt that, in his published *Narrative* of the expeditions, Thomas's correspondence was informative and to the point, but that he was far too modest about his achievements. This claim was arguable since Thomas's letters are often prolix to a fault. Alexander also suggested that Thomas shared many talents and characteristics with Sir Alexander Mackenzie, who came from the same part of northern Scotland. 'A complete exposition of the virtues, the talents, and the services of an adored brother prematurely cut off in the pride of youth and bloom of success, is the task which I undertook in penning these pages'. He also stressed the discomfort of the explorers on land and sea but he communicated something of the excitement as well.

To understand the circumstances surrounding Thomas's death, recounting earlier experiences reported by his brother may shed some light. When Alexander visited Red River (arriving on 31 December 1834) he found the mixed-blood population in a state of dangerously seething excitement. Mutinous and insolent in the eyes of the Scots, the Bois-Brûlés evinced a deep hatred of the whites. Thomas actually came to blows with one of his mixed-race voyageurs in a dispute over pay. Tempers flared as numbers gathered, but to the frustration of the Simpson brothers the Governor appeared to refuse to take control of the situation, (quite rightly) favouring negotiation over physical confrontation. The protesters allegedly 'danced the war dance of their maternal ancestors in order to keep their dastardly spirits up to the mark of bullying and threatening'. Some wanted Thomas publicly flogged, a fate from which George rescued him by supplying money and a barrel of rum to the dissidents. He also intended to ban Thomas from the colony, a plan resisted by the victim who challenged the censure upon his conduct, threatening to retire from the service, an alternative George rejected. Thomas continued to fear assassination stating that the spilling of blood would render 'the plains of Red River once more red with the blood of white men'. The brothers, armed with weapons, bedded down in a barricaded room, but the crisis had passed, George's diplomacy and pacification techniques having saved the day, even though he too was imbued with racism towards the Bois-Brûlés.

The year 1835 is a blank in Thomas's career. All that is known is that he left Red River, returning in 1836 when he was 'selected for the task of Arctic Discovery', presumably by George, who seems to have hit upon the perfect solution for Thomas's restlessness, removing him from potential harm by introducing him to the welcome dangers of the northern wilderness. Alexander reported that Thomas had never, hitherto, shown any interest in the Arctic, even though he was to display great ability and enthusiasm once he arrived there. Thomas considered Back 'a very easy, affable man' but deficient in the commanding manner required in dealing with the people 'in this savage country', while applauding his discovery of the Great Fish River.[38]

Alexander attributed his brother's 'melancholy and premature death', just two weeks short of his thirty-second birthday, to his experiences of the mixed-race protesters, who because of their *odium in logum jaciens*, literally 'long-lasting resentment', would not scruple to take revenge. Their terrifying experience at Red River had brought the brothers closer together. Alexander was now emphatically his confidant. Thomas had to maintain a public persona but could share his private concerns with his brother, as to some extent he already had. Their relationship was one of confidence and 'responsive emotion'. He pitied and scorned the frigid hearts that are incapable of such things. 'I have found many ostensible friends in this country, but my naturally warm feelings have been sufficiently chilled and tutored to distrust the friendship of the world (what is it at all compared with the love we bear each other?) and to base my hopes solely on conscious rectitude.'

Alexander's partial explanation for his brother's murder seems convincing. Thomas's own fragility and negativity combined with George's bullying and perceived lack of sympathy, together with his failure to resolve the concerns and volatility of the denizens of Red River, had already contributed to his final tragedy. Some thought Thomas a megalomaniac, which is too extreme, but he was undoubtedly a man with a good conceit of himself. In his final letter to Alexander he confided that he had suffered stomach problems and low spirits for much of the spring, which was unlike him, since he rejoiced that 'Spring – joyous, animated Spring – was returned, and the deathlike silence of winter was past'.[39] His strength of body and mind had undoubtedly been tested by the past three years of Arctic activity. And it would not be surprising if his overall wellbeing had been unsettled by the frustration of waiting to hear from HBC, London. Although it is not specifically mentioned, religion may also have played a part. Thomas had intended to return to the Kirk after a couple of years. His faith may have suffered a dent by his discoveries about First Nations and Inuit ideas and beliefs. Though he certainly invokes the Almighty in his *Narrative* he does so more sparingly perhaps than the Rosses or John Richardson.

Alexander thought that 'the long-treasured animosity (of his [brother's] half-breed companions), was likely to have shown itself in threats and insults, if not in actual attack'. Many intelligent men were allegedly of the opinion that the mixed-race voyageurs had cut short Thomas's career. Writing to George Simpson in 1839, Thomas contrived to link two of his obsessions: 'My worthy colleague on the late expedition frankly acknowledges his having been a perfect supernumerary; and to the extravagant and profligate habits of half-breed families I have an insuperable aversion.'[40] Alexander admitted that his mind 'reposed in trembling hope' that the treachery of his Bois-Brûlés companions had led to the catastrophe, an explanation he devoutly wished since it would destroy, once and for all, the rumours about suicide, but that explanation was not forgotten, namely that 'Providence had darkened the spirit' (i.e. afflicted him with mental problems) as he had hinted on his visit to Red River, incomprehensible because he had to admit 'Godly decrees are inscrutable to mortals'. This was as close as Alexander ever came to suggesting that Thomas may have suffered from derangement of some kind, though he clearly did not completely abandon the possibility. In support he quoted William Cowper:

> Man is a harp whose chords elude the sight,
> Each yielding harmony disposed aright –
> The chords reversed, (a task which if He please,
> God in a moment, executes with ease),
> Ten thousand strings at once go loose,
> Lost, till He tune them, all their power and use.[41]

Three individuals who travelled with Thomas gave their accounts of what they believed, or pretended, happened. All three, curiously, had Scottish surnames: Bruce, Logan and Flett. Was it possible that Thomas had a particular hatred of 'breeds' who were half Scottish? James Bruce of Red River stated that, along with Simpson, Antoine Legros senior, his son Antoine and John Bird, he had gone ahead of the main party on their way to St Peter's on the Upper Mississippi. Some days later Simpson felt unwell and asked his companions to return to Red River. Next day he repeated the request, offering money to each of his fellow travellers if they would turn back. Thomas appeared restless and uneasy, believing he would never recover from his illness. A physician would do no good. They agreed to return. While John Bird and Antoine Legros were erecting their tent at their camp near Turtle River, Bruce heard a shot that killed Bird and a second shot from which the victim, Legros, leaning on a cart, died in a couple of minutes. Their killer was Simpson with his double-barrelled gun. In a very poorly recorded part of Bruce's testimony, when he was asked by Simpson if he knew whether anyone planned to kill him, he denied any such intention, an assurance reiterated by the elder Legros. Simpson then allegedly told Bruce that he was perfectly safe, that he had shot the pair because they had plotted to murder him that night 'for his papers' and that the laws of England would clear him from all blame. Before he died, Legros senior asked Simpson to let his son go free, which he did. Simpson then offered Bruce £500 to return with him to Red River and keep the affair secret; Bruce, having accepted, was told to harness the horses, while Legros asked his son to kiss him for the last time. The two, Bruce and Legros junior, then left but, losing their way, did not arrive at the main camp until the following morning. Bruce then returned to the murder site with five others, shouting for Simpson but eliciting no response, before he saw him lying on a bed on the opposite side of the cart. 'The report of a gun was forthwith heard, and the whistling of a ball in the air.' Someone, unidentified, stated that Simpson must have killed himself but they continued to call his name. The party circled the cart, finding underneath it only a dog which fled when they fired at it. They also aimed at the top of the cart to ascertain whether Simpson might still be moving. Bruce thought that their quarry had killed himself. When found, the victim had been shot through the head. The three deceased were buried in the same grave. Bruce further stated that Simpson had at no time 'manifested symptoms of insanity . . . and acted through the whole affair like a man in the possession of his senses'. The deponent signed with his mark.[42]

The deposition of Robert Logan, who accompanied the main camp party after hearing the news, matched Bruce's. On arrival they saw the dog. On hearing the report of a gun, seeing 'the smoke and [hearing] the ball whistling over our heads', they assumed that Simpson had fired at them. They returned fire, shooting into the air and then all of them fired twice. Simpson lay as if dead, his body 'lying stretched out, with one leg across the other, and the butt end of his double-barrelled gun between his legs, the right hand, with the glove off, directed to the trigger, the left hand with the glove on, holding the gun, near the muzzle, on his breast'. All the head above the nose was blown off and a night cap was found with a hole in it, much singed by fire, with some of his hair sticking to it. Logan did not remember any details about the rest of the body. The three corpses were interred.

James Flett, who had an Orkney name, testified that they approached cautiously. When they were about 200 yards away they 'hallood' and called Simpson. They then heard a shot and the hissing of a ball. Individuals approached from different angles but no one found him until James Bruce and his sidekick Henry Sinclair called out that he was dead. Flett did not know how many shots were fired altogether. The victim was lying face downwards near, but not on, a blanket alongside the cart, his wounds much as already described. About half an hour lapsed from the first shot until they discovered Simpson was dead. Bruce shouted 'He is firing at us'; Flett believed the victim had fired at himself.[43]

Alexander Simpson assessed most of the incongruities in the three testimonials. He described the failure of anyone to return to Red River with the news of the murder as 'extraordinary'. The fact that they continued on their way to St Peter's suggested they had something to hide. His brother's ubiquitous diary, which accompanied him everywhere, was never found, but a pocket map, confirming events from 6 to 12 June, was recovered, leading him to suspect the accuracy of some of the dates indicated by the deponents. The whole account was a tale devised – but not cunningly. Alexander argued that Thomas turned back not because of illness but rather due to 'the treachery of his half-breed companions', notorious for their 'evil passions' and previous hostility towards him. John Bird was known to be one of the worst in such respects, 'nourished and brought up in all the fierce excitement of prairie life'. Alexander concluded that Thomas was killed for his 'papers', which were regarded as valuable in containing information about the Northwest Passage and hence wealth. It seemed most likely that Bird and Legros were shot in self-defence. Accounts of guns being fired thereafter were inventions because the assailants knew that Simpson was already dead.

There must, however, be a serious question as to why, given his antipathy towards the Bois-Brûlés, Thomas travelled with them in the first place unless the over-confident Scot had convinced himself that he could easily outwit his companions. He did not seem to realise that if you treat people like mad dogs they have a tendency to bite. The exchanges between Thomas and the dying Legros, the final kiss etc., seem to have occupied rather a long two minutes, but Legros junior, who never appeared again after he returned to the main camp, is the most likely candidate to be the murderer. Indeed, the

Métis code would have expected him to avenge the death of his own father, possibly with Bruce's assistance. It was after all the 'half-breeds' who first introduced the possibility that Thomas committed suicide, an explanation that suited the HBC, thus avoiding the sort of riots and mass activity that were later revealed in the Riel Rebellion. In her pamphlet *Thomas Simpson: Dingwall's Arctic Explorer*, Marjory Harper seems to favour suicide as an explanation of his demise.[44]

George Simpson was not exactly overcome with grief when he learned of his cousin's fate:

> A boat from our establishment brought me the journal and other papers of my late lamented relative, Mr Thomas Simpson whose successful exertions in arctic discovery and whose untimely end had excited so much interest in the public mind. By the same conveyance we got a supply of fish. This fish which is peculiar to North America, is one of the most delicious of the finny tribe, having the appearance and somewhat the flavour of trout.[45]

Combining fish with a report of his cousin's death may be regrettable but it does not suggest that George somehow commissioned Thomas's murder. There is enough controversy and speculation already without adding further complications. According to James Raffan, George's biographer, the Governor had his comeuppance. James reports that when he visited Dingwall he learned that a plaque commemorating Thomas had long ago been removed from the local church because he was a suspected suicide. However, most locals knew about Thomas but very few had heard of George.[46] It would be interesting to ascertain just what they knew about their local hero. Despite Simpson's many criticisms of his expeditionary partner, Peter Dease, Dease never wrote a bad word about Simpson.

9

MEN FOR ALL SEASONS

John Rae's Expedition of 1846–1847

Here sturdy witches of the Arctic
Kiss'd warlocks frae the far Antarctic

Robert Kerr[1]

The 1840s and 1850s were the most crowded decades in the history of Polar exploration, launched by James Clark Ross's incredible, highly successful voyage to Antarctica in 1839–43 and ending with the confirmed loss of the 129 men of the Franklin Arctic expedition in 1848 in a hell of ice, snow and incompetence, a disaster that should never have been permitted. This led to the largest Arctic search in the annals of the British Navy, featuring in the aftermath some of the worst aspects of officially promoted racism and snobbery, heinous accusations of Inuit cannibalism, and the painful recognition of national failure, despite producing a solution of a kind to the conundrum of the Northwest Passage and discovering much of unknown Arctic Canada and America.

During these years HBC promoted several expeditions led by Scots in succession to the conflicted Thomas Simpson. The best known of these was John Rae from Orkney, who was to become the subject of much attention and contention, followed by James Anderson and James Green Stewart. Scots-Canadian William Kennedy was another, though operating as the agent of Lady Franklin, as was Peterhead native and prominent whaler William Penny, who was notably influential in his trade, as well as rediscovering the Belcher Islands and becoming involved in the Franklin search. He has the distinction of having taken an Inuk, Eeenoolooapik, to Scotland; he also took his own wife, Margaret Irvine of Aberdeen, to Baffin Island. Before, during and after the years of searching, Penny remained, first and foremost, a whaler. The Scots-Irish took a much more prominent part in

John Rae, photograph by Henry Maull, c. 1862
(Public domain, via Wikimedia Commons)

this phase of operations, culminating in the achievements of Irish explorer Leopold McClintock, who confirmed John Rae's report of the fate of the Franklin expedition. English activity noticeably increased, although to little effect, while Americans made their first forays into the Arctic, and a young Frenchman, Joseph René Bellot, charmed Lady Franklin, as well as veterans of the high latitudes. The true denizens of the north were of course the enduring Inuit, who welcomed, feared and eagerly traded with the kabloonas, who usurped their traditional Inuit heritage in the name of a remote monarch, communicating lethal diseases in return.

*

James Clark Ross's achievements in the Antarctic are clearly not strictly part of the saga of the Arctic Scots but it was his Canadian experience that enabled his unsurpassed accomplishments at the ends of the Earth. On returning from Boothia he was promoted to post-captain and commissioned with overseeing the first magnetic survey of Britain, 1835–8, though he was allowed command of *Cove* to rescue eleven whaling ships beset in the Davis Strait. Before he could reach them, they had freed themselves and all returned home. One admirer described Ross as the finest officer he had ever met, 'the most persevering indefatigable man you can imagine . . . idolised by everyone'. His tally in the Arctic was an unrivalled eight winters and fifteen navigation seasons but for some reason, hopefully based on his modesty and integrity, he refused a knighthood.[2]

Having discovered the Magnetic North Pole in 1831 (see Chapter 6) his next assignment was command of an expedition to Antarctica in 1839–43 to study southern magnetism, with the aim of pinpointing the site of the Magnetic South Pole, commanding two ships, *Erebus* and *Terror*. Two of Ross's devoted friends took part, Irishman Francis Crozier, who would become second in command on the Franklin expedition, and Edward Bird, who, like Crozier and Ross himself, was trained in 'Parry's School'. Not many Scots were involved but an exception was Archibald McMurdo, born in Dumfries, 1812, lieutenant on *Terror*, who was honoured by having McMurdo Sound named for him. Ross had recommended that the lieutenant should be promoted, his conduct having been 'marked by a manifestation of zeal and talent of no ordinary character'.[3] A fellow Scot, born at Auchenblae, Kincardineshire, was David Lyall, assistant surgeon on *Terror* and later known as a botanist. His fellow assistant surgeon on *Erebus*, Joseph D. Hooker, son of Sir William Hooker, Professor of Botany at Glasgow

235

University, named the genus *Lyallia* after him. Surgeon Robert McCormick, of Scots-Irish descent, made himself conspicuous on *Erebus*. He had studied under Professor Robert Jameson at Edinburgh University, remarking that 'only Scotchmen have any chance with the head of our department'. He was recruited as naturalist by Captain Robert Fitzroy on the second voyage of *Beagle* but eventually fell out with Charles Darwin and was invalided home from Rio de Janeiro.[4] Also on *Erebus* was the ever-loyal boatswain, carpenter and gunner Thomas Abernethy, a veteran of *Fury* on Parry's third voyage, having also taken part in John Ross's 'Longest Winter', sledging with both Rosses and, as we have noted, accompanying James when he discovered the pole. He was to prove selflessly heroic on the *Erebus* voyage.[5] John Edward Davis, second master of *Terror*, an accomplished artist, surveyor and 'a right good fellow',[6] responsible for charts and pictures, considered the discipline on the leader's ship to be too lax.

The two ships were modified 'bombs' duly reinforced for southern service. George Back had taken *Terror* on his fruitless voyage to Repulse Bay, 1836–7, since when the vessel had been completely refitted and reconditioned. *Erebus*, built in 1826, was also re-strengthened. The ships were in excellent order, well supplied with food, including tinned provisions that so impressed Ross he successfully recommended that in future canned food should be supplied to all naval ships, which from 1847 they were, though with mixed results. Each ship was equipped for eighteen petty officers, twenty-six able seamen (many of whom were experienced whalers) and seven Royal Marines. The ships sailed on 2 September 1839, the crew partying when crossing the equator, while Ross investigated the magnetic equator known as the line of no dip. By mid May both ships had reached the Kerguelen Islands and the most welcome shelter of Christmas Harbour, where observatories were erected. Hooker collected plants and admired penguins. The Kerguelen cabbage fed the crews for 130 days, proving an effective anti-scorbutic while magnetic measurements went on. In mid August the adventurers reached Hobart, in beautiful Van Diemen's Land, aka Tasmania, the governor of which was none other than Sir John Franklin. Within nine days, 200 convicts built an observatory that became known as Rossbank.[7] In Hobart, Ross met Franklin's second wife for the first time, the indomitable Lady Jane Griffin.

In November the Brits were once again at sea, making for the Auckland Islands. On New Year's Day 1841 'the ships crossed the Antarctic Circle and came up with the edge of the pack'.[8] A week later they sailed into a large body of open water now named the Ross Sea. This was to prove one of JCR's true achievements, though not the chief triumph of the voyage. Robert McCormick observed that they had discovered a southern continent. C.J. Sullivan, blacksmith on *Erebus*, later wrote that the discovery was the 'most sublime but not the most dangerous'. Measurements of dip and variation suggested that the magnetic pole was at latitude 76° S, longitude 145°20' E, 500 miles to the south-west. (Today its location is 64°07' S and 135°88' E.) Next day Ross and Crozier commandeered one of the ship's boats, pulling for the ice-bound shore through a heavy surf. In haste they took possession in the name of Queen Victoria, unimaginatively naming the spot Possession Island. The sailors retreated as a heavy fog descended, but two days later they were again captivated by 'the splendour, extreme solitude and omnipotent' grandeur of the sea and the snowy mountains. Sullivan declared Mount Herschel to be 'the most perpendicular mountain in the world'. They named a totally unexpected but wondrous active volcano belching flame and smoke Mount Erebus, while its nearby extinct neighbour was dubbed Mount Terror.

A further marvel awaited them – 'As we approached the land we perceived a low white line extending from its eastern extreme point as far as the eye could discern . . . a perpendicular cliff of ice between one hundred and fifty and two hundred feet above the level of the sea, perfectly flat and level at the top and without any fissures or promontories on its even seaward face'. Sullivan reported that the discovery of this obstruction was a great disappointment; 'we might with equal chance of success try to sail through the Cliffs of Dover, as penetrate such a mass'.[9] They were to visit the phenomenon now known as the Ross Ice Barrier, twice more, reaching furthest south at latitude 78°9'30' S, longitude 161°27' W on the second voyage. Like many of his craft, the blacksmith was a man possessed of a poetic soul and a deep mindset. The 300 miles of 'nature's handiwork' that they encountered struck him as 'the most rare and magnificent sight that ever the human eye witnessed since the world was created'.[10] One great disappointment was that, although Ross identified the site of the South Pole, it was in the mountains and unreachable.

Returning to Hobart, a new play *Arctic Exploration*, honouring Ross, was performed at the theatre. The visitors organised a splendid ball; another greeted them when they visited Sydney to erect another observatory, after which they sailed to the Bay of Islands, New Zealand. The 'magnetic crusade', as it was dubbed, must represent the first truly worldwide enterprise in the history of the planet.

Re-engaging with the ice-pack in February 1842, *Erebus* and *Terror* met with a vicious storm the like of which not even Ross had ever experienced. John Davis wrote to his sister describing in detail a terrifying collision between the two ships in a horrendous sea, gouging chunks out of one another and crashing on the monumental, murderous, unforgiving ice; 'never till those moments did I in reality know what fear was'. This was truly the time, he wrote, when 'shriek'd the timid and stood still the brave'.[11] Even Ross claimed that he did not remember what went through his head during the crisis but we have to wonder if he experienced any memory of the episode, less threatening but nonetheless still terrifying, of the somewhat similar entanglement between the anchors of *Isabella* and *Alexander* back in 1818.

Shortly after his return home in 1843, Ross married the love of his life, Anne Coulman; her death in 1857 devastated him. Ross was disappointed that there did not appear to be great interest in his achievements, possibly because Antarctica completely lacked people, and he made no secret of his dislike of writing, which, taken together with a degree of exhaustion, delayed publication of his account of the expedition until 1847. A particular disappointment was his failure to reach the Magnetic South Pole but otherwise his achievements were astounding. Amundsen viewed him as 'the bright star, the man who will ever be remembered as one of the most intrepid polar explorers and one of the most capable seamen the world has ever produced'. An obituary considered his magnetic survey of the Antarctic regions 'the greatest work of the kind ever performed'.

One other consequence of the Tasmanian interlude was the deepening of the friendship between Ross and Franklin, who became Lieutenant-Governor of the colony in 1836; his tenure turned out to be a rather unenviable experience in the familiar chaotic style of antipodean administration. He tangled in particular with John Montagu, Colonial-Secretary of Van Diemen's Land, who was guilty of blocking Franklin's schemes on every possible occasion, taking care to inform London of his shortcomings as Governor. For his part Franklin accused Montagu of libelling him and Lady Franklin. Ross supported Franklin, who was relieved of his appointment in 1842. The British Colonial Secretary, Edward Smith Stanley, Earl of Derby, known as Lord Stanley, consistently favoured Montagu's complaints and observations while criticising those of Franklin. The surviving documentation makes clear Franklin's obsessive determination to defend the honour of his wife and himself during the three years prior to his departure for the Arctic. His Arctic ships sailed on 9 May 1845; his apologia or rebuttal was dated 15 May. It is impossible to believe that the whole wretched affair did not have a distractive impact on the planning of his elaborate expedition. Honour was to Franklin as important as potential glory.[12]

*

Viewed from the Scottish mainland across the frequently turbulent Pentland Firth, the hills of Hoy seem to suggest promise that the Orcadian archipelago might present images like those of the mountainous Faroes, whereas in reality they mostly guard fertile lowlands whose rich pastures have attracted migrants, cultures and civilisations since Neolithic times. A few miles east of the town of Stromness, on the edge of the natural harbour of Scapa Flow, is Hall of Clestrain, where John Rae was born 30 September 1813, the sixth child and fourth son of John Rae from the island of Wyre and Margaret Glen from Argyll.

To this day Rae is a classic example of 'Local Hero', a man who, despite contriving great achievements in the name of HBC and even greater accomplishments in the exploration of the Arctic, being credited with finding a way through the Northwest Passage, as well as becoming the first person to report on the possible fate of the doomed Franklin expedition, he has never, in the minds of his fellow Orcadians, been accorded the full recognition he is due. The folk of Orkney, fair-minded, friendly, articulate and worldly-wise as they are, do not seem to realise that more has now been written about Rae than any other Scottish Arctic explorer.

Jock, as he was known, introduces his autobiography by describing himself:

> The occupations and amusements in early life of a somewhat slow, dull and certainly very shy, sensitive and credulous boy, can be of little interest to anyone yet I shall attempt to give a brief sketch of mine, because it is the story of a part of my education for some of the work of after days – work that was offered to me partly on account of this education – which is recorded in the following narrative.[13]

He proceeds to stress the value of practical hands-on experience of boating, shooting, fishing and riding while he was taught at home by tutors, enjoying a rather privileged upbringing. The family beach was exposed to Hoy Mouth through which the tides run at 10 miles per hour. His sea adventures often recalled his favourite lines from Byron, 'She walks the waters like a thing of life / And seems to dare the elements to strife'. He compares steersmen and horse riders, both alike trained to react instantly to danger. He dislikes being hoaxed, retreating on occasion into his own solitary world accompanied only by his Newfoundland dog. His nurse tells him tales of smugglers and ghosts. One of his tutors keeps eagles in a large cage for which the Rae boys supply water birds as fodder. He became a dedicated and expert hunter, shooting seals on the rocks and occasionally indulging in whale-hunting.

He studied medicine at the University of Edinburgh, and through the Orkney connection – his father was the HBC's chief representative in Orkney – he was appointed surgeon on the company's *Prince of Wales*, sailing to Hudson Bay in June 1833. He had to deal with an on-board outbreak of typhoid fever, while learning exactly how a large ship operated. On reaching the Hudson Strait, his ship became ice-bound, introducing him to icebergs and the Inuit. Reaching Hudson Bay proper, the ship sailed on to Moose Factory (the second oldest HBC post founded in 1673) in James Bay, where he made a favourable impression upon Chief Factor J.G. MacTavish, who described him as a 'fine young man' that he wished to retain. To encourage Rae, MacTavish gave him a birchbark canoe, though Rae was too busy to use it. Scheduled to return home, *Prince of Wales* was diverted instead to Charlton Island in James Bay, an old post far to the south, where Rae prepared for his first Canadian winter. A large tent was erected and some of the crumbling houses were repaired, the ship having been beached.

Rae apparently enjoyed the adventures of winter, snow-shoeing and hunting. Of the thirty men on the island, half suffered from scurvy and two died, the ship's captain and the ship's mate, both in the doctor's opinion because they had 'taken more spirits than were good for them'. The others recovered, thanks in part to Rae's discovery of cranberries under the snow, supplemented with soup made from vetch and wild peas. When *Prince* eventually made for home in August 1834 Rae remained behind, persuaded by the lifestyle and a five-year contract as clerk and surgeon from George Simpson, paying £100 per annum, beginning a ten-year stint at Moose Factory, located on Moose Factory Island, Moose River, at the southern end of James Bay, which he considered 'the best place east of the Rocky Mountains'.

He had plenty of time for doctoring, clerking and indulging in his own particular interests, as he learned 'all the different methods of hunting, fishing, sledge-hauling, snow-shoe walking and camping out in winter, summer, spring and autumn that were afterwards so useful to me in my Arctic

Explorations'. As just one example, he gives a hair-raising account of paddling his birch-bark canoe during a snowstorm, in pitch darkness through a raging sea, employing the self-reliance he had learned as a boy. Rae's clothes and moccasins froze hard but he suffered no distress.[14] He learned how to use snow-shoes, which to this day beginners find quite difficult; like many others, he initially suffered dreadful pain in his legs, *mal de raquette*, from using them. Robert Campbell – 'Campbell of the Yukon' – once claimed to have walked 3,000 miles on snow-shoes. Though his reputation as a great self-promoter perhaps invalidated his claim, he nonetheless observed that Rae was the 'best and ablest snow-shoe walker', not only in HBC country, 'but also of the age'. Once Rae made modest adjustments to the 'shoes' he became a legend for distance and timing, believing that a 'long day's march on snow-shoes was about the finest exercise a man can take'. Boating was another recreation as well as a necessity. Rae once challenged George Simpson to a race between his boat and the Governor's canoe; Rae won. He also developed his own style of handling a canoe, paddling from the stern rather than the centre.

In 1843 Rae was given leave to visit his brothers in Ontario. He ran 'the wild and beautiful rapids' of the Ottawa River to visit George Simpson at his Lachine headquarters, before heading to Kingston on Lake Ontario. He was then promoted to take charge of the Rupert River District in the area south-east of James Bay. His predecessor mischievously suggested that he had already gained a reputation for over-generous spending, inspiring rumours that were absolutely rife in HBC. The Governor arranged to meet with him in the summer to discuss a new venture to complete the investigation that Thomas Simpson had begun, namely to explore the untraced coast between the Fury and Hecla Strait and the Gulf of Boothia. 'As regards the management of the people and endurance of toil, either in walking, boating or starving, I think you are better adapted for this work than most of the gentlemen with whom I am acquainted in the country, and with a little practice in taking observations, which might be very soon be acquired, I think you would be quite equal to the scientific part of the duty'. To be certain, Simpson insisted that Rae spend the winter of 1844–5 at Red River studying surveying and astronomy, 'filling up any spare time you may have in making yourself conversant with Geology, Botany & such other sciences as you may have an opportunity to attend to'. Anticipating his acceptance, the Governor rather cryptically added, the 'completion of the survey is reserved for you and then the world will see that Orkney has produced at all events one good man'.[15]

Another good man from Orkney and Rae's home parish of Orphir was John Corrigal, who accompanied him for the next three years. They made the long trek down the Michipicoten River to Lake Superior and on to Red River, where they discovered that Simpson's recommended tutor in surveying was on the point of death. On the Winnipeg River, Rae's path crossed that of young R.M. Ballantyne, who had joined HBC three years earlier. He was the son of an Edinburgh publisher and delighted to meet Rae whom he described as 'muscular, active, full of animal spirits [with] a fine intellectual countenance'; he had heard of his snow-shoe accomplishment, shooting skills and ability to withstand fatigue. Ballantyne's first publication was *Hudson's Bay: or Life in the Wilds of North America*, to be followed by more than 100 books, including his best known, *The Coral Island*, and several titles that introduced many young readers to the Arctic.[16] In a change of plan, Rae and Corrigal joined the Winter Express to Upper Canada, one of several fur-trading brigades, hunting when their prey were at their cold-weather best. They travelled from Fort Garry (Red River) to Sault Ste. Marie at the eastern end of Lake Superior, a distance of 1,200 miles and on to Michipicoten. En route Rae received a letter from the Governor stating that his expedition plans had been approved. At the Sault he met John Ballenden from Stromness. Simpson's letter directed Rae to Toronto to study terrestrial magnetism, among other subjects, under Lt J.H. Lefroy, who was in charge of the Toronto Magnetic and Meteorological Observatory, newly established by the British Association for the Advancement of Science; he worked on terrestrial magnetism in north-west Canada, publishing John Richardson's magnetic research on Fort Confidence and Great Bear Lake.

Rae's *Narrative* of 1850, the only book he ever published, is complemented by the much shorter account he sent to HBC on his return from the expedition in 1847. His itinerary and plan of action were devised by Governor Simpson. Volunteers proved scarce because the skilled steersmen, James McKay and George Sinclair, who had served with Back as well as Dease and Simpson, warned that if the party did not die of starvation it would freeze to death due to lack of fuel. Following the example of Thomas Simpson, Rae commissioned two clinker-built boats, *North Pole* and *Magnet*, 22 feet long and 7 feet 6 inches broad. They wintered at York Factory on Hudson Bay. Each boat was supplied with a small stove, oil lamp and an alcohol burner to save time by cooking on board. They made an oiled canvas canoe and they also carried a Halkett boat: 'This last useful and light little vessel ought to form the equipment of every expedition'. The crews were as follows: On *North Pole*, John Rae, John Corrigal (Orkneyman, steersman), Edward Hutchison (Orkneyman, middleman), Richard Turner ('half breed', middleman, carpenter and self-taught blacksmith), Hilard Mineau (Canadian, middleman), Nibitabo (Cree, middleman and hunter). On *Magnet*, George Flett (Orkneyman, steersman), John Folster (Orkneyman, middleman), William Adamson (Shetlander, middleman), Peter Matheson (Highlander), Jacques St Germain (Canadian, middleman). Orcadians were regarded as the best at coping with stormy weather and rough seas. Rae believed that volunteers were scarce because most of the Canadian-born feared sea-sickness. In tests the boats performed well.

They were instructed to complete the geography of the northern shore of America, between the western end of the Fury and Hecla Strait and the eastern limit of Dease and Simpson's expedition, proceeding as quickly as possible to 'the interesting scene of your exclusive labours'. The latitudes and longitudes of the most remarkable points were to be recorded on draft charts. Various subordinate and incidental duties involved attention to botany, geology, zoology 'in all its departments', ice and atmospheric conditions, winds, currents, depth soundings, the magnetic dip, compass variation, the Aurora Borealis and the refraction of light. Observation of 'the ethnographical peculiarities' of the Inuit were to be entered in journals. The health of the crew was entirely in Rae's hands. In the event of over-wintering, friendly relations with the Inuit were to be fostered while taking care to guard against surprise. 'For this purpose you will repeatedly and constantly inculcate on your men, collectively and individually, the absolute necessity of mildness and firmness, of frankness and circumspection'. Governor George's final flourish was to assure the expeditionaries that

> we look confidently to you for what may be deemed the final problem in the geography of the northern hemisphere. The eyes of all who take an interest in the subject are fixed on HBC; from us the world expects the final settlement of the question that has occupied the attention of our country for two hundred years; and your safe and triumphant return, which may God in His mercy grant, will, I trust, speedily compensate HBC for its repeated sacrifices and its protracted anxieties.[17]

There could be no doubt that this was an important vanity project and it was hoped also a worthwhile commercial endeavour for HBC.[18] The opportunity would also be taken to discover whether it was possible to live off the land. Rae estimated that they had food supplies for only four months to service an absence of between fifteen and twenty months. Having taken on board William Ooligbuck (whose father Ooligbuck played an important role on Franklin and Richardson's overland expedition in the 1820s) and one of his sons as Inuit interpreters, the company left Churchill on the west coast of Hudson Bay on 5 July 1846. Just before departing, Rae wrote to Simpson protesting that he seemed to credit him with all kinds of knowledge. 'The head is big enough certainly outside, but whether there is a large quantity of bone in it or not I have not yet tested. It is certainly a poor affair, but I shall endeavour to make the best use of it I can.'[19] Very few of Simpson's correspondents, if any, would have risked such levity in addressing the great man, but Rae customarily did. He also told of Orcadian hardiness, demonstrated by George Flett, who was always willing to jump into water 'and be the first at any disagreeable duty when necessary'.

Leaving Churchill, the party headed northwards. White whales swam within a few yards of their vessels. The men were all in good spirits 'there not being a melancholy look nor a desponding word to be seen or heard among them'.[20] The following day they were overtaken by three Inuit in kayaks heading for Churchill, pressed by Rae into providing a postal service to deliver a message to Simpson. Soon, however, they hit strong winds and crept along the coast coping as best as they could. The wind increased to a gale, causing *Magnet* to ship water in a heavy sea. Rae's blankets, soaked by sea water, efficiently kept out the wind, permitting sleep. Throughout, he conscientiously provided detailed accounts of his progress though there was actually little of note to record, save bird sightings about which Rae was remarkably knowledgeable; he celebrated the killing of fifty snowy owls, while perversely lamenting the death of a lapdog attacked by one of them. For food, they killed ducks, collected eggs and devoured venison. Deer made good eating as they passed Chesterfield Inlet, host to numerous seals.

At the north end of Hudson Bay, they crossed the Wager River Estuary and into Repulse Bay. Some Inuit eagerly drew a chart for them indicating that Akkoolee (the Arctic Sea) was some 40 miles to the west of Melville Peninsula. Six Inuit women visited their camp, affording an opportunity to describe their clothing, tattoos and hair styles. One female, noticing that Rae's boots were rather hard, chewed them to soften the texture. When presented with tea and biscuits, one woman said she had seen and tasted both on one of Parry's ships. Inlets were named for Flett and Corrigal. Two days were taken up with portaging the two boats. Passing two Inuit tents they met an old woman who had never before seen a European. Gifts were exchanged and another woman drew a chart. None of them had either heard or seen anything of Franklin. A sledge made of wood which appeared to come from *Fury* or *Victory* was taken for fuel. Rae now sent three men to prepare quarters for wintering at Repulse Bay. Food was becoming scarce, though he bagged eighteen brace of ptarmigan in a couple of hours: 'Knocking down those birds on this day made me half fancy myself among the grouse in my own barren native hills'. Salmon were also still plentiful. They managed to cross to Melville Peninsula but were soon defeated by ice, returning to Repulse Bay. As the 'long and dreary winter' approached, they erected an ambitious stone house, 20 feet by 14 feet, which they named Fort Hope. It had a sloping roof utilising some wood and spars from the boats and covered with oil-cloth and moose-hide. Rae had brought glass for three windows of two double panes. A curtained-off section was reserved for him and some supplies; the men shared the remainder. The structure lasted for over a century before being destroyed by tourists.[21]

The Inuit were pleased to see them return after Rae called out *Teyma* (peace). He purchased four dogs from them, trading a dagger for each. He mused that, since the weather was not favourable for observations, 'the sextant was frequently exchanged for the rifle – a not unwelcome exchange to one addicted to field-sports "from his youth upwards"'. October yielded an impressive 172 partridges, 116 salmon and trout, 63 deer, 5 hares and 1 seal. As he told an audience in Winnipeg many years later, he had never shot a deer before he arrived in Repulse Bay, where he killed sixty.[22] Rae at one point found himself facing seventeen wolves who backed down. He listened to some Inuit legends. An Inuk named Arkshuk told him about the brother-and-sister relationship of the sun and the moon, who had a falling out after he burned her face. She ran away and formed the moon, chased by her brother who never managed to catch her. It was believed that the stars represented the spirits of dead Inuit while falling stars and the aurora were the spirits visiting their friends. Additional houses were fashioned for storage linked by passages under the snow, which also served to build two observatories, one for the dip circle, the other to assess the possible effects of the aurora upon a horizontally suspended needle.

Christmas and New Year's Day were celebrated in traditional fashion with football, venison, plum pudding and brandy punch. At New Year especially, Rae could not conceive that there could be a happier company in all of

America, 'large as it is'. He would have preferred an agreeable companion to join him in a glass of punch to greet absent friends, 'to speak of by-gone times and speculate on the future', but he was not unhappy, finding compensation in the merry jokes, hearty laughter and lively songs of his men.[23] A wolf that seized one of their dogs 'by the rump' recalled Robert Burns' *Tam o Shanter*; another wounded wolf led William Ooligbuck and Rae a merry dance as they pursued it. It was so exhausted that Rae had to 'drive him on with the butt of my gun in order to get him nearer home before knocking him on the head'. An Inuit woman wore a brass wheel on her dress that, in Rae's view, must have come from some part of an instrument left by John Ross at Victoria Harbour but she would not sell it to him. However, he heard about Inuit, some now dead, who had met Ross, such as Tulluahiu of the wooden leg. The first deer of the season were shot in February. Ooligbuck wounded himself by accidently falling on his dagger. Rae treated him and stood to one side to allow Shimakuk, an angakok or shaman, to perform his healing, which consisted of questioning the patient in a loud voice, then speaking in a low tone and blowing a few puffs of breaths on the wound, a scene John considered 'irresistibly ludicrous'. The Inuit, like the First Nations, the Orcadians and the Shetlanders, all asserted that the aurora emitted an audible sound, but Rae never heard it.

On 5 April 1847 Rae's party set off on foot, with two sledges, for the north; it consisted of Flett, Corrigal, William Adamson, Ooligbuck's son and the Inuk, Ivitchuk. Poor snow conditions dictated that the building of a snow hut took three hours. Two more Inuit were recruited. Rae admired their expertise in freezing ice to their sledge runners, vowing to copy the practice. As they progressed, they named a bay Colville, in honour of the deputy-governor of HBC, just as the names of many other company servants were used to name features or places sprinkled along the Arctic coast. When they rested for a night, Ivitchuk drank enough water to satisfy an ox. Next day was one of the worst for weather that Rae had ever experienced and it did not improve greatly as he, with Flett and Corrigal, approached some of John Ross's discoveries during his forced confinement of 1829 to 1833. Flett surprisingly showed symptoms of fatigue. They struck out across country, reasonably persuaded that Ross's Lord Mayor's Bay could not be far away. While his two comrades prepared lodgings, Rae went on alone to view 'as far as the eye could reach to the northward Mayor's Bay and its islands which John Ross had curiously named the Sons of the Clergy of the Church of Scotland'. A short isthmus, one mile broad, named for JCR, linked the northward land (dubbed Sir John Ross's peninsula) to the continent. Rae gave thanks 'to Him who has thus brought our journey so far to a successful termination'. Exploring further over very difficult and energy-sapping terrain, across several hill ranges peppered with large stones, caused Flett, who was suffering lameness and blindness, all sorts of difficulties. Rae named an inlet after Franklin, of whom he remarked rather off-handedly in passing 'his protracted absence in the Arctic Sea is at present exciting . . . much interest and anxiety throughout England'.

Continuing alone, Rae met up with Inuit who were much feared by their neighbours of Repulse Bay. However, remarking that 'to anticipate Evil is often the most likely way to cause it', he plunged in to shake hands with the arrivals. They responded to his call of *teyma* (peace) with *Manig Tomig*, which were the words John Ross mentioned as 'the form of salutation employed by the natives of Boothia Felix'.[24] As anticipated, thieving was in evidence but otherwise the Inuit brought food and information. One Inuk drew a linen chart that closely resembled another drawn by the folk of Repulse Bay. Others took him to the highest point for a clear view of the surroundings. Rae had much more to relate, such as naming two bays for his 'intimate friends', James and Robert Clouston, thus reminding his readers that his expedition was emphatically Orcadian, with the exception of one or two, notably Ivitchuk who was singled out for special notice; always willing, obedient, lively and cheerful, he adapted well to the manners of the explorers, learning some English and becoming interested in learning to read and write. The party retraced their steps to reach Fort Hope on Repulse Bay, where they were gratified to find an abundance of food, on 5 May 1847. Rae recorded the successful termination 'of a journey little short of 600 English miles, the longest, I believe, ever made on foot along the Arctic coast'. He almost reached Dease and Simpson's furthest point and the Fury and Hecla Strait. He also confirmed John Ross's claim that Boothia Felix was part of the American continent. It is noteworthy that Rae was an admirer of John Ross because he had some idea of the older man's trials and tribulations, their shared nationality, their distrust of so-called naval expertise and their shared discrimination by the establishment. Both men also knew how to empathise with their followers and demonstrated genuine interest in the ways and culture of the Inuit.

Not one to hang around, Rae was off again on 13 May accompanied by Corrigal, Folster, Matheson, Mineau and Ooligbuck, the objective being the exploration of the south coast of Melville Peninsula. They followed a chain of lochs to the north until they reached Cape Thomas Simpson, which

Rae had named the previous autumn. Ooligbuck was sent back to Repulse Bay with the sledge. As they advanced in notably difficult ice conditions, conscientiously measuring longitude and latitude, Rae indulged in the usual naming of features for individuals, which may seem pointless to modern readers but was invaluable for chart-makers, because to name was in some sense to control, as had probably been the case worldwide from time immemorial, when humans took their first tentative steps in unfamiliar landscapes. Where an Inuit name existed, Rae generally recorded it but, though there was plenty of evidence of earlier Inuit visitors, there were very few names along their present track. Such names as were conferred by the explorers mean little because there is no proper context for them. The weather did not cooperate, but bays were named for Lord Selkirk and Erland Erlandson, a Danish sailor who joined HBC, while a cape honoured 'the amiable lady of our much respected governor, Sir George Simpson'. Another cape was named for John McLoughlin, who ran the Columbia Department of HBC, and an island was similarly honoured for the largest of the Orkney Islands, Pomona (now Mainland). Rae lauded Peter Matheson as one of the best men he had ever commanded.

> Always ready, willing, and obedient, he did his best in every respect, and whilst he possessed spirit enough for anything, he had a stock of good humour which never failed him in any situation, however difficult and trying. Were the walking difficult or easy, the loads heavy or light, provisions abundant or reduced to less than half allowance, it was all one to Peter Matheson; he had a joke for every occasion.

Rae was seldom so effusive while conveying a convincing idea of one he considered the consummate arctician.

Since the weather remained formidable and food supplies were seriously depleted, they decided to withdraw, embarking on a journey that Rae described as the most fatiguing he had ever experienced, this from a man who had often walked 40 or 50 and in one case 65 miles in one day. Everyone lost weight while remaining in good health. Rae was no exception; 'although we lost flesh, we kept up our spirits, and marched merrily on, tightening our belts – mine came in six inches'. Smokers vainly scoured their pockets endlessly for 'baccy'. By 9 June they were back at Fort Hope, Melville a dreadful memory.

They returned to a wild spring. The snow seemed relentless but, as temperatures rose, water appeared everywhere. They fashioned an oven from stones and clay to make excellent bread; the recipe was thoughtfully included in a footnote. On 19 July most of the men went back to North Pole Lake (north-west of Fort Hope) to bring their boat back to Fort Hope; it was floated down-river at great speed. Inuit arrived to fish for salmon and to hunt seals. They provided a concert every night, an Inuk beating on his drum as four or five women added 'their voices to the execrable sound, producing among them most horrible discord'; the drummer passed on his instrument to the next man until everyone had a turn.[25] By 25 July, the anniversary of their arrival a year earlier, mosquitoes were making their presence felt, a good if uncomfortable sign, because the break-up of the ice would soon follow. An Inuk named I-ik-tu-ang visited in August to report that as a boy he was frequently on board *Fury* and *Hecla* in 1822–3. The kabloonas on these ships had killed some walruses and black whales which were donated to the Inuit but unfortunately, they also brought a flu-like disease killing twenty-one adults.

On 12 August they set sail for 'home'. Some Inuit waded into the water to shake hands in farewell. Again, they were impeded by bad weather, gales and a stream of ice. Wildlife was abundant on reaching Chesterfield Inlet, but as they progressed, the weather made them work for every mile, seeking shelter where they could. On 31 August Churchill and its Old Fort were welcome sights. Provisions were gathered for the onward journey, but Ooligbuck and his son remained at Churchill. Gales and high seas delayed their continuation until 3 September. About 9.30pm on 6 September they arrived at York Factory, Rae praising his comrades on the recent expedition. From there he wrote a lengthy letter to his superiors summarising their achievements and experiences, including that they had proved John Ross was correct in asserting that Boothia Felix was part of the American continent. Rae travelled to London and then went home to Orkney to visit his family.

*

Rae has a well-deserved reputation. However, it is no service to his memory to make claims for him that he would have rejected himself. Rae was certainly the greatest kabloona snow-shoe expert in history and a supreme trekker for distance and speed. His reputation for travelling over vast expanses with few men owed much to the practice of HBC, harking back to Samuel Hearne and Alexander Mackenzie. When he famously stated that 'we of the HBC thought very little of our Arctic work . . . no more of it than any ordinary journey', he was as sincere as he was modest. Self-effacing though he may have been, he acted just like other HBC men, who, it should be remembered, were accustomed to tackling enormous distances from Montreal to the Pacific; the difference was that he could outpace everybody and apparently enjoyed doing so. His interest in ethnology also had HBC roots as manifested, for example, in Andrew Graham's *Observations* of 1769–91.[26] The desire to know as much as possible about the indigenous people was as commercial as it was ethnological. Potentially there were economic benefits in whatever expeditions they undertook, however distant.

Rae's famous success at living off the land has perhaps been exaggerated. He himself said that, apart from Repulse Bay, there was only one other place (unfortunately not named) at which he would attempt wintering unless he carried a full supply of provisions.[27] It is noticeable in his journals and autobiography that the further he was removed from the treeline and a plentiful supply of venison, the more apprehensive he became about the possibilities of starvation. He could feast at Repulse but many commentators seem not to have realised that there was no such abundance at Devon Island, or King William Island, where the Franklin expedition came to grief. He took exception to those who were of the view that 'wherever the native could live, there the civilized man could also maintain himself'. These individuals erred because they were not aware that the behaviour of caribou and musk-oxen could vary at different times. The Inuit could catch game in pits dug in the snow where experienced hunters failed with guns. No Europeans or First Nations could kill seals as effectively as an Inuk. None of them remotely understood the craft of hunting as thoroughly as the Inuit. All Arctic explorers were on the lookout for game whenever possible but success often evaded them. The value of fresh meat was fully realised but not everyone was a crackshot like Rae who, on occasion, supplied well over half of the shot game.[28]

Rae's ability to survive by the gun was seized upon by the Icelandic–Canadian explorer Vilhjalmur Stefansson, who was entranced by the 'friendly Arctic' thesis.[29] Stefansson articulated what has almost become a mantra for some Canadian critics when he asserted that Rae was criticised 'for having behaved on his expeditions like a menial – having done his own work – and for having lived like a savage in snow houses and so forth. This behaviour did not seem cricket to the British public which believed the object of polar exploration was to explore properly and not to evade the hazards of the game through the vulgar subterfuge of going native'.[30] This is to misrepresent both Rae and his public, while failing to understand that the Navy was concerned to maintain fit and highly trained men in peacetime for the Senior Service. In contrasting Rae's expeditions with full-blown naval voyages we are in danger of comparing grapes and potatoes. Furthermore, so far as the public was concerned, it is noteworthy that the British showed little interest in Antarctica until the beginning of the twentieth century, presumably because it lacked human interest: it had no human inhabitants. The attitudes of the Rosses, among others, prove the contrary, namely that some naval personnel interacted very well with the Inuit in pre-confederation Canada. The recently highlighted, but long known, horror stories of indigenous children condemned to die in residential schools awaited the premiership of another Scot, John A. Macdonald.

John Ross himself was strongly supportive of Rae, agreeing with him that Franklin's ships were far too large for the task in hand. What is not in doubt was Rae's ability to travel lightly, especially compared with the vast numbers of men and equipment packed into naval ships. Rae demanded respect but he did not crave or cultivate fame in the way that John Ross and some of the other naval captains did. That he did not receive a knighthood should be seen as a kind of accolade for his failure to pander to the naval and polar establishments. James Clark Ross refused a knighthood the first time it was offered, and some who did receive it, such as McClure and Collinson (see Chapter 11), were unworthy of the honour.

Beechey Island, Nunavut
(Photograph by Lizanne Henderson © padeapix)

10

A GALLIMAUFRY OF ARCTIC SCOTS

Early Rescue Missions for Franklin's Lost Expedition

And now there came both mist and snow,
And it grew wondrous cold:
And ice, mast-high, came floating by,
As green as emerald.

Samuel Taylor Coleridge

Scots were not abundant in Sir John Franklin's final expedition, launched in 1845, when discovery became disaster, and the hunter the hunted. On his ship *Erebus*, by the cruellest of ironies a ship named for the haunt of the dead in classical mythology, the officers included Lieutenant James Walter Fairholme from Kinnoull, Perth, and Assistant Surgeon Harry Duncan Spens Goodsir, born in Anstruther, Fife.[1] Other Scottish members of the crew were James Reid (ice-master), Daniel Arthur (quartermaster, Aberdeen), William Bell (quartermaster, Forfar), John Murray (sailmaker, Glasgow), Robert Sinclair (captain of forestop, Kirkwall), William Clossan (able seaman, Shetland), Robert Ferrier (able seaman, Perth), Thomas Work (able seaman, Kirkwall) and Alexander Paterson (corporal, Royal Marines). With Captain Francis Crozier on *Terror* were Scots John Peddie (surgeon, Inverkeithing), Lieutenant John Irving (born in Edinburgh to a Dumfriesshire family), Gillies Alexander MacBean (second master), David Macdonald (quarter-master, Peterhead), John Kenley (St Monans, Fife), Alexander Berry (able seaman, Fife), David Leys (able seaman, Montrose), Magnus Manson (able seaman, Shetland), William Shanks (able seaman, Dundee), William Sinclair (able seaman, Scalloway, Shetland).[2] This is not a major representation out of a total of 129 individuals. The last person to communicate with them was whaler Captain Robert Martin of Peterhead at the end of July 1845 when he talked with Franklin and ice-master James Reid, who assured him they had enough food for five years, which could if necessary be stretched to seven, supplemented by game. Martin reported the meeting to the Admiralty in November 1845 but no more was made of the revelation until December 1851 when Martin told Captain William Penny, who undertook the first search for the lost ships and realised it represented the kind of hope for which the hopeful yearned.[3]

As Ann Savours stated in 1999 there are vast numbers of publications on the Franklin mystery: 'It is almost as difficult for the writer to plot a course through this literature as it was for sailors to navigate and chart the icy seas and lands of what was eventually revealed as the Canadian Arctic archipelago', the second biggest such collection of islands in the world.[4] No attempt will be made in what follows to steer a different course except when Scots or Scots-Irish were involved. Franklin's 'Instructions' boldly stated that the object of his voyage was the discovery of a Northwest Passage, 'only a small part of which is still unknown'. He was to reach Lancaster Sound as quickly as possible, sailing through Barrow Strait to Cape Walker, on the east point of Russell Island, north of Prince of Wales Island, whence westwards towards Bering Strait. If that route was obstructed he was to consider the alternative of Wellington Channel, which separates Cornwallis Island and North Devon. Thereafter he was ordered to proceed to Hawai'i or Panama. Much of the advice was repeated from previous expeditions but the ships were on no account to separate. Commander Fitzjames was placed in charge of magnetic variations, ideally to be taken daily whenever possible. Particular attention was to be paid to matters of geography and natural history and drawings made of the larger animals observed. Once they had passed latitude 65° N, copper cylinders or bottles were to be regularly thrown overboard to check the direction of the currents while simultaneously marking their passage, the pernicious futility of which would become even starker during the frustrating search for the lost ships. Should Britain become involved in war, Franklin was to maintain strict neutrality. Since the bureaucrats back home regarded failure as impossible (because of the care lavished on the ships), there were no plans for relief.[5]

Commander James Fitzjames, of Irish descent, had been Sir John Barrow's choice to lead what became the Franklin expedition, but Fitzjames was instead appointed the 'great man's' second in command. He was a man of considerable ability, charm, popularity and recklessness, enjoying a spectacular naval career, enriched by many talents and a sense of humour. He was rather taken with a few of the Scots, describing ice-master James Reid of

Aberdeen, a Greenland whaler, as 'the most original character of all, rough, intelligent, unpolished with a broad north-country accent, but not vulgar, good humoured and honest hearted'. When *Erebus* was pitching violently, he remarked that he did not like 'to see the wind seeking a corner to blow into'. When Reid told Fitzjames 'you never seem to sleep at arl [all]; your always writin', he responded with 'I tell him that when I do sleep, I do twice as much as other people in the same time'. He also commented on Harry Goodsir:

> I can't make out why Scotchmen just caught always speak in a low, hesitating voice, which is not at all times to be understood – this is, I believe, called 'cannyness'. Mr Goodsir is 'canny'. He is long and strait, and walks upright on his toes, with his hands tucked up in each jacket pocket. He is perfectly good humoured, very well informed on general points, in natural history learned . . . laughs delightfully, cannot be in a passion, is enthusiastic about all 'ologies, draws the insides of microscopic animals with an imaginary-pointed pencil, catches phenomena in a bucket, looks at the thermometer and every other meter, is a pleasant companion, and an acquisition in the mess. So much for Mr Goodsir.[6]

Fitzjames was a talented writer. His partial journal was sent back home in the last batch of material that left the ship on 12 July 1845.

The intention here is not to rehearse the last known movements of the Franklin expedition, ably covered by legions of others, but by 1848, it was becoming clear that the expedition, which had set sail from the Thames bound for Greenland in May 1845 and was last seen by a whaling ship in Baffin Bay in July, was now lost somewhere in the Canadian Arctic. Sir John Ross had already approached the Admiralty in 1847 with detailed plans for a rescue mission to be led by him but it was initially rejected. The Admiralty was, however, persuaded the following year by Lady Franklin, among others, to commence searching expeditions. A number of prominent Scottish explorers were among those sent to find them, including Ross, Sir John Richardson, Ross's nephew James Clark Ross and John Rae.

*

Sir John Ross, sensitive as well as experienced about such matters, suggested in January 1847 that Franklin's ships were frozen up in the drift ice at the west end of Melville Island, from which they would find extrication difficult, if not entirely impossible. This idea was dismissed by John Richardson, who argued that Franklin was known as a stickler for adhering to his instructions. Richardson had engaged in many conversations with Franklin in relation to the expedition and had received a letter from him when he was on the coast of Greenland, but Franklin had not discussed wishing or expecting to store provisions on Melville Island. Nonetheless Richardson agreed on a searching expedition in the spring of 1848 if no news was forthcoming by then. He recommended building four boats, 30 feet long and 6 feet wide, somewhat larger than those he recommended in 1825. The boats were to be manned by twenty men and sent to the Mackenzie, exploring the shores of Wollaston Land and the peninsula on the south-west of Victoria Island, returning by way of the Coppermine River, thus searching the whole line of the coast to which any victims of shipwreck might naturally gravitate. However, he considered that concerns about possible difficulties for the Franklin parties were premature, so he could muster little enthusiasm for a rescue mission. He agreed with Parry (now a member of the Arctic Council planning the search for Franklin) that whalers should receive rewards for maintaining lookouts. HBC should also be approached for assistance.

After his return from Rupert's Land in 1827 Richardson had claimed he had 'laid aside forever the intention of going out again to Hudson's Bay . . . the lapse of a year or two will cause a material alteration in my power for sustaining fatigue'.[7] While working at Haslar Hospital in 1845 he suffered spasms, heart arrhythmia, a recurrence noted 'once and once only' by his second in command, John Rae, in 1848. In his autobiography, Sir John Barrow similarly reported that Richardson had an attack of paralysis in 1845, dismissed by the doctor as a fainting fit while gardening. However, the man himself wrote that he declined to carry a load of 60–70 pounds, 'distrusting to my own powers of march'.[8] At the age of 61 he could be deemed close to approaching the edge of his physical abilities, even displaying a 'lack of vigour' according to Rae,[9] but, like many physicians, the only advice Richardson respected was his own. Despite any possible misgivings, he was willing, even inwardly compelled, to return to the north once more.

Richardson's second wife, Mary Booth (niece of Sir John Franklin), sadly suffered what would now be thought a typically tragic and lengthy Victorian death in 1845, leaving five children, including a two-month-old baby. She was, like John, profoundly religious. In 1847 he married 'reasonable and romantic' Mary Fletcher, daughter of Archibald Fletcher, a well-known

Scottish radical and burgh reformer (died 1828), and his wife Eliza, the latter a very bright, independently minded blue stocking, whom Richardson adored. The couple were married in Grasmere. They inherited Lancrigg in Easedale, a stunning house in one of England's most beautiful counties, with William Wordsworth as a neighbour. Evenings at Lancrigg must have been glorious since Mrs Fletcher knew or had read the works of everybody who was anybody: writers, poets, philosophers and politicians in Britain, as well as many abroad.[10]

Richardson knew at the time of his wedding that if no information about Franklin's fate came through, he would be Arctic bound the following year. On reading Rae's account of his first Arctic journey of 1846–7 in *The Times* he announced that he had found his expeditionary companion 'if I can get him'. Luckily he could. Among Rae's attributes were his experience of fifteen years in Rupert's Land, knowing how to exploit the natural products of the region, a skilful hunting ability, expertise in 'expedients for tempering the severity of the climate' and experience in handling instruments required for latitude, longitude and the variations and dip of the magnetic needle.[11]

Richardson had the opportunity to acquire an exotic recruit, none other than Jane Franklin, née Griffin, who expressed a wish to join the expedition. This was not the crazy idea that some commentators have suggested. Jane, one of the most far-travelled women of her day, was younger than Richardson and she would have injected a much-needed and intriguing female role into the saga of the Northwest Passage. Jane was unmarried until she wed Franklin, whom she thereafter claimed to love, though he always appears something of a plodder alongside her vivaciousness. Jane sought a project, and Richardson's reputation as a naval luminary and explorer fulfilled that need. Ken McGoogan has admitted that he fell in love with Jane Franklin while writing her biography and although others were also unquestionably smitten, many men, especially those entrusted with some authority, found her persistence and demands ultimately tiresome. Arguably, however, Lady Franklin can be seen as a powerful and influential component of the driving force behind the discovery of the Northwest Passage, which she regarded as the key to her husband's legacy.

She, Richardson and Rae met, presumably to discuss her request. A recent writer describes her greeting Rae: 'she was struck by how broad and coarse his hand was'. That same author proceeds to provide a stereotypical portrait of a Scot in 1847 that revealingly appears, in the mind of the writer, to have little altered in more than 170 years:

Rae was a coarse man, speaking with a north Scottish brogue, his manners indelicate and his language unpolished. Everything about him was weather-beaten, and hard. His profile, which he was inclined to present, was bold and sharp and well-proportioned. Not by any means was he a handsome man, but nonetheless, he owned the peaty earthiness of his Scottish island roots, dressed in old tweed and moleskins, and was notable perhaps for the fact that he did not smell of tobacco.[12]

Elsewhere she alludes to Rae's 'rough-edged, manly manners, his untutored Scottish brogue and clear intelligence' – the 'untutored Scottish brogue' despite having studied for four years at Edinburgh University and becoming a licentiate of the Royal College of Surgeons before he was twenty![13]

Dr Richardson told his mother-in-law that the search for which he was preparing was a sacred trust,

a point of duty which I cannot conscientiously evade, unless I were convinced that another person could carry my plan in the way that I have conceived it. But there is no one now alive who is acquainted with the track but myself; and no one who is so bound by the ties of friendship and affection to do his utmost to find Franklin if he should unhappily be in a situation in which he and his party cannot help themselves.[14]

*

Richardson's plan was similar to that of James Clark Ross (JCR), who was to follow the route assumed to have been taken by Franklin, subject to the usual Arctic dilemma concerning the desirable and the possible. JRC was to be provided with two ships capable of tolerating the ice pressure in Lancaster Sound, 'fortified and equipped, in every respect as were *Erebus* and *Terror* for the Antarctic Seas'. These were *Enterprise*, 450 tons, built at London, and *Investigator*, 400 tons, constructed at Greenock on the Clyde. For the first time in Arctic exploration each ship was to carry a steam pinnace, or tender, of about 20 tons, so called because they 'tended' the sailing ships: for example, functioning as ice-breakers or supplying power during calms.

The seekers should progress, by either ships or boats, to Lancaster Sound and Barrow Strait and from there strike north-westwards to Wellington Channel, following which they were to examine the south coast between

Cape Clarence (Somerset Island) and Cape Walker (Russell Island at the northern end of Prince of Wales Island), possibly wintering one of the ships in the vicinity of Garnier Bay or Cape Rennell (Somerset Island). With the coming of spring, the west coast of Boothia might be investigated well to the south, while other parties explored the south-west and north-west. JCR added some refinements, such as his plan (unrealised) to sail down the west coast of Baffin Bay to Clyde River. The ships were to meet up again at Whaler Point, Port Leopold (which later became an HBC trading post), on the north-east tip of Somerset Island. When conditions permitted, a steam launch should be sent to enquire of whalers in Lancaster Sound whether there was any news of Franklin's safe return.

James Clark Ross recruited three veterans of the Antarctic expedition: Thomas Abernethy, who had accompanied him in 1827 and 1829–33, an accomplished seaman and an ice-master with a powerful thirst for alcohol; Captain Edward Bird, captain of *Investigator* and second-in-command; and John Robertson, surgeon on *Terror* in Antarctica. Irishman Robert McClure, first lieutenant on Ross's ship, *Enterprise*, had sailed with Back in *Terror* in 1836 and would, on his next expedition, earn fame as captain of *Investigator*. Another Irishman bound for glory was second lieutenant Francis Leopold McClintock, on his first visit to the Arctic, most fortuitously on *Enterprise*. Both would play their rather different roles in the searchers' story. McClintock described JCR as 'a very quick, penetrating old bird, very mild in appearance and rather flowery in his style. He is handsome still and has the most piercing black eyes.'[15]

JCR had basically written his own searching instructions, which were that both ships should scrutinise the area north-west from Lancaster Sound. He was entrusted with 'the duty of following the track of the discovery ships', should that be ascertained, which of course crucially it was not. *Investigator* was to winter near Cape Rennell, having one party explore the west coast of Boothia, while another probed the south of Prince Regent Inlet. *Enterprise* was to winter, fittingly, on Winter Island, Melville Island or at Banks Land following a route to Cape Bathurst or Cape Parry on the northern coast of the mainland in spring, whence on to the Mackenzie. Another party was to look at the east coast of Banks Land and Cape Krusenstern, meeting up with Richardson and returning home with him. The steam launches were to ensure communication with both ships, 'to transmit such information for the guidance of each other as might be necessary for the safety and success of the undertaking' but for some reason JCR had one steam pinnace removed at

Port Leopold, perhaps because he had never been a keen supporter of steam, unlike his enthusiastic uncle. The third probe from the Bering Strait involved two Navy ships: *Herald*, Captain Kellet, and *Plover*, Commander Moore. If *Erebus* was found afloat, JCR was to defer to Franklin, but if beset he should retain his own command.

*

The instructions given to Richardson for his expedition ordered him and Rae to proceed by way of New York and Montreal to consult George Simpson about supplies and other assistance.[16] Richardson's party was to follow the by now familiar route via Lake Superior, Fort William and Lake Winnipeg to overtake Chief Trader John Bell (from the Island of Mull), who was in charge of transporting the four newly built boats to Fort Confidence. On arrival Richardson was instructed to examine the coast between the Mackenzie, the Coppermine and hopefully Wollaston Land, but he was given full permission to deviate from the track if necessary. Since JCR's party was also sent westwards in *Enterprise* Richardson was required to deposit for his use suitable caches of calorie-rich pemmican, most of which was manufactured in London owing to HBC shortages. Richardson and Rae departed on 25 March 1848; James Clark Ross sailed on 12 May. Rae reported that when their ship, Cunard's *Hibernia*, broke a crank pin it was repaired by the ship's chief officer, James Anderson (born in Dumfries and later lauded for laying the first successful transatlantic cable). It is to be hoped that the two 'Doonhamers' and the Orcadian enjoyed 'guid crack' on their voyage. Rae politely declined a lady's fine gift of 'a valuable silk-lined eider-down quilt and beautiful muff'. It was expected that during the following season Richardson's men would cross some of Ross's routes; Richardson's stint was to end after a winter spent at Great Slave Lake. On no account was it to be prolonged beyond spring of 1850.

Two weeks after departing, JCR hosted a dinner party to mark the anniversary of his discovery of the Magnetic North Pole. A week later McClintock reported that he was fascinated by ever-changing images in the sea-ice and the overwhelming presence of the icebergs. On the Whale Fish Islands off the coast of Greenland he was intrigued by the wildlife as well as the Inuit, entranced as the women danced tirelessly with the crew. After ten days they sailed on to Upernavik (Woman's Island) and Cape York, where he deposited a record in a cairn, and then on to Lancaster Sound. He found a small pile of stones left by JCR in 1825. The search of the south coast of Lancaster

Sound had to be abandoned as bad weather forced both vessels to winter at desolate Port Leopold. A wall was built between the two ships and two observatories for magnetic observations were constructed using snow. The traditional 'school classes' were organised but there were no theatricals. The daily gill of spirits was doubled on Christmas Day and New Year's Day. Since they had no dogs with them, JCR depended upon sledges modelled on Greenlandic man-hauled specimens that had proved efficient and were used by future Navy sledgers, although still regarded as controversial by some commentators because man-hauling is a notoriously exhausting exercise.

James Clark Ross was in his element establishing depots some 15 miles from their base. Captain Bird, with a fatigue party numbering twenty-eight men, accompanied him for five days before returning, but the men were exhausted by the vast quantities of ice that rendered travelling difficult and dangerous. With the traditional three hearty cheers from all, JCR departed in May 1849 to cover 500 miles in thirty-nine days by way of Cape Rennell, with two sledges, twelve men and Leopold McClintock. From Cape Bunny they had views of the area between Cape Walker and Wellington Channel choked with ice, persuading them south into the unexplored Peel Sound and down the west coast of Somerset Island (Kuunganajuk), until the unforgiving ice compelled them to turn back. They travelled by night to avoid the soft daytime snow, the enemy of man-sleds. In June the party raised 'an enormous cairn of stones' at Cape Coulman, so named by JCR for his wife, then he pushed on to Bay of Four Rivers with two companions. A copper cylinder was placed inside the cairn with information about his planned route and the position of the caches. He named Cape Bird, some 50 miles away, which later proved to be the northern entrance to Bellot Strait. While JCR was away, Captain Bird had organised various short investigations of land and sea in different directions, creating and checking measurements and observations.

For a time it looked as if they might be ice-bound but they broke free, JCR deciding to return to his ship but, before doing so, he ordered the building of another cairn containing information about the whereabouts of caches. The previous year a whaler had recovered a cask thrown overboard from *Investigator*, an event that persuaded the English authorities to send a supply ship, *North Star*, to relieve JCR, but it became trapped in the ice. Ironically, JCR and his men were starving before they left the Arctic, their plight worsened by an outbreak of scurvy, caused by insufficient rations and tins of bad food, specially prepared for the expedition but proving seriously underweight, or rancid, or both. Only he and McClintock avoided disease.

Some of the men, on whom the sledging was very hard and painful, were still incapacitated when they reached home, McClintock alone remained reasonably fit; even JCR was bed-ridden for a time. The assistant doctor and *Investigator*'s cook died. Before they departed Port Leopold, they built a house and left sufficient fuel and food for a year, enough, it was reckoned, for sixty-four persons. Also abandoned was *Investigator*'s steam launch. They feared they were becoming trapped in the ice but luckily it broke up off Pond Inlet. There seemed no option except to return home.[17]

Many were puzzled by JCR's behaviour, notably Londoner Richard King, who had sailed as surgeon and naturalist on George Back's Great Fish River expedition. He wrote, with characteristic exaggeration, that 'if ever one man sacrificed another, Sir James Ross sacrificed Sir John Franklin and not only Franklin but [one hundred and twenty-nine] noble hearts with him . . . Ross rushed headlong upon a shoal and wrecked himself at once and for ever'.[18] Lady Jane Franklin was deeply disappointed by JCR's early return but still regarding him as one of her main hopes she continued to badger him about renewed attempts to find her husband and presumably the pet monkey that she had presented to him on his departure.

JCR's expedition achieved very little for a man of his standing and accomplishment. It has been suggested that some of his problems were linked to members of the crew who were attracted by the promise of double pay but were not properly vetted for fitness and experience, which would have been Ross's responsibility. There was no mention that he also might have suffered longer-term damage to his health. Neither he nor anyone else ever published an account of the voyage, while other sources are incomplete. There is a suggestion that he arrogantly refused to produce a narrative, though his log does exist. One of his officers (apparently anonymous) wrote 'we have certainly had to grapple with difficulties of no ordinary nature; but thanks to the energy and dauntless courage of our experienced commander, we have triumphantly overcome them all'.

Perhaps JCR had outlived the role of polar explorer, had experienced enough of cold and snow, and had exhausted his true interest in conquering ice barriers. Perhaps, after a lifetime of male companionship, he craved marriage and domesticity, having tired of the endless demands made of him. He had declined the offer of leading what became the Franklin expedition because he was suffering exhaustion after his Antarctic experiences and wished to spend more time with his wife, Anne Coulman. It is said that he had promised her at their marriage in 1843 that he was done with polar exploration but she agreed that, if required, he should go in search of his friend, Franklin. Scurvy, inadequate rations and disease would have been ample reason for an early return. He is credited with exploring 150 miles of the west coast of Somerset Island and with proving that Franklin failed to visit Fury Beach, not an impressive result.[19] Once described by Lady Franklin as 'the handsomest man in the Navy', he died in 1862, some said of a broken heart due to Anne's death five years earlier. Towards the end, he sought solace in alcohol, a condition not unknown among men who realise they have lost their invincibility. Edward Sabine wrote that Ross had established a claim 'to be regarded as the first scientific navigator of his country and of his age'.[20] In terms of Arctic exploration the man was indeed a colossus.

*

Richardson loved detail, reminiscent of that adopted by a well-meaning but rather boringly knowledgeable university professor. En route he imparts geography seminars, a recipe for pemmican with his own additions of currants and sugar (listing the expense of production), details of the building of his boats, lists the stores, the men's clothing, the invaluable and essential duties of voyageur wives (washing, making and mending clothes, moccasins and fishing nets, as well as netting for snow-shoes)[21] and provides a reading list for those interested in the geology, geography, hydrology, climatology and natural history he encounters. He writes sympathetically and at length about the folk that he meets – the Inuit, the First Nations Kutchin or Loucheux, the Chipewyans, the Dogribs – and their languages, represented by several vocabularies that he put together. He describes the Inuit as a littoral people who display the virtues of 'Norwegian Vikings', inhabiting 5,000 miles of coast from the Straits of Bellisle to the Peninsula of Alaska; their kayaking gear renders them 'a race of fearless seamen'.

The fact that those they encounter are starving looks ominous for the wellbeing of Franklin's men. When one Inuk states that Cape Bathurst is an island, Richardson disagrees, to receive the riposte 'Are not all lands islands?'. According to Richardson, HBC and Orkneymen still call the Inuit *Seymos*, a corruption of 'Eskimos'. He thinks that their code is 'Spartan'; 'thief' is a term of reproach among themselves but they do not hesitate to steal from strangers, an action they regard as heroic or mischievous. They are also generous with their wives where approved visitors are concerned.

Richardson's overwhelming desire to share useful knowledge whenever possible is well illustrated in a letter he sent to his daughter telling her that when he reached Fort William (Lake Superior) he would have travelled one quarter of the way round the Earth, explaining that it rotates completely every twenty-four hours, 'completing each spot in succession to the sun'.

> If the circle it makes, in turning, be divided into 24 parts, each part is equal to an hour of time; or if it be divided into 360 degrees, each hour includes fifteen degrees, and six hours are equal to ninety degrees, which is the longitude of Fort William west of Greenwich ... You are not old enough to understand this ...

'Correct, Father, for I am only six', she might have replied. Her reward was to be reminded that God was everywhere. 'Unless your papa was under the constant guardianship of His providence his long journey would be a wild and vain attempt ... I beseech you, my dear child, never to forget to pray, morning, evening and at noon-day, for your papa.'[22]

The summer of 1848 was disappointingly short, resulting in bad weather and the consequent abandoning of boats and supplies on the coast due to transportation difficulties on land and sea, described in Richardson's *Arctic Searching Expedition*. In the absence of little to report that is new, he falls back on travelogue as, for example, in his lengthy discussion of the Mackenzie. His observations are undoubtedly compelling but some are by now fairly familiar and despite their best efforts the expedition was a failure because it found no trace of the lost ships. Rae, however, found plenty to interest him. He reported that traditionally if a voyageur broke an oar or paddle he had to replace it the first time the brigade halted. The offender went into the woods, hacked down a suitable tree and shaped the wood to his satisfaction using axe and knife. A boat was lost in rapids. The party encountered a former HBC Métis who made his living by selling salt that occurred naturally in mounds. Rae experienced the most violent storm he had ever seen when 'the wind blew with great force and thunder shook the ground'. The tent he shared with Richardson blew away. Joining the Mackenzie, they viewed the Rocky Mountains after a few days. On the beach they witnessed an inundation of spiders. A white-headed eagle was spotted. Mosquitos were voracious.

In the Mackenzie estuary they encountered 200 Inuit, each in his own kayak, along with three umiaks full of women and old men. Richardson was quite wary of them. When they tried to hold on to, or possibly tip, the boats, he ordered the beating of their knuckles with a stick, rather an extreme measure that he claimed they 'respected'; Rae, on the other hand, 'without much difficulty unclasped their hands from our gunwales'. The Inuit responded by attempting to drag a cockswain named Duncan Clark overboard, testing the visitors with other 'aggressive acts', such as attempting to plunder one of the boats. Cocked muskets restored order. On more peaceful exchanges it emerged that the locals knew nothing about Franklin or his whereabouts. Rae suspected that the invaders must be responsible for the hostility of the Inuit but he specifically blamed cockswain Clark for current problems and admitted his own desire to punish some of the most daring and impudent scoundrels he had ever come across, admiring the methods adopted by Dease and Simpson.

Rae was not greatly impressed by his companions, who seemed to be almost as dismal as the weather. They complained a lot and apparently had difficulty in tolerating rain and cold; they used bad language. Some of their boat journey experiences were far from enjoyable. They had to suffer three portages in a single day. Such *esprit de corps* as had existed seems to have collapsed. Rae had expected better. One example of an irritating offender must suffice. 'One fat young fellow', Edward Dodd, possibly a Scot, announced he was afraid of contracting rheumatism because the soles of his moccasins had become slightly wet while he was standing on ice. Rae was almost incandescent: 'to one who had been wet for days together without intermission, the croaking of the young man was irresistibly ludicrous', adding that 'this feeling of taking immense care of themselves was very general among the men to a greater or less extent'.[23]

As he sailed east, Richardson made mention of places he was revisiting and recalling from 1826, while providing what he assumed would be useful information for subsequent navigators. The sky was dark and lowering as they approached Cape Hope, their boats buffeted by ice floes, generating further misery. Caches continued to be deposited as directed. Occasionally the party stayed put because of adverse weather, but serious ice in the Dolphin and Union Strait meant they could not reach Wollaston Land, forcing them south. Richardson later learned that JCR was having similar problems in Barrow Strait and he decided to abandon the ocean. The bitter weather wrecked their intention of leaving their boats up the Coppermine ready for next summer's use but it was also feared that if they were deposited on shore the vessels would be destroyed by the Inuit. In the event they were stowed at Icy Cove and Cape Krusenstern but only one survived the winter. They received generous help from the Inuit (described by Joseph Bellot as 'these unconscious subjects of Great Britain') who rigged up their kayaks to ferry them across an inlet – actually a freshwater river that was named for Rae, Richardson's 'active, zealous and intelligent companion, as a testimony of my high sense of his merits and exertions'. It was due to Rae's efforts that they had managed to progress so far by sea, thus reducing the overland journey. The appreciation was almost overdue, for Rae had hitherto played a respectable but not greatly acknowledged part in proceedings, treated somewhat as an underling, generally mentioned for his outstanding (and essential) hunting and sailing skills. The parties crossed Richardson's River to reach the Coppermine a few miles above Bloody Falls (Kogluktok), before carrying their gear across the Barren Lands, taking some thirteen days in fierce weather to arrive at Great Bear Lake and Fort Confidence in mid September 1848. They were aided by a band of First Nations who supplied them with food and a guide.[24]

Fort Confidence had to be largely rebuilt. Two Scottish carpenters, Mackay and Brodie, were assigned to furniture-making. Time was not wasted. During the winter Richardson and Rae 'recorded the temperatures hourly, sixteen or seventeen times per day', as well as recording the readings of two barometers, the declinometer and the dipping needle. Once a month, on a 'term day' of thirty-six hours, magnetic fluctuations were recorded, incredibly every two and a half minutes. Rae reported that Richardson had 'almost forgot the mode of taking observations so that the greater part of that duty devolves upon me' because Richardson was so busy with other matters. A register of winds and weather was kept and appearances of the aurora noted.[25] Rae was very impressed by Richardson's morning prayers before they set out each day. 'Our appearance with gun on shoulder and loads on our backs, reminded me much of what I had read of the covenanters of old, when they worshipped in the glens and on the hillsides, prepared at a moment's notice either to fight with or flee from their persecutors.'[26] Mail was extremely erratic. Letters posted on 31 October 1848 were delivered to the fort on the day after Richardson arrived home. American newspapers brought news of wars with the First Nations who often gave away part of their prey to the needy. When challenged they responded, 'what [else] could they do if hungry Indians came their way'? They must eat. 'This socialist practice presses heavily on the industrious hunter, and encourages the lazy individuals in their idleness; but its continuance . . . is proof of a fund at the bottom of the national character', sufficient evidence that the tribes do not make a habit of deserting the old and the sick.[27] Food was reasonably plentiful, winter feasts quite frequent. Bruce the Métis made his own fiddle and taught himself to play it. The interpreter, Albert, improved the water supply and showed the company how to ice their sledge-runners. Visiting parties of First Nations slept in the HBC dining-hall. The first geese arrived in May heralding spring. From then on birds dominated the calendar.

Richardson's thoughts now turned to his homeward journey and he left Rae at Fort Confidence on 7 May 1849 and headed for Fort Franklin. Clearly, he was losing the strength that had sustained his earlier expeditions but his instructions had told him to withdraw after over-wintering and certainly no later than spring of 1850. He admitted he was missing his wife and his sizeable family. Since only one of their boats remained serviceable it was available to either Richardson or Rae, but not both. If two boats had been available, Richardson might have been persuaded to spend another season in the Arctic: 'I could almost fancy at times that I have never been anything but an inhabitant of these wilds.' He clearly shared a recognition with Cowper's *Winter Evening on the Arrival of the Post*:

> He comes, the herald of a noisy world,
> With snowy boots, strapp'd waist, and frozen locks,
> News from all nations lumbering at his back,
> Yet careless what he brings his one concern
> Is to conduct it to the destined Fort;
> But oh the important budget, who can say
> What are its tidings?

But he was actually ready to leave. 'When one strikes the key-note of home, it has the effect of the tune of "Lochaber" on a Highland emigrant.'[28]

Rae was given his orders to explore Wollaston and Victoria Lands, 'which the state of the ice in Dolphin and Union Straits rendered inaccessible last autumn'. Richardson had no hesitation in choosing him. He considered Rae's ability and zeal unquestionable, his fitness and hunting skills admirable. Also, with only one boat in action HBC would save money, a truly Scottish concern!

Rae departed Fort Confidence on 8 June 1849 with six men, two of whom were First Nations, hauling the boat through ice and water and diverting up the south-east branch of the Dease River. After a number of exhausting portages they descended to the Dismal Lakes, the Kendal and the Coppermine. Having spent five days recovering and hunting, they pushed on to Bloody Falls, collecting a cache along the way. On 11 July, skirting the shore of Richardson Bay, they encountered seven Inuit who had been in communication with their fellows in Wollaston Land, 'none of whom had ever seen whites, large boats or ships'. Taking their leave of 'these simple and inoffensive people' they pushed on to Cape Kendall and the place they had left the boats the previous year, finding them broken up and looted, although one food stockpile, concealed by snow, was untouched. On 30 July they reached Cape Krusenstern, aiming to cross to Wollaston Land but they were delayed until 19 August waiting for the ice to clear. Signs of early winter convinced Rae that the party should return. Back at the Coppermine the interpreter Albert was drowned in rather a freak accident though Rae squarely blamed the steersman for using too small a towline; 'his cowardice where there was no danger, can admit of no excuse'. Rae grieved deeply since Albert was much liked for his lively, amiable disposition and extreme good nature. The party arrived back at Fort Confidence on 26 September.

Richardson explained that Rae's mortification on returning early was 'much more severe than he has thought proper to express in his official despatch'. He admitted his indebtedness to his activity and intelligence, sound advice and co-operation 'on every emergency'. His society 'cheered the long hours of an arctic winter's absence from my wife and family, and it was in great measure owing to his skill and assiduity in observing, that our experiments on magnetism during our stay at Fort Confidence were carried on so as to be productive of scientific results'.[29]

Richardson comes across as somewhat racist in one of his last Arctic letters to his mother-in-law, almost as if he was trying to mirror her assumptions and prejudices, which he did not wholly share. He states that the First Nations cannot be credited with achieving a single step on the road to civilisation. They enjoy their freedom but the only restraint on a man's actions is the opinion of his neighbours. He was unable to figure out whether they had any idea of a Deity, or a sense of right and wrong. None of them are truthful; because they tell lies, insignificant incidents 'swell into some dreadful calamity', a situation not entirely unknown in Scotland, as Mrs Fletcher would be well aware. Richardson's experience had taught him that 'Arcadian innocence and happiness exist only in the imaginations of the poets.'

Richardson had left Fort Confidence on 7 May 1849 but was delayed by weather for a month at Bear Lake River. Some unforgettable memories accrued: 'When the snow is filled with water it looks like frosted silver in the sunlight, and every little rising is studded with innumerable polished facets, as if sprinkled with diamonds. The intensity of all this splendour soon becomes painful to eye'. Likewise, beneath the 'immeasurable distance of the blue profound', towards the horizon blue, gradually becoming grey, 'blending beautifully with the snow of distant hills empurpled by the rays of the nearly level sun. The depth of shade which marks out the low snowy waves of the lake when the sun is low would surprise a painter brought here for the first time'.[30] He reached Sault Ste. Marie on 25 September, stopping for a few days with George Simpson at Lachine, moving on to Boston and arriving at Liverpool on 6 November. He had to report to the Admiralty in London before he could join the family at Haslar, just as the children, due to a remarkable example of surely contrived serendipity, were dancing to the tune of 'There's nae luck aboot the hoose, when Oor Guid Man's awa'!'[31] Once he was home Mrs Fletcher reflected that Richardson was to be greatly admired for devolving command to a person better fitted for the task. It was rare for such a man to think of handing over to anyone as competent as himself.[32]

John Richardson was a man of many talents. In addition to his medical knowledge and abilities, he was a fine writer, a notable geographer, ethnologer, surveyor, cartographer, Christian and supporter of the Magnetic Crusade. Above all he was a highly respected natural historian at a period when the subject was soaring in Canada and the USA, populated by numerous Scottish practitioners, many of whom, alongside Scots–Irish, found employment at the Smithsonian, Washington DC. As the American scientist Joseph Henry said, 'truth and science should know no country'.[33]

Both Rosses might have benefited from John Richardson's reliance on common sense. When he was denied the position of Director-general of the Medical Department at Haslar on grounds of age, he resigned, eventually retiring to Lancrigg. The Royal Society presented him with a medal. He was consulted by Florence Nightingale on hospital administration and doubtless other matters on which they agreed, notably that the army and the Navy were both branches of the 'Circumlocution Office', the place of endless confusion in Charles Dickens's *Little Dorrit*. He continued to produce papers on natural history, remained a member of the Arctic Council, processed findings and samples from other expeditions, wrote articles on ichthyology and Sir John Franklin for *Encyclopaedia Britannica*, celebrated the Robert Burns Centenary and became increasingly interested in the older Scots tongue, contributing to a new dictionary, published by the Philological Society, which later grew into *The Oxford English Dictionary*. His articles included 'a complete index of words used by Burns, with their significations and cognates in Norse, Icelandic, or Gaelic, as far as I could ascertain them'. Two of his children died. He travelled abroad, took an interest in the archaeology of Dumfries and Galloway and recited Burns for a penny reading in Grasmere. He died suddenly on 5 June 1865. Eleven years earlier he had lamented that 'as age steals upon me with an accelerated pace the daily duties of office become more burdensome. I feel a desire for rest and incapacity for even the slightest exertion of writing'.[34] His biographer supplied many obituaries but perhaps one of the more interesting came from George Back, the sole survivor of the first expedition:

> No one could perfectly understand the admirable qualities of his nature, who had not been with him in trials of no ordinary description, even when life itself was in question. In storm and sunshine, in plenty and famine, in moments of great danger, requiring unusual self-possession and coolness, he was ever firmly balanced and collected – an example to others. With a keen sense of humour, quick to discern, and ready to applaud, he was ever a pleasant companion, and, better than all, a moral good man.[35]

*

John Ross had assured his old friend Franklin that, if necessary, he would volunteer for his rescue 'if you are not heard of in February 1847', a notion he retained while trying to organise an expedition to Spitsbergen to measure an arc of the meridian (an imaginary circle of longitude passing through the poles). Edward Sabine, veteran of Ross's 1818 venture, had established a pendulum observatory there because he was convinced that it was an ideal place for researching the shape of the Earth. But Ross did not receive government backing for the venture and so was free for an Arctic rescue mission instead. As combative as ever, Ross complained that his opinions and plans were scorned along with his experience and knowledge. So he begins his *Narrative*, revealingly subtitled *The Circumstances and Causes which led to the Failure of the Searching Expeditions sent by Government and others for the Rescue of Sir John Franklin*, as he means to end it – in critical confrontation. He suggested that Franklin's ships were too large, the steam machinery was too heavy, canned meat was putrid; Franklin did not know how to read the weather, which was predicted to be severe. There was no provision to leave supply ships in key locations in the way that had saved Ross's 1830s expedition at Fury Beach, and there was no mention of rescue plans. Parry,

Sabine, JCR and Richardson all opposed his suggestions, though some of them were not without merit. He had urged Franklin to place a notice in a cairn wherever he wintered, indicating the routes he intended to take. When the two men parted, an emotional Franklin had said, 'you are the only one who has volunteered to look for me; God bless you', or so Ross avowed, but he found no helpful cairns.[36]

True to his word, John Ross had first mooted a search in the early months of 1847. It was rejected, along with his Spitsbergen meridian proposal. He was far from silenced as the wrangle continued for months. A stock response was, 'You will go and get frozen in like Franklin, and we shall have to send after you'. He wrote to the Board of Admiralty and the Royal Society deploring their members' most unfortunate misapprehension of duty, though a hopeful sign was that the Astronomical Society offered support if the Royal Society replied favourably. An increasingly exasperated Ross reported a meeting hosted by Lady Franklin 'at which all my proposals were sneered at and my opinions scouted [examined], while I was represented to be too old and infirm to undertake such a service'. Also, they had proposed his nephew James Clark Ross should receive command of any expedition rather than John who, needless to say, was outraged by the suggestion. He argued that Franklin was probably ice-bound, rendering the ships, and consequently the crews, far too large if abandonment proved necessary. Richardson's current foray would be no use in extricating the beleaguered vessels and could only be useful in taking some supplies to the Mackenzie, 'if they ever reach it', because he feared that if they were delayed another winter it would be too late to find any of them alive. Given that his own men on *Victory* in 1832–3 had been totally exhausted, having travelled half the distance to the American coast compared with that faced by Franklin's crews, their situation looked grim. Again, Ross was defeated by the 'stupid pertinacity' of the apparatchiks in London. Admiral and Arctic explorer Sherard Osborn once remarked that 'all propositions of a rational nature' meet with opposition 'from the persons consulted by the Admiralty' and the opinion is borne out by many an instance of 'official ignorance and near-sightedness'.[37]

The next blow landed when Ross was told his nephew was indeed to command the rescue expedition instead of him. Worse, JCR favoured two large ships over John's suggested four smaller ones which would perform much more efficiently in the ice conditions. At this point the elder Ross rather flipped since James had often been heard to claim that smaller ships were to be preferred. 'But I immediately saw through his intention, which could be no other than the survey of the western coasts of North Somerset and Boothia, and thereby [to] determine the north-west passage . . . there can be no doubt that Sir J.C. Ross and his friend Sir John Barrow had made up their minds to treat the search for poor Franklin as a secondary consideration, in order to accomplish their favourite object.' Even the names of the ships were a giveaway, *Enterprise* and *Investigator*, 'sufficiently indicative of the *double* service they had to perform'. Ross further claimed that he heard Richardson boasting that he would find Franklin.[38]

What is to be made of such accusations and reports? There is no evidence to support John Ross's allegations about his nephew's exploratory intentions. Indeed, the idea seems to originate with Sir John himself in reference to his proposal combining meridian research in Spitsbergen with a search for the missing ships. Betrayal, however, which Ross was entitled to claim after his hard work on behalf of his friend Franklin, had bred bad blood and he had reason to be angry. Many men in their seventies do not feel old until someone points out the obvious. In the tiresome flighting about who said what and when, John Ross was outraged that he had never been consulted about some of the statements he had allegedly made. 'They played only the humiliating game of a tin tied to the dog's tail, and unhappily for the cause of humanity, and the credit of the Admiralty, the dog which dragged them through the dirt was a cross-grained and sour-tempered old cur, determined to snap at my heels and bark me into a becoming state of silence.'[39] It is not exactly clear who the 'old cur' actually was, though many would have seen John Ross as a perfect fit for the scurrilous description, had it not been written by the man himself. The most likely candidate was John Barrow, who died in 1848.

With the Richardson and JCR relief expeditions now well underway, Ross having been overlooked for these positions due to his advanced years, he nevertheless continued to campaign for his own rescue mission throughout 1848. After the return of *Enterprise* and *Investigator* later that year, Ross once again approached the Admiralty with the outline of a proposed expedition under his command. Ross's plan for the relief of Franklin 'from the eastward or by way of Baffin's Bay' returned to the virtues of small vessels over large ships. He specifically recommended three: *Asp*, a Portpatrick packet with paddle wheels and a crew of twenty-four; a small clipper, *Isla* of Aberdeen, managed by a crew of thirty-eight; and his own yacht, *Mary*. The first two were dropped. To reach Ayr, *Mary*, berthed in London, was towed up the east coast of Scotland to Inverness and the entrance to the Caledonian

Canal, one of the greatest achievements of engineer Thomas Telford. She then sailed through the canal to Loch Linnhe and probably by way of the Crinan Canal to the Firth of Clyde. Rather a roundabout route for a short cut as some might have said. She never returned to Scotland since she was to be abandoned by Ross when he left the Arctic for the last time.

Ross planned that his small west-coast fleet would sail to the Arctic, using steam power when they arrived in the ice. They would stop at Lievely (Disko Island) to take on board two Danish interpreters who knew Inuktitut and acquire sledge dogs from the Greenlanders, thereafter continuing to Port Leopold, Wellington Channel and Melville Island. If no trace of Franklin was found in Barrow Strait, small parties consisting of an officer and two men were to be despatched in every likely direction. Whalers should be recruited, twenty-five of whom were awaiting Ross at Peterhead, having already volunteered to serve under him and no one else. He pledged that he would return the following year with news of Franklin and 'his devoted companions'.[40]

Ross hyped his qualifications for the job in hand. He was a senior officer with much Arctic experience. He was the only officer who promised to search for Franklin if he had not returned in 1847 and he had discussed possible locations with him (partly true, but he was not alone in this). His Danish language skills were good, reinforced by the interpreters (arguable). According to him he was perfectly acquainted with steam navigation (he was a keen advocate of steam). His constitution was well adapted to the climate (perhaps true). As a consul for six years in Sweden he was an experienced sledger on snow and ice (possibly the case). He had borrowed astronomical instruments and an 8-foot telescope. Sir Francis Beaufort (Hydrographer of the Admiralty) thought the whole plan admirable, 'if he is really able and willing to carry it into execution'; in a letter of support Beaufort more or less repeated many of Ross's immodest assessments of his own abilities. The Admiralty Secretary requested further information regarding estimated expenses, which Ross duly supplied in January 1850. But the recommendation that was returned from the Arctic Council was to send large ships, and they remained uncommitted to employing Ross for any further searches.

Scandalously, Sir John Ross is conspicuously absent from Stephen Pearce's 1851 painting of the Arctic Council planning a search for Sir John Franklin, which was supposed to show the officials, naval officers and explorers most active in the search. This omission was allegedly because Ross was differently minded to many of its subjects, whom he described as 'men pertinaciously adhering to an absurd opinion'. His revenge took the form of some critical and mischievous remarks about the painting, which no doubt increased hostilities towards him.

Ross's perseverance would eventually gain him command of a ship in 1850 when he received funds from HBC and its employees that, together with the promise of a donation from Sir Felix Booth, enabled him to purchase a schooner he named *Felix*, built by Sloan and Gemmell of Ayr. Second in command would be Commander C. Gerrons Phillips; he had recently returned from James Clark Ross's expedition to Antarctica. Chief Mate Alexander Sivewright of Peterhead was entrusted with recruiting the crew of eighteen, mainly Peterhead whalers, which included three of his own sons. Veteran Thomas Abernethy, also of Peterhead, requested employment; surgeon David Porteous ('a Scotsman') had studied at Glasgow University. A request to the Admiralty for a year's provisions was refused, although the expedition was sanctioned. Additional funds were still sought. The Earl of Hardwick was so impressed by Ross's age on committing to such a severe and arduous enterprise, 'a rare and splendid example of devotion to friendship and science', that he donated £50. 'Let it be borne in mind that this is most probably the last effort that will be made to rescue from a miserable death 140 [129] of the bravest and most devoted seamen that ever trod the deck of a ship.'[41]

Ross was still indignant about the 'unmerited contempt' showered upon his ideas and suggestions. He reviewed at length his old arguments concerning ships and routes. Despite those disappointments HBC praised him as 'a naval officer of dauntless courage and well-tried ability, who has calculated the risks of the undertaking, and in humble reliance on the protection of Providence is determined to carry it through, whatever it may cost him'. He even contributed some of his own money to the cause. It was needed because when Booth suddenly died in 1850 so did his sponsorship, leaving HBC and public subscriptions to cover the financial loss.

Ross boasted about his 'iron constitution'; 'I have no hesitation in pledging my word that I shall return in October next, after having decided the fate of Franklin and his devoted companions'. He envisaged co-operating with John Rae 'in the effectual performance of this deeply interesting service', at the least surveying the last 140 miles to determine the existence of a north-west passage. After all these years he still sought redemption for the lapse of Lancaster Sound.

At a dinner in Ayr before his departure, he explained that despite his age he was 'imperatively called upon to do all in his power to rescue the gallant

Franklin', who would have done the same for him. He claimed that he had never had to punish any man in the last three ships he had commanded: 'I glory in being the father of my crew and I treat them as if they were my own children'. Allegedly 10,000 spectators cheered his farewell. Two steamships sold tickets: cabin one shilling, steerage sixpence, to follow *Felix* a little of the way. Some crew were absent, having demanded and been refused additional pay, drinking gallons of alcohol as compensation. Abernethy was outrageously prominent among them, taking a week to recover. Other members of the crew were completely drunk at sailing time.

Ross departed from his fine house, North West Castle, Loch Ryan, Stranraer (now a hotel)[42] on 23 May 1850. *Felix* made good progress arriving at Holsteinborg (Sisimiut), Greenland, on 20 June; here Adam Beck, a Danish-Inuktitut interpreter was hired. The men stayed until the 24th, the day when Ross entered his seventy-third year 'in perfect health', a self-advertisement doubtless intended to stress his superiority to younger contemporaries such as John Richardson (born 1787) and James Clark Ross (born 1800). That summer they encountered several other ships, particularly off Cape York, on the north-western coast of Greenland, before they journeyed westwards. Ross reported Abernethy's antics to the secretary of HBC, also advising him that he had aboard potentially more useful creatures in the shape of two brace of trained carrier pigeons he hoped would provide communications between the Arctic and the home base by landing on whaleships, obtaining a free ride. Later in the voyage two of the birds were sent off with balloons and small baskets attached to them, designed to be released by a slow-match. One supposedly landed near Kilmarnock, a journey of some two thousand miles, the original donor claiming the bird was one of hers but it was minus any type of message. By 1850 pigeons were often used for communication between ships. Two thousand miles is a bit of a stretch but greater distances have been claimed. Although they had been used as messengers for centuries, they demonstrate Ross's willingness to experiment because there was great interest in pigeon potential in the dying days of the pre-telegraph. Another experiment was more successful; he sermonised on the evils of drink and allowed his men only a small spirit allowance on Saturday nights. Binges were outlawed.

In August, after visiting Union Bay, they stopped at Beechey Island and saw the graves of three of Franklin's ill-fated crew before pressing further into Wellington Channel. By 13 September they had entered Assistance Harbour, which froze over the following day, and the crew over-wintered on Cornwallis Island. Also over-wintering in Lancaster Sound were other searching parties – three ships under Captain Horatio Austin's command and two under Captain William Penny, the latter described by Ross as 'an excellent and kind neighbour'.[43] During this time, several conversations with local Inuit were had by Ross to establish if any of Franklin's expedition had been spotted. Responses varied from no sightings at all to claims the crew members had been murdered. With no hard evidence of Franklin's presence in Wellington Channel emerging, Ross concluded they would not find survivors. In August 1851, once the ice had thawed, Ross gave the order to sail back to Britain. En route they dropped interpreter Beck off at Godhaven, Disko Island, and arrived back in London by September.

This marked the last sea voyage of Captain Ross's illustrious and long-serving career that spanned sixty-five years. He was appointed Rear-Admiral on his return, eventually retiring to his home in Stranraer. During a visit to London, John passed away on 30 August 1856, leaving his nephew James to make the funeral arrangements. The hunt for the Northwest Passage and the fate of Franklin were still to be resolved.

11

THE LIONS IN WINTER

The Searches by William Penny and
William Kennedy, 1849–1851

The great sea has set me in motion,
Set me adrift,
Moving me as the weed moves in a river.

The arch of sky and mightiness of storms
Have moved the spirit within me,
Till I am carried away
Trembling with joy.[1]

By August 1850 several groups of searchers were well represented in
Lancaster Sound. As Professor W. Gillies Ross describes them: 'Ten ships
and almost three hundred men – five times as many ships and twice as many
men as on Franklin's missing expedition – were now sniffing eagerly to pick
up his trail'.[2] The total effort to save Franklin's 129 men comprised nineteen
ships and approximately 700 men, not including tugs and other vessels, as
well as transports. The men were not idle. To name but one, Peter Cormack
Sutherland (from Latheron, Caithness), surgeon on Penny's *Sophia*, was
responsible for over 2,600 temperature readings. He also measured magnetic
fields and daily records of weather, wind and water conditions.[3]

The ice forced all the ships to head in the direction of Beechey Island,
at the entrance to Wellington Channel. The island (Iluvialuit in Inuktitut)
was named for English artist William Beechey by his son, Frederick William
Beechey, lieutenant on Parry's expedition of 1819, the first known visit by
Europeans. It is a tiny, compellingly desolate, tear-drop, linked by a presqu'ile
to the grim face presented by the mighty cliffs of south-west Devon Island.
Beechey is 'almost an island'. There seems to be little record or archaeology
of its Inuit history but for a short time in the 1850s, owing to the shelter

offered by what became known as Erebus and Terror Bay, it was Arctic Central for Scottish, English and American ships hoping to find the track of the Franklin expedition.

The bay is guarded by Capes Riddle and Riley with Cape Ricketts off to the south-west. North of Beechey is Union Bay and Cape Spencer on the edge of Wellington Channel. From the beach, looking north, the ground rises to a rocky hill, the height of which is exaggerated in a well-known print that seems to memorialise Beechey as an island of the dead. In 1843 the Clyde-built *Breadalbane*, a supply ship, was holed by ice and sank half a mile south of the isle, to be discovered by Joseph MacInnis in 1980.[4] In 1852–3 Commander Pullen, leader of one of the rescue expeditions, inspired the building of Beechey's Northumberland House as a refuge and supply store for any returning members from Franklin's ships, constructed from the residue of a wrecked whaling ship. Today there are private graves and memorial sites, as well as some small mementos of the dead pinned on posts, but the house has almost entirely gone; on each visit the remains become fewer. On a visit in 2018 melting permafrost caused us some anxiety as Beechey's middling ground, in a few places, turned into dangerous sink holes resembling quicksand.

*

William Penny of Peterhead embarked on his first whaling ship to Greenland at the age of twelve.[5] He became a captain of vast experience. By the time Franklin sailed off to oblivion Penny had made at least twenty-one visits to the Arctic, often venturing into places the Navy pretended was virgin territory. He was very interested in the Inuit, famously bringing the Inuk Eenoolooapik back to Scotland with him to advertise the potential whaling opportunities of north Baffin Bay (see Chapter 7). The supercilious attitude of the naval establishment toward whalers ensured that many opportunities were lost that might have opened up the Arctic more effectively on a cooperative basis. Penny's more long-standing ambition was to abandon the highly dangerous summer whaling expeditions, favouring instead a base on Baffin Island, where he could over-winter, thus freeing up more time for hunting the whale, the 'fish' as they were known. He was to be rewarded with his rediscovery of Cumberland Sound, first named by sixteenth-century English explorer John Davis.

As we have seen, John Ross had assured Franklin that if there was no word from him after two years, he would organise a search. Franklin's

'Instructions' were dated 5 May 1845, and in 1846 Ross was urging the need for a search, as was Richard King, but Barrow turned down both ideas. Parry's recommendation of financial rewards for whalers who might acquire information was adopted instead. In 1847 Penny was in command of the whaler *St Andrew* and was the first to look for some signs of *Erebus* and *Terror* in Lancaster Sound, the search becoming a passion. He had reached Pond Inlet on 23 July 1847, 'determined to proceed to Lancaster Sound both with a view to the capture of whales and in search of H.M.S.' but was turned back by ice.[6] Such a concentration of talent suggests that already there were doubts about Franklin's competence barely two years after his departure. The conquest of the Northwest Passage had become secondary to the fate of Sir John Franklin and his team.

In March 1849, Penny sailed from Dundee on the whaler *Advice*. On board as surgeon was Robert Anstruther Goodsir, hoping to make a contribution to the search for his brother Harry, on *Erebus*. He recorded the experience in *An Arctic Voyage*. Passing Hoy Head, in Orkney, he was told there was something on his hat. He removed his hat to laughter, the captain explaining 'you have now saluted the Old Man of Hoy', the famous rock stack. Soon they were hit by a vicious storm which lashed the ship, badly damaging it, killing two men and seriously injuring two others, a truly painful introduction for Goodsir. He was intrigued by the 'Mollies', the mollemokes or fulmars, that were, according to the sailors, 'animated by the spirits of Old Greenland Skippers'.[7] Goodsir was keen on natural history having scrutinised William Scoresby's works. Everything, especially birds, fascinated him. Inuit huts were better than many homes he had seen in the West Highlands of Scotland. He much admired the Moravian missionaries, comparing the harsh environment in which they operated to 'our own missionaries in the sunny islands of the Pacific'. At Lively (Disko Island), the resident Danish mineralogist asked if the whalers had any information about the Schleswig–Holstein War between Denmark and Germany, a tall order about an almost unfathomable event of great complexity, but Goodsir did his best to oblige. He remarked on the Runic inscription discovered at Upernavik and the similarity of the Devil's Thumb to the Standing Stones of Stenness, Orkney, and those of Lundin in Fife. The 'great misshapen columns' on icebergs reminded him of Stonehenge.[8]

In June, moving north into Melville Bay, Penny's contingent hit a storm, conjuring thoughts of the 1830 'Baffin Fair' disaster in Goodsir's mind. Some twelve ships were involved in this current episode, which began when two ships were nipped in the ice and two others listed heavily. It was later reported that, of the four, two were totally destroyed. Most of the men collected their gear and sometimes their sea-chests in expectation of abandoning ship. The experience of this second 'Fair' was not to be forgotten. 'It was as if one was standing over the site of an earthquake', wrote Goodsir, 'the ponderous ice, trembling and slowly rising, would rend and rift with a sullen roar, and huge masses, hundreds of tons in weight, would be heaved up, one above the other, until, where it was before a level, an immense rampart of angular blocks became piled'. He was reminded of *The Seasons*, written by the poet James Thomson, from the Scottish Borders, who had never actually personally encountered such sights:

> And hark! The lengthening roar continuous runs
> Athwart the rifted deep: at once it bursts,
> And piles a thousand mountains to the clouds.[9]

Sherard Osborn was also soon present in the bay in his pinnace *Pioneer*. He was a writer of some talent, genuinely hoping to engage his readers as he described 'the mighty glacier, creeping on like Time, silently, yet ceaselessly; the deep and picturesque fiord pent up between precipice, huge, bleak, and barren; the iceberg! Alone a miracle; . . . and last but not least, the ruins of the Scandinavian inhabitants, and the fast disappearing race of the Inuit.'[10] He was loyal to the Navy and very proud of its achievements. When he encountered the second 'Baffin Fair' he remarked that smart things were done in the Navy but he could not think of anything that could excel the alacrity with which 500 whalers appeared to set up the triangles to which the long-saws were attached for cutting the ice. 'A hundred songs from hoarse throats resounded through the gales', including the patriotic anthem 'Rule Britannia', with words by Thomson.[11] Osborn thought the whalers' camaraderie and community spirit outclassed the Navy, a remarkable admission.

When the wind dropped, the 'fishermen' had to track along the floe edge, 'a laborious operation which is reserved for horses' on English canals. There was friendly rivalry between the ships. They were beset for forty days, yet the men remained cheerful, at least according to Osborn, who tried to give a lead:

> the hearty song, the merry laugh, and zealous labours of the crew;
> day after day the same difficulties to contend with, yet day after

day met with fresh resolution and new resources . . . The etiquette of the quarter-deck was thrown on one side for the good of the common cause; and on every side . . . the officer worked as hard as the seamen each was proud of the other, and discipline suffered naught, indeed improved, for here Jack [i.e. the ordinary sailor] had both precept and example.[12]

This was surely the British Navy at its best.

At Cape York 'two natives of the Ross tribe of Arctic Highlanders came aboard' but Goodsir saw little of them due to other duties. A Greenland whaler, speaking gently and quietly, told him of finding some twenty Inuit bodies nineteen years earlier in this vicinity. Since there was evidence of food, they had not died of starvation. As to be expected, Goodsir includes much information on the whaling process that today many find repugnant but which does not detract from the bravery displayed, and the hardship experienced, by the whalers themselves. He is a compelling chronicler, effectively communicating the horrors, as well as the exhilaration, of the whale hunts; following one chase he received 'a drenching shower-bath of hot and greasy blood'. With reference to narwhals, the whalers had a saying 'after seals, unies [unicorns], after unicorns, whales'. He noticed that in the Arctic 'there is a stir in the air around – a sort of silent music heard during day which is dumb during night'.

When he had the chance, he declined to share in the messages placed in an Admiralty cylinder, hopefully for onward transmission to the lost ships, because he would have had to communicate news that would pain Harry. A report shared with others, but rejected, avowed that Franklin had been beset for three years at the entrance to Prince Regent's Inlet, where James Ross had visited him. Rumours were as rife as they were wretched. Goodsir was desperately disappointed when the weather dictated it was time to return home; on 9 August Penny took *Advice* out of Lancaster Sound due to the thick pack ice. 'Hope's blest dominion never ends' and soon she began to whisper to him 'They will have got through, they will be home as soon you will; they will have solved the long-doubtful problem of the north-west passage, which will certainly be much more gratifying to all parties, than if they had to retrace their steps, disappointed and discomfited.' Soon, therefore, he began to 'regain spirits, and become reconciled to the bad success of his voyage'.[13]

Strangely he thought he detected the sound of 'unearthly music', though a thorough-bred Highlander might not have agreed. 'It was the bagpipes to a note – to a tone. I almost thought I could recognise a long-remembered strathspey; But where could be the bagpipes?' It turned out to be gas escaping from the swollen carcase of a whale, transforming the dead creature 'into a strange musical instrument'.[14] At the time he was close to where John Ross and his crew were picked up in 1833.

Lady Franklin and her niece Sophia Cracroft had travelled to Orkney in July 1849 hoping for some news, their hopes raised by out-of-date messages and sheer scuttlebutt, emerging from cynical psychic mediums, falsely claiming information about her husband. In Stromness, she was delighted to meet John Rae's mother. After a visit to Shetland, Lady Franklin and her niece went to Dundee in order to seek out Penny and his assistant, Alexander Stewart, for the first time, on their ship, *Advice*, a few days after their return from Baffin in the autumn of 1849. The women were greatly taken with Penny, and he with them, especially when they offered him a welcome command, a soothing prospect after his three previous whaling expeditions had proved fruitless regarding the lost ships. But the Admiralty remained intransigent in declining support for future expeditions.[15]

Having resigned from command of the whaler *Advice* in late January 1850, Penny eventually resourced two Aberdeen clipper brigs, small, fast-moving, square-rigged schooners that were named *Lady Franklin* and *Sophia*, funded of course by Lady Jane. Robert Goodsir was recruited as surgeon on *Lady Franklin*. The ships were manned by the most Scottish crew ever to join the searchers. Even before he knew he had a commission, Penny demanded 'picked men, whom I can trust'. At least one third of each crew should be Orcadians who had experience of employment with HBC: 'Fatigue had no effect upon them and for food nothing came wrong.'[16] Since he had never found naval types that suited the whaling trade, he had recruited ten capable whalers from Stromness. *Sophia* was to be captained by William Kennedy, who was thought to have qualities very similar to those of Penny's second-in-command, Alexander Stewart, son of a Peterhead whaler, though later the two Scots had a serious falling out. Also assigned to *Sophia* was Peter Cormack Sutherland of Latheron as doctor, having worked with Penny twice before; he wrote a lengthy and valuable account of the imminent voyage. In 1846 he produced a census of the tiny village of Kingmiksoke, home of Eenoo. He believed that 'we have too long judged races in heathen darkness . . . it is worthy of our intelligence now to make ourselves thoroughly acquainted with their mental constitution and, having done so, we shall be better able to return a just verdict when points in their character are disputed'.[17] He was a man with a serious interest in all that he encountered and a reliable chronicler of the voyages in which he took part, wisely observing that 'Anyone that has been in Davis Strait has learned not to lay plans for tomorrow while there'. Like many others he depicted the chaos that ice could cause: 'Huge icebergs of perhaps five hundred million tons weight, plough up floes for miles and miles without being checked in their destructive course . . . A scene is beheld by the Arctic navigator which he finds it utterly impossible to admire, a picture to him of wretchedness, misery and desolation. When such changes take place among the ice, what can the ill-fated ship expect but her share of damage?'[18] When conditions improved, he with his two fellow doctors, Goodsir and John Stuart, climbed to the top of an iceberg to measure its height.[19]

John Stuart was appointed assistant surgeon to both ships, as well as acquiring the additional position of third mate on *Sophia*. First mate on *Lady Franklin* was John Marshall, with John Leiper as second mate, both of whom were whalers. Marshall had racked up thirty-one Arctic voyages. First mate on *Sophia* was Donald Manson, Peterhead, forty-two voyages; James Reid, Peterhead whaler, was second mate. 'Of the forty-five men at least thirty-six stated they had been born in towns and villages on the Scottish mainland'.[20]

The Admiralty sought the views of prominent arcticians as to where they thought the missing explorers might be. Most favoured the area around Melville and Banks Islands, or possibly further west, especially in Lancaster Sound. The Navy's contribution was two sailing ships, backed up by two steam tenders, led by Horatio Austin with Erasmus Ommanney as second-in-command, neither of whom had much Arctic experience. When they met in London, Austin and Penny took an instant dislike to one another. Lady Jane Franklin bought *Prince Albert* to sail to Prince Regent Inlet and the Gulf of Boothia under Commander Charles Forsyth, an Englishman. After a short and disastrous voyage, he was not renewed. Lady Jane's determination was such that she succeeded in acquiring the support of wealthy American merchant Henry Grinnell, with the approval of President William McKinley, as well as having recruited the remarkable Penny. Grinnell had earlier been enthusiastic about Lady Jane's initiative in offering rewards of up to £3,000 for whalers who could assist in the search. The whaleship owners would not permit deviation from duties for would-be searchers but did agree to allow three captains – Penny, Reid of Aberdeen and Parker of Hull – to deposit messages, coal and supplies at strategic points in Lancaster Sound. Lady Franklin, increasingly concerned about her husband, continued to consult clairvoyants and mediums, as promising reports of sightings were sequentially and cruelly dashed.

Penny set sail in April 1850. Leaving Aberdeen harbour swarming with well-wishers, he negotiated Cape Wrath and a boisterous Pentland Firth, making for the Butt of Lewis to skirt quite close to Britain's lonely, most westerly sentinel, the stack that is Rockall. Soon icebergs were encountered, dubbed 'white ghost ships', as they reached the colder water round Cape Farewell, proceeding up the west coast of Greenland to Lievely, whence Penny sent a message to Lady Franklin who declared, 'Our silver Penny is worth his own weight in gold'. Much more valuable, she might have added, than the King David I of Scotland silver penny recently found in Northumberland, an archaeological treasure she may have read about in *The Times* and influenced her tribute to Penny.[21]

In May *Lady Franklin* and *Sophia* were the first ships of the season to arrive in Upernavik, and in June Penny's ships slowly picked their way northwards through the ice floes along the west coast of Greenland, reaching the ice-thick waters of Melville Bay in July. It took a full month of hard work to get the ships out of Melville and within sight of Cape York. Leaving Cape York behind in August, Penny's crew progressed towards Prince Regent Bay, where again they encountered some of the 'Arctic Highlanders', the 'most wretched creatures' that Sutherland had ever seen. Ross, who had commenced his searching expedition on *Felix* in May 1850 (see Chapter 10) for some unknown reason showed almost no interest although they had fascinated him in 1818. Mixed messages from the Greenlanders and Johan Carl Christian Petersen, the Dane recruited as an interpreter by Penny at Upernavik, compounded by the ready enthusiasm of some of the crew, fed a rumour that emerged about dead sailors and damaged ships, raising hopes for a short time about possible information concerning the Franklin expedition, only to be soon rejected.[22]

Dead Inuit were another matter, and verifiable when Austin sent Captain Ommanney ashore in Wolstenholme Sound, accompanied by Ross in *Felix*. The victims who had died of disease or starvation were pathetically huddled together in their poor huts. Scattered around the 'ghost village' were Goldner's Meat tins, alongside other evidence that the supply ship *North Star* had wintered there. Penny turned into Wellington Channel and then approached Cape Riley and Beechey Island. Ommanney followed to the eastern side of Erebus and Terror Bay where he erected a cairn and left a message. With several of his men he climbed a cliff to obtain a view to the west, though the ascent was much more of a challenge than he had anticipated. Back on the beach they found more cans, an iron bar, four tent rings, some fragments of material and a rope with a Navy marker-strand woven into it. They then crossed to Beechey, some having spotted a cairn on its summit, which they ascended, only to find the monument empty save for some slight indications of bird-shot. The views were splendid but, surprisingly, they failed to see the three graves on the beach.

John Ross had joined Penny's ships and Captain Horatio Austin's 136 officers and men in the Waygutt Channel on his way north. When the American naval ships hove into view, the first of their nation to venture Arctic exploration, their surgeon Elisha Kent Kane was pleased to meet Ross, 'an old fellow, with a cloak tossed over his night gear . . . and saluted with a voice that rose above the wind. He was a square-built man apparently very little stricken in years and well able to bear his part in the toils and hazards of life'. Kane remarked that he was scarred from head to foot. He was impressed that he had already performed the unparalleled feat of wintering four years in the Arctic: 'Here he is again in a flimsy cockle-shell, embarked himself in the crusade of search for a lost comrade'.[23] To men of the sea, snow and ice, Ross was, and remained, a legend. To others who perhaps knew him better, he was regarded as a wildcard who spoke his mind when he should have been minding his speech.

Whaler and explorer William Scoresby, a lifelong supporter of Ross, had studied with naturalist Robert Jameson at Edinburgh University and had been elected to the Royal Society of Edinburgh in 1818, two years before he published *An Account of the Arctic Regions*. Ross visited with Scoresby when he published his *Narrative of a Second Voyage*. Indeed, the example of Ross's four years in the Arctic convinced Scoresby that there was a very good chance of finding Franklin and his cohorts alive. Also he thought the crews of *Erebus* and *Terror* were too numerous to be 'summarily lost'. He argued that, considering the full range of Arctic expeditions from 1818 onwards, 'a much larger number of men have returned from these enterprises in safety and health, than would have been found alive after a corresponding period of ordinary service in a tropical climate'. Scoresby fully understood that Franklin's venture was not only a Government expedition, 'and therefore national, but by the general interest given to its objects, and the universal sympathy yielded to its perils, by the British public, we, as the people, have recognised it as our own'.[24]

He also agreed with John Ross's preference for small ships and he applauded his design for steamships with retractable paddle-wheels. He advocated employing men with Arctic experience, namely whalers, especially when the concern was humane rather than commercial. He considered sabbath observance as beneficial for the wellbeing of the men as it was for their spiritual needs. He was keen on the use of hydrogen balloons; an elevation of one mile by an aeronaut would permit a view of 86 miles, potentially invaluable, if impractical, in searching for lost mariners. (Osborn also was interested in experimenting with aids to exploration, claiming that balloons had a range of intercommunication of 20 to 50 miles in favourable conditions such as wind direction. He had some success with kites but none whatsoever with collared arctic foxes.[25]) Scoresby also completely understood how weather conditions had misled Ross in 1818 since, like Bellot, he had experienced the phenomenon himself. Ross's other remarkable accomplishment was the one over which he had no control, namely his age. In 1850 he was 73, by far the oldest Scot or Briton to be involved in Arctic exploration, and he was there because he wanted to be. All contemporaries of his age, critics and competitors alike, had abandoned exploration long before. John Ross, despite his undeniable faults, was almost mythic, the quintessential Arctic explorer of his generation.[26] On his return to Scotland in 1851 he was doubtless gratified to learn that he had been appointed a rear-admiral.

Penny's instructions from the Admiralty directed him to cross the North Water towards the West Land to push into Jones Sound, thereafter exploring into Wellington Channel, the Parry Islands and Melville Island, even though no-one knew for sure whether such a route existed. There had been reports by unreliable witnesses of a cairn on Jones Sound, possibly built on Franklin's orders, but some thought it was a phantom. It was in any case ice-blocked so Penny proceeded into Lancaster Sound, followed for a time by two American brigs led by Lieutenant Edward Jesse De Haven, who was charged with the US's first official Arctic expedition. Both companies experienced dangerous weather conditions, *Lady Franklin* having her mast torn away. Ross's *Felix* was next to appear, sensibly staying out of Lancaster Sound but viewing in the distance Cape Hay, named by him in 1818. In due course Osborn's steamer *Pioneer* towed *Resolute* and *Prince Albert* to the entrance of Lancaster Sound. The last ship to appear was Commander James Saunders' *North Star*, which had been beset for 116 days. It had been intended to replenish JCR with supplies but he had long gone homeward.

*

The story so far revealed several problems. The first was that neither Franklin nor his men had deposited any scripts about their progress or otherwise, a truly lamentable omission. Writing in 2019, Gillies Ross boldly broached questions that others may have privately pondered: 'Franklin left no evidence of his passage, not even a note in a cairn. Was it a death wish? . . . One wonders whether Franklin really did not want to be found and rescued, but rather to become a martyr in the glorious cause of arctic exploration'. Although so much has been written by and about Franklin over the years, he somehow seems a remote obsessive character sadly undeserving of the greatnesses he hoped to thrust upon himself.[27] Second, there was no attempt at any kind of methodical investigation by the searchers, who appeared to wander around the shores as their whims, or the sea conditions, dictated. Third, fierce claims broke out between the captains as to whose men had first discovered any relics. Also, returning vessels such as Forsyth's *Prince Albert*, owned by Lady Franklin, refused to share with other ships any knowledge they had about the finds, apparently wishing to keep them secret until they could reach home audiences, newspapers and hopefully fame. According to Gillies Ross, the only man who attempted any kind of systemisation of the search was his hero William Penny, and his argument is convincing. Indeed, this whole saga cloaks the Navy in an unattractive light, from the bumbling grandees at headquarters in London to the petty squabbles of the officers on the oceans of the world. There was precious little evidence of that overworked word of the time – gallantry – which in any case usually applied to naval officers and no-one else. There was controversy about ship size. Was big really better? How useful were the pinnaces (steamboats), undoubtedly of value for towing, but notorious for consuming alarming amounts of coal? There was an international element as well: English snobbery and superiority versus Yankee hype and pretention; attitudes toward Inuit and First Nations. Scottish common sense, which by no means all Scots possessed, was well represented by Penny.

*

William Parker Snow, a somewhat eccentric, if enthusiastic, itinerant, and author of *The Voyage of the Prince Albert* (1851), attended the Royal Naval College, Greenwich, and joined the Merchant Marine, resulting in a career that initially took him to India, New South Wales and Australia, but he was jailed for larceny and spent a year in prison. He claimed to have some kind of vision when he was in New York about the whereabouts of the Franklin expedition, which he communicated to Lady Franklin, who arranged for him to join Charles Forsyth's *Prince Albert*, sailing from Aberdeen on 10 June 1850, returning on 1 October. He described Penny as

> daring, pushing, ardent, enthusiastic – a thorough, frank, hearty seaman – ready and rough, and rough and ready when need be – himself a *working* hand, as well as a *directing* hand – there he stood, bronze-faced, fur-capped, jacketed with spy-glass slung around him, ready for any emergency that might suddenly meet him. Quick and prompt in his action, he denoted the man of firm nerve and inexhaustible resources.[28]

Snow clearly favoured Scots: he lauded a cook named James Glennie, known as 'the Arctic Leaper', for a stupendous vault from the quayside onto his departing ship. He also enjoyed the songs and chants of the sailors and a bagpiper who led the men over the ice, all protected by a 'rowraddy', a rope harness to prevent them falling through cracks in the ice.[29] Despite his naval training and experience, Snow's behaviour was somewhat reminiscent of a sea-going groupie, smitten by seamen of all ranks. His book, based on his diary, is full of fascinating insights as well as tedious detail. He considered Presbyterianism well suited to voyaging, 'a simple prayer, with Bible reading and exposition'. When he met John Ross he was dazzled, delighted to encounter

> the gallant old veteran, whose name and writings had latterly been so frequently before me. All ceremony was dispensed with . . . Respect, esteem, admiration, all were blended together in my mind, as in returning the friendly shake of the hand he offered me, I involuntarily gave more heartiness to my manner than is usual with strangers . . . I saw before me him who, for four long years and more, had been incarcerated, hopelessly with his companions, in those icy regions to which we ourselves were bound.[30]

In Snow's view, Ross's *Felix* was superior to Forsyth's *Prince Albert* in terms of handling and seamanship. Since the lanes opened up by Ross were freezing again by the time Forsyth reached them, Ross sent men back to help with the onerous business of tracking, alleviated by the familiar rousing songs, lively ballads, sentimental ditties and bagpipes. In the company of Severight,

Felix's mate, and Thomas Abernethy, who was a fount of information on all things ice-nautical,[31] Snow walked across the ice in search of a lead. He made the acquaintance of the naval contingent, Lieutenants Sherard Osborn, Bertie Cator and Leopold McClintock, as well as Captain Ommanney, while learning that whalers did not favour the Navy, disliking ships 'where there's always a man with a stick in his hand . . . and so many officers'.[32] He watched as *Felix* was towed by *Resolute* and as *Pioneer* was ordered to act as a battering-ram on the ice, supplemented by explosives.

Typical of the newcomer anxious to impress on the basis of inadequate knowledge, Snow was instrumental in circulating a story first hatched by Adam Beck concerning a possible explanation for the demise of Franklin's ships. Beck had been recruited by Ross as an interpreter at Holsteinborg, Greenland. Beck and Snow became quite friendly, the latter much enjoying Beck's fiddle playing. Snow became excited when Beck talked about two ships that had been destroyed somewhere to the north in 1846. Their officers wore the insignia of naval uniforms, with gold bands on their caps. Survivors, having taken to the ice, had suffered great hardship until they were 'brutally massacred'. The tale was quickly related to Ross and his commander, Phillips. Abernethy added a few details, supplemented by on-board moonshine, such as the report of a cairn containing the bones of the victims.[33] Some details were probably inspired by the previous discovery of the 'ghost village' of Wolstenholme Sound. The Navy men were informed, and soon everyone had a view about the trustworthiness of the information. John Ross believed what he heard; 'the whole affair was alas! Too True'.[34]

Others dismissed it as nonsense, but some thought, or hoped, it might contain some credence. It spread to all of the sailors, so much so that it was decided that some should return to Cape York in an attempt to verify the story. This gave Snow the opportunity to check that Ross's 'crimson cliffs' of 1818 did in fact exist, while Penny proved that the Inuit tale was bogus. It is of course entirely possible that the Inuit told a true story, couched in their own traditional fashion, which was then totally (perhaps wilfully) misunderstood, or mangled, by the visitors. Some stories never die. As hope faded for the Franklinites, parts of this rumour probably resurfaced in Inuit huts, as well as exploratory ships, creating the phenomenon of competing narratives that were 'true' in some sense. Snow was to suffer another 'heavy disappointment' when he opened cylinders at Whaler Point, Port Leopold, that had been placed there by James Clark Ross the previous year. In compensation he learned a good deal about how to read ice conditions. After climbing a hill to investigate another cairn that proved empty, some of the crew used a small glacier as a slide, the Scottish team of Wilson, Anderson, Duguid and MacCullum displaying their individual styles.[35]

Penny went ashore at Cape Spencer (north-west of Beechey) with Stewart, Goodsir and interpreter Petersen. They first found a fireplace and a hut made of stones, both estimated by Petersen to be four years old. Articles discovered included soup canisters, 'some of which had been used as cooking vessels, while others had the labels entire'. 'Golder's Patent' was a very common type, and there was one bearing the name 'Mr. McDonald, the young man that Penny had employed and assisted, written in a business style'. Other finds were part of the leaves of a notebook with some markings, and 'part of a newspaper bearing the date 1844'. Cans, of which there were hundreds, showed signs of rough opening – tinned food was so novel that nobody had yet invented a tin-opener. 'There were pieces of oak, such as staves of small casks', one inscribed 'mixed pickles'; also, large pieces of oak to be used for ship repairs, bird bones but no beef bones. Pieces of rope belonging to the Navy, torn mittens, cotton rags, blank paper, all of which the wind had hidden beneath the stones. There was some coal, bird wings and feathers, and the track of a sledge. Iron fragments were found, the site of an anvil, printed and written paper dated 1844 and 1845, sledge marks, depressions in the gravel resembling wells, and the graves of three men who had died in January and April 1847. A finger-post was picked up, like that used by Ross in 1818, and reinstated to show the way to the other ships. The site of a large storehouse was discovered. Coal-bags were scattered around; also pieces of canvas, one with *T-e-r-r-o-r* inscribed on it. Meat tins were piled up to a height of two feet, each filled with loose shingle, there being six to seven hundred of them. Their arrangement has baffled commentators ever since. Is it possible that the meat was, or was thought to be, contaminated and the tins filled with dross to stop possible Inuit, or more likely the starving denizens of the lower deck, from attempting potentially fatal consumption? At Cape Riley, Ommanney had left a paper dated 23 August simply stating that he had found 'traces of an encampment', three days earlier than Penny.[36] Speculation was rife.

Shortly thereafter a group which included Sutherland, Goodsir, Stewart and Petersen had been directed to give Beechey Island a thorough examination. They were rewarded with a find of three graves, hard evidence that Franklin had spent the first winter on the island. The deceased were John Torrington, a stoker on *Terror*, John Hartnell, able seaman on *Erebus*, both of whom died in January 1846, and William Braine, a marine on *Erebus* who passed three months later. Possible exhumation was swiftly discounted. They were not to know that a post mortem had already been carried out in 1846, most likely by Harry Goodsir. Suggestions dating from the 1980s that lead poisoning was a factor in the demise of Franklin's expedition are no longer credited.[37] An inventory of articles found during an investigation that should previously have taken place need not be fully rehearsed here. All of the finds were interesting but many duplicated items had already been retrieved on the other sites. Sutherland, curiously, was uninterested in the finds but Sherard Osborn compensated somewhat, effectively encapsulating responses that many of us have experienced. 'It needed not a dark wintry sky nor a gloomy day to throw a sombre shadow around my feelings as I landed on Beechey and looked down upon the bay, on whose bosom once had ridden *Erebus* and *Terror*. There was a sickening anxiety to the heart as one involuntarily clutched at every relic they of Franklin's Squadron had left behind, in the vain hope that some clue as to the route they had taken hence might be found'.[38]

The company found the remains of a garden and a store-house used, they surmised, to shelter a portion of Franklin's 'superabundant provisions and stores with which it was well known his decks were lumbered on leaving Whalefish Islands'. The tell-tale presence of carpenters and armourers was noted, as were old salt-meat tubs used for washing. 'I was pleased to see a pair of Cashmere gloves laid out to dry, with two small stones on the palms to stop them blowing away . . . I took them up carefully, as melancholy mementoes of my missing friends', this without doubt one of the more evocative finds and one that has inspired all sorts of speculation. Did their owner have to leave in haste, the objects almost suggesting that after four years their wearer might happen along to reclaim them? Osborn speculated that two boarding-pikes, intended to repel potential ship-attackers, were used as direction-posts for ships in association with a small cairn on the crest of the island, placed as a meridian mark, all to ensure safe, secure berths, so preventing a ship or ships being swept out to sea, 'about as probable as any stout gentleman being blown out of a house through the keyhole'! The captain once again scrutinised the cairn, because 'truth is not always reasonable'; some detail may have been overlooked but nothing was found except an excellent view.[39]

The rivalry, competition, ineffectualness and self-promotion of imaginary individual achievement continued, as the ships began to explore other features of the land- and sea-scape before the arrival of winter. By early September 1850 all of the ships had found their way to the west side of Cornwallis Island with the exception of *Felix*, which was delayed, as Abernethy renewed his acquaintance with the bottle and Beck lamented their increasing distance from Greenland. Ommanney was accused of once again 'rushing ahead so as to be first at every place, then leaving it unexamined to say that no traces of the missing are found there'. Time, effort and motivation were in short supply as thoughts turned to over-wintering and the weather inevitably worsened. The ships prepared for winter, *Lady Franklin*, *Sophia* and *Felix* sharing the ice, some sixty men altogether, in Assistance Bay on the southern coast of Cornwallis Island. Late October saw the re-opening of the Royal Cornwallis Theatre in the naval tradition inspired by Parry. The doctors were responsible for the 'Arctic Academy', offering the usual subjects. Lady Franklin had thoughtfully provided a range of books for the crews, some of whom were encountering such literature for the first time in their lives. Guy Fawkes Day was elaborately celebrated by men disguised as horses and appropriately indulging in horse-play, all accompanied by rockets, music and singing. An outbreak of scurvy affecting Ross and several of his company was curbed by Penny sharing with Ross's crew his supply of carrots, potatoes and other scorbutics. In the main, Ross and his team spent a fairly pleasant winter in the company of William Penny and Alexander Stewart, who joined in dramatics and musical evenings, while lending him novels, but they eventually fell out with one another. Sutherland later wrote that he would never forget the 'venerable appearance' of Ross's 'grey locks, as he waved his hat or fur cap' but Penny thought him 'an utterly selfish man', whose name was 'proverbial for false statements'. As the wrangles and biased reports continued, Ross came off badly. He was characterised as the chief source of mischief. The two Scots planned to share the surveying of the east and west coasts of Baffin but nothing was achieved.

A Scot seldom mentioned by Arctic writers was Lieutenant Robert Shedden whose aunt, Mrs Robertson of Ednam House, Kelso (now a hotel), gifted Shedden Park to the Border burgh in his memory in 1851, an interesting coincidental link with Captain Cook (see Chapter 1). A year later, local public subscriptions paid for the erection of a 'triumphal arch' at the gateway to the park. John Richardson mentions that Shedden sailed his private yacht, *Nancy Dawson*, to the Bering Strait as part of the search for Franklin. His somewhat idiosyncratic memorial is at St Mary's Church, Hardmead, Buckinghamshire.

Wilhelmina the bereaved mother, erects this monument to the memory of her only and well-beloved son, Robert Shedden. He built and fitted out his R.T.C. Schooner Yacht, *The Nancy Dawson*, and in this frail bark he bravely explored the frozen ocean in the Arctic regions, in a disinterested search after the long missing Sir John Franklin, and his gallant band in vain, disappointed in his generous hope, and worn down by anxiety, and sleepless watching he drooped and died as he wished on the dark blue sea. He expired on board his yacht, on 17th November 1849 aged 30 years. His noble remains are interred near the wild waves of the Pacific Ocean, in the protestant burial ground at Mazatlan. His precious soul rests with his father and his God. *Resurgam* [I shall Rise Again].[40]

A relief profile of the yacht accompanies the inscription.

*

Meanwhile John Rae had been promoted Chief Trader and posted to Fort Simpson at the point where the Liard and Mackenzie rivers join. He had been considering marriage but, 'however pleasant, charming and useful the native ladies are in some respects I do not at all fancy buckling myself for life to one of them', clearly an un*Rae*generate Scot! In 1850 Rae was ordered to explore 'that portion of the Northern Sea lying between Cape Walker on the east, Melville Island and Bank's Land to the south'.[41] In June he received a letter from Sir Francis Beaufort, advising that in terms of the search for Franklin all eyes were intensely fixed upon him, begging his best efforts 'in the great cause'. Beaufort looked to Rae 'for the solution of our melancholy suspense'; Rae responded by recruiting Hector Aeneas Mackenzie of Fort Norman as his second-in-command. From Governor Simpson he requested a leave of absence following the expedition. Continued anxiety about his many duties was impacting on his mind and memory to the point that he might have to leave HBC. Simpson grudgingly complied.

On 10 September 1850 Rae returned to Fort Confidence with two officers, fourteen men, two women and thirteen dogs. Scots included James Johnstone, Charles Kennedy, Peter Linklater and Samuel Sinclair. Another was George Kirkness, who with Rae's help and supervision, constructed two clinker-built boats each 22 feet long. As leader, Rae had to find food for about thirty additional First Nations people, a task some thought beneath his dignity, like 'the securing of the buttons and seams of my travelling breeks', not that he cared 'as long as the work is done to my mind'. During the winter, his book about the 1846–7 expedition, which he dubbed his bantling (young child), reached him 'somewhat remodelled'. He had harsh words for self-regarding naval officers who had pronounced Arctic work to be 'nothing, a mere bagatelle, an everyday work' but who changed their minds on sampling it – 'awful work, the most severe and harassing duty, ever experienced', dismissing them as 'self-sufficient donkeys' who criticised HBC for the starving, poverty-stricken First Nations, while impervious to the misery of hundreds of thousands suffering famine in contemporary Ireland.

Satisfied that he was well supplied and fortified, he set out for the Kendall River (a tributary of the Coppermine River) and Richardson Bay, crossing Coronation Gulf to Point Lockyer. The company then crossed Dolphin and Union Strait via north-west Douglas Island to arrive at Wollaston Peninsula, before turning east to explore the south shore of Victoria Island for four nights. He was searching for, but failed to find, a strait separating Wollaston from Victoria. Instead he found and named the Richardson Islands. Having reached Dease and Simpson's most westerly point, he decided to back-track along the south coast of the Wollaston Peninsula to Cape Baring and a sighting of Cape Back. By the time they returned to Fort Confidence they had travelled 824 miles in 42 days. Rae reported to Simpson 'I stood the journey much better than I anticipated. The heart did its work well and the legs also did not fail me', though he felt a few twitches in one of his knees. Like Richardson he used his own body as a subject for the study of Arctic health.

Just over a week later he was off again with Mackenzie and ten men, battling ice and high water on the Coppermine, staying on the shore of the mainland to Cape Alexander and Kent Peninsula, then crossing Dease Strait to Victoria Island west of Cambridge Bay, which they fully explored. Inuit that he met on Victoria Island knew nothing of the missing ships. Next, they sailed along the coast of Victoria, meeting with gales and ice, to Cape Alfred where Rae and three men set off on foot but the terrain was so hostile that a new pair of moccasins 'with thick undressed buffalo skin soles and stout duffle socks' lasted less than a day and 'every step I took was marked with blood'. After one more day they withdrew, halting on what became Collinson Peninsula, to build two cairns. In one they left a message describing the trip from the Coppermine. It was picked up two years later by Captain Richard Collinson approaching from the west. Rae considered crossing Victoria Strait and King William Island but weather and ice did not cooperate. His foiled destination was 40 miles away and so was the solution to the Franklin mystery. There were, however, clues. In Parker Bay, Rae picked up two pieces of timber that looked as though they had been parts of an unidentified ship. It took five days to transport one of the boats up the Coppermine to Fort Confidence. He then headed for Fort Chipewyan. There followed a 44-day walk to Red River and travel in a cariole, 'a very gay affair neatly painted and well furnished with warm robes drawn by dogs ornamented with wool and white leather saddle cloths with bells attached'. As one of his biographers notes, Rae journeyed 8,000 miles from Athabasca to St Paul, 1,730 of them on foot.[42]

*

In early 1851, William Kennedy succeeded Charles Forsyth as commander of *Prince Albert*. He was born at HBC's Cumberland House, Saskatchewan, the fifth child of Chief Factor Alexander Kennedy and his Cree wife, Aggathas. He was sent to St Margaret's Hope, Orkney, his father's birthplace, for his schooling. Returning to Canada he worked for HBC in the Ottawa valley, Ungava and Labrador before leaving the company on religious grounds, but mainly in opposition to company readiness to sell alcohol to the First Nations. He then captained a fishing boat on Lake Huron and campaigned for Canada to take over Rupert's Land. At the prompting of former Chief Trader John McLean, he volunteered to work with Lady Franklin. He was encouraged by the last letter Esther Blanky received from her husband Thomas on *Terror*, telling her he might be gone for seven years. (Thomas Blanky had served with John Ross on *Victory*.) Kennedy joined the 'small fairy-looking craft' (which others dismissed as a banana boat) at Aberdeen. Important contacts had ensured free passage to New York, and then to Liverpool. A letter of introduction from British naval officer Sir Edward Belcher opened all doors, providing hospitality and travel.

Kennedy's second-in-command was French naval officer Joseph René Bellot. The crew was entirely Scottish, save for Richard Webb, 'a dashing fellow from London', an engineer who, it was hoped, might be able to rescue a steam launch that James Clark Ross had abandoned at Port Leopold. John Leask, an experienced whaling captain, accompanied Kennedy. Four 'stalwart fellows' from the previous voyage were Henry Anderson, first mate; Robert Grate, boatswain; James Glennie, 'the Arctic leaper'; and Alexander Matheson, able seaman. All were from Aberdeen. Three Shetlanders were John Smith (clerk in charge), his brother Gideon and William Adamson. Kenneth Sutherland was six foot tall and reputedly possessed of Falstaffian

William Kennedy
(© Archives of Manitoba)

wit! Andrew Irvine, Magnus McCurrus, Andrew Linklater and William Millar would join at Stromness. Also aboard was John Hepburn, a much-lauded veteran of the first expedition of Franklin and Richardson. Ship's doctor was Robert Cowie, whose family Kennedy knew.[43]

Joseph René Bellot, another devotee who fell under the spell of Lady Franklin, was a sub-lieutenant in the French Navy who volunteered to serve for free. Their mutual admiration was instant. A number of British naval types, for whom France was their inveterate enemy, were not happy about the Frenchman's inclusion, but Kennedy insisted, boldly appointing him second-in-command. *Prince Albert* was reinforced in Aberdeen and carried a gutta-percha boat (made from resin), a mahogany boat, 'a smaller kind of boat called a dingey', sledges and kites. Bellot packed a Halkett boat, an ingenious invention much admired by explorers of the Canadian Arctic but rejected by the British Navy.[44] Kennedy also constructed a kayak made of tin. Six carrier pigeons were donated by Miss Dunlop of Annan Hill, Ayrshire, who had also provided the birds that accompanied John Ross. Queen Victoria's consort gifted an organ to the ship named for him, adding music to the mix. The vessel was very well provisioned, including a ton and a half of pemmican donated by the Admiralty. Bellot was thrilled to be part of it all:

> Hardy Scots of the Orchades, or Shetland Isles, who formed part of the previous expeditions of Rae, Richardson, and Franklin, or tried by numerous voyages in search of whales, form a chosen crew. Mr John Hepburn, who followed Franklin in his examination of the Coppermine and Mackenzie Rivers, has arrived in all haste from Van Diemen's Land, to furnish a fresh proof of his devotion to his old captain. Mr Leask, pilot of the North Star, who knows the Baffin Straits as well as you do your library, is our ice-master. At our head is Captain Kennedy, a captain in the Hudson's Company's service; a man of an ancient stock; a scion of those puritans whose dauntless courage has its source in the most lively faith; one of those models from whom [James Fenimore] Cooper has taken his Pathfinder.[45]

From Bellot's *Memoir*, we learn that, on reaching Orkney, he visited Kirkwall Cathedral (falling into ruin) and took in the Stones of Stenness, the Ring of Brodgar and the Dwarfie Stane on Hoy. He received a gift of

Walter Scott's novel *The Pirate* (1822). He danced and flirted with Orkney girls. Two Stromness ladies made him a tricoleur. He visited John Rae's mother. Lady Jane cried when he departed. His sea-sickness was hugely embarrassing to him. The Scottish sailors happily conversed with him about their favourite Shakespearean characters. Kennedy instructed him to record magnetic observations. Bellot found the captain's hundred-year-old French quaint. He had long discussions regarding religion with Kennedy, who, 'in spite of his habitual good nature, is exceedingly intolerant in such matters'. However, Bellot considered it a 'good side of religion that every man of character may officiate without having taken holy orders'. His admiration deepened when Kennedy asked God to 'inspire our resolutions and direct our understandings and I see that there is no end to the strength which so ardent a faith bestows'; we have to wonder if he encountered any of those Scots who notoriously favoured Presbyterianism as 'the least expensive way to Heaven'! 'What limit can there be', he asks, 'to the daring of a man who is not only persuaded but convinced, that whatever he does is at the suggestion and by the permission of God?'[46] – a question that recalls John Richardson's certainties in his treatment of Michel.

The search was to focus on Prince Regent Inlet and 'the passages connecting it with the Western Sea', south-west of Cape Walker as per Franklin's instructions, in which vicinity it was thought he might have abandoned his ships. Franklin had allegedly expressed a notion that there was open passage from the west into the southern part of Prince Regent Inlet. This route would have appealed because of the availability of animal resources for food, complementing the bounty still available in the wreck of *Victory* at Fury Beach. He would therefore expect any aid to arrive by way of Lancaster Sound and Barrow Strait, the opening to Regent Inlet. Otherwise no-one had a clue where to look.[47]

As Kennedy travelled north up the breathtaking coast of Greenland, he conjured Vikings and sagas in a bleak and barren landscape but realised that, 'as they say in Scotland, a stout heart always to a steep brae'. Near Upernavik his crew met two whaling captains who showed them a document signed by Kent Kane listing the finds around Beechey: the graves, the meat cans and the junk, all providing valuable information. Kennedy was impressed that the local Greenlanders appeared better housed, better fed and better clad than those in Canada, a comment still heard today. Also, most were Christian. He acquired 'six powerful Esquimaux dogs', some pairs of sealskin boots and clothing. The pigeons were trialled after a fashion. He attempted to tame a couple of otters. At sea, Kennedy's men met up with the American Squadron, travelling with them for some three weeks before they separated near the Devil's Thumb, making for Pond Inlet, where the Shetlander John Smith conversed in Inuktitut with the local residents, for whom they threw a party using the organ. One guest was a seemingly crazed Inuk, carried away by the music, whooping, yelling and leaping as if possessed by a legion of demons: a good night for all before it was closed down, fearing the Inuk's excited excesses would lead to his self-harm.

Kennedy was also gaining an ever-deepening respect for Bellot, who seems to have impressed everybody. He told the Frenchman that when John Sacheuse, John Ross's interpreter, was picked up at sea after the currents carried him off in his kayak, his friends took him for a ghost, and his sister died of grief. A doctor who examined him found a wound that suggested someone had tried to murder him. Kennedy further regaled Bellot with stories about the First Nations. One such tale may well be apocryphal. When Franklin asked an ancient 'Indian' how old he was, he did not know.

'How old were you when guns were introduced?'

'Oh I had long left off hunting when this old man's grandfather was alive; I was a man almost before he was born'.

'Well, then, at the time when the whites settled here?' (thirty years earlier).

'Oh I was as old as I am now'!

The Inuit were hard bargainers, like the Scots, according to the ship's doctor, Cowie: 'they would not sell their hens on a rainy day, because the rain makes them appear thin'. As they advanced, the sights rolled by: Cape Farewell, Cape York, icebergs, Disko, polar bears.

Bellot wrote in French of course, but even in translation he was a beguiling writer attempting to discover the wonders of the Arctic and the secrets of himself at the same time as he tried to come to terms with the British (mainly Scots) and the Inuit alike. He possessed the lively inquisitive mind of a third-generation *philosophe*, but he was also an incorrigible romantic. Lady Franklin would have applauded his observation that 'the treatment women experience from men is one of the features by the aid of which the ethnologist can classify the different peoples on the scale of civilization'. Bellot believed that, unlike other animals, 'woman alone is not exclusively the female of the male. She can move onwards, parallel, and side by side with man; and there is great common sense in calling either sex the moiety of the human race'.[48] As Kennedy, like Bellot, discovered features and traces that he knew hitherto only from published journals, recognition adjusted his gaze accordingly, almost as if he was already anticipating modern cruise guides, even quoting *The Rime of the Ancient Mariner*.[49] It is tempting to explore Bellot's ideas more fully in a way that the theme and space of this book does not really permit, but his personality, a lone Frenchman on a shipload of Scots, demands at least some attention.

Over the summer of 1851 *Prince Albert* frequently spotted the American expeditionaries. Bellot was intrigued that the ten ships seeking Franklin were 'like bees hurrying to and from the hive'. In mid July, off the northern coast of Baffin, the ice dissipated, allowing contact and the exchange of information, including gossip about William Parker Snow's recent publication about the searching expedition of *Prince Albert* the previous summer. The American contingent was surprised that a charlatan like Snow could 'publish so big a book about nothing at all'. On 18 July a pigeon was launched, with a note attached to each leg stating that 'authentic traces' of Franklin had been found at Cape Riley, but the bird was reluctant to leave. Bellot became very friendly with Dr Elisha Kent Kane of the Grinnell Arctic Expedition, refusing to believe that the Inuit were capable of wiping out the Franklin expedition, while speculating that they must have wondered what the sailors were doing in the Arctic: 'Since it is not to catch whales or unicorns, or seals, what motive can have driven from home people who seem to have everything they want in order to live.' He describes how *Prince Albert* 'bounds and dives, alternately passing over and under the waves . . . springing from one to the other like a child over furrows'. The remarkable appearance of the land to the north of Lancaster Sound and west of Croker Bay, with the sun's reflections on snow-covered masses mingled with clouds, convinced Bellot and his fellows that it was not surprising that John Ross had been deceived in 1818, 'for the clouds connect both shores and it looks as if a chain of mountains closed the strait at a distance of twenty miles from us', a point shared with Scoresby.[50]

Since Port Leopold, where James Ross had wintered on his final expedition, about ten miles south of Leopold Island off the north-east corner of Somerset Island, was completely blocked by ice, Kennedy's party sailed on to Elwin Bay, Batty Bay and Fury Beach. The ice threatened a replay of *Fury*'s fate, forcing them across the inlet to Port Bowen on Stony Island where they checked out Parry's cairn, a large fireplace and a small stone hut built over the grave of John Cottrell, a *Fury* seaman who drowned in 1825. They then returned to Leopold Island via Cape Seppings on Somerset Island's north-east coastline. With Matheson, Gideon Smith, Irvine and Sutherland, Kennedy successfully, but misguidedly, navigated a lane through wild waters to Leopold shore. After an hour they decided to return to Somerset Island. It was too late! They were cut off: 'Nothing could be seen or heard around us but huge masses of ice, grinding, tossing, and rearing furiously on every side. To attempt to reach the ship under such circumstances was to ensure certain destruction to the boat and everybody in it.'[51] Meanwhile, *Prince Albert* drifted southwards some thirty miles to Batty Bay. The situation for everyone was potentially dire. The marooned men on Leopold Island were already suffering from cold. Kennedy, as befitted a sound leader, used the upturned boat as a shelter but forbade anyone to sleep longer than an hour, forcing them to exercise the rest of the time. He set about securing better protection, utilising the launch abandoned there by James Ross; soon the sails made a useful roof and a stove was installed in the launch. They were able to draw upon the contents of the cache at Whaler Point. After seven days there was no sign of *Prince Albert*; they would not be rescued for a further five weeks. Bellot's account lacks detail, suggesting that he was trying to minimise his own part in the unfortunate affair since it appears that he lacked the necessary skills to relieve his stranded comrades.

On Sunday 21 September 1851, Kennedy rejoiced that the isolated were 'occupied in recalling to mind some of the sacred melodies of their native land, and simple hymns, stored up in their memories from childhood, as well as those exquisite cullings from the word of truth, embodied in the Shorter Catechism of the Church of Scotland'. The sailors showed their traditional ingenuity in attempting to create minimal comfort out of almost nothing. Decent footwear was badly needed but no materials were available except for bits of old canvas. Sutherland made snow-shoe frames and an Inuit-style sledge, fashioning runners out of dough and ice. The carpenter shaped a grindstone. Kennedy organised modest explorations of the island. A bear hunt was unsuccessful, doubtless to Bellot's disappointment because he was forever mentioning those fascinating creatures, the crew's treatment of whom was abominable, since they were much sought after for their pelts and their flesh. Far too often they suffered horrendous wounds from multiple bullets as, bleeding profusely, they disappeared into the wilderness.[52] Otherwise there was very little to record. Bellot, based at Batty Bay, made futile efforts to find a route to rescue in dreadful weather conditions. He tried sledging with dogs but had to give up when he fell through the ice. He achieved a more reposeful breakthrough on 17 October, the day of liberation.

Bellot was intrigued that though he was from a different country and of a different faith he was accepted as a 'countryman' united 'by a common principle' and common aims. If such mutual understanding was possible among individuals, 'to the annihilation of all differences of origin, race, religion and language', what prevented nations from forming a similar union towards a common end? Noble though his ideas were, the notion of 'mutual understanding' may well have been suspended following what he called Kennedy's 'accident' (i.e. his marooning). On yet another rescue attempt, guns were discharged on approach to Cape Seppings, to be rewarded, after an anxious pause, by a sighting of their comrades on Leopold Island. Bellot, after two attempts, managed to land. Celebration followed, with cups of chocolate and sea shanties. Arguably the men suffered because of Bellot's lack of experience, which was as culpable as Kennedy's enthusiasms but there was little evidence of recriminations. Both lacked sound knowledge of Arctic conditions. They disagreed quite frequently but retained sincere respect for one another. In the thirteenth century, France and Scotland had leagued together against the might of England. Though their *entente* was at times less than perfect, Kennedy and Bellot, representing the Auld Alliance in the Gulf of Boothia, were facing a much more formidable foe in the irreducible might and scale of the Arctic.

Port Leopold is situated at the meeting of the openings to Barrow Strait, Lancaster Sound, Wellington Channel and Prince Regent Inlet, a place chosen by the four winds for their dwelling place. It recalls a passage in the thirteenth-century book of wisdom *The King's Mirror* (*Kønungs Skuggsjá*), compiled for King Hakon of Norway, which describes 'the covenant of the winds'. The reference is to the winds in the octads (the eight sections) of the compass, personified and depicted as co-operating with one another throughout spring and summer, but in late autumn the covenant is shattered 'and the winds are stirred to stormy violence . . . the breakers swell and the shores refuse good harbours'.[53]

At the head of the bay were six graves left by James Ross's men in 1848–9. Soon Kennedy's company moved on to Batty Bay. It was now November, a time of departed sun. Bellot could not have known how much he empathised with the medieval Norwegians when he remarked on 'the sobs of the weeping winds and the mournful looks of a day without light. Ossian is truly the poet of the north – of that Nature which moulds the thoughts of men after her own image, and makes them wild and desolate like herself'. He was becoming quite sentimental about his 'washermen' (companions), and the 'lively dialogues in broad Scotch carried on in every part' of the ship. He was also increasingly attracted to the religion of nature.[54]

As second-in-command the Frenchman was faced with the problem of how to accommodate thirteen men, including the massive Kenneth, in a single little tent designed for six, making sleeping impossible. However, they eventually settled on six sitting down on each side which would leave about three feet clear to stretch their legs. 'Mr Bellot, who formed the thirteenth, being the most compact and stowable of the party, agreed to squeeze in underneath them, stipulating only for a clear foot square for his head alongside the tea-kettle.' Songs, jokes and much hilarity whiled away the time: 'Kenneth you monster, take that clumsy foot of yours off my stomach will you, cries out Mr Bellot, smothered beneath the weight of four-and-twenty-legs.'

By day, classes were run on various subjects. Kennedy lectured on how to make snow-shoes, discussing the art and mystery of *babiche*, and the creation of indispensable Arctic footwear. When they could explore their surroundings, they found traces of the Rosses from 1829–33, but they were devastated at not finding any evidence of the Franklin contingent around Fury Beach. Hepburn observed that he had known only one gale since they had entered Batty Bay – 'the gale that began when we came and ended when we went away'. Detained by shocking weather, avalanches and lack of vision due to fogs, they eventually struggled through to Brentford Bay. The cutting cold attacked feet and faces. The Inuit dogs suffered as much as the men, who were greatly troubled by scurvy.

Bellot believed that the recent expedition marked a new era of land exploration at a time of year previously avoided. It was also the first time a French officer was involved in Arctic exploration. Franklin had been instructed to investigate Cape Walker in Barrow Strait before making tracks for the northern coast of America. Three years later, the expeditions of James Clark Ross, Richardson and Captain Moore followed, later joined by Penny, John Ross and the American ships inspired by Lady Franklin. Bellot insisted that, in the search led by William Kennedy, it was Kennedy who deserved the credit for any successes. He took care of health and welfare, ensuring the absence of alcohol of any kind, which had disrupted some other ventures. Despite some setbacks due to weather, the intrepid explorers triumphed, largely due to Kennedy's insistence that they adopt the clothing and culture of the Inuit; 'garments of skin, moccasins or sealskin boots, pemmican our only food, sledges with or without dogs', and snow huts. They left their ship at the end of February 1852, returning in June to follow the coastline or crossing the ice in Cresswell and Brentford Bays and Victoria Strait. In the previous four months they passed out of constant obscurity into perpetual sunlight. They battled scurvy towards the end. 'The expedition of the *Prince Albert* has, therefore contributed to contract more and more the circle of the probable directions taken by Franklin'. On 14 June Bellot recorded rain for the first time that year, 'real rain – that is, water which passed through the atmosphere without freezing'.[55]

There was considerable discussion and disagreement as to whether the Aurora was 'accompanied with a crepitation like that of an electric machine'. Employees of HBC and Shetlanders (who called them dancing lights) certainly heard a noise; others did not. Another mysterious sound appeared to emanate from under the ship which some thought resembled a dull roaring noise like the collapse of a wall but which reminded others of earthquakes.[56] When the sound coincided with the unexpected birth of a pup, 'our superstitious Scotch maintained that such noises bode nothing good'. Yet Bellot thought the Scots better educated than the English; there was only one man aboard who could not read. He thought the subterranean sounds were due to chains under the hull of their ship, placed there for additional strength. He also disapproved of liquor at sea but noted that the issue of seasonable firewater to the crew had beneficial effects. He also noted that the Scots did not observe Christmas, saving their celebrations for New Year.[57] The arcticians were fortunate that for them there was no Santa, no Coca-Cola, no cute polar bears on cards, and reindeer were for the pot!

The first order of business for the New Year of 1852 was a winter journey to Fury Beach to ascertain whether there were any signs of the Franklin party since Lieutenant Robinson's visit with James Ross in 1849. The intention was also to deposit supplies there prior to a wider search. The travellers were Kennedy, Bellot, John Smith, William Adamson and William Millar. They were joined by Leask, Cowie and others to help with kit and supplies, as well as an Inuit, or more accurately First Nations, 'flat sledge', with four dogs, which proved highly flexible on difficult ground. They were troubled by high cliffs as they approached Fury Beach, finding some traces of John Ross's passage. Leaving the sledge behind, Bellot, Smith and Kennedy forged ahead to the sad empty ruin of Somerset House but, disappointingly, there were no signs of Franklin whatsoever. They were weather-bound for almost two months in Batty Bay before making another assault on Fury Beach which took them over a week to reach. Bellot came on later with reinforcements, raising the cohort to fourteen. In two months the principals had wandered astray, risking life and limb in impenetrable fogs, colossal gales, whiplash snowstorms and minor avalanches, all in the semi-darkness of midwinter. The question has to be: Why take these ridiculous risks? What was the point? Arctic glory was dearly won at the best of times. Why add to the woes? It was probably a Scot who concluded that it was better to serve in Hell than reign in Heaven but other nationalities were similarly inclined. The late Farley Mowat was perhaps on the mark when he described the fascination of the inexplicable as *virus arcticus*. I am a fan of some, though not all, of Farley's books but his suggestion may be pertinent because, wild and terrifying as the North can be, the air is like a tonic, the wildlife unforgettable, the sea and the rivers pristine, the people welcoming, all coalescing in the glorious infection of Arctic Fever, cod-Latin and all, which reaches south to cry 'Haste Ye Back'.

*

Kennedy joked that noses were made only to be frozen; McClintock was later to pronounce them a nuisance since they were the first part of the anatomy to be frost-bitten. Other bodily parts were just as inconvenient and just as painful. They plodded on along the shore of Cresswell Bay, camping at Cape Garry on 1 April 1852, a few days later identifying Brentford Bay from John Ross's description. Bellot and Kennedy followed different routes but both found large stretches of water to the west. On 7 April the captain probed further, walking twenty miles all day until he discovered a broad channel running north-east to south-west, first assumed to be Brentford Bay, 'until its greatest extent convinced us that we had fallen upon a western sea or channel and that the passage we had just gone through was in reality a strait, leading out of Prince Regent Inlet'. He named it Bellot Strait, 'a just tribute to the important services rendered to our expedition by Lieutenant Bellot'. The latter later claimed (wrongly) that it was the cape rather than the strait that honoured him. The inlet was named for Grinnell, the American backer of Lady Franklin's campaign, while the land celebrated Prince Albert.

According to Bellot's own version, he begged leave 'with many thanks to decline this honour and to unite with our people in bestowing it on our commander to whom I think it is due before me'. Kennedy was not to be moved: 'absolute refusal on his part'. He later added that it had been his wish 'to join together on the same day, and upon the first lands he discovered, the names of three members of the three great nations which have taken part in our expedition'. They later established that the Western Sea, onto which the channel opens, was 'the northern extremity of Victoria Strait, partially explored by Dr Rae from another direction'.[58] It was also noticed that their newly discovered strait was obviously a migration route for musk-oxen and reindeer. Overall it is striking that the important discovery of Bellot Strait was reported in such a low-key manner.

Bellot urged Kennedy to erect a cairn at the foot of Cape Walker, depositing relevant documents indicating his track and his achievements, but he had lost his notes and so could do nothing, an incredible lapse given the confusion Franklin had created with similar omissions. The relationship between the Canadian Scot and the Frenchman seems to have been quite complicated. Both liked to show a brave face but occasionally cracks appear. Bellot found in Kennedy 'that nobleness of nature I so love and revere, and that ardent enthusiasm, which alone can overcome difficulties. I long for some change which shall make me forget the vexations inseparable from life in common, in this dreadful region, amongst men of such dissimilar education and ideas'. He was beginning to believe that any Franklin survivors, especially if they had lost their officers, would be found among the Inuit. If such was the case, the news should filter out on their northern communication network since Europeans were obviously highly conspicuous in that environment. As usual Bellot had a pertinent comment to describe his surroundings. Arctic regions make a very peculiar impression on the mind: 'In this hazy weather the sun rises and sets without any of the splendour accompanying it on lighter days; a pale and enfeebled disk descends without pomp behind the whitish horizon; the scene has a character at once sweet and sad, but not without solemnity.'[59] Nature was not just observed but also experienced.

William Kennedy impresses as a modest individual that Bellot might mildly criticise but would not defy, opining that he 'does not belong to our time and his perfectly primitive education has made him too good to lead the men of our day'. Kennedy reciprocated by expressing his admiration for the Frenchman who had accompanied him throughout, utilising his superior scientific attainments 'and at the same time taking an equal share with the men in dragging the sled, and ever encouraging them in their arduous labours by his native cheerful disposition'. Despite disappointment at finding no trace of Franklin, they remained reasonably optimistic. Kennedy showed a slight irritation about the obsession the expedition organisers had with food. He was clear that most of the time the land yielded reasonably plentiful supplies. The problem was not the amount of food but its appropriateness for the harsh environment and individual metabolisms. Scurvy remained a problem, but the doctor, Robert Cowie, had a good handle on how to treat it, while Captain Kennedy dealt swiftly and effectively with any signs of frostbite.

As they set about clearing the ship for departure, Kennedy noted that 'the admirable invention of Copeland's blasting cylinders, was got through in gallant style', promising 'to effect quite a revolution in the navigation of the icy seas'. Bellot added, 'after boring through the ice, the cylinder must be sunk, and the hole filled with snow and stones as hermetically as possible'. It had to be laid in a horizontal position to 'expose the largest extent possible to the action of the powder'. No sooner was the ship released than it was trapped again for a week in the ice. When the ice cleared, they made straight for Beechey Island and news of other ships: Belcher's *Assistance*, Osborn's *Pioneer* steam tender, Kellett's *Resolute* and McClintock's tender, *Intrepid*. Kennedy and Bellot with John Smith and Kenneth Sutherland had plans to stay out for another season but these were foiled. They reached Aberdeen in exactly six weeks. In a month short of a year-long vicious winter many of the men had been out for half the time, some travelling 2,000 miles, all but three in good health. They had added something (though not much) to geographical knowledge and at least their explorations had shown where the missing expedition was *not*. Kennedy acknowledged his 'constant companion' Bellot, praising his scientific expertise and his amiable qualities, creating 'a deep personal regard which can only end with my life'.[60]

*

On Lady Franklin's recommendation, Bellot was invited to join Edward Inglefield on *Phoenix* in support of Edward Belcher's supposed searching expedition.[61] The Frenchman arrived at Beechey Island on 8 August 1853. He was sent to hand over messages to Belcher, then based in Wellington Channel, at which point events took a devastating fatal turn. On 17 August, as reported by ordinary seaman William Johnson,

> Joseph Rene Bellot said he would go and see how the ice was driving. He had only been gone about four minutes, when I went round the same hummock under which we were sheltered to look for him, but could not see him; and on returning to our shelter saw his stick on the opposite side of a crack, about five fathoms wide, and the ice all breaking up. I called out 'Mr Bellot!' but no answer (at this time blowing very heavy). After this I again searched round but could see nothing of him. I believe that when he got from the shelter the wind blew him into the crack, and that his southwester [waterproof hat] being tied down he could not rise.[62]

Belcher described Bellot's passing as 'a most mysterious, incomprehensible death' but characterised the accounts of the sailors who reported it as incoherent. He further confused their evidence by inappropriately ridiculing the witnesses,[63] who were doubtless shocked and disorientated by the suddenness of their officer's disappearance. It may seem inappropriate to mention at this juncture that Bellot was somewhat accident prone. To say the least it had been careless of him to maroon his captain, Kennedy, on Leopold Island, a very bleak place, for several weeks, described by Kennedy as a 'Robinson Crusoe detention'. In one incident, attempting to reach his beleaguered comrades using dog-sleds, he had fallen through weak ice, losing a sledge and some of its contents. On another occasion the sledge had broken down. Kennedy had noted that Bellot sometimes succeeded in his daily attempts to acquire a meridian observation of the sun, but *always* managed to freeze his fingers in the process. On another occasion, failing to dodge a snowbank in time, Bellot and his dogs had 'crashed into the bottom of an abyss, where the only indication of the catastrophe' was 6 inches of his heels above the surface: 'We dug him out a wiser and better man.' A planned visit to the American ships had turned nasty when, missing his footing on loose ice, he had plunged into water that had a temperature of 34 °F (1 °C). He had laughed at his own mishap (by now a standard response) but, in trying to run through water up to his waist, he had fallen into a second hole from which it was difficult to extract himself. Dr Elisha Kent Kane of the Grinnell Arctic Expedition had come out to hook him with his gaff, but Bellot had cut his fingers on the sharp ice, gulping mouthfuls of sea water which increased the weight of his clothes and also filled his boots before he was hauled out.[64] There were doubtless other near-run, unrecorded incidents. As a stranger in a strange navy, he also seemed to worry about gaining, and keeping, the approval of his colleagues, all of whom he reportedly related well to.

The Strait (Ikirasak) in Nunavut, named for Bellot, surely must rate as one of the most beautiful parts of the Arctic. It separates the Boothia Peninsula from Somerset Island on the north. The Murchison Promontory to the south is the northernmost point of mainland North America. My wife Lizanne and I first experienced the 25-kilometre strait in 2009, in glorious sunshine on a pristine sea, entering from Peel Sound and travelling east to Fort Ross, on the edge of Prince Regent Inlet. In two other visits the weather has been less accommodating but the place nonetheless impressive. The fort, the last post established by HBC (see Plate 25), was built in 1937, inspired and managed during its eleven-year existence by an Orcadian, Lorenz Learmonth. The company supply ship, *Nascopie*, remained for six days while the fort was constructed. There are four unmarked graves near the storehouse. A cairn in honour of Leopold McClintock, destroyed by polar bears, has been replaced but the claw marks on the sturdy door of the 'fort' testify to their continuing interest in the property. It survives as a very attractive bothy in a short summer-colourful landscape, rich in miniature Arctic flowers and plants, the human presence having been moved 250 kilometres south to Taloyoak, abandoned because the strait is so often choked by ice. On one occasion, after it had been cut off for two years, folk were evacuated by the US army. On that first visit we saw at least five polar bears, as well as narwhal, beluga, a bowhead whale and seals. It is a further pleasing circumstance that the waters of the strait comprise a blend of the Pacific and the Atlantic.

*

William Kennedy was re-engaged by Lady Franklin to search the Russian Arctic by way of the Bering Strait but neither the times (the impending outbreak of war with the 'Bear') nor his crew, who mutinied in Valparaiso, were propitious. He returned in 1856 to Canada and a busy life. His grandson, Alexander Kennedy Isbister, was educated at St Margaret's Hope, Orkney, and at the universities of Aberdeen and Edinburgh, eventually earning a deserved reputation as an educator and supporter of Métis and First Nations and establishing a trust fund at the University of Manitoba to support education for both women and men 'where the highest education is given without distinction of race, creed or nationality'. At William Kennedy's funeral in 1890, he was lauded as a man who never got his due: 'While other men far less deserving received honour and emolument, he was passed over.'[65] John Rae, however, was no admirer of Kennedy; he condemned him for failing in his three expedition objectives, namely to reach Brentford Bay, to explore west Boothia as far south as the magnetic pole and to find Franklin, although of course in the last category he had many competitors in failure.

Sir Francis Leopold McClintock, c. 1860; engraved by
D.J. Pound from a photograph by R.N. Cheyne
(Public domain, via Wikipedia Commons)

12

THE SEARCH CONTINUES

Expeditions of the 1850s and Charles Dickens's Role in
Lady Franklin's Campaign

There's some say that we wan,
And some say that they wan,
And some say that nane wan at a', man.

Battle of Sheriffmuir Ballad

John Rae had spent part of his leave time in Scotland outrunning and out-shooting everyone present on the Highland Estate, Glenquoich, belonging to Edward 'Bear' Ellis, fur-trade supremo and godfather of the NWC–HBC merger. In May 1852 Rae wrote to Archibald Barclay, Secretary of HBC, proposing a plan for the completion of the survey of the northern shores of America, only a small proportion of which, along the west coast of Boothia, remained unexplored. He envisaged one officer, two Inuit and ten men (Orkneymen, Shetlanders and 'English halfbreeds') with two boats: one a little larger than he had at Repulse Bay in 1846, to be built at York Factory; the other with a 24-foot keel, to be constructed in England. The itinerary would include the western end of Chesterfield Inlet, a descent of Back's River (Great Fish River), the west coast of Boothia, and James Clark Ross's most southerly point on the west coast of Somerset Island (Four Rivers Bay), then return to York Factory. Rae would lead the expedition.[1]

Rae spent a good deal of time planning his expedition. As his first biographer pointed out, when new charts were published by the Hydrographic Office, Rae was incensed that his discovery in 1847 that Boothia was a peninsula, and his data on the stretch between Boothia and Pelly Bay, were ignored.[2] He assumed that there were at least two reasons for this. First, Rae had worked with the Inuit, who knew the region intimately, could produce verbal testimony about, and intimate personal acquaintance with, the landscape and seascape, and had developed their own mapping system. There is something inspirational in the idea that the final proofing of the American continent's northern frontier should have been a co-operative action between Inuit and Scot. Rae's interpreter, William Ooligbuck, was fluent in Inuktitut, Cree, French and English. Second, the Navy was assuming knowledge and authority that it did not possess. Rae's facts were doubted 'merely because they differed from the opinions of more influential individuals who had nothing but conjecture and theory to guide them'. Indeed, it is entirely possible that the functionaries in London had no idea what language Scots and Inuit used in discussion with one another! Rae wrote to *The Times* in late November 1852 advertising his forthcoming expedition, concluding with a postscript that has become famous among Arctic buffs. He would feel 'a more than common interest in bringing [his findings] to a successful conclusion', adding, 'I do not mention the lost navigators as there is not the slightest hope of finding any traces of them in the Quarter to which I am going.'[3]

Rae viewed the funeral procession of the Duke of Wellington in London (18 November 1852), bought chronometers for the planned expedition and was detained in bed by an attack of lumbago and a kidney infection, before his arrival in New York in early April 1853, where he met with Henry Grinnell. He visited relatives in Ontario and then took to the Great Lakes. A postscript in a letter to George Simpson indicates how tactless Rae could be. He complained that wine supplied by Simpson at Lachine 'appears to have been the dregs of all the casks or bottles emptied there during the year for neither the port nor the Madeira were palatable'. Simpson was incensed, retorting that the wine was the same stuff Rae had praised while dining at Lachine, he himself had selected the same wine out of the same bin as a gift. Although it may have looked muddy, the flavour was not affected: 'I hope your Esquimaux friends may furnish you with better drink'! A chastened Rae knew better than to reply.

Rae reached Norway House by 12 June 1853 and wrote to Sir George Simpson with a progress report. He was able to recruit Thomas Mistegan, the talented Cree hunter who had been with him in 1848–9. The boats they ordered had reached York Factory, in time for their June arrival, Rae deciding to captain the smaller one since he thought it would be more difficult to control. Among the Scots involved were John McDonald (boatman, Red River 'halfbreed'); Murdoch McDonald (boatman, Highlander from Scotland); James Clouston (steersman, Orkney); Charles Harrison (boatman, Shetland); James Johnstone (boatman and fisherman, Red River 'halfbreed'); Murdoch McLennan (boatman, Red River 'halfbreed'); and John G. McDougald (boatman, Red River 'halfbreed'). The party left York Factory on 24 June 1853 battling relentless ice that delayed their arrival at the ruined Prince of Wales Fort (known as the Old Fort, Churchill) until 11 July. The boatmen used poles to push against the ice. One missed the target and fell overboard. He popped up at once, making a joke about his accident. When, three minutes later, the same thing happened again to the same man, Rae insisted he changed his clothes. Thin ice was unpredictable and very dangerous. Men were in the water, greeting potential danger with jokes and laughter, as the floe on which they had placed their equipment began to break up on the 'lipper' (the lip or curl) of the sea caused by the wind. Just in time they saved their cargo and one another.[4]

The boats were in need of some repair. Ooligbuck the interpreter was expected shortly; he was currently engaged on a beluga hunt. Also joining them was an Inuk named Munro, 'a very good lad, but of little use as an interpreter'. They sailed along a fairly uninteresting coast to achieve 156 miles in 56 hours. A similar distance led to Chesterfield Inlet, which hosted thick clouds of mosquitoes 'making a noise like that of a hive of bees swarming, only the little torments were perhaps 1,000 times as many in number'.

While Rae slept, the steersman took a wrong turning in foggy weather. They were clearly off course, but Rae, figuring that the large river in which they found themselves would run to the west, the direction originally intended, decided to remain with it. They were moving up the river against the flow, over rapids and falls requiring many portages; Rae named it the Quoich. When it changed direction again he decided to back-track and to split the party, sending 'home' Clouston, Murdoch McDonald, Harrison, McDougald and Munro. He decided to head for Repulse Bay with Johnstone, McLennan and John McDonald as well as Mistegan, Ooligbuck and two Métis named John and Jacob Beads. He wrote about walrus killing: 'every small vessel cut, poured forth a crimson jet, 2 or 3 feet high and this after most of the blubber had been removed had a very strange appearance. It was a disagreeable duty for my fine fellows, but they had a great deal of fun over it, and did their work well and quickly, most of them being used to skinning and cutting up buffalo on the prairies'.

The party reached Repulse Bay on 15 August, their leader reminiscing about the old haunts from six years earlier, organising the men to collect fuel and food, assessing whether there was sufficient of the latter to over-winter. Fishing was poor. Buffalo skins made effective tents. On consulting the men as to whether or not they should winter at Repulse, all voted in favour. Their activities reminded Rae of Orkney. He wore a suit of Scottish tweed with holes in elbows and knees, patched with moose skin. He shot grouse and ptarmigan. He competed with foxes that often managed to outwit the traps set for them. Less Orcadian were dwellings for the company, built with passages under the snow. Rae had a house to himself, allegedly to avoid the tobacco everyone else used. Christmas and New Year came and went. 'I have mentioned every day's occupation in a manner that may be wearisome and uninteresting to the reader', he perceptively wrote. His prose is flat, and the content familiar from earlier journals. By March 1854 the men were busy 'preparing for the hard work of arctic exploration, the sledge journeys'. Provisions were carefully measured and calculated for a journey of sixty days. Needles, buttons and thread for repairs to clothing were included, as were items of cold-weather gear: fur caps (unfortunately with deficient ear flaps), leather mittens 'with a rim of fur round the wrist part, and lined with thick blanketing, moose skin moccasins big enough for two or three blanket socks with thongs of skin stitched on the soles to prevent slipping'.

Naval critics did not understand sledges, which in their ignorance they designated as 'useless'. Rae demonstrated that snow huts built en route were far superior to tents, and that wool was not a useful material for blankets and nightwear sweaters since it was a non-conductor. Although Rae enjoyed a glass of brandy or port, he considered that grog was bad for men on the move; tea was much healthier. With care, scurvy could be avoided; the Navy was at fault in taking wrong advice on this affliction (which figured prominently in the Nares expedition of 1876, an event Rae mentions several times in his autobiography). He and his explorers set out again on 31 March: James Johnstone, John McDonald, William Ooligbuck and Jacob Beads. Part of the route was identical to that of 1847 and so did not need to be described again. Two weeks after they set out, Rae's autobiography suddenly terminates. It remained 'unfinished' for the rest of his life, but has recently been published for the first time, a valuable addition to Arctic literature.

What was unexpected was that, west of Pelly Bay, Rae, while still intent upon closing the gap on the west shore of Boothia, chanced upon an Inuk sporting a cap-band once worn by an officer. This chimed with other stories he was told about a party of kabloonas perishing for lack of food further west, 'beyond a large river containing many falls and rapids'. The following is drawn from Rae's report to the Secretary of the Admiralty:

In the spring four winters past (1850) a party of about forty white men were seen travelling southward over the ice, dragging a boat with them, by some Esquimaux who were killing seals near the north shore of King William's Land which is a large island. None of the party could speak the Esquimaux language intelligibly, but by signs the natives were made to understand that their ship or ships, had been crushed by ice, and that they were now going to where they expected to find deer to shoot. From the appearance of the men, all of whom with the exception of one officer, looked thin [described in another letter as 'tall, stout and middle aged'], they were then supposed to be getting short of provisions, and they purchased a small seal from the natives. At a later date the same season, but previous to the breaking up of the ice, the bodies of some thirty persons were discovered on the Continent, and five on an island near it, about a long day's journey to the NW of a large stream, which could be no other than Back's Great Fish River (named by the 'Esquimaux' *Oot-ko-hi-ca-lik*), as its description . . . agreed exactly with that of Sir George Back. Some of the bodies had been buried (probably those of the first victims of famine); some were in tents, others under the boat, which had been turned over to form a shelter, and several lay scattered about in different directions. Of those found on the island, one was supposed to have been an officer, as he had a telescope strapped over his shoulders and his double-barrelled gun lay underneath him. From the mutilated state of many of the corpses, and the contents of the kettles, it is evident that our wretched countrymen had been driven to the last resource – cannibalism – as a means of prolonging existence.[5]

The Inuit also reported on powder and ammunition. Some possessed broken-up objects from the site as well as cutlery bearing the crests of the owners. Rae purchased as many pieces of evidence as he could. None of the Inuit had actually visited the sad site where the objects were found but they knew of some who had. Rae then wrapped up his account by recounting that his party had obtained adequate provisions from land and water, had made clothing and bedding from deerskins, and had been reasonably comfortable in snow-houses but his 'spring journey was a failure, in consequence of an accumulation of obstacles, several of which, my former experience in

Arctic travelling had not taught me to expect'. In his journal he added that there was no reason to think that the Inuit were responsible for any violence towards the distressed sailors. He was able to identify some individuals from initials on their silver table forks – Harry D.S. Goodsir (assistant-surgeon, *Erebus*); Alexander McDonald (assistant surgeon, *Terror*); Gillies A. Macbean (second master, *Terror*); John S. Peddie (surgeon, *Erebus*). A silver plate had belonged to Sir John Franklin with his motto, *Nec aspera terrent*, rendered as 'Difficulties be Damned'.[6]

News of Rae's findings created a furore at rather an awkward time as the Crimean War had broken out in March 1854. *The Times* lamented that the ships, captains and crews dedicated to the Franklin search had achieved remarkably little except a huge cost, estimated at between £660,000 and £760,000.[7]

*

Rae arrived in London on 22 October 1854, the report of cannibalism breaking in *The Times* the next day. Within the week he was making recommendations to send a canoe expedition down the Back River, launching from Great Slave Lake. He recommended Ooligbuck as interpreter. He stressed the need for haste if all was to be in place by the following summer. Rae himself would not be involved; he had determined 'not to return to these latitudes'. The whole story of the follow-up expedition has been meticulously edited by Professor William Barr. It was to be an HBC affair, part-funded by the British Government. Rae favoured the appointment of Chief Trader James Anderson (whose grandparents were Scottish) as commander. Second-in-command was James Green Stewart, the son of a wealthy Scots businessman in Quebec City, like Anderson an employee of HBC with considerable experience of New Caledonia and the Yukon, in the company of Robert Campbell.[8] At this time HBC was stacked with Scots too numerous to mention. Governor George Simpson sent Anderson and Stewart their instructions, telling them they had been selected for 'your zeal, discretion and perseverance in surmounting difficulties, as well as your experience in dealing with native tribes, and the important fact that you are inured to the hardships and perils which must necessarily attend a service of this description'. They were to communicate with the Inuit to seek information on the doomed white men. All company interests were to be subservient to the expedition. If Anderson was delayed in any way, Stewart was to take over command and find a replacement, while as soon as he reached Athabasca, he was to supervise the building of two canoes. Members of Rae's recent expedition were to be recruited wherever possible but substitutes had to be identified, should any not be forthcoming. The Halkett boat was to be forwarded from York Factory to Athabasca. All was to be accomplished in one summer but, if that did not prove possible, arrangements should be made to over-winter on the coast. Astronomical instruments and charts were to be returned on completion of the project.

'Should you discover any traces of Sir John Franklin's party, you will carefully collect and bring back with you whatever may be portable, more especially manuscripts; such articles will most probably be found in possession of the natives, from whom they should be purchased at any cost'. Any bodies were to be interred, the spot marked by a cairn, 'in which should be deposited a written memorial of all that is known of their careers and melancholy fate'. Here, as elsewhere, literacy was prioritised over Inuit testimony. There was particular interest in paper, despite its fragility in Arctic conditions. The 'whole civilized world' would watch their proceedings with deep interest. Dr Rae was commended: 'his admirable tact in the command of his people is proverbial . . . You cannot do better than follow his example on this point, treating the men with kindness and consideration, more by your influence over them than by a resort to strict discipline'. Rae advised that his own men be hired, namely Murdoch McLellan, James Isbister, John McDonald, Jacob Beads, Charles Kennedy and Samuel Sinclair. All should be well paid. George Simpson wrote thirteen letters to other interested parties, in addition to the instructions, dealing with all manner of subjects and points of detail. As late as November 1854, Simpson vainly hoped he still might persuade Rae to take over command.

Much less impressed was Jane Franklin, who told Anderson that Rae's report was not accepted by the public or by Parry, Richardson and James Clark Ross. 'Everybody regrets, even Dr Rae, I believe, himself, that he should have reported the shocking story of cannibalism – if true it should have been buried within his own bosom – there is but one feeling on this point.' In fact, the first public reports of cannibalism had been communicated to *The Times* by the Admiralty. Lady Franklin was wrong to state that members of the Arctic Council had not accepted Rae's informative account: they had, although disgracefully they neglected to say so publicly. The response to Rae's revelations shows the English establishment at its exceptionalist and racist worst and Lady Franklin at her most self-consumed and insufferable. She was prepared to ruin Rae and his supporters, as well as the Inuit people, to assuage her own selfish (if understandable) pain in the role that she had contrived for herself in the irresistible Franklin drama. Her niece's follow-up letter added nothing. Both mentioned 'a bound quarto memorandum book [with] brass at the corners and a lock and key', Franklin's private journal for which a reward was offered, though they might have reflected that notebooks in the Arctic were rarer than needles in haystacks.

The recruitment of Charles Dickens to Lady Franklin's campaign in his magazine *Household Words* may, at first sight, appear a stroke of genius in mobilising popular opinion in favour of her, though she does not figure personally until the last issue of the magazine on 25 April 1857, which discusses the lost expeditionaries in a piece woundingly entitled 'Official Patriotism'. The magazine features the Arctic, Franklin's doom-ships and the lack of state aid, discussed by writer Henry Morley but 'conducted' by Dickens, since his name was literally in the headline. In many books and articles, Dickens has been quoted from the Arctic articles in *Household Words* with the intention of illustrating his racism concerning the Inuit but this may be a misreading of his intentions. He accepts that John Rae demonstrated that Franklin and his supporters were dead but he disputes any notion of cannibalism. He finds no fault or blame with the conscientious and modest Rae for whom he reserves great praise as a skilful, 'intrepid' Arctic explorer. He points out that none of Rae's informants had seen the evidence, all of which was second-hand through an interpreter, using language skills that were often fallible. He implies that the Franklinites could have been attacked and killed by the Inuit, from his point of view a perfectly reasonable suggestion, although, like most of his contemporaries, Dickens knew virtually nothing about the people of the Arctic. He then articulates what might be described as assumptions of imperialism:

> It is impossible to form an estimate of the character of any race of savages from their deferential behaviour of the white man while he is strong. The mistake has been made again and again; and the moment the white man has appeared in the new aspect of being weaker than the savage, the savage has changed and sprung upon him.

We have already encountered this idea that Europeans must take a tough stance when dealing with the *indigenes*, for example from James Clark Ross and Rae himself. The notion of savages taking advantage might be exemplified by the killing of Cook. Dickens continues 'there are pious persons who, in their practice, with a strange inconsistency, claim for every child born to civilisation, all innate depravity, and for every savage born to the woods and wilds, all innate virtue'. All denizens not characterised as 'noble' are aliens; alienism is in the eye of the beholder. In his next assertions Dickens appears to be throwing his readers' own common-place prejudices back in their faces: 'We believe every savage to be in his heart covetous, treacherous, and cruel; and we have yet to learn what knowledge the white man – lost, houseless, helpless, shiftless, apparently forgotten by his race, plainly famine-stricken, weak, frozen, helpless and dying – has of the gentleness of Esquimaux nature.' By gentleness he means kindness or benignity. This is an important question – what knowledge do British people have about the gentleness of Inuit nature? The implied message seems to be that we should have some regard for the condition of our own folk before we pontificate on the attributes of others.

Dickens could not become steamed up about cannibalism quite simply because he contended that, if the practice existed at all, it was very rare, as he argued in his article 'The Lost Arctic Voyagers': 'if the oaks of men's beliefs could be traced back to acorns, how rarely the practice [cannibalism], even among savages, has been proved'. He then proceeds with a section that has often been cited to highlight his racism but which rather seems intended to ironically challenge the dogmas of his readers.

> The word of a savage is not to be taken for it [cannibalism]; firstly, because he is a liar; secondly, because he is a boaster; thirdly, because he often talks figuratively; fourthly, because he is given to a superstitious notion that when he tells you he has his enemy in his stomach, you will logically give him credit for having his enemy's valour in his heart.[9]

It is very likely that when news of cannibalism reached London, the popular assumption would have been that the Inuit were the consumers of the sailors, rather than the kabloonas of one another. Stories about the practice were known from all over the world. In 1843 John Nicholson published his *Historical and Traditionary Tales . . . Connected with the South of Scotland*, which prominently featured Sawney Bean and his hideous family dwelling in a gruesome cave on the Ayrshire coast.

> The limbs o' men, women an weans on the wa's,
> Like beef that is dried were hung up in grim raws,

319

An' some laid in pickle fu' sune tae be ta'en,
By that horde in the Hades o' aul Sawney Bean.

In an article wittily entitled 'A Taste of Scotland', Fiona Black has traced such stories in eighteenth-century English broadsheets, designed as colonial fictions written to highlight Scottish savagery and inhumanity in contrast to the refinements of England. This is not to suggest that everyone was reading Nicholson's book but simply that such stories were current.[10]

As might be expected, Dickens also cites the experience of John Richardson on his first Arctic excursion of 1819–22. In weighing the probabilities and improbabilities of the 'last resource' (cannibalism), the foremost question is 'not the nature of the extremity, but, the nature of the men'.

> Utilitarianism will protest 'they are dead; why care about this?' Our reply shall be, 'Because they *are* dead, therefore we care about this. Because they served their country well, and deserved well of her, and can ask, no more on this earth, for her justice or her loving-kindness; give them both, full measure, pressed down, running over. Because no Franklin can come back, to write the honest story of their woes and resignation, read it tenderly and truly in the book he has left us. Because they lie scattered on those wastes of snow, and are as defenceless against the remembrance of coming generations, as against the elements into which they are now resolving, and the winter winds that alone can waft them home, now, impalpable air; therefore, cherish them gently, even in the breast of children. Therefore, teach no one to shudder without reason, and the history of their end. Therefore, confide with their own firmness, in their fortitude, their lofty sense of duty, their courage, and their religion.[11]

When Dickens wrote, there was no evidence whatsoever of the degree or otherwise of Inuit culpability. Europeans who encountered the Inuit often referred to their propensity for sticky fingers, but not to cannibalism, plus nobody questioned Dickens's evisceration of the works of other writers, notably in some of the memorable tags and colourful language in newspapers of the time, in order to support his own literary output. As part of his mission to promote Christmas, Dickens wrote about how it was celebrated in the 'Frozen Regions'. He contributed several articles on Arctic exploration.

'The Inuit of Hudson Bay are like the negroes of the coast, demoralised by intercourse with European traders. These are not true pictures of the loving children of the north.'

During his American tour of 1842 Dickens set out in search of 'Indians' or First Nations as they are now known but he had difficulties in finding 'real Indians', as I once noticed them described on a tourist attraction in Pennsylvania. According to Dickens they had disappeared and all that was left was sadness that they were no more, leaving only images of the 'Noble Savage'. Nonetheless, he continued to acquire books on the First Nations as he travelled, reaching the conclusion that the Indians must inevitably be swept from the earth and the Noble Savage was a myth. In this he agreed with Walter Scott who convinced himself that Scotland's own First Nations, the Gaels, faced a similar destiny when confronted by 'civilisation' and progress. If both of these peoples refused to conform they faced doom. In describing First Nations Dickens adopts the same approach of bombastic deflationary adjectivity that he later repeats with reference to the Inuit. The Indian is, 'a savage – cruel, false, thievish, murderous; addicted more or less to grease, entrails and beastly customs, a wild animal . . . a conceited, tiresome, bloodthirsty, monotonous humbug'. As Francesca Orestano has indicated, Dickens in later life argued that it was nonsensical to criticise the savage customs of primitive societies while neglecting the foibles and absurdities of his own generation. She also quotes French writer of 1845 L. Faucher, whose view, in translation, is highly relevant to some of the claims that have been made in this book. 'Englishmen seem inclined to believe that, except for their nation which has already reached maturity, all other nations are still in their infancy.' It is perhaps surprising that Dickens at no point seems to compare and contrast the Inuit and the First Nations but at least he is shown to be a man who was not afraid to change his mind.[12] As a journalist we may suspect that he also contrived to speak, as it were, out of both sides of his mouth at once, a gambit that was good for sales of his journal.

John Rae contributed two articles to *Household Words* (23 and 30 December 1854). He asserted that William Ooligbuck spoke English fluently 'and perhaps more correctly than one half of the lower classes in England or Scotland'. He proceeded to convincingly refute most of the points made by his critics. To those who suggested the bodies had been mutilated by animals he explained that it was a well-known fact that bears, foxes, wolves or wolverines would never touch a dead human body unless on the verge of starvation. He dismissed any idea that the Inuit would have killed the 'sad remnant of Franklin's gallant band'. As far as information was concerned, Rae asserted that, though the Inuit would not hesitate to tell a falsehood, 'they cannot lie with a good grace – they cannot lie like truth, as civilised men do'. They contradicted themselves and their untruths were so silly that it was easy to spot them. Rae considered that the Inuit were superior to 'all the tribes of red men in America', a view shared by very many HBC employees, who found the Inuit decorous, obliging, unobtrusive, orderly and friendly. He was certain that they were not murderers. The Franklinites undoubtedly died of starvation. He did not extend his statement to include the possibility that the explorers may also have indulged in cannibalism. In conclusion he thanked Dickens for the kind, courteous and flattering manner in which he had referred to him in his articles.

Dickens's language was not very different from Rae's. For both, the Inuit were 'savages', a catch-all for 'uncivilised'. England's most famous novelist, 'manifestly the product of his age', liked to be on the side of the angels. Rae, and before him James Clark Ross and John Ross, based their relationships with the Inuit on mutual respect. It can be doubted whether Dickens actually advanced Lady Franklin's mission, because he knew his readers would have been more interested in the hardy warriors of the ice than they were in her. There is an interesting sequentiality here. Dickens published *Hard Times* in 1854, the same year as his Arctic articles appeared in *Household Words*. The novel was dedicated to Thomas Carlyle, who has been described as the most influential British writer/thinker of the nineteenth century. Between 1849 and 1853 Carlyle made the biggest mistake in his career when, as devil's advocate, he introduced a designedly contentious essay, critiquing the general slowness of slave emancipation in the British Empire. In *Fraser's Magazine* 1849 Carlyle went much further than he intended in an article entitled 'Occasional Discourse on the Negro Question'. His readers and friends were horrified. The more he was criticised, the more entrenched his views became until, in a second article on 'The N----- Question' in 1853, he earned the shame and deserved blame of racism that still haunts his reputation. Might we suggest a potential parallelism between Carlyle and Dickens, which the latter firmly rejected, for Dickens hoped he was no racist?

In January 1857 the play *The Frozen Deep* was premiered, a joint effort by Wilkie Collins, who wrote all of it, very loosely based on recent Arctic explorations, and Dickens, who developed novel production techniques. The story concerns Clara Burnham, a coming of age orphan who is subject to trances and who falls for two men, Richard Wardour and Frank Aldersley, both sailors about to go to sea. The poor lass spent her early years in 'a lonely old house in the Highlands where the ignorant folk filled her mind with superstitions which are still respected as truths in the wild North', especially those concerning second sight. She foresees that one of her men will kill the other during the imminent voyage. After what seems like an interminable amount of both time and words, all is resolved. 'Is Clara present, in the spirit, with our loved and lost ones in the lonely North. Can mortal vision see the dead and living in the solitudes of the Frozen Deep?' Great men and stagehands allegedly suffered paroxysms of grief at the end of the show, especially when Dickens performed. Today it seems quite underwhelming and an attempt to exploit, rather than sympathise with, those who actually died.[13]

When the second act transports the audience to 'A Hut in the Arctic Regions' they are introduced to a sailor pounding dry bones to make soup, while another has an unnaturally hollow voice and a third badly swollen legs, all imported from Franklin's *First Narrative*. Some of the best lines in the play go to Clara's Scottish nurse who taught the lassie all she knows about second sight: 'The men are lost, a' lost, i' the land o' ice and snow . . . they shall never be found again'! Her appearances tend to be accompanied by 'Scotch music', such as 'Wandering Willie' and she scolds any Southern Leddy that does not believe in 'The Sight'. 'I see the lamb i' the grasp o' the lion. I see your bonnie bird alone wi' the hawk. I see you and all around you crying bluid. The stain is on you! Oh my bairn, my bairn, the stain o' that bluid is on you'. The third act opens with the tune 'Farewell to Lochaber', in which she berates a man who denied having a sour face. "Face! D'ye ca' yon stickit thing o' the top' your shoulders, a face, [aside] but why do I waste words on him? He's just a puir weak creature!'[14] Thus is the Doric deployed to put nineteenth-century males – heroic explorers at that – in their place, and to proximate the imaginary atmospheres of the Scottish Highlands and the Arctic.

*

Lady Franklin requested that James Anderson should return locks of her husband's hair, as well as all his private and public papers, sealed up; he had taken a large quantity of letters and script 'for her eyes only' when he sailed, but why is not explained. Her letter was reinforced by another from her niece, Sophia Cracroft. Anderson was also asked to look for Franklin's private journal. He was keen to oblige but the late break-up of ice was a problem; it took him twenty-three days for the journey to Fort Resolution, where he met with Stewart, and they set off on 22 June 1855.

When Anderson read Rae's notice of his finds, he predicted that the paragraph that mentioned cannibalism 'would bring a storm about his ears'. Confirmation arrived in a letter from Lady Franklin, revealing that Dickens had employed his powerful pen on the subject in two issues of his magazine *Household Words*. Anderson ironically opined that her actions constituted 'a nice recompense for all Rae's sufferings and privations. She seems to expect that we shall reach the spot where Franklin's vessels were lost – very reasonable'. In his reply he assured her that any records discovered would be 'held inviolably sacred'. Furthermore Stewart, a gentleman by birth and education, would respect her request for privacy; most of his shipmates could neither read nor write and so were in no position to betray confidences. However, Anderson had confided to another correspondent that Stewart had plenty of pluck and endurance but 'as to his foresight and prudence I have my doubts', partially borne out when the second-in-command hired a guide who proved hopeless. Anderson regretted that the mention of cannibalism had so deeply wounded Jane Franklin's feelings; Rae was a friend of his who was anxious to resolve the Franklin mystery: 'I am sure that no one will regret the circumstance more than he'. Both men had concluded that Franklin's ships had been crushed by ice but not immediately destroyed, otherwise the many objects found by Rae would not have survived. This idea was becoming quite favoured, as was the issue of why Franklin did not make for Fury Beach, where he must have known there were supplies. Captain Francis Crozier of *Terror* had been a midshipman on *Hecla* when Parry abandoned *Fury* and thus could authoritatively advise on the matter.[15]

After consulting two First Nations Yellowknife, Anderson decided to take a different route from George Back in the 1830s. Known as the 'Mountain', it involved leaving Great Slave Lake to follow a chain of lakes linked by seven portages to Aylmer Lake, which feeds the Back River (Great Fish River), thus avoiding the dangerous Hoar Frost River. Anderson claimed that this move saved the entire expedition, since it was shorter and safer than the other, which would never have allowed them to reach the sea in the time available. It was hard going. The Mountain Portage involved an 'almost continual ascent of 1500 feet'. The party set out at 3am and camped at 10pm, 'the men now laughing over their day's work!!' Since mosquitoes and sand flies kept them awake until 1.30am Anderson generously allowed them to sleep until 6.30am, trekking until 7.45pm. The day after that, they were up again at 3am covering eight portages in 35 miles. It is little wonder that the whole expedition took place in record time. They left Fort Resolution on 22 June and returned on 16 September, an achievement demanding great skill and fortitude on the part of the leaders.[16] It is remarkable how the men from different cultures and backgrounds, working in appalling and dangerous conditions, maintained 'famous spirits and many a joke and laugh, raised at the expense of those who run a risk of breaking through weak portions of the ice'. Another source of amusement was doubtless Anderson and Stewart's fondness for a daily dip, 'dreadfully cold though very refreshing, it helps to deaden the bite of the mosquitoes'. At Musk Ox Rapid, one crew member and four First Nations turned back, leaving fourteen in the party, of whom the Scots were the principals, with Donald McLeod and Murdoch McLennan from Lewis and Will Reid from Orkney.

The Back River, or Great Fish River (Thlew-ee-cho-dezeth), is 605 miles long, famous for its falls and rapids, of which George Back had counted ninety-four, providing a difficult and in places a dangerous deluge. Wherever possible, throughout their voyage, the explorers compared their experiences with those of Back as described in his book of 1834. Their canoes took a battering. At the outlet of Lake Franklin the rapids were partly portaged and partly run. There they encountered a small group of Inuit who communicated the information that a group of white men had starved to death beside the sea after their ships were wrecked. Stewart reported that a woman told him she had seen an emaciated man on an island at the point of death: 'She showed the way he was sitting on the beach his head resting in his hands', beyond help. The absence of an interpreter was a problem but two of Rae's men apparently understood something of the language.

The canoeists were shown copper and tin kettles, and pieces of wood, but as they paddled down-river their sadness at the news of the dead was reflected in dismal rain that thoroughly soaked them. It was hard to find a place to camp. At times like these, mused Anderson, alcohol was required; for himself, he craved a glass of brandy and water. Later, he strongly denied that he had ever heard anything of the woman's account. Incomparably more informative was the situation on Montreal Island which yielded bits and pieces associated with boats and a piece of wood with 'Erebus' inscribed on it, together with blacksmith's tools, rope, an iron bar and a piece from a snow-shoe. The Halkett boat was used for brief visits to other sites such as Maconochie Island, their furthest reach. Point Richardson was an inlet too far and too dangerous. Stewart was satisfied that they had done their best; 'with light hearts we turn our backs on this cold sterile region'. Anderson speculated on the absence of bodies, assuming consumption by animals, the volatile landscape or the avaricious sea. They once again interacted with the Inuit at Franklin Rapids where they were shown tin boilers, a couple of frying pans, tin soup plates (tureens to men of breeding!), part of a thermometer, a chisel and different woods, used for paddles. The miserable weather was relentless. Stewart, apparently no admirer of brevity, remarked, 'we hope to have a little dry weather so that our clothes may lose a little of the humidity contracted since our arrival at the sea & which has continued till now, a sprinkling every day to keep us fresh'. His canoe was twice damaged in the rapids. They were now attempting to travel against the current of the Great Fish River. Anderson wrote about the most severe water conditions he had ever seen. Both he and Stewart were, to use a popular Scottish word, totally 'scunnered'.

Before setting out for the Arctic Ocean, Anderson had commissioned another HBC Scot, James Lockhart, to convey supplies and men from Red River to Fort Resolution on Great Slave Lake where he was to prepare shelter and food stocks for the return of the exploring parties, as well as performing a similar service at the headwaters of the Back River. In the event, neither arrangement was required. Anderson considered Lockhart a 'remarkably clever and active officer'.

Unfortunately, Anderson could not say the same for James Stewart, whom he claimed to be 'utterly useless to me', while maintaining that the pair remained excellent friends! Anderson told Simpson that Stewart would sleep through most of the day and still slumber all night, awakening with reluctance. He never opposed Anderson but never made suggestions or encouragements either. He was 'a burden and an incumbrance'; he had expected Stewart to prove rash and imprudent but he was neither. As the company dispersed, Stewart diverted to visit Margaret, his wife of one year, at Norway House, delaying the publicising of the news about their voyage and enraging Anderson. Surprisingly Governor Simpson showed that he had a sympathetic side, asking Anderson to withdraw his complaint, which he did. However, Simpson was very soon accusing Stewart of habitual drunkenness and brawling, as well as fabricating the story about the Inuk woman who met the dying kabloona on the beach. However, as Professor Barr points out, Stewart testified that his claim was true when he later appeared before the Court of Session, Scotland's supreme civil court. It was unlikely that he would utter falsehoods to that revered body.[17]

The whole expedition was completed in a short time with some accidents but no deaths. Those who had also previously accompanied Rae attested that Repulse Bay was a paradise compared with the Great Fish River and the Montreal Islands. Anderson explored new territory when he chose the Mountain Portage route and he was probably correct in claiming it a much shorter route to the sea. He succeeded in finding evidence that supported Rae's discoveries concerning Franklin, though in his various reports and letters he rather ignores Stewart's contribution when he is not explicitly criticising him as lazy and somnolent. When he stated that Stewart's suitcase was twice the size of his own he was emphasising that Stewart was 'respectably connected', though Anderson's own family were no slouches in that department. He did not 'knock up' (succumb) concerning his troublesome leg but he asked Simpson to send him an elastic stocking and cap for his knee. While naval journals mostly tried to depict a 'happy families' atmosphere on board, the HBC men were often fighting to get to the top of the barrel in order to impress Simpson with their own skills at the expense of others.

Writing to Lady Franklin, Anderson regretted the unfortunate absence of a proper interpreter but reported what they had learned at Lake Franklin Rapids and Montreal Island. A land party found nothing between Elliot Bay and Point Pechel at the mouth of the Great Fish River. An old Inuit site at Point Ogle revealed only a small strip of cotton and a piece of fishing line. He once again referred to the atrocious weather conditions as well as sea, sand and wind capable of conspiring in the destruction of evidence of all kinds. He ended with the interesting, but baseless, speculation that they had hoped to find graves in which journals or despatches had been placed, which had been removed by the Inuit (on an analogy to the First Nations, who believed that 'paper speaks to the white men' and might be robbed by them to avoid incrimination). However, the Inuit belief system did not allow tampering with the graves of the dead, which negates this suggestion.

*

The saga had moved on but was not yet complete. In 1857 Jane Franklin recruited the assistance of Irish explorer Francis Leopold McClintock. The McClintocks traced their origins to Argyll, Leopold's branch moving to Ireland during the seventeenth-century 'Plantation'. He was described by his biographer, Clements Markham, as having 'a short, slender, but wiry and muscular frame well fitted for the endurance of long-continued exertion and hardships'.[18] McClintock had experience of previous Arctic expeditions, including an earlier search for the Franklin expedition. In 1848 he had been appointed second officer on *Enterprise* with James Clark Ross, over-wintering at Port Leopold on the desolation of Somerset Island. Departing on 11 May 1849 on two sledges, with six men on each, they had achieved 500 miles in forty days and the utter exhaustion of five men. They had travelled via Garnier Bay, naming a point Cape McClintock between it and Port Leopold; the explorers had continued south to Cape Bunny and Four Rivers Bay where they had erected a cairn in which they deposited a record. On the trail, JCR led with McClintock following, as befitted their rank, with the 'thoughtless sailors' hauling behind. All suffered from starvation, thirst and exhaustion, culminating almost inevitably in an outbreak of scurvy which affected both men. Two other men died from lengthy illnesses.[19]

McClintock and his company had returned in 1849 to a disappointed Britain and a famine-ravaged Ireland but had almost immediately set about planning another voyage. In February 1850 a small armada of searching ships was assembled by the Navy, McClintock becoming first lieutenant on *Assistance* under Erasmus Ommanney. Before departing in May 1850 he briefly met Lady Franklin, who marked him as a future accomplice. Severe ice imprisoned *Assistance* in Melville Bay for forty days, and they were forced to over-winter in Barrow Strait. Wintering close by were the ships *Lady Franklin* and *Sophia*, commanded by William Penny, and *Felix*, commanded by Sir John Ross. In March 1851 *Assistance* set out on sledges, each with six or ten men, aided by sails and kites – the latter proving useless – to plant caches that they hoped would aid later searchers. McClintock named his sledge *Perseverance* after his motto of 'Perseverance to the end'. His personal target was the exploration of southern Melville Island in eighty days. Penny headed for Wellington Channel while Ommanney was set for Cape Walker. Altogether, in early April, 102 men were assigned to fourteen sledges going off in several different directions. Before long, ten men were sent back suffering from frostbite. Once again, the main achievement was some valuable additions to the accuracy of the charts and increased sledging expertise. Markham described this as the greatest example of sledge-travelling ever undertaken, covering 7,025 miles of foot traffic and discovering 1,225 miles of new ground, but there were too many delays, which rendered McClintock's mind busy 'with a sort of magic-lantern representation of the past, the present, and the future, resisting for weary hours the necessary repose'.[20] Amid the triumphs, sledging could be brutal. In April 1851 George Malcolm, captain of the hold of *Resolute* and native of Dundee, died from exhaustion and frostbite, 'brought on while labouring as captain of the sledge *Excellent*', virtually expiring at his post. He was replaced by

James Fox, a native of Portpatrick, Wigtownshire. Even an enthusiast like McClintock must have been glad to be on the way home by August.[21]

McClintock was given his first command in February 1852. His ship was *Intrepid*, a tender, which was to function in support of Henry Kellett's *Resolute* as a unit within the flotilla that was disastrously entrusted to Edward Belcher. The venture also comprised the ships *Assistance*, *Pioneer* and *Resolute*, and was meant to represent the last searching expedition paid for by the Admiralty. Of twenty-five men on McClintock's ship, seventeen had experience of Arctic searches.[22] His excursions were certainly intense. In each successive season, we are told, he allegedly broke the record for longest distance by sledge hitherto achieved, claiming on this occasion 1,210 miles between 4 April and 18 July around the Melville Islands, partially explored by Parry in 1819. The tally might have been higher but, probably after finding prints of Parry's hand cart surviving at Cape Dundas, McClintock had been smitten with the crazy idea that wheeled carts would be a great asset in travelling overland.[23] Leopold McClintock solemnly tells his readers that

> In crossing rocky ground, when one wheel or the other was almost constantly brought up, the man whose duty it was to guide the cart by the pole in front, was tossed about from side to side like a shuttlecock; he had to cling to it to prevent being knocked over, and to exert great patience, skill and temper; in going down-hill it was a post of real danger. In every difficulty we found our nautical education a most valuable acquisition; and for downright hard tugging, no men could have endured such fatigue, unless, like seamen, they had been inured from boyhood to dragging at ropes.[24]

The kindest thing that can be said for Edward Belcher is that he was not a well man. He was an officer with wide experience of the Pacific, China and East Indies as well as the Arctic, where he was much involved in man-hauled sledging, but in later life he seemed to lose such limited charm as he allegedly once possessed, as well as suffering some sort of mental collapse. McClintock's biographer Markham held Belcher in utter contempt, convinced that he was unfit for a command that should have gone to the two much younger officers, McClintock and Osborn. Instead, the Navy chose 'the very last man who should have been selected', with a track record of misery, disaster and failure. Belcher's final visit to the Arctic, arrogantly chronicled in his two-volume *Last of the Arctic Voyages*, culminated in his orders to abandon four of the five ships for which he was responsible. Kellet objected but obeyed, as did McClintock, protesting strongly, despite his recent appointment as commander of the steam tender *Intrepid*. The automatic penalty for such treatment of one ship, let alone four, was court-martial, but all involved were exonerated. Infamously Belcher's sword was returned to him in a total silence that screamed disapproval. Little had changed since Richardson's early experience in the Navy, as the top brass closed ranks in defence.

Resolute was initially ice-bound in 1853 and subsequently drifted, an empty vessel, for 1,200 miles to be picked up in 1855 by an American whaler, James Boddington, off Cape Walsingham, Baffin Island. On boarding, the Americans discovered 'a massive table on which was a metal teapot, glistening as if new, also a large volume of Scott's family Bible [which seems unlikely], together with glasses and decanters filled with choice liquors [surprisingly]'. Nearby was Captain Kellett's chair, 'a piece of massive furniture, over which had been thrown, as if to protect this seat from vulgar occupation, the royal flag of Great Britain'.

Meanwhile Jane Franklin invested much time and energy in protecting and refining the memory of her husband. Her one and only appearance in *Household Words* occurred on 25 April 1857 in a planned pitch, drawing upon two letters she had already sent the Admiralty and a missive she addressed to Prime Minister Palmerston, attempting to persuade the Government into another expedition. She heatedly made it known that if all overtures failed she was prepared to spend her own money on the project. She thought that there might still be some survivors residing with the Inuit, who would have information about papers and letters addressed to Navy wives and children. Side benefits would be geographical discoveries and possible scientific advances, especially regarding magnetism. All thinking persons supported the proposal. The Americans had refurbished *Resolute* and magnanimously restored it to Queen Victoria in December 1856, 'as a lively token of the deep interest and sympathy felt by them in the great cause of humanity'. Lady Franklin hoped, as did her transatlantic sympathisers, that the restored ship could play a part in a new expedition but it was not to be. *Resolute* was decommissioned in 1879.[25] A further American link was represented by James Gordon Bennett whose father, also James Gordon Bennet, founded the New York Herald. Bennett senior was a Scot, born in Keith, Banffshire, who rose to become a major influence on the development of the US newspaper business. His heir, Bennett Junior, sponsored, through and for his paper, Henry Morton Stanley's meeting with David Livingstone in East

Africa. Ever in search of the sensational, he went on to fund, in association with Lady Franklin, Frederick Schwatka's search for Franklin relics. It was Schwatka who named Starvation Cove on the American mainland, where the last of Franklin's men met their doom.[26]

Lady Franklin considered it premature to assume that John Rae had finally solved the mystery of the Franklin ships in 1854. There could have been other survivors, in other locations. Others agreed, hence the commissioning of Anderson and Stewart to verify Rae's information. She dismissed this response as pathetic – a birchbark canoe sent down the Great Fish River by HBC! Also, disgracefully, Lady Franklin's missives to the Government had been ignored. Anderson was convinced that answers to their questions would be found in King William's Land. Lady Franklin was urging 'a sacred claim' upon Britain. Once more, authority was deaf to her requests; the stalling continued. She demanded that, at the very least, the bones of the dead should be gathered together, the buried records unearthed or recovered from the hands of the Inuit and 'above all, that their last written words . . . be saved from destruction. A mission so sacred is worthy of a government which has grudged and spared nothing for its heroic soldiers and sailors in other fields of warfare . . . This final and exhausting search is all I seek in behalf of the first and only martyrs to Arctic discovery in modern times . . .' Not quite all, but the lady was not for backing down. Undaunted,

> she will sacrifice her whole fortune, devote her life's blood and energy to the work cast upon her woman's hands . . . She does not ask the nation for a penny . . . Will the public suffer this request also to be refused? If it be refused, if it be churlishly left to one woman to do the duty of a people, then will one woman accept her fate? She will prepare as well as equip her own vessel. Volunteers will man it; and will bring home we trust, such tidings as will put our Admiralty Lords to eternal shame.[27]

Following the Belcher fiasco, McClintock was essentially on half-pay, out of work, until he was rescued by Lady Franklin's offer of command on *Fox*, which he accepted without hesitation. She telegraphed him 'Your leave is granted; the *Fox* is mine; the refit will commence immediately.' On 30 June 1857 he sailed from Aberdeen on *Fox* (as did William Penny, once again commanding *Lady Franklin* and *Sophia*). McClintock's second-in-command was Lieutenant R.N. Hobson, son of the first Governor of New Zealand, who joined the Navy in 1845, with Allen W. Young of the Merchant Navy as sailing-master, and David Walker from Belfast as doctor and naturalist. No Scots can be identified, with the possible exception of Robert Scott, chief stoker, but the preface to McClintock's book *Voyage of the Fox* was written by the Highland Scot Roderick Murchison, scientist and imperialist, one of the most famous and influential geologists of his day, and a great admirer of both McClintock and Lady Jane Franklin.[28] The Royal Society donated £50 for magnetic and other instruments, and McClintock was elected a member of the Royal Victoria Yacht Club, but only 'for the period of my voyage'. Lady Franklin, who was still concerned about the 'unspeakably precious documents of the expedition, public and private, hoped that he could confirm her husband's claim to the earliest discovery of the passage' by 'these martyrs in a noble cause, achieved at their last extremity, after five long years of labour and suffering'.

Then they were off by way of the familiar route – Pentland Firth, Orkney, Cape Farewell, Godthab (Nuuk) and the charming village of Upernavik. En route McClintock managed to acquire twenty-nine sledging dogs, a little Inuit help and the interpretative skills of Carl Petersen, recruited at Disko Island, where the crew dug out seven tons of coal to feed *Fox*'s furnace, increasingly aware that they were doomed to a 'long winter of absolute inutility'. The organ presented by Prince Albert was set up for a third time, helping to relieve the monotony of stasis. Extra grog was issued on Guy Fawkes Day. There was a burial after Scott the stoker's fatal fall down a hatchway on the ship. Otherwise, the winter was fairly unremarkable.

In April 1858 they visited Holsteinborg (Sisimiut). Whalers supplied them with information, advice, newspapers, potatoes and hospitality. McClintock sailed for Women's Island (Upernavik), remarking that on one of the isles a runestone had been found dated 1135.[29] In June the company met up with Captain Deuchars of *Tay*, who had lost his ship three years earlier, though all of his crew were saved. Eventually *Fox* reached Cape York where the 'Arctic Highlanders' were worrying about their reduction in numbers. This was turning into a sadly unproductive voyage. Heading across Melville Bay their ship was beset for 242 days: 'The Tinker had come round and soldered us in',[30] as the seamen say, drifting south 1,385 miles into Davis Strait, a possible record drift. The ship battled and bored through 13-foot waves, slicing large chunks of ice and dodging bergs before, on Easter Sunday 1858, they managed to return to Holsteinborg for another assault on Melville Bay.[31] McClintock understood how men's hair could turn grey in a single night!

18 'Disko Island', from John Ross, *A Voyage of Discovery* (London, 1819).

19 'Crew of *Isabella* and *Alexander* Sawing a Passage through the Ice', from John Ross,
A Voyage of Discovery (London, 1819).

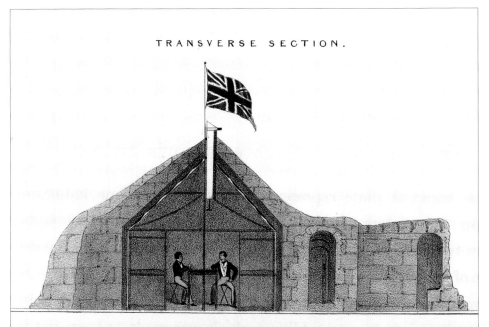

TRANSVERSE SECTION.

LATITUDE 72° 46' 46" N. LONGITUDE. 91° 47'. W.

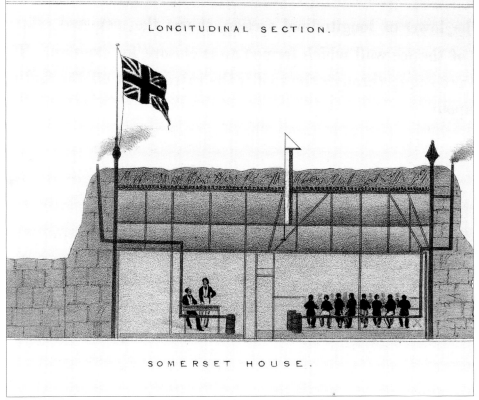

LONGITUDINAL SECTION.

SOMERSET HOUSE.

20 'Somerset House, Transverse and Longitudinal Sections', from John Ross, *Narrative of a Second Voyage in Search of the North-West Passage* (London, 1835). This building was constructed to house the officers and crew of the Ross expedition during the winter of 1832–3.

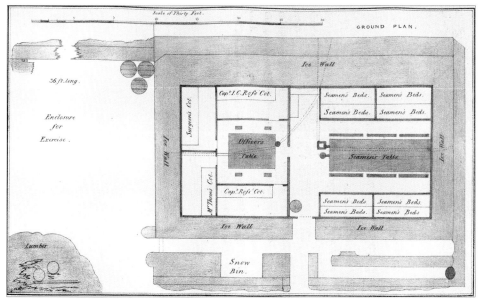

21 'Somerset House, Floor Plan', from John Ross, *Narrative of a Second Voyage in Search of the North-West Passage* (London, 1835).

22 'Victory Crew Saved by *Isabella*', from John Ross, *Narrative of a Second Voyage in Search of the North-West Passage* (London, 1835).

23 'Victoria Harbour', from John Ross, *Narrative of a Second Voyage in Search of the North-West Passage* (London, 1835).

24 'Departure of Captn. Ross from Woolwich on his last expedition May 23rd, 1829', from Robert Huish, *The Last Voyage of Capt. Sir John Ross, . . .* (London, 1835)

25 Hudson's Bay Company trading post, Fort Ross, Somerset Island, Kitikmeot, Nunavut.
(Photograph by Lizanne Henderson © padeapix)

26 Beechey Island (Iluvialiut), Wellington Channel, Nunavut: graves of John Torrington, William Braine and John Hartnell, from the lost Franklin expedition of 1845–6.
(Photograph by Lizanne Henderson © padeapix)

27 Lieutenant Joseph René Bellot, from *Memoirs of Lieutenant Joseph René Bellot* (London, 1855).
Bellot was second-in-command on William Kennedy's expedition of 1851–2 to find the lost
Franklin expedition.

28 Raven at Royal Canadian Mounted Police outpost, Port Dundas Harbour, Devon Island, Qikiqtaaluk, Nunavut. John Richardson considered ravens to be the most intriguing of the birds to haunt the Arctic. (Photograph by Lizanne Henderson © padeapix)

29 Little auk or dovekie (*Alle alle*), Flugesangen, Svalbard. These birds provided welcome food for the crews of the expeditions. (Photograph by Lizanne Henderson © padeapix)

30 Bloody Falls, Coppermine River, Kugluktuk, Nunavut. Several of the expeditions had to negotiate these falls. (Photograph by Lizanne Henderson © padeapix)

31 Thule Burial Chamber, Qilakitsoq, Greenland. (Photograph by Lizanne Henderson © padeapix)

He checked out rumours of wrecked ships from the Inuit of Pond Inlet but any reported sightings were much older than 1845 and hence irrelevant, probably referring to whaleships. No-one he consulted had heard of the discoveries of Anderson and Stewart.

Moving west, a story surfaced that some local residents had been poisoned through consuming food from a cache at Navy Board Inlet, briefly generating the speculation that Franklin's men might have sampled the same deadly fodder. When a seaman fell overboard near Cape Riley, McClintock jumped in to save him. At Beechey Island a memorial presented by Lady Franklin in honour of her husband and all on *Terror* and *Erebus* was erected. The inscription includes Crozier, Fitzjames 'and all their gallant brothers and faithful companions who have suffered and perished in the cause of science and the service of their country', whence they 'issued forth to conquer difficulties or to die'. Needless to say, death would not have been an option actively sought. This was merely Mrs Franklin's latest embellishment of her husband's bogus cultification. It also commemorates the grief of 'their admiring countrymen and friends, and the anguish, subdued by faith, of her who has lost in the heroic leader of the expedition, the most devoted and affectionate of husbands'.[32] The true significance of the memorial was that she had finally accepted the inevitable: Franklin, in his wife's imagination a conquering nonpareil but in reality no hero, was dead.

Leaving Beechey, McClintock first tried Peel Sound (to the east of Prince of Wales Island) but because of the ever-present enemy, ice, he was forced to seek the other side of the Boothia Peninsula, retreating via Barrow Strait to Port Leopold. Sailing south, opposite Fury Beach, he wondered whether Bellot Strait really existed: 'If so is it free of ice?' He found shelter at Port Kennedy. After failing for a third time to conquer the Strait he took a walk to John Ross's Possession Point of 1829, where he found a few stones piled up on two boulders, under each of which a halfpenny (ha'penny) had been deposited.[33] Here McClintock showed that the Scots part of his Scots-Irishness was alive and well: he pocketed one of the coins! (When Robert Service, the Scottish rhymer of the Yukon and Canada, asked his granny why he was given a ha'penny to put in the collection plate at the kirk, she replied, 'Cos I havnae got a farthing.' As a wise person once observed, it still costs Scots a fortune to live down stories like these!)

Currents pushed *Fox* eastwards out of Bellot Strait, the appearance of which was 'precisely that of a Greenland Fjord, twenty miles long and scarcely a mile wide in the narrowest part', with granitic shores 'bold and lofty', displaying a fine sprinkling of vegetation. McClintock enjoyed walking in 'this wondrous rough country'. On the north shore of the strait, a 10-mile-long loch was named Macgregor Laird for an interesting expedition subscriber from Greenock, who was a pioneer of steamships, an African trader and anti-slavery campaigner. The animal and bird population of Bellot Strait provided ample nourishment. Carl Petersen pronounced peregrine falcons the best of beef and the young birds 'tender and white as chicken'. When a biscuit cask (packed in 1857) was opened, completely intact and waterproof, 'a living mouse was discovered therein'. McClintock made at least six unsuccessful attempts to push through Bellot Strait to the west but had to opt for over-wintering at Port Kennedy. There was a reasonably plentiful supply of game, especially reindeer. Two observatories were built out of snow, one for hourly, the other for monthly, magnetic observations.

*

William Penny, commanding *Lady Franklin* and *Sophia*, had a combined crew of about forty. Captain John Cheyne was assigned to *Sophia*. Penny was a founder, with others, of the Aberdeen Arctic Company, which hoped to find new 'fishing' ground and bountiful whaling in Cumberland Sound. If a man is to be judged and characterised by the way he treats his wife, Penny is a fine example. In June 1857 his wife sailed with him, accompanied by their son Billie. This was Margaret's maiden voyage; a Moravian missionary, Brother Mättaus Warmow, was also on board, hoping to fish for Inuit souls. Erskine Grant, aged twenty-one, was ship's doctor, of whom Mrs P. reported 'The Dr. has managed to reach the crow's nest today', an achievement because he had recently been depressed and suicidal. She became the first-known European woman to over-winter in Cumberland Sound. Even more remarkably she was placed in charge of the ship's journal and, occasionally, of the ship. She was the sole female among twenty-five crew on *Lady Franklin*; there were seventeen crew on *Sophia*, fourteen of whom were Shetlanders, recruited in Aberdeen.[34]

Margaret met twice with Tackitrow, the younger sister of the Inuit boy Eenoo (see Chapter 7), whom she had previously met in the UK. As a result of encountering Charles Francis Hall, who called her Hannah, Tackitrow became, for a time, probably the most famous representative of her people. When left in charge, Margaret admitted she felt 'strange to be left alone in this wild country, though everybody on board is kind to me'. She disapproved of Brother Warmow laughing at St Peter for thinking he could walk upon

334

the sea. Penny and Margaret had serious problems with Alexander Stewart, who was now part of the company and captain of *Alibi* (an Aberdeen whaling ship), no longer a valued comrade but a tiresome and outspoken challenger of Penny's authority. As Professor Ross points out, Margaret's journal is most illuminating on the mutual dependency of the whalers and the Inuit of Cumberland Sound (though he suggests that she may have suffered seasonal affective disorder in the depths of midwinter). She admired their snow-houses ('I could live in one very well') and did not detect any disagreements among her Inuit friends; all were devoted to their children. Her snug deerskin trousers and boots, a sealskin bonnet and her husband's greatcoat enabled her to enjoy the outdoors. Penny insisted that everyone should exercise. On 12 December all, including the Inuit, were given a half-day holiday to celebrate Margaret's birthday with three hearty cheers and dancing from 4 till 10. Erskine Grant proposed her health after dinner, though she reported 'I must not for a moment suppose I was entitled to all the compliments he paid me'. Son Billie, developing his own interests, disappeared for a couple of days on different occasions when he was off with the Inuit hunters.

On New Year's Day a splendid dinner was enjoyed by all, including the sailors and seventy Inuit, who contributed six salmon and two quarters of deer. Throughout Margaret's visit to the Arctic, she held nightly tea parties, making twenty to thirty cups for the women who were 'my Esquimaux friends'. These women copied some of her (indoor) clothes, and she sampled some of theirs. She became involved, along with the rest of the community, in floe whaling, where the sea meets the ice, which melts, opening up the water to beluga, narwhal and bowhead caught on the shore. Penny proudly reported that his wife had been a blessing for all on board. On their return in 1858, the Aberdeen Arctic Company presented her with a silver tea set but her most valued gift was her year in the north: the beauty, the mystery, the challenge of the Arctic and her interaction with its people.[35]

*

Fox spent eight months during the winter of 1857 trapped in the ice off Melville Bay, and the crew found themselves drifting southwards with the floes. In 1858 the voyage was able to continue towards Bellot Strait where they would over-winter. Preparatory to planned searches in 1859, McClintock, his second-in-command Hobson and sailing-master Young organised dog-sledges to establish caches and to meet any Inuit who might have useful information, before spreading out to Arcedeckne Island (off the south-west corner of Somerset Island) and Prince of Wales Island to the west, and Fury Beach to the east. Arcedeckne was named for the commodore of the Royal London Yacht Club; there was no relief from the dismal desecration of Arctic onomastics. The captain developed a scheme of four men to one sledge, each responsible for 200 lb weight starting out, plus one dog-sledge with a driver and seven dogs, each with 100 lb weight. Hobson was assigned to the north coast of King William Island, while the south coast of Prince of Wales Island, and the stretch between Four Rivers Bay (JCR's furthest in 1849), Cape Bird and Bellot Strait was allocated to Allen Young. In early November 1858, things were so dull that McClintock lamented that 'no amount of ingenuity could make a diary worth the paper it is written on'. George Brand the engineer died of apoplexy. By early December, animals were scarce. No school was organised, but Allen Young taught a few men navigation. There was a general appetite for fresh meat and vegetables, 'perhaps because they cannot be obtained'. On only four days out of fourteen was it possible to walk outside. There was some largesse at Christmas, the temperature offering seasonal cheer of between 76 and 80 °F below zero. New Year was greeted with music and song. The sun was glimpsed at the end of January.[36]

By 1 March 1859 McClintock and Carl Petersen had almost reached the site of the Magnetic North Pole at Cape Adelaide on the Boothia Peninsula when, to their delight, they fell in with four Inuit, though the effect was rather spoiled when they both buckled on revolvers, while, in contrast, the Inuit put down their spears and received them without any hint of surprise or hostility.

The Inuit were paid a needle each to build a snow-house in less than half the time it took McClintock and Petersen. They noticed a naval button worn by an Inuk, and soon there appeared some forty Inuit women, children and men, who displayed relics from the lost ships that were traded. Items acquired included six silver spoons and forks, a silver medal belonging to Alexander McDonald (assistant surgeon on *Terror*), part of a gold chain, some buttons, knives, bows and arrows made of wood, and metal from a wrecked ship, found on 'an island where there are salmon', which signified a river. The Inuit knew there had been starving white men on this island but they had never seen them (although, surprisingly, one Inuk had been to Repulse Bay, where he had met seven members of Rae's party). The older folk remembered the appearance, in 1829, of John Ross's ship *Victory*. An old man told McClintock that his name was Ooblooria and he had been employed by James Clark Ross as a guide. Indeed, he asked after Ross by his Inuit name of

'Aglugga'. McClintock enquired if the Inuk who had been given the wooden leg was still to the fore. Petersen explained that the villagers did not favour mention of the dead, but he identified the man's daughter. Another man had seen human bones on the island, as well as kabloona graves. Petersen was told of a three-masted ship that was crushed by the ice to the west of King William's Island (named 'Land' by John Ross, who mistakenly thought it was a peninsula). When the ship sank, all potential booty was lost, although all aboard were saved. There was no information about the other ship.[37]

The dog-sleds proved invaluable, if occasionally difficult. McClintock returned to *Fox*. Allen Young, sailing-master, collected 8 hundredweight (cwt) of sugar from Fury Beach. The dogs took matters into their own paws when the going became really tough, bringing all to a standstill, suggesting the humans themselves should portage over hummocks and other obstacles. McClintock remarked that 'wild living' in the Arctic made the tame work of writing up a journal difficult.

McClintock confides that he did not look at his journal between 25 March and 24 June 1859 but states that in the momentous interval he had visited Montreal Island, completed the encirclement of King William Island (Qikiqtaq), walked through 'the only feasible Northwest Passage' and discovered the fate of *Erebus* and *Terror*. His party advanced by way of Long Lake, or Macgregor Laird, penetrating beyond Arcedeckne Island. This presumably was the walk through the Northwest Passage to which he referred. With his associates he met up once again with the folk they had encountered in February who told him that the other ship had been wrecked at a place called Oot-loo-lik; from it the Inuit had acquired a good deal of wood and some other objects and scraps. More interesting to the Britons were knives that they bought, thought to be made from naval swords or cutlasses. The surviving whites had departed for the 'large river'. A young man told them that the body of very large man with long teeth had been found in the ship.

McClintock entered Wellington Strait, crossing thereafter to Matty Island, where they found evidence that the few residents had left for Neitchillee. They next tried the south shore of King William Island, where they found a snow-village and about a dozen huts housing thirty or forty Inuit. From them they made a number of purchases – six pieces of silver plate bearing the crests of Franklin, Crozier, Fairholme and McDonald, bows and arrows fashioned from English woods, uniform buttons, silver spoons and forks, and a heavy sledge which they had no means of transporting. Though McClintock described the Inuit as 'good-humoured' they indulged the by now expected predilection to thieve, while assuring the whites '*Kammik toomee*' ('we are friends'). He was told he would find more Inuit on the west coast of King William Island only five days away.

On the wrecked ship, the Inuit of Qikiqtaq told them, there had been many books but all were destroyed by the weather. An old woman told Petersen that many whites never made it to the Great Fish River; some dropped, some were buried and some not. Visits to the Great Fish River and Montreal Island (in the mouth of the river) by McClintock's party did not yield much more enlightenment on the fate of Franklin's ships, though Inuit who were questioned seemed nervous and anxious, almost as if they were suspected of playing a role in their demise. A day at Barrow's Inlet at the mouth of the river added nothing to their knowledge, nor did Dease and Simpson's Strait. West of Point Richardson they crossed King William Island, examining the south coast as they made for Cape Herschel. On a gravel ridge near the shore, McClintock found a skeleton lying face-down, the bones bleached, with scraps of clothing attached. There was also a pocket-book frozen solid. The remains were those of a steward or officer's servant, who wore a blue jacket and pilot cloth greatcoat, also known as a 'p' or 'pea' jacket or coat. Nearby were a clothes brush and a horn pocket-comb. Here was corroboration of what an old Inuit woman had reported, as translated by Petersen: 'they fell down and died as they walked along'.

The captain continued to explore along the south shore of King William Island, an opportunity to visit Simpson's cairn, built 1839, at the summit of Cape Herschel. It was partially destroyed, only some 4 feet of height remaining. It revealed no information, much to McClintock's disappointment; there was no record of those 'martyrs of their country's fame'. However, compensation was very close. Hobson proved to be the hero of the hour or, as some would claim, of the century. McClintock had assigned him the west of King William Island, having a shrewd suspicion that it would reveal important information, the discovery of which would give the younger man's career a significant boost. As anyone interested in the Franklin catastrophe knows, at Victory Point on the north-west coast of King William Island, Hobson discovered incontrovertible evidence of the greatest Arctic disaster in British history, two separate messages on one piece of paper, constituting the first written testimony that *Erebus* and *Terror* had wintered on Cornwallis Island, having spent the previous winter at Beechey.

Twelve miles from Cape Herschel, in May 1859, McClintock found the cairn built by Hobson's party only a week earlier. The two messages contained within were written on one of the forms designed to be placed in a Navy messenger bottle and thrown overboard as sea-mail, the only truly comprehensible written evidence to emerge so far.

28 of May 1847

H.M.S. ships *Erebus* and *Terror* Wintered in the Ice in Lat. 70°5' N Long. 98°23' W Having wintered in 1846–7 [sic] at Beechey Island in Lat 74°43'28' N Long 91°39'15' W

After having ascended Wellington Channel to Lat 77° and returned by the West side of Cornwallis Island.

Sir John Franklin commanding the Expedition.

All well

Party consisting of 2 Officers and 6 Men left the ships on Monday 24th May 1847.

[signed] Gm. Gore, Lieut.

[signed] Chas. F. Des Voeux, Mate

25th April 1848

HM Ships *Terror* and *Erebus* were deserted on the 22nd April 5 leagues NNW of this having been beset since 12th Sept 1846.

The officers and crews consisting of 105 souls under the command of Captain F.R.M. Crozier landed here – in Lat. 69°37'42' Long. 98°41'.

This paper was found by Lt Irving under the cairn supposed to have been built by Sir James Ross in 1831 – 4 miles to the Northward – where it had been deposited by the late Commander Gore in ~~May~~ *June 1847.*

Sir James Ross' pillar has not however been found and the paper has been transferred to this position which is that in which Sir J. Ross' pillar was erected.

Sir John Franklin died on the 11th of June 1847 and the total loss by deaths in the Expedition has been to this date 9 officers and 15 men.

[signed] F. R. M. Crozier Captain & Senior Offr

And start on tomorrow 26th for Backs Fish River

[signed] James Fitzjames Captain HMS Erebus[38]

McClintock lamented that only twelve short months separated 'All Well' from dreaded hard news of the disaster. He surmised that Captain Crozier endeavoured to save his starving men, 105 souls in all, from a terrible death by retreating to the Hudson Bay territories up the Great Fish River. Of course, there is no certainty about how many men were in a position to make the attempt, or how many had already died in addition to the twenty-four mentioned in the document. As McClintock wrote, 'A sad tale was never told in fewer words; there is something deeply touching in their extreme simplicity.' He believed the men abandoned ship because the food supplies were exhausted, and scurvy almost certainly played a part, but his suggestion that the refugees had shed clothing as they retreated is not convincing. Did these items represent a desperate attempt by the crew to garner some warmth, knowing something of the horrendously exposed area into which they were headed, or had they been collected for some reason by, or for, the Inuit who often coveted pieces of cloth as adornments and who possibly regarded them as future objects of barter? Neither suggestion seems convincing.

As Hobson immediately noted, there was a mistake in the first message. The ships wintered at Beechey 1845–6, not 1846–7. The overwhelming matter was of course the report of Franklin's death on 11 June 1847, but it is interesting that two officers and six men left the ships a month earlier, without explanation. Also, as the message states, the paper was found by Lieutenant John Irving under the cairn supposed to have been built by Sir James Ross in 1831 but which no longer existed. The true site of Ross's 'pillar' had been moved from 4 miles north to its present position where the messages were found. The great trek to Back's River was to begin next day, 26 April 1848. In one year Hallelujah had become Hell.

Franklin's ships had sailed the Greenland coast by way of Disko, crossing Baffin Bay into Lancaster Sound to Beechey Island where they wintered 1845–6. They next sailed up the Wellington Channel somewhat to the north of Cornwallis Island before turning south to follow the west coast of the island, returning to Beechey in 1846–7. Next, they sailed down Peel Sound, which separates Prince of Wales Island and Somerset Island, to what is now Franklin Strait, west of the Boothia Peninsula. Ahead of them was King William Island, where they came to grief.

Confronting this moving example of 'the medium is the message' a century before Canadian thinker Marshall McLuhan articulated the concept, it is tempting to pause.[39] If, as McLuhan seems to say, the 'medium' is anything that extends our understanding as human beings, then we have an iconic assemblage of peerless icons coalescing into one extraordinary metaphor representing the sublimation of the Franklin phenomenon. Here was a message in a rusting tin, the final communications of dying men on the rock-shattered coast of King William Island, Nunavut, at the centre of the Canadian Arctic, named for a far-off British king (a pathetic specimen of kingship, William IV) for no reason save that he and the island existed. It is separated from the Boothia Peninsula by the James Ross Strait to the north-east and Rae Strait to the east, which commemorate two Scots who were among the greatest Arctic explorers of the century. To the west is Victoria Strait and, beyond, Victoria Island. South is Simpson Strait with, further on, the Adelaide Peninsula, while south-west is Queen Maud Gulf named by Roald Amundsen for a Norwegian queen, Maud of Wales.

The wreck of *Erebus* is at the bottom of the gulf west of O'Reilly and south of King William Island. Sammy Kogvik, an Inuit Canadian Ranger, recalled a mast sticking through the ice in, appropriately enough, Terror Bay on the south coast of King William Island. Both finds are important in strengthening Canada's Arctic claims. Over the years, Inuit suggestions about the whereabouts of both ships were consistently ignored. Parks Canada is quoted as expressing 'the hope that written materials may be found' in what is thought to have been Crozier's cabin. *Plus ça change, plus c'est la meme chose.* The obsession with finding a paper trail, while understandable, was tedious in 1850 and has become more so with the passing of time, though of course any such information will be welcomed. Hopefully the two ships, together representing the palladium of British and Canadian Arctic exploration, will eventually reveal their secrets to Inuit and kabloonas alike.[40]

On the west coast of King William Island, McClintock's company investigated a large boat, 28 foot long and 7 foot 3 inches wide, another of Hobson's discoveries. It was mounted on a sledge containing lots of tattered clothes. The location of the boat suggested it was intended for the Great Fish River. The boat also contained two skeletons, so how much space was left for the abandoned clothes? Near one of the victims was a pair of worked calfskin slippers, 'the edges bound with red silk ribbon'; also a pair of shooting half-boots. Beside the other, better preserved, fur-clad remains were five watches and two double-barrelled guns, each having one barrel cocked. The collection was much too large and varied for itemisation but the following may suffice as a sample: shoes, toiletries, tools, ammunition, cooking stoves, shovels, medicines, a dip circle with two needles, bar magnets and a light horizontal needle, cutlery and twenty-six pieces of plate, of which eight bore

Franklin's crest, other items displayed the insignia of nine different officers, including Franklin, Crozier, Fairholme and McDonald. McClintock was interested in 'eight to ten fir poles' from 5 to 10 feet long and 2½ inches in diameter, converted into spear handles and tent poles, as well as a kayak paddle and two large snow-shovels possibly made from a boat's bottom boards. There were no graves. The boat was 150 miles from Montreal Island. Ever since these relics were discovered, pundits have been trying to invent stories to explain them.

McClintock seems to have been a decent individual, a loyal and competent but unremarkable sailor who was promoted to lieutenant after fourteen years in the Navy. Two lucky breaks greatly enhanced his profile. The first was in 1848–9 when he had the good fortune to serve on the searching expedition led by James Clark Ross, who taught him a great deal about sledging techniques when the two explored the north and west coasts of Somerset Island, mapping some 150 miles. McClintock, following Ross, truly sledged his way to glory; he made much greater use of man-sledging, largely because of the difficulty of acquiring and training dogs. He claimed that during the Franklin search a total of over 40,000 miles had been sledged, including 8,000 miles of coastline. He calculated that on long journeys the men lost around 12 lb, making about 13 miles a day, while the same number of canines could drag half the same load for 27 miles. The reward for the information on the fate of the Franklin expedition was £5,000, £1,500 of which was his, with the rest divided among his men. His knighthood was awarded in 1860; his *Voyage of the 'Fox' in the Arctic Seas*, published in 1859, is a very readable classic. He undoubtedly made a valuable contribution and he succeeded where many others had failed, but he depended greatly upon his predecessors because, in truth, the conquest of the Northwest Passage was demonstrably incremental. After the achievements of Rae, Anderson and Stewart it was fairly obvious what had to be done, and he did it.

13

DISCOVERING THE
NORTHWEST PASSAGE

What matters the name of the conqueror, provided the
victory is gained?

Joseph René Bellot

The search for Franklin became one of the largest rescue efforts in history.
Spread over two decades, it entailed over thirty expeditions, by land and sea,
and resulted in a few concrete clues but little circumstantial details as to the
fate of the doomed crew. What it did achieve was charting of the labyrinthine
Arctic waterways (including confirming the route of a Northwest Passage),
mapping of vast areas of the Canadian Arctic and laying the foundations that
would allow for Norwegian explorer Roald Amundsen's successful navigation
through the Northwest Passage in 1903–6. Throughout the entire period of
searching for a navigable route through the Arctic, there were also substantial
scientific and natural history discoveries made, as well as ethnological reports
on Inuit and Greenlandic culture garnered.

The first indications of possible Franklin whereabouts were discovered
by William Penny on the 1850 expedition. Penny's surgeon, Peter Cormack
Sutherland (from Latheron, Caithness), a graduate of Aberdeen University,
was a man with a serious interest in all that he encountered and a reliable
chronicler of the voyage. The most difficult period in the Arctic year for
ice-bound ships was the three months following Christmas. For scientists
like Sutherland there was the opportunity to probe the impact of deadly
cold on the content of his medical chest and glass bottles, frozen and
then shattered by ice. He also keenly investigated the properties of snow.
By way of diversion from the tedium of dark months spent on the ice the
men contrived to celebrate the anniversary of Penny's wedding anniversary.
A week later Queen Victoria's eleventh year of wedlock was also an excuse
for jollifications. As Gillies Ross points out, April, May and June were the

best months for expeditions on foot, before major ice-melt created serious impediments.[1]

The Rosses had pioneered sledging during their four years' confinement (1829–33), and James Clark Ross had subsequently refined techniques that were passed on to Leopold McClintock. The Navy gradually moved from dog haulage to men. Few Brits could master dogs as successfully as the Inuit but JCR worked hard to become proficient. Penny and Petersen brought these skills with them. As befitted a whaler, Penny also excelled on the sea but, despite his efforts and those of others, the *Erebus* and *Terror* were never located.[2] When they decided to head for home in mid August their major concern was the reception that awaited them and the expected disdain of a public that was hungry for positive news, of which there was none.

John Ross paid a final visit to Beechey in 1850 but there is no information why he did so, or the thoughts that the island may have engendered. He then sailed to Disko Island, where his interpreter Adam Beck made a deposition concerning the reports he had heard from the 'Arctic Highlanders'. Ross still adhered to the truth of Beck's story that Franklin, after wintering at Beechey, sailed to Northwest Greenland where all were murdered. He reflected that 'this may detain me another winter, and with 16 men I am not very able to cope with a numerous tribe of hostile savages; but I must and will try'. It is very sad to witness a man who, at first meeting had been greatly impressed by the Greenlanders, now losing his mind and his empathy. His claims became even more outrageous on his homeward return when, cheered on by hundreds, he played the role of conquering hero to the full. At an Ayr dinner he claimed his crew had discovered the graves on Beechey Island and Franklin's wintering place. He had sailed further up Wellington Channel than anyone else, sighting land beyond. *Felix* was the only ship that was not damaged. Second-in-command, Charles Phillips, had taken the flag, made by the bonnie lasses of Auld Ayr, 'to the utmost extremity of Cornwallis Island'.

Ross was also extremely critical of James Clark Ross, whose 1848–9 expedition he said had achieved 'absolutely nothing'; he maintained JCR's search parties were puny and lacking in ambition. JCR wasted time that could have been essential to a successful outcome, thus squandering resources and deploying men ineffectively. The whole rescue effort was 'one of the greatest calamities that has ever befallen our happy country'. Why did JCR arrive in Lancaster Sound so late and leave so early? How did it come about that at one point there were six ships in Wellington Channel? Those organisations (such as the Admiralty) and individuals responsible for authorising the expeditions did not consult sufficiently widely, impacting upon John Ross himself; 'it is quite manifest why such hostile and determined opposition met my pertinacious endeavours to realize my own particular views upon the subject . . . patronage and personal considerations were not entirely overlooked, in a case that involved the lives of so many men'.[3] Jane Franklin hit the mark when she observed that John Ross could not speak the truth but she erred in thinking he was 'deranged' in only one point. However, as already suggested, John Ross has some claim to be remembered as one of the greatest 'Arctics' of the nineteenth century, just on the crazy side of right and the right side of crazy, and famed for having rescued most of his crew from certain death during his second exploratory voyage.

*

The initial puzzle concerning the search for the Northwest Passage is why John Ross was selected in the first place since he had clearly stated, after the 1818 expedition, that he did not believe that it existed. Surely someone more receptive should have been in charge. He considered that, even if a narrow strait existed somewhere, 'it must be forever navigable, and there is not even a chance of ascertaining its existence, since all approach to the bottom of these bays are filled with ice'. The following year, in 1819, Parry asserted that 'of the existence of a Northwest Passage to the Pacific it is now scarcely possible to doubt'. In 1827 Beechey had reported that, 'the extent of land left unexplored between Point Turnagain and Icy Cape is comparatively so insignificant that, as regards the question of the northwest passage, it may be considered to be known'.[4] On the second Ross expedition (1829–33), John was able to report that 'we were sure we were on the continent of America'. Much of the hard work was down to JCR, who was later given leave from the Navy to assist his uncle in the production of his *Second Voyage* publication. In 1830, he ironically asked 'Will it be believed that I was not anxious to complete the survey of the north coast of America, that with so important an object almost within my very reach, I was not desirous to attain this great triumph?' He had accumulated enough information 'to succeed entirely in completing the survey of the north shore of America'.[5]

By sailing into Coronation Gulf in 1826, John Richardson claimed his men had the honour of 'completing a portion of the north-west passage, for which the reward of five thousand pounds was established' but unfortunately, since it was not contemplated 'that the discovery should be made from west to east, and in vessels so small as the *Dolphin* and *Union*, we could not lay claim to the pecuniary reward'. On a later occasion, Richardson reflected on his visit with Franklin, Back and Kendall in 1826, confiding that they had hoped to claim the parliamentary reward for those who navigated the Arctic Sea 'up to certain meridians'. His party 'accomplished the whole space' between the said meridians but the authorities ruled that the prize was for ships, not boats.[6]

In a letter to his brother in 1836, Thomas Simpson expected Alexander to congratulate him for finding the last link through the Arctic to the Pacific. He then wrote to his cousin, Governor George Simpson, in hopes of securing a financial reward for his success at reaching Point Barrow and solving a quest that had evaded European explorers since the sixteenth century. The achievements of Simpson and Dease in the 1830s included the determination of the long-sought Northwest Passage.

Robert McClure, a sadly troubled individual who searched for the Northwest Passage (as well as the lost Franklin expedition) via the Pacific during 1850–4 confided to his private journal: 'Can it be possible that so humble a creature as I am will be permitted to perform what has baffled the talented and wise for hundreds of years?' Describing the voyage, Sherard Osborn had no doubts that the captain's feelings would be properly appreciated, namely his 'chivalrous dependence upon God and a good cause', citing a misguided Belgian writer who later compared McClure's achievement to that of Moses' conquest of the Promised Land! In both journal and commentary, the propaganda level was clearly turned up to full power.[8]

Captain Allen Young, among many others, extended sympathy for the deceased of the Franklin expedition while celebrating heroic endeavour: 'They all perished and . . . their dearest consolation must have been that Englishmen would not rest until they had followed their footsteps'. The hype grew as the news of 'the holy cause' seeped out. In 1859 McClintock had 'rent the veil' to prove that Franklin had discovered the Northwest Passage, 'the last link, to forge which he sacrificed his life'.

> The cry was taken up by the press (to its honour) and perpetuated in all forms and in all types; thousands of pages were devoted to record it. Science wore a gladsome smile. The learned and the elegant in literature embalmed the glorious theme in undying

language; and the poet sung paeans exultant, in every number of which verse is capable.[9]

John Brown, who had published *The North-West Passage and the Plans for the Search for Sir John Franklin* (1860), a book which the *Bengal Hurkaru* pronounced 'full of the deepest interest, both scientific and human', bragged about England's great achievement. He rejoiced that Franklin and his gallant followers had 'fairly won the reward they have sealed with their lives'. *Fraser's Magazine* stated that Franklin had forged the wanting link in the chain, these comments leading to John Richardson's inspiring words placed on Franklin's statue in Waterloo Place, London: 'They sealed the last link with their lives.' It originally appeared in the eulogy of Franklin that Richardson wrote for the eighth edition of *Encyclopaedia Britannica* in 1856. It was also cited in a pamphlet that Lady Franklin sent to Dickens, who described Richardson's friendship and love of Franklin as 'one of the noblest things I ever knew in my life. It makes one's heart beat high, with a sort of sacred joy.'[10] It is not difficult to believe that, but for Richardson, Franklin's career could have ended in the Barrens. *Blackwood's Edinburgh Magazine* had 'no doubt that Franklin died knowing that the great work of his life was accomplished'. Most commentators came around to the view that 'Franklin before he died, enjoyed the comfort of knowing that he had done what he was sent to do', though of course nobody could prove it.[11]

There can be no doubt that John Rae was the first person to discover, by chance and unexpectedly, the first hard evidence of the fate of Franklin and his following. His success was dazzling compared with the dismal failures of other searchers. Rae enjoyed a full life after he left HBC in 1856, working for a while in a family business in Ontario. His plans to return to the Arctic were foiled when a ship commissioned for the purpose was wrecked in the Great Lakes. He advised on the future of HBC and guided some commercial trips, for example, on railway routes in Canada and the US. He married Kate Thomson, an 'Irish colleen' in 1860. He worked extensively, planning and visiting potential routes for the Atlantic Telegraph Company. He published on various topics drawn from his Canadian experience, lectured frequently and picked up honours (although not a knighthood), occasionally becoming upset when others claimed, or were given credit for achievements that were rightfully his. The British Navy never fully forgave him for his transcendence: the disturbing revelation of cannibalism.

Rae has a superb monument in Kirkwall Cathedral, and a plaque in Rae Strait. His birthplace in Orkney, the Hall of Clestrain, is currently undergoing restoration, and plaques in his honour have been placed in Westminster Abbey, at Hamilton, Canada, and at Lower Addison Gardens, London, his home from 1869 until his death in 1893. The proceedings of an excellent conference to mark the 200th anniversary of his birth have been published by the Orkney Heritage Society. On that occasion a statue was unveiled in Stromness. Several other books and publications have appeared over the years.

While not wishing to detract from his undoubted achievements, some of his admirers may have advanced claims that Rae would not himself have made. In recent years a most active supporter in this respect has been the Canadian writer Ken McGoogan. He has been challenged by Professor William Barr, a highly respected authority on Arctic exploration, who correctly notes, in opposition to McGoogan, that Rae never claimed to have discovered the Northwest Passage, nor could he have discovered the Rae Strait, which Leopold McClintock eventually detected five years later. It therefore follows that John Rae did not discover, nor did he ever claim to have discovered, the 'final link' in the passage.[12]

Canadian historian Janice Cavell has performed a useful service in pointing out a side of Rae often overlooked by the legions of admirers in his home country. He was a plain-speaking man who 'would tell it like it was' but was sometimes less willing to accept criticism than he was to dish it out. Hindsight indicated that he would have been well advised to suppress the issue of cannibalism until he arrived home in person. The leaking of that information to the press by the Admiralty was unforgivable, but equally *The Sun* went too far in stating that Rae seemed to be more concerned about his own reputation than he was about the emotions of victims. He alienated legions of mourners for Franklin, led by Lady Jane, who continued to clutch at smooth ice, but understandably he must have been extremely irritated by the views of people who did not know the first thing about the Arctic but were full of opinions, advice and platitudes. Rae's defence of the Inuit caused further offence because their supposedly primitive characteristics were regarded as the antithesis of English fortitude, duty, courage and religion. Additionally, Rae appeared to contradict himself in careless remarks about Inuit deception and morality. He also questioned the 'moral character and discipline of some of Franklin's crews' when berthed at Stromness. Some critics suspected that he schemed to acquire a reward from the Admiralty, for which he was nominated by HBC, but payment was refused on the grounds that his discoveries benefited the government more than the company. Also Rae retained, possibly by accident, some of the relics he brought back with him, which it was thought should have gone to the families.[13] His greatest offence was the one that was never mentioned, namely that he far outclassed the British Navy's finest, a fact that renders much of the case against him suspicious, since as we have seen the Senior Service was highly accomplished in sailing close to a truth of its own creation. Rae was a victim of English exceptionalism, nationalism and superiority.

Both Rosses were, like John Richardson, interred in England. John Ross died in 1856 and was buried in Kensal Green Cemetery, Kensington. James Clark Ross died only six years later to be buried in Aston Abbots, Buckinghamshire. Two islands in the lake of the local abbey are named Terror and Erebus. JCR also has a small plaque at his London home in Blackheath. None of these three men are revered in the land of their birth for their remarkable achievements, though moves are afoot to rectify this. Like John Rae they made the mistake of surviving their outstanding Arctic experiences, uncelebrated by a culture which inexplicably preferred its heroes dead rather than alive and flourishing, although, as naval officers and recognised heroes of exploration, all three received knighthoods. Rae did not. Their story does not detract from Rae's undoubted achievements but serves to place his talents and accomplishments in a wider context of Arctic endeavour than has often been the case among some of Rae's more dedicated devotees. I would propose that, irrespective of race, class, nationality, personal quarrels, rivalries and disagreements, all of those involved in this unprecedented epic of exploration and adventure, Inuit and kabloonas alike, were members of Team Arctic.[14]

*

The saga of course continues. There is now no doubt that the doomed mariners were reduced to cannibalism. Bones showing cut marks as a concomitant of de-fleshing have been meticulously examined to show proof of the last resort, to indicate that naval officers and crew were reduced (as were Inuit and First Nations), rarely but inevitably, to the supposedly unthinkable, in the final futile attempt to preserve life. The scientific evidence is incontrovertible, irrespective of the denials and disbeliefs of those who, lacking empathy or imagination, considered their countrymen utterly beyond such possibilities. Another persistent problem throughout the Arctic adventure was scurvy, even though John Ross had been well aware of the issue since 1818. It is remarkable, given that so many medical men were engaged on the ships, the disease continued to prove lethal, not least to those heading for Starvation Cove.

Few bones were returned to the homeland but it has been suggested that, in two cases, those repatriated were Scots. An Inuk by the name of In-nook-poo-zhee-jook informed the American explorer Charles Francis Hall in 1869 about sites where piles of bones had been found, some smashed open, presumably in search of marrow, together with mutilated corpses, the flesh of which had been hacked off, as well as skulls with holes in them. Hall also heard corroboratory evidence of similar discoveries. He took one complete skeleton back to the USA. It was clearly that of an officer who had worn a silk vest and who had a gold filling. The remains were shipped to England where they were examined by T.H. Huxley, who pronounced them to be those of Lieutenant Henry Thomas Dundas Le Vesconte of *Erebus*. They were interred below the Franklin Memorial at the Royal Naval College, Greenwich, to be exhumed and scrutinised once more when the monument underwent repair. Analysis of the tooth indicated that its owner had been brought up in east central Scotland, whereas Le Vesconte hailed from Devon. Furthermore, gold fillings were unusual in the 1840s. Facial reconstruction matched a daguerreotype of Harry Goodsir, surgeon and naturalist on *Terror*; his father was a close friend of Robert Nasmyth, the 'father of Scottish dentistry'. Harry's brother John was a leading anatomist who investigated the development and composition of teeth. Harry himself had researched anatomy and natural history and was conservator of Surgeons' Hall Museum, Edinburgh 1843–5, and collaborated with his brother John on a book on pathology.[15]

The second case of a Scot whose bones were possibly repatriated was John Irving, lieutenant on *Terror*. Irving was born in 1815, in Princes Street, Edinburgh, into a family originally from Dumfriesshire. He attended Edinburgh Academy and the Royal Naval Academy at Portsmouth, where he earned a silver medal for second place in mathematics, later found on what was thought to be his grave on King William Island.[16] Irving was not a natural seaman: he left the Navy to become a sheep rancher in New South Wales between 1836 and 1840, returning to Scotland in 1843 and was signed up for the Franklin expedition in 1845. Personality wise, he was regarded in the 1830s as hot-tempered, domineering and dictatorial, and his biographer, Benjamin Bell, concurred. However, an Orkney lady who shook hands with him as he sailed off to the Arctic in 1845 was impressed by his appearance of strength and calm decision and pronounced that 'A general feeling of sure success pervaded all'. Irving's captain on *Terror*, Francis Crozier, writing what would prove a final letter to James Clark Ross, confessed: 'In truth I am sadly lonely and when I look back to the last voyage I can see the cause and therefore no prospect of having a more joyous feeling.' Crozier was referring to his doomed love affair with Sophia Cracroft, but JCR was more concerned that Franklin's officers had very little experience of the Arctic. Crozier was afraid that *Erebus* and *Terror* would blunder into the ice and 'make a second 1824 out of it', a reference to Parry's abandonment of *Fury*. Furthermore, Crozier reputedly did not expect to return: 'Look at the state our commander's ship is in, everything in confusion; he is very decided in his own views but has not good judgement'. It was not a good sign when an important officer had apparently lost faith in his captain.

In February 1845, Irving told his sister-in-law Katie (with whom he corresponded on a wide range of topics) that he was hoping to go to the Arctic on a discovery voyage currently projected as 'not a service of much danger'. In April he reported to her that he had been engaged for the anticipated two-year expedition. He hoped Katie, like himself, would not 'labour under any presentiment of evil', but she could hardly have felt reassured when in the next sentence he recalled that in 1822 'only one half of Sir John Franklin's former party returned with him and our *Terror* in her last voyage with Captain Back was so crushed by the ice that she could not have kept afloat another day, before they managed to reach Loch Swilly'. As they prepared to sail, the ships were overloaded. He wrote for the last time from the Whalefish islands, Greenland. By then they had met their first Inuit. He reported that the expeditionaries had the advantage of the experience of all their predecessors, thus saving much time in uselessly looking for a passage where none exists. 'Everyone is suffering from chilblains due to the shift from summer to winter; feet and hands are swollen.' He included a small piece of *tripe-de-roche*, 'the fruit of Sir John Franklin', with the letter.[17]

He is next recorded on the precious message found by Lieutenant Hobson at Victory Point (see Chapter 12). Then Lieutenant Frederick Schwatka, while searching for Franklin relics in 1878–80, identified a grave at Terror Camp on the west side of King William Island as that of John Irving because of the presence of Irving's silver medal and some scraps of clothing that might have belonged to him. His fork was also found. Why would an explorer take a class medal to the Arctic? Several individualised silver plates were purchased by Rae from the Inuit, including a small silver plate with

Franklin's name engraved on it and his star of the Hanoverian Guelphic Order awarded in 1836 by William IV. The idea may have been that these objects identified their owners if the worst happened. Cutlery with insignia may have performed a similar function.[18] The Americans arranged for Irving and his attributed identifiers to be returned to Scotland.

Irving's native city conferred upon this unassuming young man, half-hearted sailor and accidental national hero, a memorable funeral in Dean Cemetery, Edinburgh, in 1881, attended by the great, the good, representatives of the Navy, the military and members of learned societies. The streets were lined with folk anxious to see the coffin go by. Irving's biographer remarked that many observers, who had considered the event as little more than 'a melancholy episode in our naval history', developed a 'not unnatural curiosity in regard to the individual, hitherto little known, who had suddenly and unexpectedly become the representative of a whole company of heroic men, whose memory their country had pleasure in honouring'.[19] They avoided, however, the clinging religiosity and sacral lexis that had been applied in England to Franklin and his cohorts. Many would have sympathised with the view of *The Times*: 'There must be an end to all things; we have paid our debt.'[20]

However, it is not certain that Irving actually belonged to the Arctic grave with which he was associated. A number of investigators have pointed out that his 'narrow hoose' (as graves were known in Scotland) would have consisted of very large stones that starving, forlorn and exhausted men would have been incapable of lifting. Also, the lair appeared over-elaborate for its purpose and the medal was found on the lip of the grave, possibly moved from somewhere else through the passing of the years. The remains in Edinburgh may therefore be those of a much loftier figure than poor Irving, interred when the men still had the strength to build the structure. Who that individual may be is at present unknown.

In 1846 John Ross wrote a farewell to the world which could well stand as a plea from so many of the 'Hyperborean heroes' that some of us seek to historicise or reduce. 'The past is now nearly the whole of my life, and I am naturally tenacious of all that concerns it. I can no longer, as in the days of my youth, look with comparative indifference on the past, flushed with a proud confidence of the honours which the future would bring me.' He hoped that any future biographer of his life would 'have a regard to honour, truth and justice', so that he would not have to complain, as he did of John Barrow, 'that when I looked for an historian I found a calumniator'.[21]

History is perhaps the greatest calumniator of all since it can always find some person, event or monument to shred or diminish, even when any of them might have been held up to posterity as inspirational. It is somehow appropriate that, while the tedious Franklin cult was growing, the Scottish contribution was largely ignored. There was an attempt, only partially successful, to ridicule John Ross's two books out of existence. Thomas Simpson's book was not greatly consulted and seems to have been as unpopular as he was. William Kennedy and Joseph René Bellot (posthumously) published interesting accounts of their experiences. John Rae wrote one small book and was seldom heard of outside of Orkney until R.I. Richards published Rae's biography in 1985. The major authorial success was John Richardson with several publications, notably his outstanding *Fauna Boreali-Americana*. Leopold McClintock also enjoyed great success with his *Voyage of the 'Fox' in the Arctic Seas*. I have been privileged to have visited many of the places mentioned in this book with my wife Lizanne, and I have enjoyed becoming acquainted with some of the nineteenth-century folk who, like John Ross, were calumniated. As the Bard wrote, 'Facts are chiels that winna ding.' To this day most of Scotland's Arctic explorers are not well known in their own country, yet their contribution is significant. It is to be hoped that this book serves as somewhat of a corrective.

APPENDIX: TIMELINE OF KEY EVENTS AND EXPEDITIONS

1576: Martin Frobisher's First Arctic Expedition

1610: Henry Hudson enters Hudson Bay and James Bay

1670: Founding of the Hudson's Bay Company

1770–1: Samuel Hearne, Coppermine River Expedition to the Arctic Ocean

1773: Constantine Phipps, Skeffington Lutwidge, North Pole Expedition, HMS *Carcass* and HMS *Racehorse*

1776–80: James Cook, Third Voyage to Pacific Ocean and Bering Strait, HMS *Resolution* and HMS *Discovery*

1779: James Cook killed in Hawai'i

1779: Founding of the North West Company

1789: Alexander Mackenzie, Mackenzie River Expedition to the Arctic Ocean

1791–5: George Vancouver, Pacific Northwest Expedition, HMS *Discovery*

1793: Alexander Mackenzie reaches Bella Coola, Pacific coast

1803–15: Napoleonic Wars

1818: David Buchan, John Franklin, Spitsbergen Expedition, HMS *Dorothea* and HMS *Trent*

1818: John Ross, James Clark Ross, William Parry, First Expedition, *Isabella* and *Alexander*

1818: John Ross encounters 'Arctic Highlanders' Etah Inughuit

1818: Publication of Mary Shelley, *Frankenstein*

1819–20: William Parry, James Clark Ross, Northwest Passage Lancaster Sound Expedition, HMS *Hecla* and HMS *Griper*

1819–22: John Franklin, George Back, John Richardson, Coppermine Expedition

1821: Merger between HBC and NWC

1821–3: William Parry, Francis Crozier, James Clark Ross, Northwest Passage Foxe Basin Expedition, HMS *Hecla* and HMS *Fury*

1822: William Scoresby completes his survey of Greenland coastline

1824–5: William Parry, Francis Crozier, James Clark Ross, Northwest Passage Prince Regent Inlet Expedition, HMS *Hecla* and HMS *Fury*

1825–7:	Mackenzie River Expedition: John Franklin, *Lion* and *Reliance*; John Richardson, *Dolphin* and *Union*
1825–7:	David Douglas, Second Expedition Fort Vancouver to Hudson Bay
1827:	William Parry, James Clark Ross, North Pole Spitsbergen Expedition, HMS *Hecla*
1829–33:	John Ross, James Clark Ross, Second Northwest Passage Expedition, *Victory* and *Krusenstern*
1829–37:	Publication of John Richardson, *Fauna Boreali-Americana*
1830:	'Baffin Fair', whaling fleets trapped in Melville Bay
1831:	James Clark Ross discovers Magnetic North Pole
1833–5:	George Back, Great Slave Lake to King William Island Expedition
1833–43:	John Rae is surgeon at Moose Factory, James Bay
1836–42:	John Franklin is Lieutenant-Governor of Tasmania
1836–7:	George Back, Frozen Strait and Repulse Bay Expedition, HMS *Terror*
1836–9:	Thomas Simpson, Peter Warren Dease, HBC Expedition
1839–43:	James Clark Ross, Francis Crozier, Antarctic Expedition, HMS *Erebus* and *Terror*
1839–40:	Eenoolooapik visits Scotland (William Penny), *Bon Accord*
1840:	Death of Thomas Simpson
1845–7:	John Franklin, Francis Crozier, Northwest Passage Expedition, *Erebus* and *Terror*
1846–7:	John Rae, Gulf of Boothia, Pelly Bay and Repulse Bay Expeditions, *Magnet*
1847:	William Penny, Searching Expedition, *St Andrew*
1848:	John Richardson, John Rae, Mackenzie and Coppermine River Searching Expeditions
1848–9:	James Clark Ross, Francis Crozier, Searching Expedition, HMS *Enterprise* and HMS *Investigator*
1849:	John Rae, Coppermine to Wollaston Land Searching Expedition
1849:	William Penny, Lancaster Sound Searching Expedition, *Advice*
1849:	Jane Franklin visits Orkney
1850–1:	William Penny, William Kennedy, Beechey Island and Cornwallis Island Searching Expedition, HMS *Lady Franklin* and HMS *Sophia*
1850–1:	John Ross, Searching Expedition, *Felix*
1850–1:	Edwin De Haven, First Grinnell Searching Expedition, USS *Rescue* and USS *Advance*
1850–4:	Robert McClure HMS *Investigator* and Richard Collinson HMS *Enterprise,* Northwest Passage Expedition
1851–2:	William Kennedy, Joseph R. Bellot, Somerset Island and Prince of Wales Island Searching Expedition, *Prince Albert*

1852–4: Edward Belcher, HMS *Assistance*; Henry Kellet, HMS *Resolute*; William Pullen, HMS *North Star*; Leopold McClintock, *Intrepid*; Sherard Osborn, *Pioneer*: last Admiralty Searching Expedition

1853–4: John Rae, HBC west coast of Boothia Searching Expedition

1853–5: Elisha Kent Kane, Second Grinnell Expedition, USS *Rescue* and USS *Advance*

1853–6: Crimean War

1854: Charles Dickens publishes Arctic articles in *Household Words*

1856: Death of John Ross

1857–8: William and Margaret Penny over-winter in Cumberland Sound

1857–9: Francis Leopold McClintock, Searching Expedition, *Fox*

1862: Death of James Clark Ross

1865: Death of John Richardson

1880: Arthur Conan Doyle joins an Arctic whaling ship

1890: Death of William Kennedy

1892: Death of William Penny

1893: Death of John Rae

1903–6: Roald Amundsen, first official complete navigation of Northwest Passage

NOTES

Chapter 1

1   James Montgomery (1771–1854) was born at Irvine, Ayrshire. He was known as a poet, reformer, newspaper editor and anti-slavery writer of hymns, of which he allegedly wrote 400, including 'The Lord is My Shepherd' based on Psalm 23: Tabernacle Choir Blog, 'The Lord is My Shepherd': https://www.thetabernaclechoir.org/blog.html.

2   Murdoch, *Britain, Denmark–Norway and the House of Stuart*, 196–7.

3   Equiano, *The Interesting Narrative of the Life of Olaudah Equiano*.

4   Irving, *The Irvings, Irwins, Irvines or Erinveines or any other Spelling of the Name*, 220, which indicates Irving's Scottish identity, something that does not seem to concern any other investigator. On board Irvine had an assistant surgeon named Alexander Mair. On the relationship between Irving and Equiano see Lovejoy, 'Autobiography and Memory', 332–3, 336–7.

5   Explorers and seamen in the area were often known as 'Arctics'. Since there are now far fewer true explorers but many more scientists, tourists, artists, musicians, writers, adventurers, etc. crowding in upon the original inhabitants, the Inuit, 'arctician' is modestly proposed as an alternative catch-all for anyone and everyone interested in the Arctic.

6   Spitsbergen, or Svalbard as it is now known, seems promising territory for those in search of Arctic Scots, for the archipelago is littered with Scottish place-names. However, most of these are late since the islands never had any permanent human inhabitants. See Anon., *The Place Names of Svalbard*.

7   There is a substantial bibliography of books on HBC. See e.g. Rigg, *Men of Spirit and Enterprise*, and numerous edited texts by E.E. Rich.

8   Lubbock, *The Arctic Whalers*, 52 and index. See also Jackson, *The British Whaling Trade*, and W. Gillies Ross, *Arctic Whalers, Icy Seas*. Some excellent books about specific Scottish whaling ports such as Dundee and Lerwick are also available.

9   Cavell, *Tracing the Connected Narrative*, 197.

10   Doyle, 'Dangerous Work'.

11   Welky, *A Wretched and Precarious Situation*, 64–5.

12   Van Kirk, *'Many Tender Ties'*, 4; W. Gillies Ross, *This Distant and Unsurveyed Country*, 137. Lest the reader assume that Professor Ross's unmistakable Scottish name may have influenced his judgement on this matter, he was a Canadian who also wrote, 'Penny was a staunch nationalist, not merely in a narrow Scottish sense but in a wider British context'! His notion of 'narrow Scottish' and 'wider British' can easily be challenged. W. Gillies Ross, *Hunters on the Track*, 36.

13   W. Gillies Ross, *This Distant and Unsurveyed Country*, 137.

14   Mackenzie, *Voyages from Montreal*, xvi.

15   Gough, *Distant Dominion*, 20–39; Robson, *The Captain Cook Encyclopaedia*, 155–6.

16   Justice, *Mr Menzies' Garden Legacy*, 91–2. Menzies had several quarrels with Vancouver, who was reputed to be 'a very good fellow but very passionate', 211. See also Olson and Thilenius, *The Alaska Travel Journal of Archibald Menzies*.

17   Vancouver, *A Voyage of Discovery*, vol. 1, 255; vol. 4, 1635.

18   Gibson, *Otter Skins, Boston Ships and China Goods*, 37.

19   Mackenzie, *Voyages from Montreal*, 259.

20   Hayes, *First Crossing*, 220–1.

21   Mackenzie, *Voyages from Montreal*, 345.

22   Fry, *Alexander Dalrymple and the Expansion of British Trade*, 31 note.

23   Mackenzie, *Voyages from Montreal*, i–xvii.

24   Mackenzie, *Voyages from Montreal*, 411.

25   Chambers, *A Biographical Dictionary of Eminent Scotsmen*, vol. 1, 427–9; Mackie, *Trading Beyond the Mountains*, 7–11.

26   *Scots Magazine* (1798), 894. On sailors and soldiers see Cowan and Paterson, *Folk In Print*, 251–300.

27   Armstrong, *A Personal Narrative of the Discovery of the North-West Passage*, xx–xxi.

28   John Ross, *A Treatise on Navigation by Steam*.

29   It has been suggested Scoresby lacked sufficient tact in his dealings with Barrow, and his distaste for the Royal Navy may have furthered the clash. Another factor may have been Barrow's strong conviction of an open and navigable Arctic sea while Scoresby found the idea ridiculous, suggesting the only way through the Arctic ocean would not be by ship but by sled dogs. Martin, 'William Scoresby Jr and the Open Polar Sea – Myth and Reality', 43–6.

30   Stamp and Stamp, *William Scoresby*, 32.

31   Leslie, John, *ODNB*.

32 Lambert, *Franklin, Tragic Hero of Polar Navigation*, 62–3.

33 See M.J. Ross, *Polar Pioneers,* 313–14; John Ross, *A Short Treatise on the Deviation of the Mariner's Compass.*

34 *Oxford English Dictionary.*

35 Quoted in James Clark Ross, *A Voyage of Discovery and Research in the Southern and Antarctic Regions*, vol. 1, x. See also Mawer, *South by Northwest.*

36 For example, Zeller, *Inventing Canada*; Levere, *Science and the Canadian Arctic*; Dickenson, *Drawn from Life*. See also Binnema, *Enlightened Zeal.*

37 Cunningham, *Poems and Songs of Allan Cunningham*, 97.

38 Willis, *Fighting Ships*, 152.

39 Fleming, *Barrow's Boys*, 11.

40 Daines Barrington (1727–1800) was an English judge and a dilettante with many interests including Arctic exploration. He was instrumental in setting up the Phipps expedition of 1773. The following year he persuaded the Royal Society to attack the Northwest Passage from the Pacific, leading to Captain Cook's third and last expedition: Barrington, Daines, *ODNB*. Mark Beaufoy (1764–1827) was an astronomer and physicist who eloped to Gretna Green to marry his cousin Margaretta, a talented mathematician. He was the first known Englishman to climb Mont Blanc. A founder member in 1791 of the Society for the Improvement of Naval Architecture, he also worked on ship resistance to water and wind: Beaufoy, Mark, *ODNB*.

41 Croker, 'Frankenstein or the Modern Prometheus', 379–85; the Mary Shelley Chronology and Resource site. See also Shelley, *Frankenstein*, and Bann, *Frankenstein, Creation and Monstrosity*. An edition of the novel published in 2008 controversially attributed authorship to both Mary and Percy.

Chapter 2

1 *NSA*, vol. iv, *Dumfries–Kirkcudbright–Wigton*, Parish of Inch, Wigtonshire, 85. Some sources place his birth at Barsalloch (Barscalloch on OS map) in Kirkcolm parish. The confusion arises because John Ross's parents, Rev. Andrew Ross and Elizabeth Corsane, had sasine (infeftment) of the lands of Barsalloch, the old house of which no longer exists, but which stood almost at the most northerly point of the Corsewall peninsula. Barsalloch is some 15 miles from Soulseat and so rather inconvenient for the minister. The Rev. James Fergusson, minister of Soulseat, in 1839 stated that Ross was born at Soulseat manse. He may have had access to written evidence but in any case Ross was still alive when this volume of the *NSA* was published. Ross would have agreed with Fergusson's observation that Inch 'enjoys facility of communication with all parts of the world' because it was on the coast and so offered

a means of egress! See *NSA*, vol. iv, 89, 92; M'Kerlie, *History of the Lands and their Owners in Galloway*, vol. 1, 127–8; Hume, *Dumfries and Galloway*, 209, which has an illustration of Barsalloch House.

2   Of his brothers, George, the eldest, was an adventurous businessman in London. Andrew fought at Waterloo and became colonel in the 54th regiment. Robert, like many boys from Galloway, spent some time in Virginia learning the tobacco trade, later finding employment in the Cape Colony and Dutch Guiana. He made enough money to build himself a fine house at Cargenholm, Dumfries.

3   M.J. Ross states, citing 'Ross family papers', that John Ross went to sea on *Pearl* serving for three years and one further year on *Impregnable*: M.J. Ross, *Polar Pioneers*, 11. This seems to be the same period for which Ross differently accounts in his memoir. The latter is preferred here as the better indicator of Ross's self-regard.

4   This selection of activities in his younger life is drawn from his memoir and consequently cannot be verified. A partial copy of the memoir is in the Ewart Library, Dumfries.

5   John Ross, *Narrative of a Second Voyage*, 396–7.

6   Franklin, *Journals and Correspondence*, lv–lxxviii.

7   John Ross, *A Voyage of Discovery* (1819a edn), Intro., xxiv–xxxii. The first edition of this book (by John Murray, 1819a) is cited throughout from now on, except where the second edition (2 vols, 1819b, published by Longman, Hurst, Rees, Orme, and Brown) is specifically indicated.

8   Sacheuse was a stowaway on whaler *Thomas and Ann* in 1816. M.J. Ross, *Polar Pioneers*, 40.

9   Fisher, *Journal of a Voyage of Discovery to the Arctic Regions*, vii–viii.

10   John Ross, *A Voyage of Discovery*, 1–14.

11   Fisher, *Journal of a Voyage of Discovery to the Arctic Regions*, 2.

12   William Scoresby senior is credited with the invention of this contraption which was much more elaborate than the lookout platforms on masts depicted in some medieval manuscripts.

13   John Ross, *A Voyage of Discovery* (1819b edn), 51.

14   Peary refers to Sir John Ross as an 'English explorer'. Peary, *North Pole*, 73.

15   Fisher, *Journal of a Voyage of Discovery to the Arctic Regions*, 41.

16   John Ross, *A Voyage of Discovery*, 68–72.

17   Fisher, *Journal of a Voyage of Discovery to the Arctic Regions*, 42, 47.

18   John Ross, *A Voyage of Discovery*, 76–7. The bower anchors were the two anchors attached to their cables, each carried on either side of the ship's bow. Also known as sheet anchors. Formerly named as the 'best bower', starboard, and the 'small bower', port.

19 On the people of Greenland see Sonne, *Worldviews of the Greenlanders*. The author often takes issue with the classic and absorbing Knud Rasmussen, *Across Arctic America*. I must admit to having been fascinated by the books of Peter Freuchen in my younger days. See also King and Lidchi, *Imaging the Arctic*; Bennett and Rowley, *Uqalurait: An Oral History of Nunavut*; Hulan, *Northern Experience and the Myths of Canadian Culture*, especially Chapter 5, 'Everybody Likes the Inuit'; and McGhee, *The Last Imaginary Place*.

20 John Ross, *A Voyage of Discovery*, 152–3.

21 M.J. Ross, *Polar Pioneers*, 45.

22 John Ross, *A Voyage of Discovery*, 158.

23 John Ross, *A Voyage of Discovery*, 172.

24 John Ross, *A Voyage of Discovery*, 174–5.

25 John Ross, *A Voyage of Discovery* (1819b edn), viii. This passage does not appear in the 1819a edition.

26 John Ross, *A Voyage of Discovery*, 186.

27 No specific suggestions at present for the inspiration for other names: Brodue, Bruce, Caledon, Campbell, Duneira, Jamson, Mcleay, Meikleham.

28 John Ross, *A Voyage of Discovery*, 208.

29 John Ross, *A Voyage of Discovery*, 226.

30 M.J. Ross, *Polar Pioneers*, 102.

31 See Hamilton, *Arctic Fox*, 163–76.

32 M.J. Ross, *Polar Pioneers*, 161–3.

33 M.J. Ross, *Polar Pioneers*, 52.

34 M.J. Ross, *Polar Pioneers*, 55.

35 M.J. Ross, *Polar Pioneers*, 52.

36 Fisher, *Journal of a Voyage of Discovery to the Arctic Regions*, 73–4, Appendix 7.

37 Smith, *Arctic Expeditions*, 100.

38 John Ross, *A Voyage of Discovery*, 160.

39 Having reached this tentative conclusion I was delighted to find some support in Patten, *George Cruikshank's Life, Times, and Art*, vol. 1, Preface. 'Cruickshanks' prints often point overtly to one reading while conveying different, even contradictory, implications through allusions, design, dialogue and captions, or the energy of composition, drawing, and empathy'. Unfortunately in his ambitious survey Patten does not mention the 'Treasures' print.

40 Regard, 'Eskimaux, Officers and Gentlemen', 58; Potter, *Arctic Spectacles*, 46–51.

41 Regard, 'Eskimaux, Officers and Gentlemen', 58.

42 *Edinburgh Review* No. 62 (1819) 31.

43 M.J. Ross, *Polar Pioneers*, 65.

44 Fleming, *Barrow's Boys*, 48–51.

45 It seems at times as though John Ross's life was one long battle. See 'On the Expedition to the Arctic Seas, Minutes of Evidence', 9–29, House of Commons Parliamentary Papers Online.

46 Regard, 'Eskimaux, Officers and Gentlemen', 38.

47 Cowan and Gifford, *The Polar Twins*. See also, Cowan, 'Scottish History: Competing Pathways to the Past'.

48 Barrow, *Voyages of Discovery*, 19–55; Regard, 'Eskimaux, Officers and Gentlemen', 41–3.

49 Regard, 'Eskimaux, Officers and Gentlemen', 37–60; Young, *The Idea of English Ethnicity*, 30–1. Why, we must wonder, has Young selected a quote from Carlyle's 'Occasional Discourse on the Negro Question', which was a disgraceful, unforgivable and racist lapse, or evidence of increasing mental confusion, or both? Was the professor by chance attempting, Barrovian-like, to further demonise the Scots? As a matter of fact some learned Scots did argue that since the Scots language was unaffected by the Great Vowel Shift, a purer form of English was actually spoken in Lowland Scotland than in England. See also Ferguson, *The Identity of the Scottish Nation*, 314–15, and Kidd, *Subverting Scotland's Past*, 2–4, 7. Also useful is Langford, *Englishness Identified*.

50 John Ross, *Observations on a Work*, 13. The title page also has the epigraph 'Oh! That mine enemy would write a book!'

51 M.J. Ross, *Polar Pioneers*, 70.

52 Barker, *Description of a View of the North Coast of Spitzbergen*.

53 See Potter's fascinating book *Arctic Spectacles*.

54 Beechey, *A Voyage of Discovery*, 7.

55 Beechey, *A Voyage of Discovery*, 6–23.

56 Beechey, *A Voyage of Discovery*, 46.

57 Stange, *Spitsbergen–Svalbard*, 321.

58 Beechey, *A Voyage of Discovery*, 47–52.

59 This was in the first week of June 1818: Beechey, *A Voyage of Discovery*, 58. Ross did not encounter his red snow until 17 August: John Ross, *A Voyage of Discovery*, 191.

60 Umbreit, *Spitsbergen, Svalbard, Franz Josef Land and Jan Mayen*, 137.

61 Beechey, *A Voyage of Discovery*, 76–7.

62 Beechey, *A Voyage of Discovery*, 108.

63 Beechey, *A Voyage of Discovery*, 117, 119.

64 Beechey, *A Voyage of Discovery*, 128.

65 Beechey, *A Voyage of Discovery*, 157.

66 Beechey, *A Voyage of Discovery*, 201–11.

Chapter 3

1   M.J. Ross, *Polar Pioneers*, 106–7.

2   M.J. Ross, *Polar Pioneers*, 5, 107, 135, 371.

3   M.J. Ross, *Polar Pioneers*, 71.

4   M.J. Ross, *Polar Pioneers*, 81.

5   Cf. M.J. Ross, *Polar Pioneers*, 73.

6   Sabine, *The North Georgia Gazette and Winter Chronicle*, 28, 29, 38, 51, 63. Sabine claimed that the weekly issues were published due to public demand on the return of the expedition.

7   An identical incident in almost identical language is described in Vancouver's *A Voyage of Discovery* though the cook John Brown, a Scot, escapes punishment apparently because he knew of Sir Joseph Bank's opinion that grease mixed with pulse was an excellent antiscorbutic: Vancouver, *A Voyage of Discovery*, vol. 4, 1471–2.

8   Parry, *Journals of the First, Second and Third Voyages*, vol. 1, 236–82.

9   M.J. Ross, *Polar Pioneers*, 79.

10 Lyon, *The Private Journal of Captain G.F. Lyon of H.M.S. Hecla*, 293 and throughout.

11 Parry, *Journal of a Second Voyage*, 6.

12 M.J. Ross, *Polar Pioneers*, 86.

13 Parry, *Journal of a Second Voyage*, 239.

14 Lyon, *A Brief Narrative*, 4, 7–8.

15 Parry, *Journals of the First, Second and Third Voyages*, vol. 5, 51–2. Aldebaran is the brightest star in the constellation Taurus (the Bull) and is orange in colour.

16 Parry, *Journals of the First, Second and Third Voyages*, vol. 5, 68–9.

17 M.J. Ross, *Polar Pioneers*, 93.

18 Scoresby, *An Account of the Arctic Regions*, vol. 1, 54–5.

19 Parry, *Narrative of an Attempt*, xi–xiii.

20 Barrington, *The Possibility*, Appendix.

21 Parry, *Narrative of an Attempt*, 6.

22 Parry, *Narrative of an Attempt*, 48.

23 Parry, *Narrative of an Attempt*, 52.

24 Parry, *Narrative of an Attempt*, 61.

25 Parry, *Narrative of an Attempt*, 89.

26 Parry, *Narrative of an Attempt*, 105.

27 Parry, *Narrative of an Attempt*, 121.

28 M.J. Ross, *Polar Pioneers*, 95, 106–7 (slightly modified).

Chapter 4

1   Houston, *Arctic Ordeal*, 140–3.

2   McIlraith, *Life of Sir John Richardson*, 24–8, 40.

3   McIlraith, *Life of Sir John Richardson*, 1–61. See also Sweet, 'Robert Jameson and the Explorers', 21–47.

4   Lambert, *Franklin*, 26.

5   Lambert, *Franklin, Tragic Hero of Polar Navigation*, 34.

6   Condon et al., *The Northern Copper Inuit*, 3–65.

7   Steele, *The Man Who Mapped the Arctic*, 62–3.

8   Franklin, *Narrative of a Journey*, 35.

9   Franklin, *Narrative of a Journey*, 167–92. This chapter was written by Hood. A useful study of the expedition is Lanone, 'John Franklin and the Idea of North', 119–30.

10   Franklin, *Narrative of a Journey*, 51.

11   McIlraith, *Life of Sir John Richardson*, 72.

12   Franklin, *Narrative of a Journey*, 61. This section was written by Richardson.

13   Houston, *Arctic Ordeal*, 59–87.

14   McIlraith, *Life of Sir John Richardson*, 74.

15   Franklin, *Narrative of a Journey*, 166.

16   'The food of the mosquito is blood, which it can extract by penetrating the hide of a buffalo; and if it is not disturbed, it gorges itself so as to swell its body into a transparent globe. The wound does not swell, like that of the African mosquito, but it is infinitely more painful; and when multiplied an hundred fold, and continued for so many successive days, it becomes an evil of such magnitude, that cold, famine, and every other concomitant of an inhospitable climate, must yield the pre-eminence to it. It chases the buffalo to the plains, irritating him to madness; and the reindeer to the sea-shore, from which they do not return till the scourge has ceased': Franklin, *Narrative*, 189.

17   Franklin, *Narrative of a Journey*, 181, 193.

18   Franklin uses the spelling Akaitcho, while Richardson uses Akaicho. Franklin, *Narrative of a Journey*, 203-7; Davis, *Sir John Franklin's Journals and Correspondence*, 29–30.

19   Franklin, *Narrative of a Journey*, 209.

20   McIlraith, *Life of Sir John Richardson*, 76–85.

21   Craciun, *Writing Arctic Disaster*, 94: I have italicised the words that McIlraith omitted in *Life of Sir John Richardson*, 84.

22   Scott, *Guy Mannering*, 14, 43, 287.

23   Steele, *The Man Who Mapped the Arctic*, 113.

24   Houston, *To the Arctic by Canoe*, xxix, xxxv; Steele, *The Man Who Mapped the Arctic*, 103–4, 113–14, 179, 239; Franklin, *Narrative of a Journey*, 254.

25   Steele, *The Man Who Mapped the Arctic*, 119.

26   Houston, *Arctic Ordeal*, 77–8.

27   Houston, *Arctic Ordeal*, 80.

28   Houston, *Arctic Ordeal*, 116.

29   Houston, *Arctic Ordeal*, 126.

30   There is confusion in the sources about how many canoes or pieces thereof they still had.

31   Houston, *Arctic Ordeal*, 129, 133, 196.

32   Houston, *Arctic Ordeal*, 142–8.

33   Houston, *Arctic Ordeal*, 153.

34   Houston, *Arctic Ordeal*, 156.

35   Richardson, *The Polar Regions*, 149.

36   Bellot, *Memoirs*, vol. 1, 263.

37   Houston, *Arctic Ordeal*, 148–60; Franklin, *Narrative of a Journey*, 449–61.

38   Houston, *To the Arctic by Canoe*, xxvii.

39   Houston, *Arctic Ordeal*, 218.

40   Houston, *Arctic Ordeal*, 218. It is somewhat odd that Houston, who has produced so much valuable material on Richardson and the Arctic, does not have much to say about the Teroahauté slaying. For a factual but non-analytical account see his 'Epilogue: The Death of Hood' in Houston, *To the Arctic by Canoe*, 157–64.

41   Houston, *Arctic Ordeal*, 140–2.

42   There were a remarkable number of doctors from Dumfriesshire and the south-west; see, for instance, Schwarz, 'Scottish Surgeons in the Liverpool Slave Trade', 145–65.

43   Steele, *The Man Who Mapped the Arctic*, 98; Houston, *To the Arctic by Canoe*, 141.

44   Houston, *Arctic Ordeal*, 133.

45   McIlraith, *Life of Sir John Richardson*, 113, 202.

46   Craciun, *Writing Arctic Disaster*, 96.

47   Bellot, *Memoirs*, vol. 1, 263.

48   Franklin, *Narrative of a Journey*, 491–4.

Chapter 5

1   Cowan, 'Sober Attentive Men', 18–19. Dixon, *The Enlightenment of Cadwallader Colden*.

2   McIlraith, *Life of Sir John Richardson*, 130–1.

3   Washington Irving, *Astoria*, 4–11.

4   McIlraith, *Life of Sir John Richardson*, 130, 142.

5   Franklin, *Narrative of a Second Expedition*, 94; McIlraith, *Life of Sir John Richardson*, 138.

6   Franklin, *Narrative of a Second Expedition*, 69.

7   Ooligbuck, or Ouligbuck, did not speak English but was recruited to Franklin's 1820s overland expedition as company for fellow Inuit Tattannoeuk, or Augustus, who did speak English. After the expedition, Ooligbuck returned to Churchill in 1827, was employed by the HBC and, having now learned English, acted as interpreter for subsequent expeditions. His son, William Ooligbuck, was interpreter on John Rae's HBC expedition in 1846.

8   Letter to mother, 6 Sept. 1825, McIlraith, *Life of Sir John Richardson*, 142–4; Normand, *Scottish Photography*.

9   Letter to sister, 6 Feb. 1826, McIlraith, *Life of Sir John Richardson*, 144–9.

10 Franklin, *Narrative of a Second Expedition*, 84–5.

11 Franklin, *Journals and Correspondence*, 169–80; Franklin, *Narrative of a Second Expedition*, xxvii–xxviii.

12 Franklin, *Narrative of a Second Expedition*, xxvii.

13 Franklin, *Narrative of a Second Expedition*, xxxvii.

14 Franklin, *Journals and Correspondence*, 120, note 470.

15 Franklin, *Narrative of a Second Expedition*, 127; Beechey, *Narrative of a Voyage*, vol. 1, 324–470, vol. 2, 256–317.

16 Franklin, *Narrative of a Second Expedition*, 183–4. The Loucheux were also known as the Kutchin, later described and beautifully illustrated in Richardson's *Arctic Searching Expedition*, 1851.

17 Franklin to Richardson, Holograph, Dumfries and Galloway Archives, 21 September 1826; Franklin, *Narrative of Second Expedition*, 95–185.

18 Franklin, *Narrative of a Second Expedition*, 168; Cunningham, the brother of the poet Alan Cunningham, was born at Dalswinton near Dumfries. He was a naval doctor who specialised in conveying convicts to Australia: Cowan, 'The Emigrant Experience', 403–5.

19 Franklin, *Narrative of a Second Expedition*, 178–84.

20 Franklin, *Narrative of a Second Expedition*, 233.

21 Almost all books on the Arctic contain maps but those in Franklin, *Journals and Correspondence*, and in the map pocket of Franklin, *Narrative of a Second Expedition*, are particularly useful.

22 Franklin, *Narrative of a Second Expedition*, 276.

23 Franklin, *Narrative of a Second Expedition*, 305–6.

24 Franklin, *Narrative of a Second Expedition*, 258.

25 Cowan, 'The Scots Imaging of Canada', 5–7.

26 Mitchell and House, *David Douglas*, 49–140. See also Douglas, *Journal kept by David Douglas*; Davies, *Douglas of the Forests*; Houston, *Arctic Ordeal*, 220.

27 Brown, *Scurvy*.

28 McIlraith, *Life of Sir John Richardson*, 179–80.

29 Baillie, *From Boston to Dumfries*.

30 All references are from Richardson, Swainson and Kirby, *Fauna Boreali-Americana*.

31 Richardson, Swainson and Kirby, *Fauna Boreali-Americana, Part 2, The Birds*, x, xi, 12–19, 82–5.

32 Richardson, Swainson and Kirby, *Fauna Boreali-Americana, Part 3, The Fish*, 140–4, 148–50, 163–4, 174.

33 Letter of John Richardson to Captain Beaufort Admiralty Hydrographer, 6 February 1836, Ewart Library, Dumfries GD 109.3.

Chapter 6

1 Henry Morley was Editor and contributor to *Household Words* 12 November 1853 but Dickens was the 'Conductor'. This quote (p. 246) represents the romanticism and chauvinism of a writer who had no first-hand experience of Arctic reality.

2 John Ross, *Narrative of a Second Voyage*, ix. See also Cowan, 'The Longest Winter: The Ross Expedition, 1829–33', 34–46.

3 John Ross, *Narrative of a Second Voyage*, 10–17.

4 John Ross, *Narrative of a Second Voyage*, 17–18.

5 M.J. Ross, *Polar Pioneers*, 125.

6 John Ross, *Narrative of a Second Voyage*, 63–77.

7 Huish, *Last Voyage*, 109.

8 Huish, *Last Voyage*, 129, 145. According to contemporary lore, tailors sat cross-legged on a table or the floor when practising their craft.

9 Huish's informant was Englishman William Light, purser's steward to the expedition. Huish, *Last Voyage*, 125, 126, 129, 139, 141.

10 For a fuller discussion see Cowan, 'The Longest Winter: The Ross Expedition, 1829–33', 36–7.

11 For a popular account see Edinger, *Fury Beach*.

12 John Ross, *Narrative of a Second Voyage*, 107.

13 John Ross, *Narrative of a Second Voyage*, 108.

14 Lyon, *A Brief Narrative*, 104.

15 John Ross, *Narrative of a Second Voyage*, 152–3.

16 John Ross, *Narrative of a Second Voyage*, 197–203.

17 John Ross, *Narrative of a Second Voyage*, 191.

18 Inuksuit (singular inuksuk or inukshuk, meaning 'to act in the capacity of a human', an extension of 'human being') are piled stones or cairns used to

communicate information to passersby. Some may be as old as 2400 BCE but others have been dismissed as way-markers or follies built by whalers, explorers and other interlopers. Authoritative discussion by Inuit would be most valuable. One elder explained they were made by people who wished to attach their thoughts to 'distant and familiar places'. Sometimes they take the form of large uprighted stones some of which are venerated as having association with shamans and spirits, but this is a complex subject: Norman Hallendy, 'Inuksuk (Inukshuk)' in *The Canadian Encyclopedia* (Historica Canada, 2013); John Ross, *Narrative of a Second Voyage*, 186, 193. https://www.thecanadianencyclopedia.ca/en/article/inuksuk-inukshuk

19 Though questions later endured as to what had happened to the rest of the generous liquor supply originally taken on board, Ross had a not entirely convincing answer to hand, namely that most of the wine and spirits were abandoned along with *Victory* in 1833. John Ross, *Narrative of a Second Voyage*, 209–10.

20 In a blatantly self-indulgent passage he described how a black cloud at the centre of the sun projected rays like those of the star on the Order of the Bath. 'If there was anyone on board who imagined that this appearance was ominous of that, or any other knighthood, to any of us, the secret was kept; fortunately for the prognosticator, who might have lost his fame by trusting to a fallacious omen.' As it happened and as he must have hoped, Ross was later to be knighted and made a member of the Order of the Bath on 24 December 1834, on the very day that, back home, he was allegedly correcting the page of his book which mentioned the so-called prognostication. John Ross, *Narrative of a Second Voyage*, 222.

21 John Ross, *Narrative of a Second Voyage*, 227–31.

22 House of Commons, *Narrative of the Second Voyage of Captain Ross to the Arctic Regions*, 23–5.

23 Huish, *Last Voyage*, 185–8.

24 John Ross, *Narrative of a Second Voyage*, 464.

25 Credland, *Baffin Fair*, 30.

26 John Ross, *Narrative of a Second Voyage*, 470, 480, 497.

27 John Ross, *Narrative of a Second Voyage*, 489–90.

28 John Ross, *Narrative of a Second Voyage*, 555.

29 John Ross, *Narrative of a Second Voyage*, 550.

30 James Clark Ross, 'On the Position of the North Magnetic Pole', 47–52.

31 John Ross, *Narrative of a Second Voyage*, 559.

32 Bomann-Larsen, *Roald Amundsen*, suggests that Amundsen was not greatly interested in magnetism, 39, 41.

33 John Ross, *Narrative of a Second Voyage*, 593, 597, 608, 609.

34 John Ross, *Narrative of a Second Voyage*, 589–91.

35 John Ross, *Narrative of a Second Voyage*, 597–603.

36 John Ross, *Narrative of a Second Voyage*, 619–20.

37 John Ross, *Narrative of a Second Voyage*, 632–9.

38 James Ross and Savelle, 'Retreat From Boothia', 179–94.

39 Huish, *Last Voyage*, 614–17.

40 James Ross and Savelle, 'Retreat From Boothia', 182; John Ross, *Narrative of a Second Voyage*, 643.

41 Huish, *Last Voyage*, 621.

42 John Ross, *Narrative of a Second Voyage*, 640.

43 James Ross and Savelle, 'Retreat From Boothia', 185.

44 James Ross and Savelle, 'Retreat From Boothia', 191.

45 John Ross, *Narrative of a Second Voyage*, 671–3.

46 James Ross and Savelle, 'Retreat From Boothia', 193–4.

47 John Ross, *Narrative of a Second Voyage*, 695–6.

48 John Ross, *Narrative of a Second Voyage*, 701. The story is told at much greater length in Huish, *Last Voyage*, 665–9, wherein Ross and Nelson are humorously compared.

49 Huish, *Last Voyage*, 659.

50 Chapman, *James Boswell and Samuel Johnson: Journal*, 349.

51 John Ross, *Narrative of a Second Voyage*, 715.

52 John Ross, *Narrative of a Second Voyage*, 720–1.

53 John Ross, *Narrative of a Second Voyage*, 724–5; *Household Words* (1851), 79.

54 Huish, *The Last Voyage of Capt. Sir John Ross*, 171.

55 Huish, *The Last Voyage of Capt. Sir John Ross*, 466.

56 Huish, *Last Voyage of Capt. Sir John Ross*, 208–12.

57 Potter, *Arctic Spectacles*, 66–113. One other Scotsman, nurtured as an engraver in a similar milieu to the others, but much more famous, was William Simpson, born in Glasgow, known as 'Crimean Simpson' who was commissioned to produce a painting of *Resolute* when it was returned to Britain by the Americans (see Chapter 13).

Chapter 7

1 Colombo, *Poems of the Inuit*, 104. This song, collected by Knud Rasmussen, is anonymous.

2 The earliest contact between Inuit and Scots, though very little is known about it, dates from Viking times in the tenth century when a few Scots accompanied Norwegians in longships westwards to Greenland and America: see Magnusson and Palsson, *The Vinland Sagas*. The first reported sightings of

'Finnmen' in Scottish waters date from the seventeenth century. Lone paddlers in kayaks allegedly appeared in Orkney and Aberdeen. How they managed the journey from Greenland or Arctic Canada is the subject of debate. It has been suggested, unconvincingly, that they were blown off course by storms. A favoured explanation is that they were kidnapped by whalers or other sea-farers who, as they approached Scottish shores, put them overboard with their kayaks. In some cases the vessels survived but details about their owners, whether Greenlanders or Inuit, did not: Idens, 'Eskimos in Scotland', 161–74.

3   Neatby, 'Exploration and History of the Canadian Arctic', 379. See also Oswalt, *Eskimos and Explorers*. I was visiting Mittimatalik (Pond Inlet) where I was sampling the community library, when someone came in to excitedly tell me that a group of Inuit girls were demonstrating my culture in the neighbouring hall. Sure enough a young lass explained that they were about to perform dances and tunes that their ancestors had learned from the Scottish whalers. There followed a cross-cultural concert that was deeply moving. This was the same occasion on which I met for the first time my friend David Reid from Bishopton near Glasgow, the last Scot to be recruited for the HBC.

4   John Ross, *A Voyage of Discovery*, 80–114.

5   John Ross, *A Voyage of Discovery*, 126.

6   Ross also discussed clothing, food and hunting practices. John Ross, *A Voyage of Discovery*, 124–5.

7   John Ross, *A Voyage of Discovery*, 133.

8   John Ross, *A Voyage of Discovery*, 109.

9   John Ross, *A Voyage of Discovery*, 123–4.

10 Vaughan, *Northwest Greenland*, 16–18.

11 John Ross, *A Voyage of Discovery*, 98.

12 John Ross, *A Voyage of Discovery*, 121.

13 John Ross, *A Voyage of Discovery*, xxxii.

14 John Ross, *A Voyage of Discovery*, 129.

15 John Ross, *A Voyage of Discovery*, 134–5.

16 John Ross, *Narrative of a Second Voyage*, 73.

17 John Ross, *Narrative of a Second Voyage*, 242–6.

18 John Ross, *Narrative of a Second Voyage*, 246–8.

19 John Ross, *Narrative of a Second Voyage*, 249–56.

20 Macfie, *Vancouver Island and British Columbia*, 378, 388, 492; Sproat, *Scenes and Studies of Savage Life*, xxx.

21 John Ross, *Narrative of a Second Voyage*, 257.

22 John Ross, *Narrative of a Second Voyage*, 322–3.

23 John Ross, *Narrative of a Second Voyage*, 287.

24 John Ross, *Narrative of a Second Voyage*, 321.

25 John Ross, *Narrative of a Second Voyage*, 290–9.

26 John Ross, *Narrative of a Second Voyage*, 390.

27 John Ross, *Narrative of a Second Voyage*, 392.

28 John Ross, *Narrative of a Second Voyage*, 446–7.

29 John Ross, *Narrative of a Second Voyage*, 391. The *sipak* reference is from Kane, *The Far North*, 100.

30 John Ross, *Narrative of a Second Voyage*. In 1822 Parry encountered an Inuit boy named Aglooka 'about ten years of age': Parry, *Journal of a Second Voyage*, 367. Huish, *Last Voyage* spelt the word Augliecock.

31 John Ross, *Narrative of a Second Voyage*, 331–2.

32 John Ross, *Narrative of a Second Voyage*, 517.

33 John Ross, *Narrative of a Second Voyage*, 519, 530–48. Ross refers to Neitchillee as Lady Melville's Lake while Knud Rasmussen places it on the shores of Netsilik Lake: Rasmussen, *The Netsilik Eskimos*, 93–4.

34 John Ross, *Narrative of a Second Voyage*, 573–4.

35 John Ross, *Narrative of a Second Voyage*, 578–9.

36 McDonald, *A Narrative of Some Passages in the History of Eenoolooapik*. Another Inuk who was taken to Scotland was Aukuttook Zininnuck. The Scots called him Kookie-Eekie: see W. Gillies Ross, *Hunters on the Track*, 58.

37 McDonald, *A Narrative of Some Passages in the History of Eenoolooapik*, 9, 25–32.

38 Eenoolooapik (Bobbie), *Dictionary of Canadian Biography*.

39 McDonald, *A Narrative of Some Passages in the History of Eenoolooapik*, 103.

Chapter 8

1 Simpson, *The Life and Travels of Thomas Simpson*, 180.

2 Back, *Narrative of the Arctic Land Expedition*, 8.

3 Back, *Narrative of the Arctic Land Expedition*, 33.

4 *Encyclopedia Arctica*, vol. 15, 6.

5 Binnema, *Enlightened Zeal*, 143–5.

6 Back, *Narrative of the Arctic Land Expedition*, 338.

7 Back, *Narrative of the Arctic Land Expedition*, 366.

8 Back, *Narrative of the Arctic Land Expedition*, 386–7, 389, 425.

9 Steele, *The Man Who Mapped the Arctic*, 235–46.

10 Simpson, *The Life and Travels of Thomas Simpson*, 169–70.

11 *Encyclopedia Arctica*, vol. 15, 7.

12 Rich, *Part of a Dispatch from George Simpson*, 233–4; Belyk, *John Tod*, 31–2. On Simpson, see also Raffan, *Emperor of the North*.

13   *Encyclopedia Arctica*, vol. 15, 23–5.

14   A capot was a long hooded coat adopted from the Métis, which is slightly ironic given Simpson's later difficulties with these people. He presumably also learned the Métis language, Michif, which, like Bungee, is a mixed language incorporating elements from French, Cree, Ojibwa, English, Gaelic, Scots and Norn (*Canadian Encyclopedia*).

15   Simpson, *The Life and Travels of Thomas Simpson*, 32.

16   Simpson, *The Life and Travels of Thomas Simpson*, 32–3.

17   Barr, *From Barrow to Boothia*. This is a very substantial work containing a great deal of detail about the day-to-day organisation of HBC.

18   Simpson, *Narrative of the Discoveries on the North Coast of America*, 3–4; Beechey, *Narrative of a Voyage to the Pacific and Beering's Strait*, vol. 2, 274. His voyage involved sailing 73,000 miles in three and a half years during which fifteen men died, 329.

19   Simpson, *Narrative of the Discoveries on the North Coast of America*, 4–7; Simpson, *The Life and Travels of Thomas Simpson*, 90–4.

20   Simpson, *The Life and Travels of Thomas Simpson*, 113, 116, 131, 256, 227.

21   Simpson, *The Life and Travels of Thomas Simpson*, 276; Dease, Peter Warren, *DCB*, Vol. IX (1861–1870).

22   Simpson, *The Life and Travels of Thomas Simpson*, 159.

23   Johnson, *York Boats of the Hudson's Bay Company*.

24   Franklin, *Narrative of a Second Expedition*, 179–80.

25   Simpson, *Narrative of the Discoveries on the North Coast of America*, 112 and note.

26   Simpson, *Narrative of the Discoveries on the North Coast of America*, 121.

27   There may be some overlap in these events since Alexander Simpson's dates seem a little confused at this point but the first episode is said to have taken place at Franklin's Return Reef and the second at Point Barrow. Simpson, *The Life and Travels of Thomas Simpson*, 132, Simpson, *Narrative of the Discoveries on the North Coast of America*, 153–4. The description in the *Narrative* of female dancers wearing only deer-skin breeches as 'land mermaids' may have been referring to the same occasion.

28   One gadget Simpson and the others admired was a kind of bird sling, six perforated ivory balls attached to sinew cords 3 feet long. It was thrown in the air to bring down birds in flight.

29   Simpson, *Narrative of the Discoveries on the North Coast of America*, 223.

30   Simpson, *The Life and Travels of Thomas Simpson*, 132.

31   Simpson, *The Life and Travels of Thomas Simpson*, 141.

32   Simpson, *The Life and Travels of Thomas Simpson*, 133–4.

33   Beechey, *Narrative of a Voyage to the Pacific and Beering's Strait*, vol. 2, 298.

34   Simpson, *Narrative of the Discoveries on the North Coast of America*, 255.

35   Simpson, *The Life and Travels of Thomas Simpson*, 162.

36   Simpson, *The Life and Travels of Thomas Simpson*, 172.

37   Simpson, *Narrative of the Discoveries on the North Coast of America*, 14.

38   Simpson, *The Life and Travels of Thomas Simpson*, 100–6.

39   Simpson, *Narrative of the Discoveries on the North Coast of America*, 72.

40   Simpson, *The Life and Travels of Thomas Simpson*, 353, 339; Barr, *From Barrow to Boothia*, 296.

41   Simpson, *The Life and Travels of Thomas Simpson*, 189; Cowper, 'Retirement', 48–55.

42   Simpson, *The Life and Travels of Thomas Simpson*, 354–60.

43   Simpson, *The Life and Travels of Thomas Simpson*, 360–6.

44   Simpson, *The Life and Travels of Thomas Simpson*, 366–73; Harper, *Thomas Simpson*, 10.

45   Simpson, *An Overland Journey Round the World*, 31.

46   Raffan, *Emperor of the North*, 313–23; see also McArthur, 'A Tragedy of the Plains: The Fate of Thomas Simpson'.

Chapter 9

1   Robert Kerr, 'Maggy o' the Moss', in Nicholson, *Historical and Traditional Tales*, 235.

2   He may have considered that he had not done enough to justify the supposed honour of a knighthood but he was possibly staggered by the realisation that to accept the knighthood by patent would have cost him £400. In a letter of 1844 he rejected an offer to lead the planned Northern Expedition later commanded by Franklin. He stated that he had no wish to return to 'the severe and arduous service to which I have already devoted four and twenty years of my life with considerable pecuniary sacrifice and without the smallest equivalent advantage . . .' M.J. Ross, *Ross in the Antarctic*, 72, 111, 212, 248–9.

3   M.J. Ross, *Ross in the Antarctic*, 140.

4   McCormick, Robert, in *DCB*.

5   M.J. Ross, *Polar Pioneers*, 216, 221.

6   M.J. Ross, *Ross in the Antarctic*, 34.

7   Savours and McConnell, 'The History of Rossbank Observatory, Tasmania', 527–64.

8   M.J. Ross, *Ross in the Antarctic*, 81.

9   M.J. Ross, *Ross in the Antarctic*, 93.

10   M.J. Ross, *Ross in the Antarctic*, 93–7.

11   M.J. Ross, *Ross in the Antarctic*, 159–65.

12 Franklin, *Narrative of Some Passages in the History of Van Diemen's Land*. See also Fitzpatrick, *Sir John Franklin in Tasmania 1837–1843*.

13 Barr, *John Rae: The Unfinished Autobiography*, 1.

14 Smith, *Arctic Expeditions from British and Foreign Shores from Earliest Times to the Expedition of 1876–7*, 629–30.

15 Rich and Johnson, eds. *John Rae's Correspondence*, 301–2, 313–16; Barr, *John Rae: Unfinished Autobiography*, 91–3.

16 Rich and Johnson, *John Rae's Correspondence*, xix.

17 Barr, *John Rae: Unfinished Autobiography*, 121; my account of the 1846–7 saga closely follows Rae, *Narrative of an Expedition*, supplemented by Barr, *John Rae: Unfinished Autobiography*.

18 Fitzpatrick, *Franklin in Tasmania*.

19 Barr, *John Rae: Unfinished Autobiography*, 121.

20 Rae, *Narrative of an Expedition*, 19.

21 Richards, *Dr John Rae*, 41.

22 Rae, 'The Arctic Regions and Hudson Bay Route'.

23 Rae, *Narrative of an Expedition*, 84.

24 Rae, *Narrative of an Expedition*, 122.

25 Rae, *Narrative of an Expedition*, 169–70.

26 Graham, *Andrew Graham's Observations on Hudson's Bay*.

27 Richards, *Dr John Rae*, 185.

28 Barr, *John Rae: Unfinished Autobiography*, 142.

29 Stefansson, *The Friendly Arctic*, was written in support of arguments in favour of Arctic colonisation.

30 Stefansson, *Unsolved Mysteries of the Arctic*, 181.

Chapter 10

1 Harry Goodsir's family represented a dynasty of medical doctors. His father and grandfather both practised in Fife. Three of his brothers also became practitioners. John became Professor of Anatomy at Edinburgh University, and Archibald, after study at Edinburgh and Leipzig, became a member of the Royal College of Surgeons of England. Robert graduated as a doctor from St Andrews University. He sailed on two separate searches to find Franklin led by whaler William Penny. See Kaufman, 'Harry Goodsir and the Last Franklin Expedition of 1845'.

2 'List of Officers, Seamen and Marines of Her Majesty's Discovery Ships "Erebus" and "Terror"', retrieved Feb 2018.

3 Cyriax, *Sir John Franklin's Last Arctic Expedition*, 64–8.

4 Savours, *The Search for the North West Passage*, 193.

5   Cyriax, *Sir John Franklin's Last Arctic Expedition*, 45–52.

6   *Capt. Fitzjames Journal* in Mangles, *Papers and Despatches*, 77–81.

7   Crombie Collection, Ewart Library, Dumfries, Folder A, GD 109 No. 2625.

8   McIlraith, *Life of Sir John Richardson*, 185, 217; Richardson, *Arctic Searching Expedition*, vol. 1, 308. He later confessed that 'the last two or three days' march proved to me that I overcalculated my strength, in loading and clothing myself too heavily', p. 326.

9   Wallace, *The Navy, the Company, and Richard King*, 85.

10   Fletcher, *Autobiography of Mrs Fletcher*. On Richardson see 261ff.

11   McIlraith, *Life of Sir John Richardson*, 192–3.

12   Baxter, *After the Lost Franklin Expedition*, 114, 219.

13   McIlraith, *Life of Sir John Richardson*, 194–5. Another luminary famed for his northern brogue and idiosyncrasies was Thomas Carlyle. Richardson and wife Mary, with Mrs Fletcher, were enjoying a dinner party with Lady Franklin at which Carlyle was among the guests. On the announcement that 'Louis Philippe (King of the French) had fled, and France had declared herself a Republic, there was complete silence until Carlyle threw himself back in his chair, clasped his hands, burst into a loud laugh, and left the room. We did not see him again'. At the time Carlyle was becoming Dumfriesshire's most famous son, and Britain's most celebrated, if flawed, seer.

14   McIlraith, *Life of Sir John Richardson*, 194.

15   M.J. Ross, *Polar Pioneers*, 303–4.

16   In a letter, Richardson noted that poor Irish children in a foreign land were much better treated than in Scotland, 'which is apt glory in the moral and religious character of its inhabitants'. The folk of Massachusetts had concluded that it was cheaper to educate the poor rather than to maintain large prisons for criminals. Idleness and drunkenness are less in evidence than in Scotland. Religious education is 'well cared for though there is no state religion', revealingly noting that 'the voluntary principle works well there – and quietly'! He would have been quite relaxed if his sons chose to work in the US. Richardson Correspondence, 28 November 1849, Ewart Library Dumfries, 2658.

17   They departed Baffin Bay in September and returned to Scarborough, England, on 4 November 1849. Ross, *Polar Pioneers*, 231–3.

18   King, *The Franklin Expedition from First to Last*, 71–2.

19   Markham, *Life of Admiral Sir Leopold McClintock*, 49–67.

20   M.J. Ross, *Polar Pioneers*, 384–7; Jones, 'Sir James Clark Ross and the Voyage of the *Enterprise* and *Investigator*, 1848–49'. I have profited from this helpful reconstruction of Ross's last voyage by Jones, but some problems remain.

21   Richardson, *Arctic Searching Expedition*, vol. 1, 46.

22   McIlraith, *Life of Sir John Richardson*, 199–200.

23 Barr, *John Rae*, 155–84.

24 McIlraith, *Life of Sir John Richardson*, 197–215.

25 Barr, *John Rae*, 154; Richardson, *Arctic Searching Expedition*, 2, 66–7.

26 McIlraith, *Life of Sir John Richardson*, 216.

27 Richardson, *Arctic Searching Expedition*, 75.

28 McIlraith, *Life of Sir John Richardson*, 223, 230; *Lochaber No More* is an eighteenth-century song and pipe tune.

29 Richardson, *Arctic Searching Expedition*, 118–33.

30 McIlraith, *Life of Sir John Richardson*, 236.

31 There are several candidates for the composer of *Nae Luck Aboot the Hoose*. One of the leading contenders is William Julius Mickle of Langholm (1736–1827). See Cowan, *The Chronicles of Muckledale*.

32 McIlraith, *Life of Sir John Richardson*, 225–7, 239.

33 For an excellent discussion of this absorbing subject see Binnema, *Enlightened Zeal*, 129–293.

34 Richardson Correspondence, 9 October 1854, Ewart Library, Dumfries, 2667.

35 McIlraith, *Life of Sir John Richardson*, 269. See also 246–80.

36 M.J. Ross, *Polar Pioneers*, 223–4.

37 Smith, *Arctic Expeditions from British and Foreign Shores from Earliest times to the Expedition of 1876–7*, 658.

38 John Ross, *Rear Admiral Sir John Franklin*, 48.

39 John Ross, *Rear Admiral Sir John Franklin*, 32.

40 M.J. Ross, *Polar Pioneers*, 234–5.

41 John Ross, *Rear Admiral Sir John Franklin*, 72. The correct number was 129.

42 An Irish friend of mine always used to wonder why it was that when he alighted from the Irish ferry at Stranraer in south-west Scotland, the first building he saw was the North West Castle. In the hotel bar, designed as the captain's cabin, there is a mural copying that illustrated in John Ross's *Narrative of a Second Voyage*, 720. I have speculated whether this could be a survivor from the panoramas discussed by Potter in *Arctic Spectacles*. The owner of the hotel confided that in the process of several touch-ups of the painting over the years the original black guillemots in the foreground had been transformed into penguins!

43 Dodge, *The Polar Rosses*, 239.

Chapter 11

1 A story told by Aua about a woman named Uvavnuk, recorded by Rasmussen, *Across Arctic America*, 34.

2 W.G. Ross, *Hunters on the Track*, 175.

3 W.G. Ross, *Hunters on the Track*, 113, 119.

4 MacInnis, *The Search for the Breadalbane*.

5 W.G. Ross, *Hunters on the Track*, 29–30.

6 W.G. Ross, *Hunters on the Track*, 30.

7 Goodsir, *An Arctic Voyage*, 1–7.

8 Lively was the name British whalers gave to Liefde Bai (Bay of Love), also called Godhavn by the Danes: Ross, *Hunters on the Track*, 81; Goodsir, *An Arctic Voyage*, 41.

9 Goodsir, *An Arctic Voyage*, 48ff.

10 Osborn, *Stray Leaves*, 10.

11 Osborn, *Stray Leaves*, 57–9.

12 Osborn, *Stray Leaves*, 57–77.

13 Goodsir, *An Arctic Voyage*, 113.

14 Goodsir, *An Arctic Voyage*, 126–7.

15 Penny's application for a further expedition was submitted to the Admiralty in December 1849, but their response, in January 1850, was to delay him by requesting more information. The episode is explained in W.G. Ross, *Hunters on the Track*, 63–7.

16 W.G. Ross, *Hunters on the Track*, 65.

17 W.G. Ross, *Hunters on the Track*, 27.

18 Sutherland, *Journal of a Voyage in Baffin's Bay*, vol. 1, 66.

19 W.G. Ross, *Hunters on the Track*, 120–1.

20 W.G. Ross, *Hunters on the Track*, 72–6.

21 *The Times* (28 May 1850); W.G. Ross, *Hunters on the Track*, 82–3.

22 W.G. Ross, *Hunters on the Track*, 152–3.

23 Kane, *The U.S. Grinnell Expedition*, 153.

24 Scoresby, *The Franklin Expedition*, 14–15.

25 Osborn, *Stray Leaves*, 171–8.

26 Scoresby, *The Franklin Expedition*; Stamp and Stamp, *William Scoresby*, 73–81, 101, 125, 126, 131.

27 W.G. Ross, *Hunters on the Track*, 462–3.

28 Snow was second-in-command on the schooner *Prince Albert*, part of the British Franklin Search expedition in 1850 led by Charles Forsyth and sponsored by Lady Franklin. Snow, *The Voyage of the Prince Albert*, 224.

29 This is the earliest reference to 'rowraddy' according to the *Oxford English Dictionary*. The word does not appear in the *Scottish National Dictionary*.

30 Snow, *The Voyage of the Prince Albert*, 112–13.

31 Snow, *The Voyage of the Prince Albert*, 122–33.

32 Snow, *The Voyage of the Prince Albert*, 169–71.

33 Snow, *The Voyage of the Prince Albert*, 207–23.

34 Snow, *The Voyage of the Prince Albert*, 214.

35 Snow, *The Voyage of the Prince Albert*, 328.

36 Sutherland, *Journal of a Voyage in Baffin's Bay*, vol. 1, 299–314.

37 Geiger and Beattie, *Frozen in Time*; Solly, 'Lead Poisoning Wasn't a Major Factor'.

38 Osborn, *Stray Leaves*, 107.

39 Osborn, *Stray Leaves*, 107–20.

40 See Maritime Memorials. The children's playpark now includes a 'bespoke galleon', *Nancy Dawson*. See also Richardson, *Polar Regions*, 172. Robert's aunt referred to him as 'The Philanthropic Shedden'. His father, who died when Robert was only a year old, seems to have been a wine merchant. Matzatlan is on the west coast of Mexico.

41 Rich and Johnson, *Rae's Arctic Correspondence*, lix.

42 Richards, *Dr John Rae*, 84.

43 Kennedy, *A Short Narrative*, 27, 29–31.

44 Designed by Lieutenant Peter Halkett whose father was an HBC director posted to Canada. The boat included a waterproof cloak and an umbrella used as a sail, as well as a paddle. It was made in four airtight sections. All who used it, such as John Richardson and John Rae, were greatly impressed. Rae's boat survives in Stromness Museum. It could carry eight people. Bellot recommended additional airtight pockets. See Visions of the North website.

45 Bellot, *Memoirs*, vol. 2, 374–5. Cooper, *The Pathfinder, or The Inland Sea*, was published in 1840. The 'Sea' is Lake Ontario. Cooper visited Walter Scott at Abbotsford.

46 Bellot, *Memoirs*, vol. 1, 232, 313.

47 Kennedy, *A Short Narrative*, v–43.

48 Bellot, *Memoirs*, vol. 2, 354–5.

49 Kennedy, *A Short Narrative*, 46.

50 Bellot, *Memoirs*, vol. 1, 197, 213, 216, 284, 299, 302.

51 Kennedy, *A Short Narrative*, 60.

52 Kennedy, *A Short Narrative*, 65–8. On human/animal encounters in the Arctic see Henderson, 'Incidents of Great Importance'.

53 *The King's Mirror*, chapter 22, 160.

54 Bellot, *Memoirs*, vol. 2, 36–53. For the *King's Mirror* see Cowan, *The Battle of Largs*, 90–1. The Ossian reference is to the sensational 'translations' from Gaelic by James Macpherson, *Fragments of Ancient Poetry Collected in the Highlands of Scotland* (1760), which purported to be of great antiquity, older than Rome or Greece. Further translations fed into the Romantic Movement and a European craze for rescuing ancient histories and cultures; Sher, *Church*

and University in the Scottish Enlightenment, 242–61; Cowan, 'The Poetics of Robert Heron', 7–17.

55 Bellot, *Memoirs*, vol. 1, 108, vol. 2, 274.

56 Bellot, *Memoirs*, vol. 2, 62, 66–7.

57 Christmas Day did not become a public holiday in Scotland until 1958, and Boxing Day until 1974. Bellot, *Memoirs*, vol. 2, 68–71.

58 Bellot, *Memoirs*, vol. 2, 222–8. Kennedy, *A Short Narrative*, 126–9, 132–3.

59 Bellot, *Memoirs*, vol. 2, 110, 116, 159, 202.

60 Kennedy, *A Short Narrative*, 162, 171; Bellot, *Memoirs*, vol. 2, 323–4.

61 British naval officer Sir Edward Belcher was in command of the last expedition to search for Franklin organised and funded by the Admiralty between 1852 and 1854.

62 Bellot, *Memoirs*, vol. 1, 78–81; Hodgson, 'Bellot and Kennedy', 55–8.

63 Belcher, *The Last of the Arctic Voyages*, vol. 2, 3–4.

64 Kennedy, *A Short Narrative*, 60, 74, 80, 87, 97; Bellot, *Memoirs*, vol. 1, 253–4.

65 'William Kennedy', *DCB*. See also 'Alexander Isbister', *DCB*.

Chapter 12

1 Rich and Johnson, *John Rae's Correspondence with the Hudson's Bay Company*, 222–4; While Rae was in Orkney, he described a visit by the preposterous Archibald McNab, 17th Chief of McNab, who founded a Highland 'colony' in the Ottawa Valley, the autocratic, arrogant and anachronistic, self-appointed, swindler and custodian of values and ideas that were almost as totally redundant as his personal self-regard and his mouldering kilts. 'McNab, Archibald', *DCB*.

2 Richards, *Dr John Rae*, 102.

3 Rich and Johnson, *John Rae's Correspondence with the Hudson's Bay Company*, 152.

4 Barr, *John Rae: Unfinished Autobiography*, 416–31; Rich and Johnson, *John Rae's Correspondence with the Hudson's Bay Company*, 212–52.

5 Barr, *Searching for Franklin*, 18–24.

6 Anon., *The Melancholy Fate of Sir John Franklin*, iv–vi. A much fuller account is Rae's report of 1 September 1854, in Rich and Johnson, *John Rae's Correspondence with the Hudson's Bay Company*, 265–87.

7 Bellot, *Memoirs*, vol. 1, 66.

8 Wilson, *Campbell of the Yukon*.

9 Charles Dickens, *Household Words* 9 and 2 Dec 1854, 362; 9 and 10 Dec 1854, 385–93.

10 Black, 'A Taste of Scotland', 154–70.

11   Dickens, 'Lost Arctic Voyagers', *Household Words* 9 Dec 1854, 392.

12   Orestano, 'Dickens on the Indians', 277–86.

13   Collins, *The Frozen Deep: A Drama in Three Acts.*

14   Collins, *The Frozen Deep: A Drama in Three Acts.*

15   Barr, *Searching for Franklin*, 85–7, 92–3, 95. All of my information on the Anderson/Stewart expedition is drawn from this study.

16   Malcolm, *The Life of Sir John Malcolm*, 24. There are several versions of this anecdote. Anderson suffered from varicose veins but he demonstrated a kind of inner resilience still legendised (rightly or wrongly) in Scottish jokes and sayings to this day, such as 'Rome wasnae built in a day but I wasnae gaffering' or 'Wha dar meddle wi me?' When a practical Scottish mother was told that her son had been captured, chained and imprisoned at Seringapatam, her response was 'pity the poor man who is shackled to our Davie'.

17   The case arose to ascertain whether Lieutenant James Walker Fairholme, born in Kinnoull, Perth, serving on *Erebus*, was in fact dead. His heir was his brother George. Evidence was taken from John Rae, who cited the find of a fork with the Fairholme crest. The opinions of James Anderson and James Green Stewart were also submitted. John Richardson deponed that he was personally acquainted with Lieutenant Fairholme and he believed that he had perished with the others. He also was well acquainted with John Rae, 'a man of great acuteness of mind; I confide implicitly in his powers of observation and veracity'. He completely dismissed any suggestion that the Inuit could have been responsible for some kind of murderous attack on the explorers. William Penny also gave supporting evidence. *Cases Decided in the Court of Session* No. 161, 18 March 1858, 813. Author's Collection.

18   Markham, *Life of Admiral Sir Leopold McClintock*, 77.

19   McClintock, *Voyage of the 'Fox'*, 317–18.

20   McClintock, *Voyage of the 'Fox'*, 146–7.

21   'Captain Austin's Despatches', in Mangles, *Papers and Despatches*, 28, 29.

22   McClintock, *Voyage of the 'Fox'*, 7.

23   Murphy, *The Arctic Fox*, 70.

24   McClintock, 'Reminiscences of Arctic Ice-Travel in Search of Sir John Franklin and His Companions', 216–17.

25   A desk was fashioned out of her timbers and presented to President Hayes to be used by some, but not all, presidents, in the Oval Office. Sandler, *Resolute*, 3–5.

26   Klutschak, *Overland to Starvation Cove*, xxv, 16; Fermer, *James Gordon Bennett and The New York Herald*, 313.

27   *Household Words* 15, 389–90. See also McGoogan, *Lady Franklin's Revenge*, and Elce, *As Affecting the Fate of My Husband: Selected Letters of Lady Franklin.*

28 Stafford, *Scientist of Empire*.

29 This may be a reference to the discovery in 1824 by the Inuk named Pelimut on the island of Kingigtorssuaq near Upernavik, which records that in 1333 three Norse Greenlanders wintered there: Jones, *A History of the Vikings*, 294.

30 Murray, *Arctic Expeditions*, 661.

31 McClintock, *Voyage of the 'Fox'*, 109–10.

32 McClintock, *Voyage of the 'Fox'*, 174.

33 McClintock, *Voyage of the 'Fox'*, 190.

34 I refer the reader to Margaret's journal, edited by Gillies Ross, as I cannot do it justice here. Gillies Ross, *This Distant and Unsurveyed Country*, Appendix I.

35 Gillies Ross, *This Distant and Unsurveyed Country*.

36 McClintock, *Voyage of the 'Fox'*, 189, 196.

37 McClintock, *Voyage of the 'Fox'*, 208–9, 211.

38 Raymond, *A Very Special Piece of Paper*. Lieutenant Graham Gore's namesake and grandfather served with Cook on *Endeavour* and his father became a Rear Admiral. Graham was born in Plymouth, served on Back's expedition of 1836, fought in the First Opium War and volunteered for *Endeavour*, the ship of Captain Stokes and Charles Darwin, serving as unofficial artist. Charles Des Voeux was an Irishman who also served in the Opium War. Among the items recovered by Rae in 1847 was a piece of flannel on which was marked 'F.D.V. 1845'. Francis Crozier, captain of *Terror*, was also Irish, an officer with vast experience of the Arctic, having served three times with Parry and as a prominent member of James Ross's Antarctica expedition. The origins of James Fitzjames are hazy but he was raised in a Scotch-Irish household. At age 6 he joined the Navy, beginning an adventurous career in many venues that did not include the Arctic until he became commander of *Erebus* under Franklin. On Irving, a member of an old Dumfriesshire family, see Bell, *Lieutenant John Irving* and Chapter 13 below.

39 McLuhan, *The Medium is the Message*; Federman, 'What is the meaning of the Medium is the Message?'. According to my friend Bill Somerville of Toronto, who made a documentary about McLuhan, he used to sport a tartan waistcoat on Scottish occasions to celebrate his heritage.

40 For further details see Hutchison, *Sir John Franklin's Erebus and Terror Expedition Lost and Found*.

Chapter 13

1 W.G. Ross, *Hunters on the Track*, ch. 20.

2 The location of the long-lost ships, *Erebus* and *Terror*, were finally discovered in 2014 and 2016, thanks largely to Inuit testimonies and oral history.

3   Ross, *Rear Admiral Sir John Franklin*, 80, 85, 93.

4   Simmonds, *Sir John Franklin and the Arctic Regions*, 101; Beechey, *Narrative of a Voyage to the Pacific*, vol. 2, 298.

5   John Ross, *Narrative of a Second Voyage*, 414–16.

6   Franklin, *Narrative of a Second Expedition*, 258; Richardson, *Arctic Searching Expedition*, 138.

7   Alexander Simpson, *Life and Travels*, 132–41.

8   Irishman Robert McClure was a strange amalgam of excellent seamanship, bravery, hopelessness and psychosis. He was knighted and financially rewarded for his discovery of 'a Northwest Passage' but he really did not qualify because he was forced to abandon his ship, *Investigator*, in Mercy Bay and consequently all aboard had to walk out, although the rules specified that ships had to sail through the whole passage in order to claim rewards. The entire voyage is well described in considerable detail by Osborn, *The Discovery of the North-West Passage*, Armstrong, *A Personal Narrative* and Neatby, *Frozen Ships*, 196.

9   John Brown, *A Sequel to the North-West Passage*, 17.

10   Quoted in Cavell, *Tracing the Connected Narrative*, 223.

11   John Brown, *A Sequel to the North-West Passage*, 45–7.

12   Barr, *John Rae: Unfinished Autobiography*, 511–12; McGoogan, *Fatal Passage*, 257–9. See also Barr, 'John Rae to be Honoured in Westminster Abbey – but not for Discovering the Northwest Passage', 219–20; Barr, *John Rae: Unfinished Autobiography*, 218, xxvii, 511–12; McGoogan, 'Defenders of Arctic orthodoxy turn their backs on Sir John Franklin', 220–2. Professor Barr is also my source for Rae's later life.

13   Cavell, *Tracing the Connected Narrative*, 208–29, an excellent study.

14   Cowan, 'The Longest Winter', 45.

15   Potter, *Finding Franklin*, 26–33. 'Lost to science in Victorian Britain, he would have ranked with [Edward Forbes, Professor of Natural History, Edinburgh] and Darwin'. See Cook, 'Harry Goodsir, Lost Naturalist of the Franklin Expedition', 47–59.

16   John Irving became a lifelong friend of William Elphinstone Malcolm son of Sir Pulteney Malcolm of Burnfoot, Langholm, one of the famed 'four knights of Liddesdale'. Sir Pulteney was charged with guarding Napoleon on St Helena, his wife preserving an underwhelming record of their discussions. Another friend was George Kingston a Cambridge graduate, later appointed Director of the Magnetic Observatory, Toronto and Superintendent of the Meteorological Service of Canada. Irving also corresponded with his sister-in-law Katie on a wide range of topics. He belonged to a small band of Christians nicknamed 'the Holy Ghost boys' by their shipmates. On one occasion he climbed Mount Etna. He quit the Navy intending to spend five years as a

sheep rancher in New South Wales, re-joining in 1843, two years later, when he signed up as a lieutenant on *Terror*. Posted to Cork, he observed an Ireland in turmoil and swarming with beggars. He estimated that 30,000 troops, fully supported by the Navy, had been sent to Ireland where the rebels were allegedly looking for assistance from America and Canada. Cork reminded him of Portobello, Edinburgh. He yearned for information about the Disruption which was tearing the Scottish Kirk apart, as it struggled to find its place between faith, charity and the exigencies of the contemporary world.

17 Bell, *Lieutenant John Irving*, 113–28.
18 Rich and Johnson, *John Rae's Arctic Correspondence with the Hudson's Bay Company*, 285.
19 Bell, *Lieutenant Irving*, 158.
20 Cavell, *Tracing the Connected Narrative*, 226.
21 John Ross, *Observations on a Work Entitled 'Voyages of Discovery'*, 62.

BIBLIOGRAPHY

Anon., *The King's Mirror* (Speculum Regale – *Kønungs Skuggsjá*), trans. Laurence Marcellus Larson. New York: Twayne Publishers, 1917.

Anon., *The Melancholy Fate of Sir John Franklin and his party as disclosed in Dr. Rae's report; together with the Despatches and Letters of Captain McClure, and other officers employed in the Arctic Expedition*. London, 1854.

Anon., *Northward Ho! A Voyage Towards the North Pole 1773*. Catalogue to the exhibition at the Captain Cook Memorial Museum, Whitby, 2010.

Anon., *The Place Names of Svalbard*. Tromsø: Norwegian Polar Institute, 2002.

Anon., 'Review of *Narrative of a Voyage to Hudson's Bay*'. *Quarterly Review* 18 (October 1817): 212.

Armstrong, Alex. *A Personal Narrative of the Discovery of the North-West Passage; with Numerous Incidents of Travel and Adventure During Nearly Five Years' Continuous Service in the Arctic Regions while in Search of the Expedition Under Sir John Franklin*. London, 1857.

Back, George. *Narrative of the Arctic Land Expedition to the Mouth of the Great Fish River and Along the Shores of the Arctic Ocean*. London, 1836.

Baillie, Thomas W. *From Boston to Dumfries: The First Surgical Use of Anaesthetic Ether in the Old World*. Dumfries: Robert Dinwiddie, 1969.

Bann, Stephen, ed. *Frankenstein, Creation and Monstrosity*. London: Reaktion Books, 1994.

Barker, Henry Aston. *Description of a View of the North Coast of Spitzbergen*. London, 1819.

Barr, William. *Searching for Franklin: The Land Arctic Searching Expedition, 1855, James Anderson's and James Stewart's Expedition via the Back River*. London: Hakluyt Society, 1999.

Barr, William, ed. *From Barrow to Boothia: The Arctic Journal of Chief Factor Peter Warren Dease, 1836–1839*. Montreal and Kingston: McGill-Queen's University Press, 2002.

Barr, William. *Arctic Hellship: The Voyage of HMS Enterprise, 1850–1855*. Edmonton: University of Alberta Press, 2007.

385

Barr, William. 'John Rae to be Honoured in Westminster Abbey – but not for Discovering the Northwest Passage'. *Polar Record* 51/2 (2014): 219–20.

Barr, William, ed. *John Rae, Arctic Explorer: The Unfinished Autobiography.* Edmonton: University of Alberta Press, 2019.

Barrington, Daines. *The Possibility of Approaching the North Pole Asserted.* London, 1818.

Baxter, Peter. *After the Lost Franklin Expedition: Lady Franklin and John Rae.* Barnsley: Pen and Sword History, 2019.

Beechey, F.W. *Narrative of a Voyage to the Pacific and Beering's Strait to Co-operate with the Polar Expeditions in His Majesty's Ship Blossom, under the command of Captain F.W. Beechey in the years 1825, 26, 27, 28,* 2 vols. London: Henry Colburn and Richard Bentley, 1831.

Beechey, F.W. *A Voyage of Discovery Towards the North Pole, Performed in His Majesty's Ships Dorothea and Trent, Under the Command of Captain David Buchan, R.N.,1818; to which is added a summary of all the early attempts to reach the Pacific by way of the Pole.* London: Richard Bentley, 1843.

Belcher, Edward. *The Last of the Arctic Voyages; Being A Narrative of the Expedition in H.M.S. Assistance,* 2 vols. London, 1855.

Bell, Benjamin, ed. *Lieutenant Irving of H.M.S. Terror, In Sir John Franklin's Last Expedition to the Arctic Region.* Edinburgh, 1881.

Bellot, Joseph R. *Memoirs of Lieutenant Joseph Rene Bellot,* 2 vols. London, 1855.

Belyk, Robert C. *John Tod: Rebel in the Ranks.* Victoria: Horsdal and Schubart, 1995.

Bennett, John and Susan Rowley, eds. *Uqalurait: An Oral History of Nunavut.* Montreal and Kingston: McGill Queens University Press, 2004.

Binnema, Ted. *Enlightened Zeal: The Hudson's Bay Company and Scientific Networks, 1670–1870.* Toronto: University of Toronto Press, 2014.

Black, Fiona. 'A Taste of Scotland: Historical Fictions of Sawney Bean'. In Edward J. Cowan and Douglas Gifford, eds, *The Polar Twins.* Edinburgh: John Donald, 1999.

Bomann-Larsen, Tor. *Roald Amundsen.* 1995; Stroud: History Press, 2006.

Brown, John. *A Sequel to the North-West Passage, and the Plans for the Search for Sir John Franklin: A Review.* London, 1860.

Brown, R.N. Rudmose. *Spitsbergen: An Account of Exploration, Hunting, the Mineral Riches & Future Potentialities of an Arctic Archipelago.* London: Seeley, Service and Co., 1920.

Brown, R.N. Rudmose, J.H. Pirie and R.C. Mossman, *The Voyage of the Scotia: The Story of Scotland's Forgotten Polar Heroes.* Edinburgh: Mercat Press, 2002 [Edinburgh, 1906].

Brown, Stephen R. *Scurvy: How a Surgeon, a Mariner and a Gentleman Solved the Greatest Medical Mystery of the Age of Sail.* London: London Bridge Books, 2006.

Canadian Encyclopedia (Historica Canada, 2013): https://www.thecanadianencyclo
pedia.ca/en

Cases Decided in the Court of Session. No. 161, 18 March 1858. Author's Collection.

Cavell, Janice. *Tracing the Connected Narrative: Arctic Exploration in British Print Culture, 1818–1860.* Toronto: University of Toronto Press, 2008.

Chambers, Robert. *A Biographical Dictionary of Eminent Scotsmen*, 3 vols. Edinburgh, 1875.

Chapman, R.W., ed. *James Boswell and Samuel Johnson: Journal of a Tour to the Hebrides with Samuel Johnson, 1785.* Oxford: Oxford University Press, 1979.

Collins, Wilkie. *The Frozen Deep: A Drama in Three Acts*, 1856. Project Gutenberg. Produced by James Rusk and David Widger, 2016.

Colombo, John Robert, ed. *Poems of the Inuit.* Ottawa: Oberen, 1981.

Condon, Richard G., Julia Ogina and the Holman Elders. *The Northern Copper Inuit: A History.* Toronto: University of Toronto Press, 1996.

Cook, Andrew. 'Harry Goodsir, Lost Naturalist of the Franklin Expedition'. *New Orkney Antiquarian Journal. Special Edition: John Rae 200 Conference Proceedings.* Eds. Sarah Jane Gibbon and James Irvine. Vol. 7 (Orkney Heritage Society, 2014). 47–59.

Cooper, James Fenimore, *The Pathfinder, or The Inland Sea*, 2 vols. Philadelphia, PA: Lea and Blanchard, 1840.

Cowan, Edward J. 'Prophecy and Prophylaxis: A Paradigm for the Scotch-Irish'. In H. Tyler Blethen and Curtis W. Wood Jr, eds, *Ulster and North America: Transatlantic Perspectives on the Scotch-Irish.* Tuscaloosa, AL: University of Alabama Press, 1997, 15–23.

Cowan, Edward J. 'The Scots' Imaging of Canada'. In Peter E. Rider and Heather McNabb, eds, *A Kingdom of the Mind: How the Scots Helped Make Canada.* Montreal and Kingston: McGill-Queen's University Press, 2006.

Cowan, Edward J. 'Scottish History: Competing Pathways to the Past'. *Tay and Fife Archaeological Journal* 14 (2008): 99–104.

Cowan, Edward J. '"Sober Attentive Men": Scots in Eighteenth-Century America'. In V. Habib, J. Gray and S. Forbes, eds, *Making for America Transatlantic Craftmanship: Scotland and the Americas in the Eighteenth and Nineteenth centuries.* Edinburgh: Society of Antiquaries, 2013.

Cowan, Edward J. 'The Longest Winter: The Ross Expedition, 1829–33'. In Sarah Jane Gibbon and James Irvine, eds, *New Orkney Antiquarian Journal. Special Edition: John Rae 200 Conference Proceedings*, Vol. 7. Orkney Heritage Society, 2014, 34–46.

Cowan, Edward J., ed. *The Chronicles of Muckledale, being the Memoirs of Thomas Beattie of Muckledale.* Edinburgh: European Ethnological Research Centre, 2016:https://www.ed.ac.uk/. . ./celtic-scottishstudies/research/eerc/sources-in-local-history

Cowan, Edward J. 'The Poetics of Robert Heron'. *Review of Scottish Culture* 28 (2016): 7–17.

Cowan, Edward J. *The Battle of Largs*. Ayr: Ayrshire Archaeological and Natural History Society (Ayrshire Monographs, 42), 2017.

Cowan, Edward J. 'The Emigrant Experience'. In Edward J. Cowan and Kenneth Veitch, eds, *Dumfries and Galloway: People and Place c.1700–1914*. Edinburgh: John Donald, 2019, 428–66.

Cowan, Edward J. and Douglas Gifford, eds. *The Polar Twins*. Edinburgh: John Donald, 1999.

Cowan, Edward J. and Mike Paterson, *Folk in Print: Scotland's Chapbook Heritage, 1750–1850*. Edinburgh: John Donald, 2007.

Cowan, Edward J. and Lizanne Henderson, eds. *A History of Everyday Life in Medieval Scotland, 1000 to 1600*. Edinburgh: Edinburgh University Press, 2011.

Cowper, William. 'Retirement'. In *The Works of Cowper and Thomson*. Philadelphia, PA: Lippincott, Grambo and Co., 1850.

Craciun, Adriana. *Writing Arctic Disaster: Authorship and Exploration*. Cambridge: Cambridge University Press, 2016.

Credland, Arthur C., ed. *Baffin Fair: Experiences of George Laing, a Scottish Surgeon in the Arctic Whaling Fleet 1830 and 1831, transcribed with an historical introduction by his great-grandaughter, June Starke*. Beverley: Hutton Press, 2003.

Croker, John. 'Frankenstein or the Modern Prometheus'. *Quarterly Review* 36 (January 1818): 379–85.

Crombie Collection. Ewart Library, Dumfries. Folder A, GD 109 No. 2625.

Cunningham, Peter, ed. *Poems and Songs of Allan Cunningham*. London, 1847.

Cyriax, Richard J. *Sir John Franklin's Last Arctic Expedition: The Franklin Expedition. A Chapter in the History of the Royal Navy*. Plaistow and Sutton Coldfield: Arctic Press, 1997 [London: Methuen, 1939].

Cyriax, Richard J. 'Adam Beck and the Franklin Search'. *The Mariner's Mirror* 48 (1962).

Davies, John. *Douglas of the Forests: The North American Journals of David Douglas*. Edinburgh: Paul Harris, 1979.

Davis, Richard C., ed. *Sir John Franklin's Journals and Correspondence: The First Arctic Land Expedition 1819–1822*. Toronto: Champlain Society, 1995.

Dickenson, Victoria. *Drawn from Life: Science and Art in the Portrayal of the New World*. Toronto: University of Toronto Press, 1998.

Dixon, John M. *The Enlightenment of Cadwallader Colden: Empire, Science, and Intellectual Culture in British New York*. Ithaca and London: Cornell, 2016.

Dodge, Ernest S. *The Polar Rosses: John and James Clark Ross and their Explorations*. London: Faber and Faber, 1973.

Douglas, David. *Journal kept by David Douglas during his Travels in North America*. London: W. Wesley and Son, 1914.

Doyle, Arthur Conan. *'Dangerous Work': Diary of an Arctic Adventure*, ed. Jon Lellenberg and Daniel Stashower. Chicago, IL, and London: University of Chicago Press, 2012.

Dunlop, Andrew. *The Life of Vice-Admiral Sir Robert John LeMesurier McLure C.B. Arctic Explorer and Discoverer of the North West Passage (1807–1873)*. Salisbury, Rhodesia [Zimbabwe], 1977.

Edinburgh Review, or Critical Journal (1802–1929). No. 62 (1819).

Edinger, Ray. *Fury Beach: The Four-Year Odyssey of Captain John Ross and the Victory*. New York: Berkley Books, 2003.

Elce, Erika Behrisch. *As Affecting the Fate of my Husband: Selected Letters of Lady Franklin Concerning the Search for the Lost Franklin Expedition, 1848–1860*. Montreal and Kingston: McGill-Queen's University Press, 2009.

Encyclopedia Arctica. Dartmouth College Library: https://collections.dartmouth.edu/arctica-beta/index.html

Equiano, Olaudah. *The Interesting Narrative of the Life of Olaudah Equiano*. London, 1789.

Federman, Mark. 'What is the meaning of the Medium is the Message?' 2004: http://individual.utoronto.ca/markferderman/MeaningTheMediumistheMessage.pdf

Ferguson, William. *The Identity of the Scottish Nation: An Historic Quest*. Edinburgh: Edinburgh University Press, 1998.

Fermer, Douglas. *James Gordon Bennett and The New York Herald: A Study of Editorial Opinion in the Civil War Era 1854–1867*. Woodbridge: The Boydell Press and New York: St. Martin's Press, 1986.

Fisher, Alexander. *Journal of a Voyage of Discovery to the Arctic Regions performed between the 4th of April and the 18th of November, 1818, in His Majesty's Ship Alexander, Wm. Edw. Parry, Esq. Lieut. and Commander*, 2nd edn. London: Longman, Hurst, Rees, Orme and Brown, 1821 [first edn London, 1819].

Fitzpatrick, Kathleen. *Sir John Franklin in Tasmania 1837–1843*. Carlton, Victoria: Melbourne University Press, 1949.

Fleming, Fergus. *Barrow's Boys: The Original Extreme Adventurers*. London: Granta Books, 1998.

Fletcher, Eliza Dawson. *Autobiography of Mrs. Fletcher: With letters and other family memorials edited by the survivor of her family*, 3rd edn. Edinburgh: Edmonston and Douglas, 1876.

Franklin, John. *Narrative of a Journey to the Shores of the Polar Sea in the Years 1819, 20, 21, and 22 with an Appendix on Various Subjects Relating to Science and Natural History Illustrated by Numerous Plates and Maps*. Edmonton: Hurtig, 1986 [London, 1823].

Franklin, John. *Journals and Correspondence: The Second Arctic Expedition, 1825–1827*, ed. Richard C. Davis. Toronto: Champlain Society, 1998.

Franklin, John. *Narrative of a Second Expedition to the Shores of the Polar Sea in the Years 1825, 1826, and 1827*. Edmonton: Hurtig, 1971.

Franklin, John. *Narrative of Some Passages in the History of Van Diemen's Land, during the Last Three Years of Sir John Franklin's Administration of its Government*. London, 1845.

Fry, Howard T. *Alexander Dalrymple and the Expansion of British Trade*. Abingdon: Routledge, 2015 [Toronto: University of Toronto Press, 1970].

Geiger, John and Owen Beattie. *Frozen in Time: The Fate of the Franklin Expedition*. Vancouver: Greystone Books, 1998 [1987].

Gibson, James R. *Otter Skins, Boston Ships and China Goods: The Maritime Fur Trade of the Northwest Coast, 1785–1841*. Seattle, WA, and Montreal: University of Washington Press, 1992.

Goodsir, Robert Anstruther. *An Arctic Voyage to Baffin's Bay and Lancaster Sound in Search of Friends with Sir John Franklin*. London: John Van Voorst, 1850.

Gough, Barry M. *Distant Dominion: Britain and the Northwest Coast of North America, 1579–1809*. Vancouver: University of British Columbia Press, 1980.

Graham, Andrew. *Andrew Graham's Observations on Hudson's Bay, 1769–1791*, ed. Glyndwr Williams. London: Hudson's Bay Record Society, 1969.

Hackler, Rhoda E.A., ed. *The Story of Scots in Hawai'i*. Honolulu: Caledonian Society of Hawai'i, 2000.

Hagen, Rune. 'At the Edge of Civilisation: John Cunningham, Lensmann of Finnmark, 1619–51'. In Andrew Mackillop and Steven Murdoch, eds, *Military Governors and Imperial Frontiers c. 1600–1800*. Leiden and Boston: Brill, 2003.

Hallendy, Norman, *Inuksuit: Silent Messengers of the Arctic*. London: British Museum Press, 2000.

Hamilton, Garry. *Arctic Fox: Life at the Top of the World*. Richmond Hill: Firefly Books, 2008.

Harper, Marjory. *Thomas Simpson: Dingwall's Arctic Explorer*. Dingwall: Dingwall Museum Trust, n.d.

Hayes, Derek. *First Crossing: Alexander Mackenzie, His Expedition Across North America, and the Opening of the Continent*. Vancouver: D & M Publishers, 2009 [2001].

Henderson, Lizanne. '"Incidents of Great Importance": Animal Observation in Nineteenth Century Polar Explorations'. In Sarah Jane Gibbon and James Irvine, eds, *New Orkney Antiquarian Journal. Special Edition: John Rae 200 Conference Proceedings*, vol. 7. Orkney Heritage Society, 2014, 20–33.

Hodgson, Maurice. 'Bellot and Kennedy: A Contrast in Personalities'. *The Beaver Magazine of the North*. Winnipeg: Hudson's Bay Company (Summer, 1974): 55–8.

House of Commons. *Narrative of the Second Voyage of Captain Ross to the Arctic Regions*, London: Henry Renshaw, 1834.

Houston, C. Stuart, ed. *To the Arctic by Canoe 1819–1821: The Journal and* Houston, C. Stuart, ed. *Arctic Ordeal: The Journal of John Richardson Surgeon–Naturalist With Franklin, 1820–1822.* Montreal and Kingston: McGill-Queen's University Press, 1984.

Paintings of Robert Hood Midshipman with Franklin. Montreal and Kingston, 1974.

Huish, Robert. *The last Voyage of Capt. Sir John Ross, R.N. Knt to the Arctic Regions for the Discovery of a North West Passage; Performed in the Years 1829–30–31–32 and 33 to which is Prefixed An Abridgement of the Former Voyages of Captns Ross, Parry, & Other Celebrated Navigators to the Northern Latitudes Compiled From Authentic Information and Original Documents, Transmitted by William Light Purser's Steward to the Expedition, Illustrated by Engravings From Drawings Taken on the Spot.* London: John Saunders, 1835.

Hulan, Renée. *Northern Experience and the Myths of Canadian Culture.* Montreal and Kingston: McGill-Queen's University Press, 2002.

Hume, John R. *Dumfries and Galloway: An Illustrated Guide.* Edinburgh: RIAS Publishing, 2000.

Hutchison, Gillian. *Sir John Franklin's Erebus and Terror Expedition Lost and Found.* London: Adlard Coles Nautical, 2017.

Idens, Dale. 'Eskimos in Scotland, c.1682–1924'. In Christian F. Feest, ed., *Indians and Europe: An Interdisciplinary Collection of Essays.* Lincoln, NE: 1989, 161–74.

Irving, John Beaufin, of Bonshaw. *The Irvings, Irwins, Irvines or Erinveines or any other Spelling of the Name: An Old Scots Border Clan.* Dumfries: Dumfries and Galloway Libraries, 1996 [Aberdeen, 1907].

Irving, Washington. *Astoria: Adventure in the Pacific Northwest.* Intro by Kaori O'Connor. London and New York: KPI, 1987 [1839].

Jackson, Gordon. *The British Whaling Trade.* Hamden: Archon Books, 1978.

Johnson, Dennis F. *York Boats of the Hudson's Bay Company: Canada's Inland Armada.* Calgary: Fifth House, 2006.

Jones, A.G.E. 'Sir James Clark Ross and the Voyage of the *Enterprise* and *Investigator*, 1848–49'. *Geographical Journal* 137/2 (1971): 165–79.

Jones, Gwyn. *A History of the Vikings.* Oxford: Oxford University Press, 1968.

Justice, Clive L. *Mr Menzies' Garden Legacy: Plant Collecting on the Northwest Coast.* Vancouver: Bigleaf Maple Books, 2000.

Kane, Elisha Kent. *The U.S. Grinnell Expedition in Search of Sir John Franklin: A Personal Narrative.* New York: Harper and Bros, 1854.

Kane, Elisha Kent. *The Far North: Explorations in the Arctic Regions.* Edinburgh: Echo Library, 1879.

Kaufman, Matthew H. 'Harry Goodsir and the Last Franklin Expedition of 1845'. *Journal of Medical Biography* 12/2 (2004): 82–9.

Kennedy, William. *A Short Narrative of the Second Voyage of the Prince Albert in Search of Sir John Franklin*. London: W.H. Dalton, 1853.

Kidd, Colin. *Subverting Scotland's Past: Scottish Whig Historians and the Creation of an Anglo-British Identity, 1689–c.1830*. Cambridge: Cambridge University Press, 1993.

King, J.C.H. and Henrietta Lidchi, eds. *Imaging the Arctic*. London: British Museum Press, 1998.

King, Richard. *The Franklin Expedition from First to Last*. Cambridge: Cambridge University Press, 2014 [1855].

Klutschak, Heinrich. *Overland to Starvation Cove: With the Inuit in Search of Franklin, 1878–1880*, ed. William Barr. Toronto: University of Toronto Press, 1993.

Laing, John. *An Account of a Voyage to Spitzbergen; Containing a Full Description of the Country, of the Zoology of the North, and of the Shetland Isles; with an Account of the Whale Fishery*. London, 1815.

Lamb, W.K., ed. *The Journals and Letters of Sir Alexander Mackenzie*. Cambridge: Cambridge University Press, 1970.

Lambert, Andrew. *Franklin, Tragic Hero of Polar Navigation*. London: Faber and Faber, 2009.

Lamont, James. *Seasons with the Sea-Horses, or, Sporting Adventures in the Northern Seas*. New York: Harper and Brothers, 1861.

Lamont, James. *Yachting in the Arctic Seas, or Notes of Five Voyages of Sport and Discovery in the Neighbourhood of Spitzbergen and Novaya Zemlya*. London: Chatto and Windus, 1876.

Langford, Paul. *Englishness Identified: Manners and Character, 1650–1850*. Oxford: Oxford University Press, 2000.

Lanone, Catherine. 'John Franklin and the Idea of North: Narrative of a Journey to the Shores of the Polar Sea in the Years 1819–1822'. In Frederic Regard, ed., *British Narratives of Exploration*. London: Pickering and Chatto, 2009, 119–30.

Levere, Trevor H. *Science and the Canadian Arctic: A Century of Exploration, 1818–1918*. Cambridge: Cambridge University Press, 1993.

'List of Officers, Seamen and Marines of Her Majesty's Discovery Ships "Erebus" and "Terror"' (1845). National Maritime Museum, Greenwich, London. Uncatalogued material. MSS/84/140.

Lovejoy, Paul E. 'Autobiography and Memory: Gustavus Vasa, alias Olaudah Equiano, the African'. *Slavery and Abolition* 27/3 (2006): 317–47.

Lubbock, Basil. *The Arctic Whalers*. Glasgow: Brown, Son and Ferguson Ltd, 1937.

Lyon, George Francis. *The Private Journal of Captain G.F. Lyon, of H.M.S. Hecla: During the Recent Voyage of Discovery Under Captain Parry*. Digitally reprinted edition, Cambridge: Cambridge University Press, 2014 [London: John Murray, 1824].

Lyon, G.F. *A Brief Narrative of an Unsuccessful Attempt to Reach Repulse Bay, through Sir Thomas Rowe's 'Welcome' in His Majesty's Ship Griper in the year MDCCCXXIV*. London, 1825.

Macfie, Matthew. *Vancouver Island and British Columbia: Their History Resources and Prospects*. London, 1865.

MacInnis, Joe. *The Search for the Breadalbane*. Newton Abbot: David & Charles, 1985.

Mackenzie, Alexander. *Voyages from Montreal on the River St. Lawrence through the Continent of North America to the Frozen and Pacific Oceans in the Years 1789 and 1793 with a Preliminary Account of the Rise, Progress, and Present State of the Fur Trade of that Country*, 2 vols. Edmonton: Hurtig, 1971 [London, 1801].

Mackie, Richard Somerset. *Trading Beyond the Mountains: The British Fur Trade on the Pacific, 1793–1843*. Vancouver: University of British Columbia Press, 1997.

Magnusson, Magnus and Hermann Palsson, trans. *The Vinland Sagas: The Norse Discovery of America*. London: Penguin, 1965.

Malcolm, John. *Malcolm: Soldier, Diplomat, Ideologue of British India. The Life of Sir John Malcolm (1769–1833)*. Edinburgh: John Donald, 2014.

Mangles, James, ed. *Papers and Despatches Relating to the Arctic Searching Expeditions of 1850–51–52. Together with a few Brief Remarks as to the Probable Course Pursued by Sir John Franklin*, 2nd edn. London: Francis and John Rivington, 1852.

Maritime Memorials: Commemorating Seafarers and Victims of Maritime Disasters: memorials.rmg.co.uk

Markham, Clements R., ed. *The Voyages of William Baffin 1612–1622*. London: Hakluyt Society, 1881.

Markham, Clements R. *Life of Admiral Sir Leopold McClintock, by an Old Messmate*. London: Murray, 1909.

Martin, Constance. 'William Scoresby, Jr. (1789–1857) and the Open Polar Sea – Myth and Reality'. *Arctic* 41/1 (1998): 39–47.

Mary Shelley Chronology and Resource Site: https://romantic-circles.org/reference/chronologies/mschronology/mws.html

Mawer, Granville Allen. *South By Northwest: The Magnetic Crusade and the Contest for Antarctica*. Edinburgh: Birlinn, 2006.

McArthur, Alexander. 'A Prairie Tragedy: The Fate of Thomas Simpson, the Arctic Explorer'. *Manitoba Historical Society* Series 1, No. 27 (1886).

McClintock, Francis Leopold. 'Reminiscences of Arctic Ice-Travel in Search of Sir John Franklin and His Companions'. *Journal of the Royal Dublin Society* 1 (1858): 216–17.

McClintock, Francis Leopold. *The Voyage of the 'Fox' in the Arctic Seas: A Narrative of the Discovery of the Fate of Sir John Franklin & His Companions*. London: John Murray, 1859.

McDonald, Alexander. *A Narrative of Some Passages in the History of Eenoolooapik, a Young Esquimaux who was brought to Britain in 1839, in the Ship 'Neptune' of Aberdeen etc.* Edinburgh, 1841.

McGhee, Robert. *The Last Imaginary Place: A Human History of the Arctic World.* Oxford: Oxford University Press, 2005.

McGoogan, Ken. *Fatal Passage: The Untold Story of John Rae, the Arctic Adventurer who Discovered the Fate of Franklin.* Toronto: HarperCollins, 2001.

McGoogan, Ken. *Lady Franklin's Revenge: A True Story of Ambition, Obsession, and the Remaking of Arctic History.* Toronto: HarperCollins, 2005.

McGoogan, Ken. 'Defenders of Arctic orthodoxy turn their backs on Sir John Franklin'. *Polar Record* (2014): 220–2.

McIlraith, John. *Life of Sir John Richardson.* London: Longman, Green and Co., 1868.

McLuhan, Marshall. *The Medium is the Message: An Inventory of Effects.* London: Allen Lane/Penguin, 1967.

Mitchell, Ann L. and Syd House, eds. *David Douglas: Explorer and Botanist.* London: Aurum Press, 1999.

M'Kerlie, P.H. *History of the Lands and their Owners in Galloway,* 5 vols. Edinburgh: 1870–9.

Murdoch, Steve. *Britain, Denmark–Norway and the House of Stuart, 1603–1660.* East Linton: Tuckwell Press, 2000.

Murphy, David. *The Arctic Fox: Francis Leopold McClintock, Discoverer of the Fate of Franklin.* Cork: Collins Press, 2004.

Murray, Smith D. *Arctic Expeditions from British and Foreign Shores from the earliest times to the expedition of 1875–76.* London: John G. Murdoch, 1877.

Neatby, L.H., trans., *Frozen Ships: The Arctic Diary of Johann Miertsching, Diary 1850–1854.* Toronto: Macmillan, 1967.

Neatby, L.H. 'Exploration and History of the Canadian Arctic'. In William C. Sturtevant, ed., *Handbook of North American Indians,* Vol. 5. Washington: Smithsonian Institute, 1984.

Nicholson, John. *Historical and Traditional Tales in Prose and Verse Connected with the South of Scotland, Original and Select.* Kirkcudbright, 1843.

Normand, Thomas. *Scottish Photography: A History.* Edinburgh: Luath Press, 2007.

Olson, Wallace M. and John F. Thilenius, *The Alaska Travel Journal of Archibald Menzies, 1793–1794.* Fairbanks, AK: University of Alaska Press, 1993.

Orestano, Francesca. 'Dickens on the Indians'. In Christian E. Feest, ed., *Indians and Europe: An Interdisciplinary Collection of Essays.* Lincoln, NE: University of Nebraska Press, 1989, 277–86.

Osborn, Sherard. *Stray Leaves from an Arctic Journal; or, Eighteen Months in the Polar Regions in Search of Sir John Franklin's Expedition in the years 1850–51.* London: Longman, 1852.

Osborn, Sherard, ed. *The Discovery of the North-West Passage by H.M.S. 'Investigator', Capt. R. M'Clure, 1850, 1851, 1852, 1853, 1854, ed. Captain Sherard Osborn from the logs and journals of Capt. Robert Le M. M'Clure*, 2nd edn. London, 1857.

Oswalt, Wendell H. *Eskimos and Explorers*. Novato, CA: Chandler and Sharp, 1979.

Parry, William Edward. *Journal of a Second Voyage for the Discovery of a North-West Passage from the Atlantic to the Pacific Performed in the years 1821–22–23 in His Majesty's Ships Fury and Hecla*. New York: Greenwood Press, 1969 [London, 1824].

Parry, William Edward. *Journals of the First, Second and Third Voyages for the Discovery of the North-West Passage from the Atlantic to the Pacific in 1819–20–21–22–23–24–25 in His Majesty's Ships Hecla, Griper and Fury*, 5 vols. London, 1828.

Parry, William Edward. *Narrative of an Attempt to Reach the North Pole, in Boats Fitted For the Purpose, and Attached to His majesty's Ship Hecla in the year MDCCCXXVII*. London, 1828.

Patten, Robert L. *George Cruikshank's Life, Times, and Art*, 2 vols. London: Lutterworth Press, 1992 and 1996.

Peacock, Thomas Love. *Crotchet Castle*, ed. Henry Morley. London: Cassell and Company, 1887 [1831].

Peary, Robert E. *The North Pole*. New York: Frederick A. Stokes, 1910.

Phipps, Constantine John. *Voyage Towards the North Pole Undertaken by His Majesty's Command, 1773*. Dublin, 1775.

Potter, Russell A. *Finding Franklin: The Untold Story of a 165-Year Search*. Montreal and Kingston: McGill-Queen's University Press, 2016.

Potter, Russell A. *Arctic Spectacles: The Frozen North in Visual Culture, 1818–1875*. Seattle, WA: University of Washington Press, 2007.

Rae, John. *Narrative of an Expedition to the Shores of the Arctic Sea in 1846 and 1847*. London, 1850.

Rae, John. 'The Arctic Regions and Hudson Bay Route'. *MHS Transactions* Series 1, No. 2. Winnipeg: Manitoba Historical Society, 1882.

Raffan, James. *Emperor of the North: Sir George Simpson and the Remarkable Story of the Hudson's Bay Company*. Toronto: HarperCollins, 2007.

Rasmussen, Knud. *Across Arctic America: Narrative of the Fifth Thule Expedition*. Fairbanks, AK: University of Alaska Press, 1999 [New York, 1927].

Rasmussen, Knud. *The Netsilik Eskimos*. Copenhagen: Guldendal, 1931.

Rattray, W.J. *The Scot in British North America*, 4 vols. Toronto: Maclear and Company, 1880–4.

Raymond, Sylvia. *A Very Special Piece of Paper*. Canadian Museum of History: https://www.historymuseum.ca/blog/a-very-special-piece-of-paper/

Regard, Frédéric. 'Eskimaux, Officers and Gentlemen: Sir John Ross in the Icy Fields of Credibility (1818–46)'. In F. Regard, ed., *Arctic Exploration in the*

Nineteenth Century Discovering the Northwest Passage. London: Pickering and Chatto, 2013, 37–60.

Regard, Frédéric, ed. *Arctic Exploration in the Nineteenth Century Discovering the Northwest Passage*. London: Pickering and Chatto, 2013.

Rich, E.E., ed. *Part of a Dispatch from George Simpson, Esq. Governor of Rupert's Land, to the Governor and Committee of the Hudson's Bay Company, London, March 1 1829, Continued and Completed March 24, and June 5, 1829*. London: Champlain Society, 1947.

Rich, E.E. and A.M. Johnson, eds. *John Rae's Correspondence with the Hudson's Bay Company on Arctic Exploration 1844–1855*. London: Hudson's Bay Record Society, 1953.

Richards, R.L. *Dr John Rae*. Whitby: Caedmon, 1985.

Richardson, John. *Arctic Searching Expedition: A Journal of a Boat-Voyage through Rupert's Land and the Arctic Sea, in Search of the Discovery Ships under Command of Sir John Franklin. With an Appendix on the Physical Geography of North America*, 2 vols. Cambridge: Cambridge University Press, 2013 [New York: Harper and Brothers, 1852].

Richardson, John. *The Polar Regions*. Edinburgh: A. & C. Black, 1861.

Richardson, John, William J. Swainson and William Kirby. *Fauna Boreali-Americana or the Zoology of the Northern Part of British America Containing Descriptions of the Objects of Natural History Collected on the Late Northern Land Expeditions Under the Command of Captain Sir John Franklin, R.N.*, 4 vols. London: J. Murray, 1829–37.

Richardson, John. Letter to Captain Beaufort Admiralty Hydrographer, 6 Feb 1836. Ewart Library, Dumfries GD 109.3.

Rigg, Suzanne. *Men of Spirit and Enterprise: Scots and Orkneymen in the Hudson's Bay Company, 1780–1821*. Edinburgh: John Donald, 2011.

Robinson, Edwin Arlington. *Collected Poems of Edwin Arlington Robinson*. 1896; New York: Macmillan, 1937.

Robson, John, ed. *The Captain Cook Encyclopaedia*. London: Chatham Publishing, 2004.

Ross, James Clark. 'On the Position of the North Magnetic Pole'. *Philosophical Transactions of the Royal Society of London* 124 (1834): 47–52.

Ross, James Clark. *A Voyage of Discovery and Research in the Southern and Antarctic Regions during the years 1839–43*, 2 vols. New York: Augustus M. Kelly, 1969 [London: John Murray, 1847].

Ross, James and James Savelle. 'Retreat From Boothia: The Original Diary of James Clark Ross, May to October 1832'. *Arctic* 45/2 (1992): 179–94.

Ross, John. *A Voyage of Discovery, Made Under the Orders of the Admiralty in His Majesty's Ships Isabella and Alexander, for the Purpose of Exploring Baffin's Bay and Inquiring into the Possibility of a North-West Passage*. London: John Murray, 1819a.

Ross, John. *A Voyage of Discovery, Made Under the Orders of the Admiralty in His Majesty's Ships Isabella and Alexander, for the Purpose of Exploring Baffin's Bay and Inquiring into the Probability of a North-West Passage*, 2 vols, 2nd edn. London: Longman, Hurst, Rees, Orme, and Brown, 1819b.

Ross, John. *A Treatise on Navigation by Steam Comprising a History of the Steam Engine, and an Essay Towards a System of the Naval Tactics Peculiar to Steam Navigation, as Applicable both to Commerce and Maritime Warfare*. London, 1828; reprinted 1837.

Ross, John. *Narrative of a Second Voyage in Search of a North-West Passage and of a Residence in the Arctic Regions during the years 1829, 1830, 1831, 1832, 1833, Including the Reports of Commander, Now Captain, James Clark Ross R.N. F.R.S, F.L.S. &c and The Discovery of the Northern Magnetic Pole*. London, 1835.

Ross, John, ed. *Memoirs and Correspondence of Admiral Lord de Saumarez*, 2 vols. London, 1838.

Ross, John. *Observations on a Work Entitled, 'Voyages of Discovery and Research Within the Arctic Regions' Being a Refutation of the Numerous Misrepresentations Contained in that Volume*. Edinburgh and London, 1846.

Ross, John. *A Short Treatise on the Deviation of the Mariner's Compass, with Rules for its Correction and Diagrams*. London, 1848.

Ross, John. *Rear Admiral Sir John Franklin: A Narrative of the Circumstances and Causes which led to the Failure of the Searching Expeditions sent by Government and others for the Rescue of Sir John Franklin*, 2nd edn. London: Longmans, Green, Brown and Longmans, 1855.

Ross, M.J. *Ross in the Antarctic: The Voyages of James Clark Ross in Her Majesty's Ships Erebus & Terror, 1839–1843*. Whitby: Caedmon, 1982.

Ross, M.J. *Polar Pioneers: John Ross and James Clark Ross*. Montreal and Kingston: McGill-Queen's University Press, 1994.

Ross, W. Gillies. *Arctic Whalers, Icy Seas: Narratives of the Davis Strait Whale Fishery*. Toronto: Irwin, 1985.

Ross, W. Gillies. *This Distant and Unsurveyed Country: A Woman's Winter at Baffin, 1857–58*. Montreal and Kingstone: McGill-Queen's University Press, 1997.

Ross, W. Gillies. *Hunters on the Track: William Penny and the Search for Franklin*. Montreal and Kingston: McGill-Queen's University Press, 2019.

Sabine, Edward, ed. *The North Georgia Gazette and Winter Chronicle*. London, 1821.

Sandler, Martin W. *Resolute: The Epic Search for the Northwest Passage and John Franklin, and the Discovery of the Queen's Ghost Ship*. New York: Sterling, 2006.

Savours, Ann and Anita McConnell. 'The History of Rossbank Observatory, Tasmania'. *Annals of Science* 39 (1982): 527–64.

Savours, Ann. *The Search for the North West Passage*. New York: St. Martin's Press, 1999.

Schwarz, Suzanne. 'Scottish Surgeons in the Liverpool Slave Trade in the Late Eighteenth and Early Nineteenth Centuries'. In T.M. Devine, ed., *Recovering Scotland's Slavery Past: The Caribbean Connection*. Edinburgh: Edinburgh University Press, 2015, 145–65.

Scoresby, William. *An Account of the Arctic Regions with a History and Description of the Northern Whale-Fishery*, 2 vols. Edinburgh, 1820.

Scoresby, William. *The Franklin Expedition: or Considerations on Measures for the Discovery and Relief of our Absent Adventurers in the Arctic Regions*. London, 1850.

Scots Magazine 60 (1798).

Scott, Robert F. *The Voyage of the Discovery*, 2 vols. New York: Greenwood Press, 2001 [New York: Elder and Co., 1905].

Scott, Walter. *Guy Mannering or The Astrologer*. London: Melrose Edition, 1900 [1815].

Shelley, Mary. *Frankenstein*, ed. J. Paul Hunter. New York: Norton Critical Edition, 2012 [1818].

Sher, Richard. *Church and University in the Scottish Enlightenment. The Moderate Literati of Edinburgh*. Edinburgh: Edinburgh University Press, 1985.

Simmonds, Peter Lund. *Sir John Franklin and the Arctic Regions*. Buffalo, NY: Derby and Co., 1852.

Simpson, Alexander. *The Life and Travels of Thomas Simpson: The Arctic Discoverer*. Toronto: Baxter, 1963 [London: Richard Bentley, 1845].

Simpson, George. *An Overland Journey Round the World, During the Years 1841 and 1842*. Philadelphia, PA: Lea and Blanchard, 1847.

Simpson, Thomas. *Narrative of the Discoveries on the North Coast of America: Effected by the Officers of the Hudson's Bay Company During the Years 1836–39*. London: Richard Bentley, 1843.

Smith, D. Murray. *Arctic Expeditions from British and Foreign Shores from Earliest Times to the Expedition of 1876–7*. Glasgow: T. Liddell, 1877.

Snow, William Parker. *The Voyage of the Prince Albert in Search of Sir John Franklin: A Narrative of Everyday Life in the Arctic Seas*. London: Longman, 1851.

Solly, Meilan. 'Lead Poisoning Wasn't a Major Factor in the Mysterious Demise of the Franklin Expedition'. *Smithsonian Magazine*, 28 August 2018: https://www.smithsonianmag.com/smart-news/lead-poisoning-wasnt-major-factor-mysterious-demise-franklin-expedition-180970150/

Sonne, Birgitte. *Worldviews of the Greenlanders: An Inuit Arctic Perspective*. Fairbanks, AK: University of Alaska Press, 2017.

Southey, Robert. *The Life of Nelson*. London, 1813.

Speak, Peter. *William Speirs Bruce: Polar Explorer and Scottish Nationalist*. Edinburgh: NMSE, 2003.

Sproat, G.M. *Scenes and Studies of Savage Life*. London, 1868.

Stafford, Robert A. *Scientist of Empire: Sir Roderick Murchison, scientifc exploration and Victorian inperialism*. Cambridge: Cambridge University Press, 1989.

Stamp, Tom and Cordelia Stamp. *William Scoresby: Arctic Scientist*. Whitby: Caedmon, 1976.

Stange, Rolf. *Spitsbergen–Svalbard: A Complete Guide around the Arctic Archipelago: Nature, Places and Regions, Useful and Important Information*. Spitsbergen: Rolf Stange, 2008.

Steele, Peter. *The Man Who Mapped the Arctic*. Vancouver: Raincoast Books, 2003.

Stefansson, Vilhjalmur. *The Friendly Arctic*. London: Macmillan, 1921.

Stefansson, Vilhjalmur. *Unsolved Mysteries of the Arctic*. London: George G. Harrap, 1939.

Sutherland, Patricia D., ed. *The Franklin Era in Canadian Arctic History 1845–1859*. Ottawa: National Museums of Canada, 1985.

Sutherland, Peter Cormack. *Journal of a Voyage in Baffin's Bay and Barrow Straits in the years 1850–51*, 2 vols. Cambridge: Cambridge University Press, 2014.

Sweet, Jessie M. 'Robert Jameson and the Explorers: The Search for the North-West Passage Part 1'. *Annals of Science* 31/1 (1974): 21–47.

Tabernacle Choir (blog): https://www.thetabernaclechoir.org/blog.html

Umbreit, Andreas. *Spitsbergen, Svalbard, Franz Josef Land and Jan Mayen*, 4th edn. Chalfont St Peter: Bradt Travel Guides, 2009.

Vancouver, George. *A Voyage of Discovery to the North Pacific Ocean and Round the World, 1791–1795*, ed. W. Kaye Lamb, 4 vols. London: Hakluyt Society, 1984.

Van Kirk, Sylvia. *'Many Tender Ties': Women in Fur-Trade Society, 1670–1870*. Winnipeg: Watson and Dwyer, 1980.

Vaughan, Richard. *Northwest Greenland: A History*. Orono, ME: University of Maine Press, 1991.

Visions of the North (blog): https://visionsnorth.blogspot.com/

Wallace, Hugh N. *The Navy, the Company, and Richard King: British Exploration in the Canadian Arctic, 1829–1860*. Montreal: McGill-Queen's University Press, 1980.

Welky, David. *A Wretched and Precarious Situation: In Search of the Last Arctic Frontier*. New York: W.W. Norton, 2017.

Willis, Sam. *Fighting Ships, 1750–1850*. London: Quercus, 2007.

Wilson, Clifford. *Campbell of the Yukon*. Toronto: Macmillan, 1970.

Young, Robert J.C. *The Idea of English Ethnicity*. Oxford: Blackwell, 2008.

Zeller, Suzanne. *Inventing Canada: Early Victorian Science and the Idea of a Transcontinental Nation*. Toronto: University of Toronto Press, 1987.

INDEX